Goddesses in World Culture

Goddesses in World Culture

Volume 2
Eastern Mediterranean and Europe

Patricia Monaghan, Editor

 PRAEGER

AN IMPRINT OF ABC-CLIO, LLC
Santa Barbara, California • Denver, Colorado • Oxford, England

Library of Congress Cataloging-in-Publication Data

Goddesses in world culture / Patricia Monaghan, editor.
p. cm.
Includes bibliographical references and indexes.
ISBN 978-0-313-35465-6 (set : alk. paper) — ISBN 978-0-313-35466-3 (ebook)
1. Goddesses. I. Monaghan, Patricia.
BL473.5.G64   2011
202′.11409—dc22   2010017298

ISBN: 978-0-313-35465-6
EISBN: 978-0-313-35466-3

15   14   13   12   11   1   2   3   4   5

This book is also available on the World Wide Web as an eBook.
Visit www.abc-clio.com for details.

Praeger
An Imprint of ABC-CLIO, LLC

ABC-CLIO, LLC
130 Cremona Drive, P.O. Box 1911
Santa Barbara, California 93116-1911

This book is printed on acid-free paper (∞)

Manufactured in the United States of America

Contents

Introduction

Patricia Monaghan

Any museum in which great art is exhibited includes statuesque women, some nakedly beautiful, some clothed in symbols of power and prestige. Some bear names of historically known goddesses, like Isis and Hera, Xiwang Mu and Epona, but others remain nameless or are labeled as "fertility figures" or "ancestor idols." The earliest of these artworks go back to the dawn of humanity's emergence in the Paleolithic or Old Stone Age, approximately 35,000 years ago. The latest might be only a few years old, crafted by an artist in one of the many lands where feminine divinity is still honored.

Goddesses have been part of human culture for millennia. They appear not only in visual art but also in literature, both oral and written. At times they are clearly divine powers such as Greek Athena in *The Iliad* or White Buffalo Calf Woman in the sacred stories of the Lakota. Or they may be disguised and diminished, appearing as queens and other heroines: Guinevere in the legends of King Arthur and Vashti in the Hebrew scriptures. Alternatively, they may be so removed from cultural centrality that they have become figures of folklore, appearing in children's stories as the fierce witch Baba Yaga in Russian tales or in local legend to explain names of places, as does the Irish cow of abundance, the Glas Ghaibhleann.

These powerful female figures also appear in religious rituals and liturgies. In some cases, the rituals remain only in historical records, for worship of the goddess in question died out or was suppressed. Such is the case with the great goddesses of Greece and Rome, known now only through ancient literature and archaeological remains. No one alive has seen a man castrate himself with a stone knife in honor of the Magna Mater, the "great mother" Cybele, or seen the vast procession of worshipers seeking initiation into the mysteries, threading their way to the shrine of Greek Demeter at Eleusis. The number of goddesses lost to history through deliberate persecution is impossible to know, although historical evidence points to the elimination of some divinities such as Berecynthia in Gaul, known only through documentation that her wagon-borne procession ceased when the Christian Martin of Tours destroyed all her images and threatened her followers. In other cases, as with many indigenous peoples around the globe, colonization and forced conversion, together with destruction of culturally important sites and monuments, have meant that the name and mythology of the goddess have been lost to history.

But in many cases, goddess rituals are still celebrated today. Such is the case with Divali, the Indian feast of the goddess of wealth, Lakshmi, which is part of the yearly cycle of Hindu devotion in Chicago as well as Calcutta. In Ireland the old Celtic feast of the goddess Brigit continues to be marked on February 1; although she now appears as a Christian abbess and saint, the same holy wells are visited in her honor as when she was acknowledged as divine. Finally, some goddesses are honored in reconstructed rituals, such as that dedicated to Isis in Southern California or those to Diana across the United States. Far removed in time and place from earliest worshipers, these new devotees create rituals; they walk to the Pacific Ocean rather than to the Nile, wearing gold lamé rather than hand-woven linen, chanting the name of Isis the all-mother; or they join in drum circles on a midwestern farm and call down to Diana to empower their daily lives. Even more startlingly, a worldwide movement to honor Celtic Brigit's ancient fire worship exists entirely online; people who never see or speak to each other share a living vigil by a virtual flame.

When scholars address the role of the feminine in religion today, they do so most frequently from the point of view of monotheistic religions. Annually, hundreds of articles and books, both learned and popular, address questions of the status of women in Judaism, Christianity, and Islam. But an underlying question arises among scholars who question how women can ever be equal in religion based on a single male divinity. Although orthodox believers argue that such a god represents all humanity, male and female, others point out that monotheism is almost invariably associated with a male clerical hierarchy whose edicts impact the lives of countless voiceless women. While the presence of a goddess within a religion is no guarantee of better status for women, her absence provides an opportunity for oppression. In countries that offer a vote to their citizens, only two do not allow women to vote: Saudi Arabia and Vatican City, both centers of monotheistic patriarchal religions.

Monotheism is based on a male divine image. The opposite is not, however, true. There is no known case of a monotheistic religion based on a goddess; all religions where goddesses are honored employ both male and female imagery in describing divinity. Scholars of goddess religion have argued that by creating a "god/nongod" dualism, monotheisms encourage an exclusionary and divisive worldview. When "woman" is placed on the side of "nongod," spiritual gender segregation can result, with women excluded from religious power.

Yet even within monotheisms, images remain of powerful women: mothers, sisters, lovers, warriors. Although not accepted as divine, these figures hold much the same place in art and narrative as goddesses in nonmonotheistic cultures do. Christianity deliberately adopted the images and symbols of powerful goddesses for saints and the Virgin Mary. Slavic Europe still honors many "black Madonnas" in areas where the black-skinned earth goddess Mokosh was once worshiped; when the Spanish conquered Mexico, the figure of Aztec Tonan was absorbed into the Christian Guadalupe. Such goddess-like figures often attract more popular devotion than the official male divinity, as is suggested by the fact that more Catholic churches in America are named for the Virgin Mary than for her divine son.

These volumes offer an introduction to the ways in which images of the feminine divine have appeared in world culture. Rather than attempting to discuss only the best-known figures in world religion, the chapters address figures of varying centrality within their cultures. Sedna, the "great food-dish" who assures survival to the Inuit, appears here, but so does Sôlmundae Halmang, a Korean goddess who exists only in place-name stories of the island of Cheju. Some goddesses suggest a bridge between several cultures; the Matronae, for instance, were honored in Roman-occupied areas where Celtic and Germanic peoples lived and thus reveal some of all three cultures; and Cinderella, familiar to readers from Germanic fairy tales, is shown to have come originally from Asia by way of Egypt. Some cultures that are especially rich in goddess lore, such as India, are represented by more than one chapter, while due to limitations of space, other cultures are not covered. In every case, the figure is not intended to represent all aspects of the female divine in a specific culture; rather, each offers an illuminating view of a culture's views of the feminine.

Similarly, the chapters exemplify a variety of methods for goddess study, from new translations of liturgical hymns to the living goddess Lakshmi to interpretation of archaeological remains in examination of the related Egyptian goddesses Bast, Sekhmet, and Hathor. Among the methods employed by the authors of these chapters are ethnography, textual analysis, and visual reconstruction. Several authors are primarily poets and bring a trained poetic sensibility to the examination of goddesses, such as Greek Helen and Mexican Guadalupe. Others employ a psychological framework, especially relying on archetypal theories articulated by Carl Jung and Toni Wolff in examining the feminine divine. Many of the contributors deliberately select or create cross-disciplinary methods in order to better define and describe their topics. The writers themselves include both women and men from various religious and ethnic backgrounds. Within these volumes are Christians and Mormons, Jews and pagans, women in religious orders and those who follow indigenous religions. Some approach their subjects as devoted followers of the goddess in question, others as disinterested observers, but all employ critical analysis in discussing their subjects.

Volume 1 discusses figures from Asia and Africa. Here several important Hindu divinities are found, including the wealth-goddess Lakshmi and the death-dancer Kali. As well as orthodox Hinduism, this volume includes discussion of goddesses from pre-Hindu traditions, the "village goddesses" known only with a limited geographical area and perceived as protectors of both land and people. In the nearby lands of Tibet and Nepal, female Buddhist figures appear who hold great power, both spiritual and political. Similar imagery is found in China, where the "goddess of mercy" Guanyin melds an indigenous tradition with images from the immigrant Buddhism. In Japan and Korea, contributors describe geographically located goddesses who are seen as embodied in the land itself. In Egypt and Africa scholars attest to important female divinities whose influence continues despite recent attempts to discourage their worship.

Volume 2 discusses goddesses from the eastern Mediterranean and Europe. Goddesses of the Babylonians and the Assyrians, such as Inanna-Ishtar and Nisaba, testify to the power and prestige such deities had among people of the lands that are now Iraq and Iran. Another chapter describes the controversial Asherah, now believed by many scholars of the Old Testament to be an original primary divinity of the Hebrews, consort to Jehovah. That a now-monotheistic religion may have once honored a goddess is unsettling to some believers, but contemporary archaeological evidence points to monotheism as having been created during the Babylonian captivity. Similarly, the figure of Mary Magdalene, either a saint or sinner (or both) in Christian legend, is shown to hold the power of earlier goddesses despite being positioned within a monotheistic religion, while Lilith, "Adam's first wife," shows how female power was demonized with the rise of monotheism. In Europe, despite a common assumption of an overarching "Western way of thinking" that upholds linear and patriarchal values, our authors reveal an ongoing and powerful substrata of goddess worship. Even such an apparently familiar figure as Helen of Troy is revealed to descend from a powerful earth divinity. From the Celtic lands, evidence of several important goddesses appears in iconography and literature, suggesting the power of the feminine in that ancient culture, while in the Germanic culture we find a number of similarly powerful figures including the fate-goddesses called Norns who sit at the foot of the world-tree and control human destiny. In the Alps, place-names and legends hold in memory an ancient goddess of the white peaks, whose worshipers may have included the "Ice Man" found sacrificed on her glaciers.

Volume 3 brings together myths of Australia and the Americas. The volume begins with reflections on goddesses of Australia, including an indigenous figure rarely discussed in scholarly literature and the unnamed goddesses who appear in pre-Aboriginal rock art; these chapters only graze the surface of a rich and complex goddess mythology in the world's most ancient continent. The volume then explores some of the goddesses of North, Central, and South America. These range from White Buffalo Calf Woman, whose myth is today used to inspire a new generation of Lakota with reverence towards living women, to the frightening snake-skirted Aztec goddess Coatlicue, whose visage can be seen in magnificent ancient art. Several chapters reflect the syncretic impulse that led, in Mexico and the Caribbean, to the emergence of figures that include aspects of ancient goddesses under the guise of Christian figures. The volume also includes chapters on contemporary American interpretations of goddess myths: the adoption of Roman Diana as the matron divinity of women's religious groups in America, the self-creation as a goddess of a Wiccan priestess, the creation of a temple to Egyptian Sekhmet on the western American desert. The volume also includes commentary on the use of goddess imagery by contemporary American writers, whose projects of reclamation suggest the importance of the feminine divine to the creative artist.

Were all the world's important goddesses to be discussed in such depth, dozens more volumes would be needed; were we to add the intriguing but lesser-known divinities, the volumes would cover many shelves. Goddesses and goddess-like figures have been known in every culture and every era. Their stories and images offer an immense variety of possibilities for ways to interpret women's realities. They speak both to men and to women about human as well as divine potential. These volumes offer a glimpse of the richness of goddess mythology throughout the world and, it is hoped, will inspire more such efforts as well as more general awareness of the diversity of approaches possible in study of such mythic figures.

Nisaba of Eresh: Goddess of Grain, Goddess of Writing

Betty De Shong Meador

this shining house of stars
bright with lapis stones
has opened itself to all lands
a whole mix of people in the shrine
every month
lift heads for you Eresh
all the primeval lords[1]

With these lines the world's first poet known by name, Enheduanna, begins her hymn to Nisaba's temple in Eresh; the poem is the last of the forty-two hymns in her collection, known as *The Sumerian Temple Hymns*. In 2300 BCE Enheduanna was the eminent high priestess at the ancient temple of the moon god Nanna in Ur. Situated on the banks of the Euphrates near the present Persian Gulf, the Ur temple was famously restored in the 20th century by Saddam Hussein of Iraq before his reign was overthrown. Enheduanna lived most of her long life in the *gipar* area, located at the site of this very temple. The *gipar* was reserved for the women officials in the entourage of the high priestess.

Enheduanna may have traveled by boat on the elaborate system of irrigation canals, from Ur in the far south of the country of Sumer, north toward present-day Baghdad, writing or collecting hymns from each of forty-two temples along the way. Eresh, the city that held Nisaba's principal temple, lay in the plain between the two great rivers, the Tigris

Figure 1.1 Sumerian priestess in traditional dress, praying with the gesture called "folded-hand prayer." (Oriental Institute, University of Chicago. Photo by Patricia Monaghan.)

and the Euphrates. Its exact location has never been found, but it is thought to have been north of the Sumerian's great religious center, Nippur, and south of present-day Baghdad.

First mention of the city of Eresh appears in an archaic list of geographical names from the late fourth millennium BCE. The scant records indicate that the city flourished in the third millennium. One of the last references to Eresh occurs in a grain inventory of King Shulgi in the Ur III period before 2000 BCE, a reference scholars speculate may indicate that the city was abandoned and its various temples moved to Nippur.[2] In the last extant mention of Eresh, King Sinmuballit commemorates the building of a wall around Eresh (1797 BCE), suggesting its reconstruction. Nevertheless, Nisaba's temple at Eresh, called Ezagin, "house of lapis lazuli," remained the center of her worship in Sumer for over a thousand years. Her role as goddess of writing continued in the many scribal schools that trained primarily young men to write. After 1600 BCE an Akkadian god, Nabû, took her place as god of writing and granter of wisdom, but Nisaba's original position was never forgotten. She was often invoked along with Nabû until late in the Neo-Babylonian era at the end of the seventh century BCE.

Nisaba's name appears on ancient Sumerian god lists from Fara and Abu Şalābīkh, 2600 and 2550 BCE, on Old Babylonian lists, 2000 to 1600 BCE, and finally on divinity lists from the first millennium BCE. She appears in literary texts of the oldest literature so far discovered. Archeologists found a trove of ancient clay tablets at a site known as Tell Abu Şalābīkh dating from the mid-third millennium BCE. Among them were twenty-one fragments of a composition known as the *zà-mì* or praise hymns, a series of verses honoring Sumerian deities and their principal temples. Nisaba of Eresh is acclaimed in a three-line verse, ending "^dNisaba zà-mì," "praise divine Nisaba."[3] A second group of texts found at Abu Şalābīkh, known as UD.GAL.NUN, are written in an orthography so unlike traditional Sumerian that scholars are as yet unable to read them. The words that can be read suggest that this important group of texts had to do with temple rituals.[4] Nisaba's name clearly appears a number of times in the UD.GAL.NUN texts particularly in the colophon, "Praise be to Nisaba." Another hymn from the mid-third millennium, also discovered at Abu Şalābīkh, praises the temple of the mother goddess Ninhursag at her city of Kesh and is known as the Kesh Temple Hymn. The hymn states that Nisaba took down the words of the hymn, spoken by the great god Enlil, and wrote them on a tablet held in her hands.

> Establishing of the standard version there of
> was Nisaba
> she spun, as it were, a web
> out of those words
> and writing them down on a tablet
> she laid them (ready) to hand[5]

A copy of this Kesh hymn, written down a thousand years later, is almost identical to the original, except for changes in orthography.[6]

Goddess of Grain, Goddess of Writing

The Sumerians' invention of writing evolved over a period of several hundred years. Their creation of a useful script is the first instance in history of a successful writing system. The earliest pictographic signs from the end of the fourth millennium BCE include a simple stalk of grain. One of the meanings this image represents is the goddess Nisaba. She *was* the grain, and the sign drawn into damp clay "was an immediate reflection, as a real substitute for what it represented."[7] Jean Bottèro emphasizes the intrinsic emanation of meaning in the pictographic signs themselves:

> It was precisely this "realism" of their writing system that so strongly marked, even modeled, the minds of its inventors and users. Being in the habit of taking their written signs as an immediate reflection, as a real substitute for what they represented, it was much easier for them to pass from the written sign to reality, and from the name to the object.[8]

The significance of the written sign lay in its identification with the divine being, the sign being inseparable from the goddess herself. Naturally, the question arises, why was the goddess of grain also the divine being who gave writing to human beings? The answer may lie in the conjunction of grain cultivation with the building of early settled communities.

An ancient Sumerian myth tells the tale that in the beginning the people ate only grass, as do sheep. In this myth the great god of heaven, An, sends down to earth grains for the humans.[9] Archeological evidence indicates that in the period from 15,000 to 11,500 BCE, early occupants of the ancient Near East (now Israel, Jordan, Lebanon, and Syria) experimented with the cultivation of grains that grew naturally in the wild around them. Agriculture that could sustain a community's food needs, however, required daily tending, technological skills, and a favorable conjunction of natural elements. Not until around 9000 BCE were groups in the ancient Near East able to cultivate enough grain to feed a whole village successfully. With the added food supplies from hunting, herding, and fishing, they could then support year-round settlements. The dependability of a stable community and an adequate food supply allowed additional time for the deliberate development of governance and religious practices, and for artistic expression.

Recordkeeping actually began in these settlements as early as 8000 BCE. Not only were sustainable communities dependent on grain, but the necessity of recordkeeping related to grain storage and allotment led to the invention of various forms of accounting, the precursor to writing.

By 4000 BCE, the interaction of these settled communities over a large area is apparent in the discovery of a similar style of pottery decoration from both southern and northern Mesopotamia and Syria. A gradual increase in the complexity of the communities led to their evolution into urban areas. Assyriologist Hans Nissen describes the evolution by the mid-fourth millennium.

> In one part of the Near East there now arose the features that consti-tute the distinguishing marks of Babylonian civilization, whereupon the building blocks essential for later development became available. In a short time there arose an urban culture with the necessary economic and social structure, with differentiated large buildings, with major art, and finally with writing. While each of these phenomena can without exception be traced to earlier stages, their transformation into a specifi-cally urban form was a matter of a few hundred years . . . a very short time in light of the preceding slow and steady development.[10]

By the late fourth millennium BCE, Nisaba had become the divine pres-ence in life-sustaining grain. Its organized storage and equitable distribu-tion required that transactions be recorded in some elementary fashion. Nisaba watched over the cultivation, storage, and distribution of grain and over the essential records. Her divine sanction formed the basis of organized community life. Her essential role is described in a late third millennium hymn to the king Išbi-Erra of Isin that praises Nisaba "greater than all." Following are excerpts from this hymn:

> The Lady—in the place which she approaches there is writing! . . .
> Nisaba, the place which you do not establish,
> [There] humanity is not established, cities are not built,
> The palace is not constructed, the king is not elevated,
> The purification rites of the gods are not performed!

> Nisaba, the place which you do not approach,
> [There] no stall is constructed, no sheepfold erected,
> The shepherd does not soothe the heart with the flute,
> The tending staff is not set up, [the stall's] cleaning is not performed
> The little shepherd does not churn the milk, does not shake the churn
> From it, fat and cream do not issue,
> And the table of the gods is [thus] not made perfect! . . .

> For Enlil, the king of all the lands,
> You are his great storage room, you are his seal keeper . . .

> Your growth is indeed the furrow,
> Your form is indeed the grown grain,
> Your features, all of them, are good,
> Your figure is indeed that grain![11]

From Tokens to Pictographs to Cuneiform Script

Records of transactions taking place in grain storage and distribution areas began with the use of small, differently shaped clay pieces an inch or less in size. The use of the so-called tokens began in the ancient Near East around 8000 BCE about the same time that the first settlements developed. The tokens occur in uniform shapes, some sixteen types, as studied by Denise Schmandt-Besserat. The shaped clay was lightly baked. Some tokens are marked "with fine pitting produced with a point as sharp as a needle, small circles done probably with a reed, or a deep circular impression made with the blunt end of a stick."[12]

By the beginning of the fourth millennium more complex tokens began to be used adding new geometric forms as well as images of some natural objects such as tools, furnishings, and human beings. These new forms, like the older ones, have been found all across the inhabitable areas of the Near East, sites far distant from each other, yet the shapes and types of tokens are identical. Schmandt-Besserat came to the conclusion that these uniform geometric shapes were precursors of early cuneiform script in southern Iraq, where the same shapes were carved or stamped into damp clay "envelopes."[13]

The envelopes consisted of a ball of clay hollowed in some manner; the correct tokens for the transaction were deposited inside before the envelope was sealed with more clay. On the outside of the envelope the sender stamped his "signature" or seal impression, and could also draw or stamp into the moist clay the particular shapes of tokens sealed inside. The envelope could then be delivered with the product being sent, and the recipient could "read" the identification of the sender and the accounting information held inside the envelope in the form of the sealed tokens. As Schmandt-Besserat says, "The accountants who initiated the new method of impressed markings to communicate information probably never realized the importance of the event: they had invented writing."[14]

The more complex tokens did not lend themselves to being impressed on the face of the envelope. Accountants began to incise the shapes with a sharp instrument, first on the envelopes themselves and eventually onto flat slabs of damp clay. Once the process of drawing the tokens began, the process of drawing or stamping pictures into clay to express ideas took hold and was no longer limited simply to the repertory of the accountant. Using pictographs to express objects and ideas had evolved into a medium that eventually became the means of writing cuneiform script, history's first script, which began to be used at the end of the fourth millennium and continued almost to the Christian era.

By the end of the fourth millennium, the use of pictographs had evolved into an elaborate system that communicated consensual meaning with uniform pictures of things. This first appearance of writing was used exclusively for administrative purposes. As the pictographs evolved over time, they began to conceal complex meanings related to the object they pictured. The image, essentially a name of an entity or a thing, implicitly contained the meaning imparted to it by the deities in their divine purpose.

> Each name, in the opinion of the authors, was the expression of a will and of a particular decision of the gods concerning that which was the subject of naming. . . . [E]ach name precisely stated that *destiny* of the named object . . . because the name was nothing but the translation of the destiny, in other words, the proper and authentic expression of the nature.[15]

The name of a thing, Bottèro says, was "comparable to the genetic code" because it contained information that could reveal the divine nature of what was pictured.[16] Because the name was an emanation of divine destiny inseparable from the pictograph, naming was essential for existence. One creation myth begins,

> When, on high, the heaven had not [yet] been named [and], below, the earth had not been called by name.[17]

Not having been named meant that neither heaven nor earth could have existed. Existence depended on naming. To exist was to be named. The deities themselves determined names, that is, they determined the existence of everything that is. To know the essence of reality was to know its divine origin, its given divine destiny.

The pictographs as a whole successfully communicated complex information, but they did not express the sounds of spoken language. The evolution of a script that would specify spoken sounds began a hundred years after the development of pictographs. Its creators discovered that the names of certain pictographs, for instance, the two parallel wavy lines that meant water, pronounced "ah," was identical to the sound "ah" that appeared in numerous words in the Sumerian language. The written pictograph of two wavy lines could be substituted for the sound "ah" whenever it appeared in spoken speech. Slowly, the homophony between sign and sound developed a new way of writing that eventually became a script of sounds of spoken words, no longer simply a script of things.

This process of transition from drawing on clay tablets pictures of things, to drawing images that indicated spoken sounds, evolved over many years. The presence in Sumer of a large group of inhabitants who spoke a Semitic language, Akkadian, influenced the evolution from pictographs to phonemes in writing. The Akkadian language was in no way related to Sumerian, an isolate language of unknown ancestry. As cuneiform script developed into a writing of phonemes, it could be used to record the similar and identical sounds of an entirely different language, and the Akkadian population quickly adapted the script to their own. Cuneiform did become the first script in the world to record the sounds of the spoken word. Not only was it used to write Sumerian and Akkadian, but it was eventually used to write Hittite, Elamite, Eblaite, and Hurrian, among other languages of Asia Minor. All these cultures adapted cuneiform script to their unique and unrelated languages. Even when the alphabet was established in Phoenicia in the 15th century BCE, evidence exists that it was at first influenced by cuneiform script.[18] Nevertheless, even as the form of the script evolved, cuneiform always retained for the Sumerian scholars some of its original profound connection to divine revelation that was evident in its original pictographic manifestation. They never forgot that Nisaba was "the Lady—in the place which she approaches there is writing."

Scribes and Schools

With the spread of writing from simple accounting to a multiplicity of uses—literature, communication, law, temple and palace records—the education of scribes became a necessity. Scribal schools, called È-DUB-A, "tablet house," proliferated in cities and towns. The territory of Sumer boasted a formal school system by 2000 BCE. The schools trained students to read and to write cuneiform. Most were young men, but evidence on ancient tablets reveals that women were scribes as well.[19] The "signature" of the high priestess at Ur, Enheduanna, occurs on a number of hymns and poems that include her vivid descriptions of personal interactions with her goddess Inanna.[20] Among the naditu cloister for women in Sippar, 600 years after Enheduanna, were scribes who served the business and personal needs of other women in the group.[21] From the many tablets archeologists uncovered, particularly in the religious capital of Nippur, scholars have been able to determine much of the sequence of the curriculum that the students followed in the scribal schools. For the first time in history, the orderly recording of acquired knowledge became a common practice.

Among the oldest tablets were elaborate lexical lists, the earliest dating from the last centuries of the fourth millennium, and a number from the third millennium. These lists, essentially lists of categorized names, again stress the power of naming to the Sumerian mindset. The lists include names of animals, plants, trees, metals, textiles, vessels, proverbs, incantations, and particularly names of professions, place names, and divine names. Each list began with the most important element in the category, and the items that followed were sorted in descending order of value. Already at this early date, the thirteen sections of "The Names, Professions, and Toponym List" ends with a doxology to Nisaba, goddess of writing, "patron-goddess of scholars."[22] Assyriologist Miguel Civil comments on the importance of the lexical lists.

> The lexical texts and the educational system of scribes associated with them are the backbone of Mesopotamian culture. Despite local, political, and cultural differences, and their changes through time, the body of lexical compilations tends to be extremely uniform. The very same compilations that are first attested in the earliest Uruk tablets were copied, with very minor changes, for more than one millennium.[23]

Along with the tablets of lexical lists from the mid-third millennium, found at the site of Fara, were the first literary texts. Robert Biggs, who has translated some of these early tablets, calls the find "the first great flowering of Sumerian literature and the culmination of the archaic Sumerian tradition of scholarship."[24]

The purpose of the scribal schools was to protect and conserve knowledge as well as to cultivate literacy. By the early second millennium, literacy was surprisingly widespread.[25] Nisaba was the goddess of literacy and the goddess of the students and the literate elite alike. A young student wrote on one ancient tablet, "I am the creation of Nisaba."[26] The king whom Sargon conquered, Lugalzagesi, claimed Nisaba as his mother, saying he was born from his personal goddess Nisaba.[27] She epitomized godly wisdom and the gift of learning. King Lipit-Eshter wrote in a hymn to Nisaba these lines.

> Nisaba . . . Embellished the writing on the tablets
> Made the hand resplendent with a golden stylus.[28]

Finding Sumer, Finding Nisaba

The discovery of the Sumerian language written in cuneiform script began in the 1850s when a British diplomat copied a trilingual engraving on the precipice of a cliff in Persia. The inscription was written in ancient Persian, Elamite, and a third unknown language. By 1857 three scholars independently translated the third text, after deducing that it was a Semitic language, related to Hebrew and Arabic. It actually was Assyrian written with cuneiform script. This same type of writing had been found several years earlier on stone inscriptions and clay tablets dug up in several ancient Assyrian cities. Controversy over the identity of the actual language continued until 1900 when a British cuneiformist argued that it was not, as some had insisted, "a secret writing used by priests," a language no one had ever really spoken, but rather that it was an "original language" never before discovered. The language was Sumerian.[29] The language, its literature, and its culture had been forgotten for almost 2000 years. The last original texts in Sumerian had been written in ancient temples just before the Christian era.

The rich written treasures of the Sumerian civilization have been deciphered and translated only in the past fifty to seventy-five years. Scholars have now been able to connect the origin of Western civilization back to the land between the two rivers, to the original Sumerian culture whose ancestors first occupied that land around 5000 BCE. The earliest settlers, known as the Ubaidians, began to form villages whose archeological remains connect them to the Sumerians in the Uruk culture, 4000 to 3000 BCE. There, in the Uruk culture, writing began.

As soon as writing appeared in the third millennium, Nisaba's name was there as a simple stalk of grain. She was said to be the daughter of Urash, earth, and An, heaven, the original godly pair. Her husband was Haia, a god of livestock, connected with grain. Nisaba was known by other names, NUNBARŠEGUNU, meaning "noblewoman with a body of speckled barley," and Nanibgal, a word whose meaning is uncertain. Her daughter was Sud, who was renamed Ninlil, the prominent wife of the leading god, Enlil.

Although her principal temple was in the city of Eresh, called "an ancient town," she also occupied temples in other important locations. In the pantheon of the territory of Lagash, she was known as the daughter of Enlil, the chief god of the land. In the third-millennium territory of Umma, she became the personal goddess of the rulers. About the same time, Enheduanna's nephew, the powerful Akkadian king Naram-Sin, dedicated a mace head to Nisaba. King Shulgi in the Ur III dynasty at the end of the third millennium enlarged the literary canon with numerous hymns, even inserting one of his hymns into copies of Enheduanna's Temple Hymns, written 300 years earlier. Whether Shulgi himself or his scribes wrote the hymns is unknown. In a poem praising himself, Shulgi says, "I am a knowledgeable scribe of Nisaba," and ends his poem, "Praise be to Nisaba."[30]

Nisaba had many attributes related to her primary features as goddess of grain and goddess of writing. In Temple Hymn 42, Enheduanna calls her "faithful woman exceeding in wisdom." Already mentioned was her close relationship to scholars and scholarly activities. Mathematics and astronomy were in her repertoire. She was said to be a "lady with cunning intelligence."[31] She was the goddess of creative inspiration, goddess of creative mind.

In one myth her inspiration saved King Enmerkar, ruler of Uruk, in his struggles with the Lord of Aratta, a fictitious land far to the east. The Lord of Aratta agreed to submit to Enmerkar if he would transport grain to Aratta held in open net sacks on the backs of donkeys. Enmerkar was taken aback. How could he carry grain in open-weave sacks? Nisaba came to his aid.

> That day did she who is [like] shining brass,
> the refulgent reedstalk, the aureate shape. . . .
> Nisaba, the lady of vast intelligence,
> open for him her "Nisaba's holy house of understanding."
> . . . The king took out from the grain his old grain,
> soaked with water
> the malt spread on the ground, and its lips locked together.[32]

Enmerkar had turned the grain into malt, easily held in the net sacks. Nisaba had come to him as he tossed and turned in the night, struggling with his problem. When morning came, he performed a sacred ritual that successfully bid Nisaba to present him with a solution.

The celebrated late third millennium ruler of the Lagash territory in southern Sumer, Gudea, called on Nisaba to let him know when the time was propitious for him to begin building his temple for the god Ningirsu.

> Being that the maiden coming to the fore,
> who had places with sheaves made on her,
> who held a stylus of fine silver in the hand,
> set a star tablet on the knee, and consulted it,
> surely was my sister Nisaba
> She will have announced to you
> the holy star above for the building of the house.[33]

Nisaba had determined that the rising star signaled the beginning of the month, a propitious time for the start of a new building. Later the same text says that for Gudea "did Nisaba open the house of understanding." As he built his temple, "He placed the brick, paced off the house / laid out the plan of the house, / (as) a very Nisaba knowing the inmost (secrets) of numbers."[34] Nisaba offered her knowledge of the movement of the stars and her proficiency in mathematics to the builder king Gudea.

Nisaba continued to be invoked in the doxology of many hymns, myths, and legends beginning with the UD.GAL.NUN texts of the earliest known literature. Later texts, such as the myth of the warrior god Ninurta called Lugal-e, end with a long tribute to Nisaba. Its twenty-one line ending record her attributes: "unique adviser, adept counselor, . . . queen taking care of the dark-headed people, . . . consulting with the stars above . . . praise be unto you."[35] In a composition known as a dialogue, a Sumerian literary form, a learned scribe gives advice to a young scribe. The poem ends with, "Priase to Nisaba who has brought order to . . ., and fixed districts in their boundaries, the lady whose divine powers are divine powers that have no rival."[36]

Nisaba was the overseer of surveying. In Temple Hymn 42 of Enheduanna, she "measures the heavens by cubits / strikes the coiled measuring rod on the earth."[37] Enki, the great god of wisdom and the sweet waters under the earth, when organizing the world, gave Nisaba as her domain the powers of recordkeeping and surveying. Carvings of kings often present the monarch holding the coiled measuring rod and line, symbols of his royal power, the same "coiled measuring rod" that belongs to Nisaba.

A hymn, "The Blessing of Nisaba by Enki," was carved on a monumental stone that dates to the third millennium era of Gudea. A tablet found at Ur, dating some 300 years later, contains the same hymn, while another copy dating between the two appeared in the tablet collection at Yale. William Hallo translated the Yale tablet, which praises Nisaba "colored like the stars of heaven, holding the lapis lazuli tablet." She is "Honest woman, chief scribe of Heaven, record-keeper of Enlil, / All-knowing sage of the gods."[38] In the hymn a high priest prepares a festival for Nisaba, "He verily opened the House of Learning of Nisaba, / Has verily placed the lapis lazuli tablet on (her) knee."[39] Parallels in the Gudea hymn to Nisaba as a goddess of wisdom and to the tablet on her knee are characteristic of repetition of important aspects of this deity across Sumerian poetry.

Nisaba maintained her prominence throughout the 3000-year history of Mesopotamia. She was identified with writing, but carried other important aspects as goddess of the divine grain, the rudiment of civilization. In the Išbi-Erra hymn she is the "great storage room" that guards the grain. Every household had an area for storage of grain. This part of the house was under the auspices of women. The gipar, the residence of the high priestess and the women in her entourage, was also a storehouse for grain, a communal storehouse. The Išbi-Erra hymn says of Nisaba, "You are his great storage room." The Sumerian word for storehouse is ama. It is the word used to designate the communal storehouse in the temple as well the women's quarters of a house. The gipar as a storehouse and as a house for women was sacred space.

Nisaba, who blesses women as guardians of the storerooms in homes and temples, also assists in facilitating pregnancies and births. "You place good semen in the womb," one hymn testifies.[40] A divination incantation of the god Asalluhi "which Mami, the wise one, as medication . . . gave to Nisaba in order to make the vagina give birth well" calls upon the birthing mother:

May her taut mooring rope be slackened,
. . . May the sealed one ease, may the creature come forth.[41]

Nisaba's daughter Sud is the subject of the mythical tale "The Marriage of Sud." The stability of Sumerian literary culture is revealed, as Miguel Civil, who created an edition of the text, reports, by its "wide diffusion attested not only by the relatively high number of sources preserved and their geographical distribution, but also by its long survival through Middle-Babylonian times and into the Assyrian libraries." In the tale the great god Enlil sends his messenger, Nusku, to propose marriage to Nisaba's daughter. Enlil first saw Sud walking in the streets alone and consequently seems to have assumed she was a woman of ill repute. This breach of propriety is the cause of Nusku, at Enlil's instructions, giving Sud his gift with his left hand. The myth is rich with suggestive details of the ancient culture's conventions. Enlil does marry Sud, making her an honest woman, and renames her Ninlil, who becomes a significant deity in the pantheon. She becomes mistress of the house of Enlil, "Lady, the woman of his choice . . . [he gives her] the functions of the nu-gig, everything pertaining to women that no man must see." Nisaba in this hymn plays the proper role of the bride's mother. She replies to Nusku's request, "Who could reject the one who bestows such exceedingly great favors? / [The message] from your House gladdens our hearts and livers. Let us consider that amends have been made. / By bringing the bridal gifts and his personal presents, the insult is wiped away. / Tell him: 'Let me be your mother-in-law, do what you wish.'"[42]

The culture of ancient Sumer is the repository of the oldest literature in history, made available because of the Sumerians' exceptional invention of writing. Discovered less that two hundred years ago and only recently understood with any facility at all, this treasure is available through the extraordinary gift of the goddess Nisaba—her appearance into the resonant psyches of the Sumerian people who recorded her deeds. The late respected Assyriologist Jeremy Black, along with colleagues at Oxford University, in their desire to make Sumerian literature more available, created on the Web the Electronic Text Corpus of Sumerian Literature.[43] In tribute to a kind and generous man, Jeremy Black, here are verses from the ETCSL version of a hymn to Nisaba. This hymn was part of the scribal curricular group known as the Tetrad, copies of which come from third-millennium Lagash.

> Lady coloured like the stars of heaven, holding a lapis lazuli tablet.

> Nisaba, great wild cow born of Uraš, wild sheep nourished on good milk among holy alkaline plants, opening the mouth for seven . . . reeds! Perfectly endowed with fifty great divine powers, my lady, most powerful in E-kur! (ll.1–6)

> O Nisaba, good woman, fair woman, woman born in the mountains! Nisaba, may you be the gutter in the cattle-pen, may you be the cream in the sheepfold, may you be keeper of the seal in the treasury, may you be a good steward in the palace, may you be a heaper up of grain among the grain piles and in the grain stores! Because the Prince cherished Nisaba, O Father Enki, it is sweet to praise you![44]

Notes

1. Betty De Shong Meador, *Princess, Priestess, Poet—The Sumerian Temple Hymns of Enheduanna* (Austin: University of Texas Press, 2009), 237. Reprinted with permission.

2. Piotr Michalowski, "Nisaba," in *Reallexicon der Assyriologie* (Berlin: Walter de Gruyter, 1998–2001), 576.

3. Robert D. Biggs, *Inscriptions from Tell Abu Ṣalābikh* (Chicago: University of Chicago Press, 1974), 48. See also Miguel Civil, "Enlil and Ninlil: The Marriage of Sud," *Journal of the American Oriental Society* 103, no. 1 (1983): 45.

4. Biggs, *Inscriptions*, 32.

5. Thorkild Jacobsen, *The Harps That Once* . . . (New Haven, CT: Yale University Press, 1987), 378–379.

6. R. D. Biggs, "An Archaic Sumerian Version of the Kesh Temple Hymn from Tell Abu Şalābīkh," *Zeitschrift fur Assyriologie* 61, no. 2 (1972): 196.

7. Jean Bottèro, *Mesopotamia—Writing, Reasoning, and the Gods* (Chicago: University of Chicago Press, 1992), 4.

8. Ibid.

9. Jean Bottèro and S. N. Kramer, *Lorsque les dieux faisaient l'homme: Mythologie mesopotamienne* (Paris: Gaillnard, 1989), 515–517.

10. Hans J. Nissen, "Western Asia Before the Age of Empires," in *Civilizations of the Ancient Near East*, ed. Jack Sasson, vol. 2 (New York: Charles Scribner's Sons, 1995), 796–797.

11. Daniel Reisman, "A 'Royal' Hymn of Išbi-Erra to the Goddess Nisaba," in *Kramer Anniversary Volume*, ed. Barry L. Eichler (Kevelaer, Germany: Verlag Butzon and Bercker, 1976), 359. Reprinted with permission.

12. Denise Schmandt-Besserat, "Record Keeping Before Writing," in *Civilizations of the Ancient Near East*, ed. Sasson, 4:2097.

13. See also Denise Schmandt-Besserat, *Before Writing*, vol. 1 (Austin: University of Texas Press, 1992).

14. Schmandt-Besserat, "Record Keeping," 2101.

15. Bottèro, *Mesopotamia*, 98.

16. Ibid.

17. Ibid., 97.

18. Ibid., 85, 86.

19. William W. Hallo, *Origins* (Leiden: E. J. Brill, 1996), 262–263. See also Laurie E. Pearce, "The Scribes and Scholars of Ancient Mesopotamia," in *Civilizations of the Ancient Near East*, ed. Sasson, 4:2305.

20. Betty De Shong Meador, *Inanna—Lady of Largest Heart* (Austin: University of Texas Press, 2000), 134, 176.

21. Rivkah Harris, *Gender and Aging in Mesopotamia* (Norman: University of Oklahoma Press, 2000), 149–150.

22. Ibid., 87.

23. Miguel Civil, "Ancient Mesopotamian Lexicography," in *Civilizations of the Ancient Near East*, ed. Sasson, 4:2305.

24. Biggs, "An Archaic Sumerian Version," 28.

25. H. L. J. Vanstiphout, "Memory and Literacy in Ancient Western Asia," in *Civilizations of the Ancient Near East*, ed. Sasson, 4:2188.

26. William Hallo, *Journal of the American Oriental Society* 88 (1968): 82; quoted in M. Stol, *Birth in Babylonia and the Bible* (Groningen: Styx, 2000), 86.

27. Stol, *Birth in Babylonia*, 89.

28. H. L. J. Vanstiphout, "Lipit-Eshtar's Praise in the Edubba," *Journal of Cuneiform Studies* 30 (1978): 33–61, l.18ff.

29. Jeremy Black, Graham Cunningham, Eleanor Robson, and Gábor Zólyomi, *The Literature of Ancient Sumer* (Oxford: Oxford University Press, 2004), lii–liv.

30. Ibid., 307.

31. Åke Sjöberg, "The Old Babylonian Eduba," *Sumerological Studies in Honor of Thorkild Jacobsen* (Chicago: University of Chicago Press, 1975), 175.

32. Jacobsen, *The Harps That Once . . .*, 301.

33. Ibid., 394.

34. Ibid., 409, 412.

35. Ibid., 272.

36. Black et al., *Literature of Ancient Sumer*, 227.

37. Meador, *Temple Hymns*, 238.

38. W. W. Hallo, "The Cultic Setting of Sumerian Poetry," in *Actes de la XVIIe Rencontre Assyriologique Internationale* (Bruxelles: Universitè Libre de Bruxelles), 128.

39. Ibid., 129.

40. Reisman, "A 'Royal' Hymn," 360.

41. Stol, *Birth in Babylonia*, 65.

42. Civil, "Enlil and Ninlil," 43, 60, 61.

43. For access to this material, see http://www-etcsl.orient.ox.ac.uk.

44. Black et al., *Literature of Ancient Sumer*, 293–294.

Bibliography

Biggs, Robert D. "An Archaic Sumerian Version of the Kesh Temple Hymn from Tell Abu Şalābīkh." *Zeitschrift fur Assyriologie* 61, no. 2 (1972).

Biggs, Robert D. *Inscriptions from Tell Abu Şal'ābikh*. Chicago: University of Chicago Press, 1974.

Black, Jeremy, and Graham Cunningham, Eleanor Robson, and Gábor Zólyomi. *The Literature of Ancient Sumer*. Oxford: Oxford University Press, 2004.

Bottèro, Jean. *Mesopotamia—Writing, Reasoning, and the Gods*. Chicago: University of Chicago Press, 1992.

Bottèro, Jean, and S. N. Kramer. *Lorsque les dieux faisaient l'homme: Mythologie mesopotamienne*. Paris: Gaillimard, 1989.

Civil, Miguel. "Ancient Mesopotamian Lexicography." In *Civilizations of the Ancient Near East*, ed. Jack Sasson, vol. 4. New York: Charles Scribner's Sons, 1995.

Civil, Miguel. "Enlil and Ninlil: The Marriage of Sud." *Journal of the American Oriental Society* 103, no. 1 (1983).

Hallo, William W. "The Cultic Setting of Sumerian Poetry." *Actes de la XVII e Rencontre Assyriologique Internationale*. Bruxelles: Universitè Libre de Bruxelles, 1970.

Hallo, William W. *Origins*. Leiden: E. J. Brill, 1996.

Harris, Rivkah. *Gender and Aging in Mesopotamia*. Norman: University of Oklahoma Press, 2000.

Jacobsen, Thorkild. *The Harps That Once . . .* New Haven, CT: Yale University Press, 1987.

Meador, Betty De Shong. *Inanna—Lady of Largest Heart*. Austin: University of Texas Press, 2000.

Meador, Betty De Shong. *Princess, Priestess, Poet—The Sumerian Temple Hymns of Enheduanna*. Austin: University of Texas Press, 2009.

Michalowski, Piotr. "Nisaba." In *Reallexicon der Assyriologie*. Berlin: Walter de Gruyter, 1998–2001.

Nissen, Hans J. "Western Asia Before the Age of Empires." In *Civilizations of the Ancient Near East*, ed. Jack Sasson, 2:796–797. New York: Charles Scribner's Sons, 1995.

Pearce, Laurie E. "The Scribes and Scholars of Ancient Mesopotamia." In *Civilizations of the Ancient Near East*, ed. Jack Sasson, vol. 4. New York: Charles Scribner's Sons, 1995.

Reisman, Daniel. "A 'Royal' Hymn of Išbi-Erra to the Goddess Nisaba." In *Kramer Anniversary Volume*, ed. Barry L. Eichler. Kevelaer, Germany: Verlag Butzon and Bercker, 1976.

Schmandt-Besserat, Denise. *Before Writing*. 2 vols. Austin: University of Texas Press, 1992.

Schmandt-Besserat, Denise. "Record Keeping Before Writing." In *Civilizations of the Ancient Near East*, ed. Jack Sasson, vol. 4. New York: Charles Scribner's Sons, 1995.

Sjöberg, Åke. "The Old Babylonian Eduba." In *Sumerological Studies in Honor of Thorkild Jacobsen*. Chicago: University of Chicago Press, 1975.

Stol, M. *Birth in Babylonia and the Bible: Its Mediterranean Setting*. Groningen: Styx Publications, 2000.

Vanstiphout, H. L. J. "Lipit-Eshtar's Praise in the Edubba." *Journal of Cuneiform Studies* 30 (1978).

Vanstiphout, H. L. J. "Memory and Literacy in Ancient Western Asia." In *Civilizations of the Ancient Near East*, ed. Jack Sasson, vol. 4. New York: Charles Scribner's Sons, 1999.

2

Queen of Heaven and Earth: Inanna-Ishtar of Mesopotamia

Johanna Stuckey

Goddess of "Infinite Variety," "Paradox and a Coincidence of Opposites," ambiguous and contradictory, complex and conflicting—these are among the words scholars have used to describe the popular and powerful Mesopotamian goddess Inanna-Ishtar.[1] One of the seven great deities of the Mesopotamian pantheon, she was "the most important female deity of ancient Mesopotamia at all periods."[2] Sumerian Inanna is the earliest goddess about whom written evidence exists.[3] Semitic-speaking people, also living in Mesopotamia in early times, worshiped a similar goddess, Ishtar. Gradually the two goddesses became so identified that scholars usually refer to them together as Inanna-Ishtar.[4] Finally, with the first-millennium BCE Assyrians and later, Inanna had all but disappeared, but Ishtar was still widely known. Later, the goddess influenced Canaanite, Phoenician, and Carthaginian Astarte, the biblical Ashtoreth, and also the "Syrian Goddess" Atargatis. All of the latter were worshiped well into Greco-Roman times. Via Cyprus, she also influenced Greek Aphrodite and, through her, Roman Venus.[5]

Mesopotamia is the ancient name for Iraq, particularly the part that lies between the Tigris and Euphrates rivers. Scholars studying the ancient world usually call southern Iraq, from near modern Baghdad to the Persian Gulf, "Babylonia," and the part north of Baghdad "Assyria." In the southern half of Babylonia, a people speaking a language known as Sumerian founded one of the world's first civilizations. By around

Figure 2.1 The complex figure of Inanna-Ishtar emerged in the ancient Babylonian-Sumerian region that is today's Iraq. She represented love, but also war; fertility, but also death. Such complex mythologies often accrue to important divinities in a polytheistic religion. (Copyright © Stephane Beaulieu. Used by permission.)

3000 BCE, they were constructing large cities with defensive walls, monumental art and architecture, and sophisticated irrigation systems. They were worshiping deities who were to have a wide influence throughout the eastern Mediterranean. Further, the Sumerians had developed writing that they and Semitic-speakers of Akkad, the northern part of Babylonia, used to record administrative, legal, and religious/literary texts.

Disagreements between the male-dominated cities over such matters as water rights led to increasing warfare, and men who had perhaps once acted as temporary war leaders gradually became kings.[6] Soon relations between city-states were marked by chronic warfare. It is therefore not surprising that many of the surviving literary texts focus on males and their heroic deeds and struggles.

Around 2300 BCE, the Semitic-speaking ruler Sargon the Great founded the Akkadian Empire and, for about 150 years, his dynasty asserted military control over not only Babylonia but also much of what is now northern Iraq, eastern Syria, and western Iran.[7] To help keep the Sumerians in line, he arranged for his accomplished daughter Enheduanna to become high priestess of the moon god Nanna, protector of Ur, an important southern city.[8] Enheduanna served Ur for over forty years and was extremely influential, especially as a poet. Indeed she is the first poet in history whose name is known. Forty-two temple poems are attributed to her, and in them she "spread her influence and her beliefs"[9] In addition, she is cited as author of three poems to the goddess Inanna which "effectively defined a new hierarchy of the gods" and helped Sargon's unification project by strengthening the identification of Inanna with Ishtar.[10]

After a period of foreign incursions lasting about fifty years, a Sumerian Renaissance occurred under the Third Dynasty of Ur (ca. 2100–ca. 2000 BCE). When that dynasty collapsed, Mesopotamia suffered a protracted struggle for dominance, which Babylon finally won around 1800 BCE under the leadership of its great king Hammurapi. As a result Babylon remained an important power in the area for over a millennium. By about 1350 BCE, the Assyrians to the north of Babylonia began to emerge as a major player but were held back by incursions from foreign groups until about 930 BCE. The Assyrian empire, led by its warrior kings and its war goddess Ishtar, expanded widely, even briefly conquering Egypt in the seventh century BCE.

Derivation of the Goddess's Name

Almost certainly the name Inanna was derived from Sumerian Nin-Ana(k) "Lady or Queen of Heaven."[11] The written sign for her name looks like a post or standard with a large ring on top and streamers or a scarf hanging down from it.[12] It occurs in the earliest writings, and very early in the archaeological record, and might have been her primary symbol.[13] Ishtar, by contrast, has a Semitic name closely related to Athtar, the Southern Arabian male deity. The latter appears, among other places, in texts from the ancient Syrian city Ugarit, where there seems to have been a grammatically feminine equivalent, Athtart. Some scholars have argued that Athtar was the morning star and Athtart the evening star; later, Inanna-Ishtar had strong masculine qualities that she might have absorbed from Athtar.[14] An earlier form of her name was Eshtar. In late periods, "Ishtar" came to be understood as the generic word for "goddess." Originally, then, Inanna and Ishtar were two separate goddesses who, particularly in the Old Akkadian period (2334–2154 BCE), became equated.

A comparison of the Sumerian with the Akkadian/Babylonian story of the encounter between the great Mesopotamian hero Gilgamesh and, first, the goddess Inanna and then the goddess Ishtar illustrates one aspect of the difference between the two goddesses. In the earlier Sumerian fragment, "Gilgamesh and the Bull of Heaven," the hero follows his mother's instructions to display himself in the temple of Inanna and catches the goddess's eye. She wants him to stay with her, and she forbids him "to decide legal cases in [her] Eanna temple" and elsewhere at Uruk. Again following his mother's advice, Gilgamesh refuses. The furious goddess persuades the sky god An to give her the Bull of Heaven to destroy Uruk. Eventually the hero and his friend Enkidu kill the Bull, and Gilgamesh tells Inanna that he would like to kill her also.[15] In the Akkadian/Babylonian epic, Ishtar boldly makes sexual advances to Gilgamesh when she catches sight of him dressed in all his royal finery.[16] Indeed, she offers him marriage, riches, and other gifts. However, Gilgamesh refuses Ishtar's advances in the most insulting terms. As in the Sumerian fragment, Ishtar's subsequent anger leads to the unleashing and killing of the Bull of Heaven. The section ends with Gilgamesh celebrating and gloating at Ishtar's expense.[17]

In the Sumerian version it is Gilgamesh who is the manipulator and the goddess who expects her spouse to stay at her side and, in one interpretation, not try to rule in her sanctuary and city. In the Babylonian version Ishtar is depicted as a lascivious and untrustworthy female whom, no longer on the advice of his mother, Gilgamesh spurns and then succeeds in further humiliating. Already in the Sumerian story, Gilgamesh is undermining the powerful goddess's authority; in the Babylonian version he does not hesitate to defy her, and his killing of the Bull becomes another of his heroic deeds.

Family of the Goddess

As to Inanna-Ishtar's family, in one tradition her father was An/Anu, the sky god and supreme deity. In another tradition, she was daughter of the moon god Nanna-Suen and sister of the sun god Utu/Shamash. Still other traditions considered her as daughter of the powerful god Enlil or the wisdom god Enki/Ea. Her older sister and likely twin, Ereshkigal was goddess of the Underworld. In most sources Inanna/Ishtar had no permanent divine spouse, but her bridegroom was the disappearing god Dumuzi. However, in one very old tradition Inanna-Ishtar was spouse of the sky god An/Anu and thus was equated with the earth goddess Ki/Antum.[18] Although she was not primarily a mother, in certain traditions, she had three offspring, who were very minor deities.[19]

In Mesopotamian literature, Inanna-Ishtar comes across as "a beautiful, rather willful young aristocrat." As Jacobsen points out, the roles she takes include young and troublesome sister, young and rebellious daughter, young woman being wooed, happy young bride, and sorrowful young widow. He adds that she never appears as wife or mother. The only two female roles she does not fulfill, he says, are the two that demand "maturity and a sense of responsibility."[20] Notably, all these descriptions include the word "young." Inanna-Ishtar is a *young* woman. Indeed, one of her epithets is "the Maiden." The social roles Jacobsen lists are appropriate for a female in late adolescence. Inanna-Ishtar is forever fixed at the threshold of womanhood, not yet tied down by marriage and motherhood. Not surprisingly, she behaves like a male and enjoys what feminist scholar Tikva Frymer-Kensky calls "essentially the same existence as young men," delighting in warfare and looking for sexual experiences.[21] In addition, the roles that Jacobsen examines connect a woman to men and the patriarchal family. Thus, her sexuality and ability to reproduce are carefully controlled.

Nonetheless, Frymer-Kensky argues that Inanna-Ishtar does have a significant social role and function; she is the divine model for an undesirable social role: "the non-domesticated woman." Inanna-Ishtar represents "all the fear and attraction" of such a female. As an independent woman, she is not committed to the patriarchal family, which cannot therefore restrict her sexuality. In addition, Inanna-Ishtar embodies sexual attraction and sexuality "regardless of its social purpose or value."[22] It is no puzzle, then, why Inanna-Ishtar was patron of prostitutes.[23]

Visual Depictions of Inanna-Ishtar

In visual depictions, Inanna-Ishtar is normally frontally posed. She sits enthroned, stands erect and proud, or strides out as a warrior. Sometimes she has wings, and she is associated with birds, for example, the owl. She wears the high horned crown of a major deity and either a flounced or tiered dress or a split skirt over a warrior's short tunic. Occasionally she is nude. Above her shoulders protrude a number of what look like carved "rods," which have been interpreted variously as weapons, vegetation, rays of light, symbols of authority, and even representations of the *me*, the divine attributes of culture and civilization. Often she stands on a lion, her sacred animal, or controls the roaring beast with a rope. She is the only Mesopotamian goddess called *labbatu*, "lioness." A star, usually eight-pointed, is one of her symbols, signifying her identification with the planet Venus. Probably another is the rosette, a symbol that goes back into Mesopotamian prehistory. The post or standard with ring and usually streamers signals both the presence of the goddess and the entrance to her shrine. The semiprecious stone carnelian was sacred to her, and red was her color.[24]

Inanna/Ishtar was the tutelary deity of the southern city of Uruk, one of the world's first urban centers. In Uruk stood the great temple Eanna "House of Heaven," which was the center of her cult. The Eanna, the oldest preserved shrine in the sacred precinct, seems to have been also dedicated to the sky god An/Anu. There, archaeologists unearthed clay tablets with some of the earliest writing.[25] Inanna-Ishtar had important sanctuaries at most other towns and cities, and her temples were often named Eanna.[26] Her temple at Babylon was called "Ishtar of the Star" (Venus). Festivals and rituals for the goddess took place regularly throughout the year.[27] Uruk held festivals for her as both aspects of the Venus star, and, at New Year festivals throughout Mesopotamia, devotees almost always made offerings to her. Sometimes the New Year Festival focused on her. In general, she received offerings including cows, sheep, oil, and flour. As protector of towns and cities where she had active cults, she was known by such names as Belet-Lagaba (or Lagabitu[m]) "Mistress of Lagaba," Belet-Sippar "Mistress of Sippar," and Supalitu(m) as "She of Zabala(m)." She was also Belet-Akkade, "Mistress of Akkade," and Belet-Ninua, "Mistress of Nineveh."

Epithets, Titles and Associated Goddesses

Inanna-Ishtar enjoyed many epithets, "Queen of Heaven (Sky) and Earth" being the most common.[28] Her oldest one was *nun*, "Princely." Others included "Lady of Battle," "Amazement of the Land," "Lady Who Ascends into the Heavens," "Heroic Woman," "Ornament of Heaven," "Maiden," and often simply "the Woman." She also bore the Sumerian priestess title *nu-gig*, the exact meaning of which is not clear. In addition, as protector deity of a number of cities, she was often identified by their names, for instance, Ishtar of Arbela and Ishtar of Nineveh. It is possible that the "Inanna-Ishtars" of specific places represented local goddesses who were equated with this great goddess and absorbed into her. Ishtar of Nineveh was identified with Shaushka, a north Syrian and north Mesopotamian goddess who was revered at Nineveh for close to 1500 years.

The goddesses Anunitu(m), Nanay(a), and Kilili were closely associated or actually identified with Inanna/Ishtar. Anunitu(m), whose name probably meant "the skirmisher,"[29] was first and foremost a battle goddess. As such she was patron of the Akkadian Dynasty (c. 2350–2150 BCE), which was founded by Sargon the Great. King Naram-Sin (c. 2260–2223 BCE), described himself as her husband, "*mut* Ishtar-Anunitum."[30] Nanay(a) was a Sumerian goddess of erotic love and sexual attractiveness and thus connected with Inanna/Ishtar. One of her titles was "Lady of Sensuality." In later cultic texts she was treated as another aspect of Inanna/Ishtar, though she was "more enduring" than Ishtar, being worshiped as Nanaya well into Greek times.[31] Kilili was the famous "Woman in the Window." Her Semitic name probably means "Garlanded One." The Sumerians called her Aba-shushu, "(One) Who Leans in (or Looks out of) the Window." There are many beautiful ivory depictions of Kilili. The most famous of them is the "Mona Lisa of Nimrud." In most of these images, the ornately coiffed goddess looks straight ahead. The "Woman at the Window" has normally been interpreted as a prostitute displaying her wares.[32]

Sexuality, Prosperity, and War

Among Inanna-Ishtar's many powers, aspects, and spheres of influence were sexuality and love, the prosperity of the land under the king's rule, war and warfare, and the planet Venus as both morning and evening star. She also had strong underworld connections and was goddess of prophecy. Further, she controlled the *me*, the divine attributes of culture and civilization.

As goddess of sexuality and love, Inanna-Ishtar is the focus of a group of charming and erotic hymns and songs that tell of her courtship by the disappearing and returning god Dumuzi and his becoming her bridegroom. Scholars have usually regarded her as the goddess of prostitutes, though recently this has been questioned. However, she never tires of sexual intercourse and can outlast a large number of young men. Nonetheless, Inanna-Ishtar was also considered a "patron of marital sexuality." She was often invoked in rituals and incantations intended to cure male impotence. Cross-dressing was part of her cult, and many of her personnel were transvestites and eunuchs. She was able to change a man into a woman and vice versa: "A woman . . . [is] holding a bow / A man carries a hairpin. . . ." In Mesopotamian treaties, breakers of the agreement would be cursed with lines like the following, from an

Assyrian vassal treaty: "may Ishtar, the goddess of men, the lady of women, take away their 'bow,' cause their steri[lity]." Inanna-Ishtar confused the bounds that separate not only the sexes, but also the generations, the classes, and the species, human and animal.[33]

The goddess was also the central figure in an important rite known as the Sacred Marriage, which probably began in Inanna's special city Uruk. The ritual united the king embodying Inanna's bridegroom Dumuzi with the goddess, probably incarnated in a priestess. Through the rite, the goddess bestowed power on Uruk's ruler, which, it is generally agreed, was the main aim of the ceremony.[34] In addition, it guaranteed prosperity for the land. The Sacred Marriage ritual was adopted by other Mesopotamian cities and became one of the central ways of validating a king. The question of who the participants in the Sacred Marriage actually were is still being asked. Literary material from the period 2112–2004 BCE attests that various rulers called themselves spouses of Inanna-Ishtar. One poem describes a Sacred Marriage Festival in considerable detail and elucidates a king's seemingly significant role in it.[35] The female partner was referred to simply as "Inanna." In later times the rite was symbolic, with the deities' statues being put to bed together in a room in a shrine.

There is some agreement among scholars that the scenes on the famous Uruk Vase might be a depiction of part of the Sacred Marriage rite.[36] The beautiful alabaster vase, which is around three feet high, features a procession of naked priests led by what seems to be a man (possibly Dumuzi) in a ceremonial net tunic. The priests are carrying offerings to a shrine flanked by two of Inanna-Ishtar's standards. Between them stands a female figure, the goddess herself or her priestess, receiving the tribute.[37] Indeed, this procession is very like the ones later described in hymns about the Sacred Marriage ritual.[38]

As goddess of war Inanna-Ishtar delighted in the chaos of battle. She reveled in violence. One of her tasks was to punish and destroy. Battle was her festival.[39] One of her titles, Agushaya, probably referred to a whirling dance that she performed madly on the battlefield. In the Akkadian "Agushaya Poem," Ishtar's aggression and battle frenzy became so extreme that the deities decided to create a female counterpart Saltu, "Discord," to challenge and outdo the blood-thirsty goddess. When Saltu began raging, Ishtar got the point and asked for Saltu to be sent back "to her lair." "The lioness Ishtar quieted."[40] Later, as often in earlier periods, Ishtar's warlike qualities were definitely emphasized by warrior conquerors like the Assyrians, for whose kings Ishtar was not only "Lady of Battle" but also often a personal deity. She fought beside them in battle and led them to victory. Ishtar of Arbela (modern Erbil) was an especially warlike figure.[41]

Morning and Evening Star

In her astral form Inanna-Ishtar was the planet Venus, and as such she was revered mainly as the evening star. In one of her poems, Enheduanna addresses Inanna-Ishtar as a light in the darkness: "Your torch lights up the corners of heaven." Another hymn describes Ishtar as "Torch of heaven and earth." Two temple hymns address the goddess in her evening and morning manifestations. Interestingly, in the early period at Uruk, Inanna received offerings in both her morning and evening aspects, and these appear to have been "two different cults." Ninsianna, "Lady Russet Brown of Heaven," perhaps originally one of Inanna-Ishtar's epithets, was also understood as the Venus star and was equated with Inanna-Ishtar. Indeed, Ninsianna was one of the Sumerian names for the planet.[42]

Unlike Inanna-Ishtar, who was predominantly female although often quite androgynous, Ninsianna took both male and female forms, likely the male morning star and the female evening star. Ninsianna's Semitic name was Ishtar-kakkabi, "Ishtar of the Stars." The ancient Mesopotamians knew the planet well, and they saw the morning and evening stars as distinct but related deities. They recorded Venus's movements in detail, primarily for purposes of divination.[43] Priests made observations from temples and sent reports to kings. One cuneiform text, usually called the Venus tablets, purported to date to around 1600 BCE, is known only in later copies.[44]

Surprisingly, the "Queen of Heaven" had strong underworld connections, for her twin sister Ereshkigal was goddess of the netherworld and Inanna-Ishtar was able to descend to the "Great Below" and return. In "Inanna's Descent to the Underworld," the goddess took it upon herself to go down to Ereshkigal's realm, where she quickly became a corpse-like object hanging on a nail.[45] With the wisdom god Enki's help she was revived and ascended to earth, but she had to offer a substitute. When she realized her bridegroom Dumuzi's indifference to her supposed death, she turned him over to the Underworld in her place. Some have interpreted the poem as explaining the cycle of the seasons. In the Akkadian/Babylonian version, "Descent of Ishtar to the Netherworld," Ishtar's absence in the Underworld caused all fertility on earth to cease.[46]

The fact that Ereshkigal and Inanna-Ishtar were sisters suggests that they might originally have been one goddess. One scholar says that

Ereshkigal "can be seen as deriving from Inanna/Ishtar" and that an Assyrian version of the poem, "Ishtar's Descent," identifies Ereshkigal as Ishtar "who resides in the midst of Irkalla [the Underworld]."[47] In addition, after two fly-like beings sent by the god of wisdom to retrieve Inanna's corpse succeed in commiserating with Ereshkigal, the Underworld goddess tried to reward them with life—river water and grain. In Mesopotamia, fresh water produced life and fertility, and they seem to have been Ereshkigal's to give. Further, the misery for which the flies were sympathizing with Ereshkigal was birth pains! Was the underworld the source of life? Did Inanna-Ishtar and Ereshkigal originate from a goddess of life, death, and renewal?

There is some visual evidence from Mesopotamia that supports this hypothesis. For instance, a Babylonian seal shows a nude woman with high, horned crown, wings, and claws of a bird.[48] She stretches across the seal from top to bottom, with her head among "deities and their human worshippers" and her feet among "demonic creatures." This overarching figure might be Inanna-Ishtar, and the "hierarchical arrangement" perhaps states "her dual nature, partially of 'heaven and earth' and partially of the underworld."[49] Another similar image occurs in the famous "Burney plaque," displaying a nude, claw-footed goddess, almost certainly Inanna-Ishtar and not Lilith, standing on a lion and flanked by owls.[50] Yet another theory, based on analysis of five sets of elite grave goods, suggests that Inanna-Ishtar served as psychopomp, the deity who escorted the human dead to the underworld.[51]

Prophesy and Ecstasy

Prophesy, especially that resulting from ecstatic behavior, was another of Inanna-Ishtar's concerns.[52] Since the goddess mediated between deities and between deities and humans, it was normally she who possessed a prophet and spoke through her.[53] The goddess caused ecstasy in her devoted followers. Any "possession cult in Mesopotamia" would have been associated with her.[54] The Semitic word for one kind of prophet meant "shouter," whereas another kind was designated "ecstatic."[55] Both were normally temple personnel of the deity for whom they spoke.

Surviving Mesopotamian oracular reports consist primarily of two groups dated about 1000 years apart. Scribes wrote down the prophecies, but they are purported to be a deity's words. For instance, the goddess speaking through one of the prophets identifies herself: "I am the Gr[eat

Lady. I am Ishtar o]f Arbela."[56] In the Mari letters (second millennium BCE), which the king of Mari received from members of his family and courtiers, the prophets numbered slightly more women than men.[57] They served several deities, among them Annunitu(m), a form of Inanna-Ishtar. The other collection was preserved at Nineveh in the great library of the Assyrian king Assurbanipal and recorded in the seventh century BCE.[58] In this collection, female prophets outnumbered males by two to one. Furthermore, the majority of the Assyrian prophets worked at Arbela, a city in northern Mesopotamia (681–669 BCE).[59] Not surprisingly, Arbela's tutelary deity was Ishtar. Assyrian warrior kings Esarhaddon (668–627 BCE) and his son Assurbanipal, whom most of the prophecies concerned, regarded Ishtar of Arbela, "Lady of Battle," as their personal deity. A number of other cities also had prophets attached to their Ishtar temples.

One of Inanna-Ishtar's titles was "Lady of all the *Me*," and one of Enheduanna's hymns to Inanna begins with the epithet.[60] The term *me* is a plural noun meaning the godly powers that allowed the central activities that constituted civilized life to happen and ensured their continuation. Jacobsen described them as "cosmic offices."[61] In one Sumerian poem, Inanna visited the god Enki and drank beer with him until he got very drunk. Then he started giving her the *me*, which the poem lists in detail. Later, Enki, no longer drunk, tried to stop her from taking them back to Uruk, but she won through to her city.[62] That they should be held by Inanna-Ishtar seems appropriate since they are full of antitheses and represent "the delicate balancing of order and disorder."[63]

Inanna-Ishtar's holding of the oppositional but carefully balanced *me* is a clue to resolving questions about her "infinite variety" and contradictory nature. Undoubtedly, the Mesopotamians saw Inanna-Ishtar as a single and unified deity. In the literature about her, she is definitely "a coherent and believable if complex personality."[64] Is there one element or trait that runs through all her functions, roles, and powers? What is there that unifies sexuality and love, war and warfare, morning and evening stars, relations with the Underworld, and control of the *me*, not to mention permanent late adolescence and independence? Some of her symbols provide hints. Her bird flew in the sky, but rested on earth. Her standard often marked the entrance to her shrine and its exit. Her star indicated the transitions between light and dark, day and night. All designate boundaries, and Inanna/Ishtar was very much a boundary crosser: female warrior, sometimes cross-dresser, often androgyne. Among her cult servants were "transvestites and castrates."[65]

Inanna-Ishtar as Border-Crosser

Almost all of her seemingly contradictory aspects, functions, and spheres of influence involve boundary crossing, transition, or transformation. Women and men can be deeply altered by love and sexuality. Inanna-Ishtar's dance of war can cause huge political and social changes, as well as the ultimate change of death, with its shift of focus from earth to netherworld. Morning and evening stars are visible at the boundary of dark and light, light and dark. The *me* include the contradictions in culture that are to a large extent what Inanna-Ishtar represents. Late adolescence is a dangerous time of transition, and the independent, non-domestic woman is marginal, as is the prostitute. Both defy limitation. It is, then, change that is the key to the unity of the seemingly paradoxical goddess. She is "the dynamic principle of change."[66] Forever a late teenager hovering at the transition to womanhood, Inanna-Ishtar was herself a threshold, the way in and the way out, the Lady of Transformation.[67]

Notes

1. Thorkild Jacobsen, *The Treasures of Darkness: A History of Mesopotamia Religion* (New Haven, CT: Yale University Press, 1976); Rivkah Harris, "Inanna-Ishtar as Paradox and a Coincidence of Opposites," *History of Religions* 30 (1991): 261–278; Amélie Kuhrt, "Women and War," *NIN: Journal of Gender Studies in Antiquity* 2 (2001): 1–2; Tzvi Abusch, "Ishtar's Proposal and Gilgamesh's Refusal: An Interpretation of The Gilgamesh Epic, Tablet 6, lines 1–79," *History of Religions* 26 (1986): 143–187.

2. Jeremy Black, Graham Cunningham, Eleanor Robson, and Gábor Zólyomi, eds. and trans., *The Literature of Ancient Sumer* (Oxford: Oxford University Press. 2003), 108.

3. William W. Hallo and J. Van Dijk, *The Exaltation of Inanna* (New Haven, CT: Yale University Press, 1968).

4. J. J. M. Roberts, *The Earliest Semitic Pantheon: A Study of the Semitic Deities Attested in Mesopotamia before UR III* (Baltimore: Johns Hopkins University Press 1972), 153.

5. Jacqueline Karageorghis, *Kypris, the Aphrodite of Cyprus: Ancient Sources and Archaeological Evidence* (Nicosia, Cyprus: Levantis Foundation, 2005); Budin, Stephanie L. Budin, *The Origins of Aphrodite* (Bethesda, MD: CDL Press, 2003); Miroslav Marcovich, "From Ishtar to Aphrodite," *Journal of Aesthetic Education* 30 (1996): 43–59; Paul Friedrich, *The Meaning of Aphrodite* (Chicago: University of Chicago Press, 1978).

6. Piotr Steinkeller, "Inanna's Archaic Symbol," in *Written in Clay and Stone: Ancient Near Eastern Studies Presented to Krystyna Szarynska on the Occasion of Her 80th*

Birthday, ed. J. Braun, K. Lyczkowska, M. Popko, and P. Steinkeller (Warsaw: Agade, 1998), 87–100.

7. Samuel Noah Kramer, "Sumerian History, Culture and Literature," in Diane Wolkstein and Samuel N. Kramer, *Inanna, Queen of Heaven and Earth: Her Stories and Hymns from Sumer* (New York: Harper and Row, 1983), 117.

8. Joan G. Westenholz, "Eneduanna, En-Priestess, Hen of Nanna, Spouse of Nanna," in *DUMU-E2-DUB-BA-A: Studies in Honor of Åke Sjöberg*, ed. H. Behrens, D. Loding, and M. T. Roth (Philadelphia: Samuel Noah Kramer Fund, University Museum, 1989), 539–556; Hallo and van Dijk, *Exaltation of Inanna*.

9. Betty De Shong Meador, *Inanna, Lady of Largest Heart: The Poems of the Sumerian High Priestess Enheduanna* (Austin: University of Texas Press, 2000), 6, 49, 50.

10. Ibid., 51; Elizabeth Williams-Forte, "Annotations of the Art," in Wolkstein and Kramer, *Inanna, Queen of Heaven and Earth*, 174–199.

11. Gebhard J. Selz, "Five Divine Ladies: Thoughts on Inana(k), Ištar, In(n)in(a), Annunitum, and Anat, and the Origin of the Title 'Queen of Heaven,'" *NIN: Journal of Gender Studies in Antiquity* 1 (2000): 29–59; I. J. Gelb, "The Name of the Goddess Innin," *Journal of Near Eastern Studies* 19 (1960): 72–79.

12. Steinkeller, "Inanna's Archaic Symbol," 92; Wolkstein and Kramer, *Inanna, Queen of Heaven and Earth*, 47.

13. Beatrice L. Goff, *Symbols of Prehistoric Mesopotamia* (New Haven, CT: Yale University Press, 1963), 84.

14. Abusch, "Ishtar," 23; Selz, "Five Divine Ladies," 32; Wolfgang Heimpel, "A Catalog of Near Eastern Venus Deities," *Syro-Mesopotamian Studies* 4 (1982): 65.

15. Douglas Frayne, trans., "The Sumerian Gilgamesh Poems," in *The Epic of Gilgamesh: A Norton Critical Edition*, ed. and trans. Benjamin R. Foster (New York: Norton, 2001), 120–127.

16. Tzvi Abusch, "Ishtar's Proposal and Gilgamesh's Refusal: An Interpretation of The Gilgamesh Epic, Tablet 6, lines 1–79," *History of Religions* 26 (1986): 173.

17. Benjamin R. Foster, trans., *The Epic of Gilgamesh: A Norton Critical Edition* (New York: Norton, 2001), 46–52.

18. Abusch, "Ishtar," 23; Hallo and van Dijk, *Exaltation of Inanna*, 61, 97.

19. Tikva Frymer-Kensky, *In the Wake of the Goddesses: Women, Culture, and the Biblical Transformation of Pagan Myth* (New York: Free Press, 1992), 189.

20. Jacobsen, *Treasures of Darkness*, 141.

21. Frymer-Kensky, *In the Wake of the Goddesses*, 29.

22. Ibid., 25.

23. Julia Assante, "The kar.kid/[k]harimtu, Prostitute or Single Woman? A Reconsideration of the Evidence," *Ugarit-Forschungen* 30 (1998): 5–96.

24. Jeremy Black and Anthony Green, *Gods, Demons, and Symbols of Ancient Mesopotamia* (Austin: University of Texas Press, 2003), 108; Wolkstein and

Kramer, *Inanna, Queen of Heaven and Earth*, 52, 102, 36, 100, 92; Pirjo Lapinkivi, *The Sumerian Sacred Marriage in the Light of Comparative Evidence* (Helsinki: The Neo-Assyrian Text Corpus Project, University of Helsinki Press, 2004), 140; Douglas Frayne, University of Toronto, 2007, personal communication; Brigitte R. M. Groneberg, *Lob der Ištar: Gebet und Ritual an die altbabylonische Venusgöttin. TANATTI IŠTAR* (Groningen: Styx, 1992), 125; Harris, "Inanna-Ishtar as Paradox," 272; Williams-Forte, "Annotations of the Art," 187, 188; Goff, *Symbols of Prehistoric Mesopotamia*; Krystyna Szarzyńska, "Cult of the Goddess Inana in Archaic Uruk," *NIN: Journal of Gender Studies in Antiquity* 1 (2000): 63–74, 67; Caitlin E. Barrett, "Was Dust Their Food and Clay Their Bread? Grave Goods, the Mesopotamian Afterlife, and the Liminal Role of Inanna/Ishtar," *Journal of Ancient Near Eastern Religions* 7 (2007): 25.

25. Williams-Forte, "Annotations of the Art," 174–175.

26. Abusch, "Ishtar," 24; Andrew R. George, *House Most High: The Temples of Ancient Mesopotamia* (Winona Lake, IN: Eisenbrauns 1993).

27. Mark E. Cohen, *The Cultic Calendars of the Ancient Near East* (Bethesda, MD: CDL Press, 1993).

28. Szarzyńska, "Cult of the Goddess Inana in Archaic Uruk," 64; Françoise Bruschweiler, *Inanna. La Déesse triomphante et vaincue dans la cosmologie sumérienne. Recherche lexicographique* (Leuven, Belgium: Peeters, 1987), 160; Annette Zgoll, "Inana als Nugig," *Zeitschrift für Assyriologie und vorderasiatische Archäologie* 87 (1997): 87; Abusch, "Ishtar," 24; Gary Beckman, "Ištar of Nineveh Reconsidered," *Journal of Cuneiform Studies* 50 (1998): 8; Ilse Wegner, *Gestalt und Kult des Ištar-Shawuška. Kleinasien und Hurritologische Studien* (Neukirchner-Vluyn/Kevelauer: Butzon und Zerker, 1981).

29. Selz, "Five Divine Ladies," 34–35; Roberts, *Earliest Semitic Pantheon*, 147.

30. Rivkah Harris, *Ancient Sippar: A Demographic Study of an Old Babylonian City (1894–1595 B.C.)* (Istanbul: Nederlands Historisch-Archaeologisch Instituut te Istanbul, 1975), 150.

31. Joan Aruz with Ronald Wallenfels, *Art of the First Cities: The Third Millennium B.C. from the Mediterranean to the Indus* (New York: Metropolitan Museum of Art Press, 2003); 206 #133 detail.

32. Joan G. Westenholz, "Nanaya: Lady of Mystery," in *Sumerian Gods and Their Representations*, ed. I. L. Finkel and M. J. Geller (Groningen, The Netherlands: Styx, 1997), 79.

33. Lapinkivi, *Sumerian Sacred Marriage*, 232–240.

34. Yitschak Sefati, *Love Songs in Sumerian Literature: Critical Edition of the Dumuzi Inanna Songs* (Ramat Gan, Israel: Bar-Ilan University Press, 1998); Wolkstein and Kramer, *Inanna, Queen of Heaven and Earth*, 29–49; Julia Assante, "From Whores to Hierodules: The Historiographic Invention of Mesopotamian Female Sex Professionals," in *Ancient Art and Its Historiography*, ed. A. A. Donahue and M. D. Fullerton (Cambridge: Cambridge University Press, 2003); Assante, "The kar.kid/[k]harimtu; Benjamin R. Foster, ed. and trans., *Before the*

Muses: An Anthology of Akkadian Literature, 3rd ed. (Bethesda, MD: CDL Press, 2005), 284, 678; Frymer-Kensky, *In the Wake of the Goddesses*, 47–48; R. D. Biggs, *Ancient Mesopotamian Potency Incantations* (Locust Valley, NY: Augustin, 1967), 27, 28; Zainab Bahrani, "The Whore of Babylon: Truly all Woman and of Infinite-Variety," *NIN: Journal of Gender Studies in Antiquity* 1 (2000): 95–106; Will Roscoe, "Priests of the Goddess: Gender Transgression in Ancient Religion," *History of Religions* 35 (1996): 195–230; Erica Reiner, *Ancient Near Eastern Texts Relating to the Old Testament: Third Edition with Supplement*, ed. James B. Pritchard (Princeton, NJ: Princeton University Press, 1969), 533.

35. Joan G. Westenholz, "King by Love of Inanna—An Image of Female Empowerment," *NIN: Journal of Gender Studies in Antiquity* 1 (2000): 75, 77.

36. Wolkstein and Kramer, *Inanna, Queen of Heaven and Earth*, 107–110.

37. Black and Green, *Gods, Demons, and Symbols*.

38. Szarzyńska, "Cult of the Goddess Inana," 67–68.

39. Black et al., *Literature of Ancient Sumer*, 262–269.

40. Ibid., 91; Kuhrt, "Women and War," 1–2; Groneberg, *Lob der Ištar*, 128.

41. Foster, ed. and trans., *Before the Muses*, 814.

42. Ibid.

43. Heimpel, "A Catalog of Near Eastern Venus Deities," 62; Black et al., *Literature of Ancient Sumer*, 98; Foster, ed. and trans., *Before the Muses*, 674; Wolkstein and Kramer, *Inanna, Queen of Heaven and Earth*, 101, 103; Szarzyńska, "Cult of the Goddess Inana," 64, 65; G. E. Kurtik, "The Identification of Inanna with the Planet Venus: A Criterion for the Time Determination of the Constellations in Ancient Mesopotamia," *Astronomical and Astrophysical Transactions* 17 (1999): 501–513; Frayne, personal communication, 2007.

44. Piotr Bienkowski and Alan Millard, *Dictionary of the Ancient Near East* (Philadelphia: University of Pennsylvania Press, 2000), 40–41.

45. Wayne Horowitz, *Mesopotamian Cosmic Geography* (Winona Lake, IN: Eisenbrauns, 1998), 158, 253–254.

46. Black et al., *Literature of Ancient Sumer*, 65–76.

47. Foster, ed. and trans., *Before the Muses*, 498–505.

48. Lapinkivi, *Sumerian Sacred Marriage*, 179.

49. Wolkstein and Kramer, *Inanna, Queen of Heaven and Earth*, 51.

50. Williams-Forte, "Annotations of the Art," 189.

51. Black and Green, *Gods, Demons, and Symbols*, frontispiece.

52. Barrett, "Was Dust Their Food?" 56.

53. Simo Parpola, *Assyrian Prophecies* (Helsinki: Helsinki University Press, 1997), xv.

54. Martii Nissinen, "The Socioreligious Role of Neo-Assyrian Prophets." in *Prophecy in Its Ancient Near Eastern Context: Mesopotamian, Biblical, and Arabian*, ed. M. Nissinen (Atlanta: Society of Biblical Literature, 2000), 96.

55. Karel van der Toorn, "Mesopotamian Prophecy between Immanence and Transcendence: A Comparison of Old Babylonian and Neo-Assyrian

Prophecy," in *Prophecy in Its Ancient Near Eastern Context: Mesopotamian, Biblical, and Arabian*, ed. M. Nissinen (Atlanta: Society of Biblical Literature, 2000), 76.

56. Martii Nissinen, *Prophets and Prophecy in the Ancient Near East* (Atlanta: Society of Biblical Literature, 2003), 6–7.

57. Parpola, *Assyrian Prophecies*, 4.

58. Herbert B. Huffmon, "A Company of Prophets: Mari, Assyria, Israel," in *Prophecy in Its Ancient Near Eastern Context*, ed. Nissinen, 51.

59. M. deJong Ellis, "Observations on Mesopotamian Oracles and Prophetic Texts: Literary and Historical Considerations," *Journal of Cuneiform Studies* 41 (1989): 141.

60. Parpola, *Assyrian Prophecies*, xlviii.

61. Black et al., *Literature of Ancient Sumer*, 315–320; Hallo and van Dijk, *Exaltation of Inanna*, 14ff.

62. Jacobsen, *Treasures of Darkness*, 84.

63. Wolkstein and Kramer, *Inanna, Queen of Heaven and Earth*, 11–27.

64. Harris, "Inanna-Ishtar as Paradox," 267.

65. Abusch, "Ishtar," 24.

66. Lapinkivi, *Sumerian Sacred Marriage*, 159.

67. Abusch, "Ishtar," 26.

68. Since I cannot read Sumerian, Akkadian, or Assyrian, I have to work with translations. However, my training in ancient Greek, Latin, and biblical Hebrew has taught me that critical comparison of a number of different translations produces a good understanding of an original text. I also check my understanding with a colleague, Professor Douglas Frayne of the University of Toronto, who does read the original languages and for whose help I am deeply indebted. Nonetheless I am responsible for any errors and especially for interpretations.

Bibliography

Abusch, Tzvi. "Ishtar." *NIN: Journal of Gender Studies in Antiquity* 1 (2000): 23–27.

Abusch, Tzvi. "Ishtar's Proposal and Gilgamesh's Refusal: An Interpretation of The Gilgamesh Epic, Tablet 6, lines 1–79." *History of Religions* 26 (1986): 143–187.

Aruz, Joan, with Ronald Wallenfels. *Art of the First Cities: The Third Millennium B.C. from the Mediterranean to the Indus.* New York: Metropolitan Museum of Art Press, 2003.

Assante, Julia. "From Whores to Hierodules: The Historiographic Invention of Mesopotamian Female Sex Professionals." In *Ancient Art and Its Historiography*, ed. A. A. Donahue and M. D. Fullerton, 13–47. Cambridge: Cambridge University Press, 2003.

Assante, Julia. "The kar.kid/[k]harimtu, Prostitute or Single Woman? A Reconsideration of the Evidence." *Ugarit-Forschungen* 30 (1998): 5–96.

Bahrani, Zainab. "The Whore of Babylon: Truly All Woman and of Infinite Variety." *NIN: Journal of Gender Studies in Antiquity* 1 (2000): 95–106.

Barrett, Caitlin E. "Was Dust Their Food and Clay Their Bread? Grave Goods, the Mesopotamian Afterlife, and the Liminal Role of Inanna/Ishtar." *Journal of Ancient Near Eastern Religions* 7 (2007): 7–65.

Barton, George A. *The Semitic Ishtar Cult.* 1893–1894. Piscataway, NJ: Gorgias, 2007.

Beckman, Gary. "Ištar of Nineveh Reconsidered." *Journal of Cuneiform Studies* 50 (1998): 1–10.

Bienkowski, Piotr, and Alan Millard. *Dictionary of the Ancient Near East.* Philadelphia: University of Pennsylvania Press, 2000.

Biggs, R. D. *Ancient Mesopotamian Potency Incantations.* Locust Valley, NY: Augustin, 1967.

Black, Jeremy, and Anthony Green. *Gods, Demons, and Symbols of Ancient Mesopotamia.* Austin: University of Texas Press, 2003.

Black, Jeremy, Graham Cunningham, Eleanor Robson, and Gábor Zólyomi, eds. and trans. *The Literature of Ancient Sumer.* Oxford: Oxford University Press, 2004.

Bruschweiler, Françoise. *Inanna. La Déesse triomphante et vaincue dans la cosmologie sumérienne. Recherche lexicographique.* Leuven, Belgium: Peeters, 1987.

Budin, Stephanie L. *The Origins of Aphrodite.* Bethesda, MD: CDL Press, 2003.

Cohen, Mark E. *The Cultic Calendars of the Ancient Near East.* Bethesda, MD: CDL Press, 1993.

Ellis, M. deJong. "Observations on Mesopotamian Oracles and Prophetic Texts: Literary and Historical Considerations." *Journal of Cuneiform Studies* 41 (1989): 127–186.

Foster, Benjamin R., ed. and trans. *Before the Muses: An Anthology of Akkadian Literature.* 3rd ed. Bethesda, MD: CDL Press, 2005.

Foster, Benjamin R., trans. *The Epic of Gilgamesh: A Norton Critical Edition.* New York: Norton, 2001.

Frayne, Douglas, trans. "The Sumerian Gilgamesh Poems." In *The Epic of Gilgamesh: A Norton Critical Edition*, trans. Benjamin R. Foster, 99–155. New York: Norton, 2001.

Friedrich, Paul. *The Meaning of Aphrodite.* Chicago: University of Chicago Press, 1978.

Frymer-Kensky, Tikva. *In the Wake of the Goddesses: Women, Culture, and the Biblical Transformation of Pagan Myth.* New York: Free Press, 1992.

Gelb, I. J. "The Name of the Goddess Innin." *Journal of Near Eastern Studies* 19 (1960): 72–79.

George, Andrew R. *House Most High: The Temples of Ancient Mesopotamia.* Winona Lake, IN: Eisenbrauns, 1993.

Goff, Beatrice L. *Symbols of Prehistoric Mesopotamia.* New Haven, CT: Yale University Press, 1963.

Groneberg, Brigitte R. M. *Lob der Ištar: Gebet und Ritual an die altbabylonische Venusgöttin. TANATTI IŠTAR.* Groningen: Styx, 1992.

Hallo, William W., and J. Van Dijk. *The Exaltation of Inanna*. New Haven, CT: Yale University Press, 1968.

Hallo, William W., and William K. Simpson. *The Ancient Near East: A History*. New York: Harcourt Brace Jovanovich, 1971.

Harris, Rivkah. *Ancient Sippar: A Demographic Study of an Old Babylonian City (1894–1595 B.C.)*. Istanbul: Nederlands Historisch-Archaeologisch Instituut te Istanbul, 1975.

Harris, Rivkah. "Inanna-Ishtar as Paradox and a Coincidence of Opposites." *History of Religions* 30 (1991): 261–278.

Heimpel, Wolfgang. "A Catalog of Near Eastern Venus Deities." *Syro-Mesopotamian Studies* 4 (1982): 59–72.

Horowitz, Wayne. *Mesopotamian Cosmic Geography*. Winona Lake, IN: Eisenbrauns, 1998.

Huffmon, Herbert B. "A Company of Prophets: Mari, Assyria, Israel." In *Prophecy in Its Ancient Near Eastern Context*, ed. M. Nissinen, 47–70. Atlanta: Society of Biblical Literature, 2000.

Jacobsen, Thorkild. *The Treasures of Darkness: A History of Mesopotamian Religion*. New Haven, CT: Yale University Press, 1976.

Karageorghis, Jacqueline. *Kypris, the Aphrodite of Cyprus: Ancient Sources and Archaeological Evidence*. Nicosia, Cyprus: Levantis Foundation, 2005.

Kramer, Samuel Noah. "Sumerian History, Culture and Literature." In Diane Wolkstein and Samuel N. Kramer, *Inanna, Queen of Heaven and Earth: Her Stories and Hymns from Sumer*, 115–126. New York: Harper and Row, 1983.

Kuhrt, Amélie. "Women and War." *NIN: Journal of Gender Studies in Antiquity* 2 (2001): 1–2.

Kurtik, G. E. "The Identification of Inanna with the Planet Venus: A Criterion for the Time Determination of the Constellations in Ancient Mesopotamia." *Astronomical and Astrophysical Transactions* 17 (1999): 501–513.

Lapinkivi, Pirjo. *The Sumerian Sacred Marriage in the Light of Comparative Evidence*. Helsinki: The Neo-Assyrian Text Corpus Project, University of Helsinki Press, 2004.

Leick, Gwendolyn. *Sex and Eroticism in Mesopotamian Literature*. London: Routledge, 1994.

Marcovich, Miroslav. "From Ishtar to Aphrodite." *Journal of Aesthetic Education* 30 (1996): 43–59.

Meador, Betty De Shong. *Inanna, Lady of Largest Heart: The Poems of the Sumerian High Priestess Enheduanna*. Austin: University of Texas Press, 2000.

Nissinen, Martii. *Prophets and Prophecy in the Ancient Near East*. Atlanta, GA: Society of Biblical Literature, 2003.

Nissinen, Martii. "The Socioreligious Role of Neo-Assyrian Prophets." In *Prophecy in Its Ancient Near Eastern Context: Mesopotamian, Biblical, and Arabian*, ed. M. Nissinen. Atlanta: Society of Biblical Literature, 2000.

Parpola, Simo. *Assyrian Prophecies*. Helsinki: Helsinki University Press, 1997.

Pollock, Susan. "Women in a Men's World: Images of Sumerian Women." In *Engendering Archaeology: Women and Prehistory*, ed. Joan M. Gero and Margaret W. Conkey, 366–387. Oxford: Blackwell, 1994.

Reiner, Erica. *Ancient Near Eastern Texts Relating to the Old Testament: Third Edition with Supplement*, ed. James B. Pritchard (Princeton, NJ: Princeton University Press, 1969).

Roberts, J. J. M. *The Earliest Semitic Pantheon: A Study of the Semitic Deities Attested in Mesopotamia before UR III*. Baltimore: Johns Hopkins University Press, 1972.

Roscoe, Will. "Priests of the Goddess: Gender Transgression in Ancient Religion." *History of Religions* 35 (1996): 195–230.

Sefati, Yitschak. *Love Songs in Sumerian Literature: Critical Edition of the Dumuzi Inanna Songs*. Ramat Gan, Israel: Bar-Ilan University Press, 1998.

Selz, Gebhard J. "Five Divine Ladies: Thoughts on Inana(k), Ištar, In(n)in(a), Annunitum, and Anat, and the Origin of the Title 'Queen of Heaven.'" *NIN: Journal of Gender Studies in Antiquity* 1 (2000): 29–59.

Steinkeller, Piotr. "Inanna's Archaic Symbol." In *Written in Clay and Stone: Ancient Near Eastern Studies Presented to Krystyna Szarynska on the Occasion of Her 80th Birthday*, ed. J. Braun, K. Lyczkowska, M. Popko, and P. Steinkeller, 87–100. Warsaw: Agade, 1998.

Steinkeller, Piotr. "On Rulers, Priests, and Sacred Marriage: Tracing the Evolution of Early Sumerian Kingship." In *Priests and Officials in the Ancient Near East: Papers of the Second Colloquium on the Ancient Near East, The Middle Eastern Culture Center in Japan*, ed. K. Watanabe, 103–137. Heidelberg: Winter, 1997.

Stuckey, Johanna H. "'Inanna and the *Huluppu* Tree': An Ancient Mesopotamian Narrative of Goddess Demotion." In *Feminist Poetics of the Sacred: Creative Suspicions*, ed. Frances Devlin-Glass and Lyn McCredden. New York: Oxford University Press, 2001.

Szarzyńska, Krystyna. "Cult of the Goddess Inana in Archaic Uruk." *NIN: Journal of Gender Studies in Antiquity* 1 (2000): 63–74.

Toorn, Karel van der. "Mesopotamian Prophecy between Immanence and Transcendence: A Comparison of Old Babylonian and Neo-Assyrian Prophecy." In *Prophecy in Its Ancient Near Eastern Context: Mesopotamian, Biblical, and Arabian*, ed. M. Nissinen, 71–87. Atlanta: Society of Biblical Literature, 2000.

Wegner, Ilse. *Gestalt und Kult des Ištar-Shawuška. Kleinasien und Hurritologische Studien*. Neukirchner-Vluyn/Kevelauer: Butzon und Zerker, 1981.

Westenholz, Joan G. "Eneduanna, En-Priestess, Hen of Nanna, Spouse of Nanna." In *DUMU-E2-DUB-BA-A: Studies in Honor of Åke Sjöberg*. ed. H. Behrens, D. Loding, and M. T. Roth, 539–556. Philadelphia: Samuel Noah Kramer Fund, University Museum, 1989.

Westenholz, Joan G. "King by Love of Inanna—An Image of Female Empowerment." *NIN: Journal of Gender Studies in Antiquity* 1 (2000): 75–89.

Westenholz, Joan G. "Nanaya: Lady of Mystery." In *Sumerian Gods and Their Representations*, ed. I. L. Finkel and M. J. Geller, 56–84. Groningen: Styx, 1997.

Williams-Forte, Elizabeth. "Annotations of the Art." In Diane Wolkstein and Samuel N. Kramer, *Inanna, Queen of Heaven and Earth: Her Stories and Hymns from Sumer*, 174–199. New York: Harper and Row, 1983.

Wolkstein, Diane, and Samuel N. Kramer. *Inanna, Queen of Heaven and Earth: Her Stories and Hymns from Sumer*. New York: Harper and Row, 1983.

Zgoll, Annette. "Inana als Nugig." *Zeitschrift für Assyriologie und vorderasiatische Archäologie* 87 (1997): 181–195.

3

Asherah: Hidden Goddess of the Bible

Daniel Cohen

In recent years, scholars have become more and more convinced that a goddess was part of ancient Hebrew religion, and that this religion was thus not, as generally believed, resolutely and profoundly monotheistic. Not long ago, the question "Was there a Hebrew goddess?" was widely discussed among biblical scholars, with a minority, though a sizeable one, arguing that there was. Now it seems to be largely accepted that there was such a goddess, and the questions are "What is the nature of the Hebrew goddess? How does she relate to earlier goddesses in the same area and to goddesses of nearby peoples?"[1]

In looking into this question, various sources are reliable. The Bible can be read critically. For instance, denunciations of cult images of the goddess Asherah are repeated so often that they lead one to deduce that such images were common. Other sources are nonbiblical texts found in archaeological excavations, as well as at the mythology of other cultures in the same region; and archaeological remains, especially figurines and plaques, and their iconography. In combining these different approaches, one needs to avoid circular arguments where, for instance, biblical texts lead one to conclusions about figurines, and the resulting understanding of the figurines is fed back into interpretations of the texts. Nonetheless, there is an interplay of approaches, in which careful consideration of one aspect can illuminate others.

Texts from Ugarit, which contain the first mention of the goddess Asherah, then biblical references and some crucial nonbiblical Hebrew

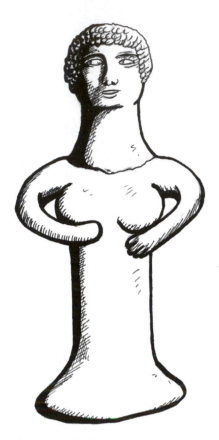

Figure 3.1 Asherah figurine, ceramic, from Lachish, Judah, eighth–seventh century BCE. After R. Patai, The Hebrew Goddess, plate 1. (Copyright © Stephane Beaulieu. Used by permission.)

writings will be examined; then archaeology will be explored to find the presence of a Hebrew goddess.

Texts from Ugarit

In 1929 and subsequent years, texts were found in Ras Shamra in Northern Syria, the site of the ancient city of Ugarit near the Mediterranean coast. These clay tablets, written in the 14th and 13th centuries BCE, contained myths of the deities and also god lists, records of rituals and offerings, and similar material.[2] There were a large number of these tablets, but many of them were found in a damaged or fragmentary condition. These form the principal body of texts relating to Asherah. Some mentions occur elsewhere, but they are scanty and do not add much knowledge of her. Also, the Ugaritic texts are close in location and fairly close in time to the biblical texts. Though the language, which is related to Hebrew, has been deciphered, it is often difficult to determine precisely which symbol a particular mark represents. Consequently, debate persists among scholars of Ugaritic as to the meaning of various phrases and texts. Though most scholars would accept in broad outline the account given here, and the details would be acceptable to many, each detail can be challenged.[3]

The term "Canaanite myths" is often used to refer simply to the texts from Ugarit, although the word "Canaan" when used in its widest sense refers to the whole area of the Levant (also referred to as the ancient Near East). The Canaanites mentioned in the Bible are perhaps best thought of as "the people living near us whose culture is different from ours."[4] The principal goddesses of Canaan were Asherah (also referred to as Athirat) and Anath, while the principal gods were El and Baal. The word "El" functions as a name and also as the word for "god," while "Baal" by itself just means "Lord"; it too is used as a name and also as a title.[5] Similarly Asherah may well be a title, such as "goddess," functioning as a name. Among the titles of Asherah were "Lady of the Sea" and "creatrix of the gods." She is sometime referred to as "Elat," which just means "goddess." In the myths Asherah performs various functions. When Baal requires a palace, he asks Asherah to intercede for him with El. When Baal appears dead, El asks her to nominate a new heir, and this appears to be one of her functions. She also appears in the myth of Keret/Kirta as the wet nurse of human royal heirs, legitimating an heir by suckling him.

The discovery of the Ras Shamra texts with their many references to the goddess Asherah transformed understanding of the term *asherah* in the Bible, and writings that are too early to take these into account cannot be considered reliable.

Background to the Bible

Many people who are not biblical scholars believe that the Bible is an accurate history of the ancient Hebrews. It is not. Rather, it is a mix of legend, history, and propaganda. Berlin and Brettler say

Although many of the texts in the Bible have been characterised as historical texts, they certainly are not historical in our sense. The biblical authors, unlike modern professional historians, made no attempt to be objective or complete in recording events from the past; instead, they constructed narratives of the past for religious and/or didactic purposes. Certainly, these narratives incorporated many facts, but it is often difficult to disentangle fact from fiction, truth from myth or legend. Unfortunately, relatively little writing outside the Bible has been preserved that might help us confirm what is historically accurate or fill in historical gaps. Though much archeological effort has gone into studying ancient Israel, the evidence is often ambiguous and open to different interpretations.[6]

The biblical description of the conquest of Canaan is now rejected by scholars, although they disagree as to the actual origin of the Israelites. There are no historical references in the texts of other nations to Israel until after the death of Solomon, apart from one very early source; after that time, references are common. Solomon was certainly not the great king he is portrayed as in the Bible, and some scholars even deny the existence of David and Solomon.[7] Finkelstein and Silberman express one of the minority views.[8]

Working backward and forward from that first known reference, and relying on the Bible for length of reigns, the following are approximate dates for the Hebrew kings. The kings of the United Monarchy of Israel and Judah were Saul (1025–1005 BCE), David (1005–965 BCE) and Solomon (965–928 BCE).[9] After Solomon's death, the kingdom was divided into two. The rich northern kingdom of Israel with capital Samaria had a succession of different dynasties until its conquest and destruction by the Assyrians in 722 BCE. Descendants of David ruled the poorer southern kingdom of Judah with its capital Jerusalem. Judah suffered through Assyrian invasions, but Jerusalem and the kingdom survived until Nebuchadnezzar of Babylon, who had previously conquered Assyria, conquered it and destroyed the temple in 586 BCE. At that time the upper classes and some of the skilled workers were deported to Babylon, though the majority of the population remained in Judah. When Cyrus of Persia conquered Babylon in 539 BCE, many of the exile families returned to Judah some fifty years after they had left, though others had by now settled in Babylon and remained there.

The main biblical texts at issue come from what is known as the Deuteronomistic History (Deuteronomy through 2 Kings), which had been composed during the later years of the Judean monarchy and updated during the exile. Another version of that history (1–2 Chronicles) was written a couple of centuries later. As to the religion of the peoples,

[B]iblical religion was a minority, dissident phenomenon, always at odds, as the Bible itself states, with the actual religions of the small kingdoms of Israel and Judah. . . . The actual religion of the states of Israel and Judah from ca. 900 to 600 BCE can be partially reconstructed from archeological and inscriptional evidence and from some evidence in the biblical text, which must be interpreted with caution, because the Bible stands in a polemical relationship to the contemporary religions of Israelites and Judeans, consistently distorting the real meaning of such features as the "high places" (*bamot*).[10]

The cult of "Yahweh alone," complete monotheism, only became significant during the Babylonian exile and was transplanted back to Judah on the return from exile.[11] The Deuteronomistic History is in large part an attempt to backdate this monotheism to an earlier period where it was not truly present.

Asherah in the Hebrew Bible

The Hebrew Bible uses the word *asherah* or the plural *asherim* forty times (see appendix).[12] Between three and five uses, depending on decisions made in the translation, refer either directly to the goddess Asherah or to images of the goddess. The vast majority of references are to cult objects presumably connected with the goddess. In many English translations this connection is completely lost. For instance, the Authorized (King James) version usually translates *asherah* as "groves," whereas the Revised Standard Version prefers "sacred poles."[13] "Grove" is a direct translation of the Greek *alsos*, which is the word used in the Septuagint, the original Greek translation of the Hebrew Bible, made by Jewish scholars between the third and first centuries BCE.

The best-known reference to the goddess occurs in 1 Kings 18:19, where the prophet Elijah meets with "the 450 prophets of Baal and the 400 prophets of the goddess Asherah." Elijah engages in a contest with the prophets of Baal and utterly defeats them, but the prophets of Asherah play no part in the story. It is likely that the purpose of this story as regards Asherah is to associate her with the foreign god Baal and to distance her from the god of the Hebrews.

In 1 Kings 15:13, repeated in 2 Chron. 15:16, King Asa "removed his mother Maacah from being queen mother because she made an abominable image for Asherah." In 2 Kings 21:7 King Manasseh ordered that "[t]he carved image of Asherah that he had made he set in" the temple. The exploits of King Josiah in 2 Kings 23:4–15 include removing and destroying vessels made for Asherah and an image of Asherah. He also "broke down the houses of the male temple prostitutes that were in the house of the Lord, where the women did weaving for Asherah."[14]

The prophet Jeremiah warned those Judeans who went to Egypt after the Babylonian conquest, saying that Judah was conquered because its people made offerings and served other gods. The response of both women and men (Jer. 44.16–19; also Jer. 7:17–18) was that they intended to continue making offerings to the Queen of Heaven, pouring out libations, with the women making cakes for her in her image "just as we and our ancestors, our kings and our officials, used to do in the towns of Judah and in the streets of Jerusalem."

Who is the Queen of Heaven? She may well be the Babylonian goddess Ishtar (see Johanna Stuckey's chapter in this volume), one of whose titles was "Queen of Heaven and Earth"; some of whose ceremonies seem similar to the ones mentioned. But there is no direct account of worship of Ishtar among the Judeans. Similar ceremonies for Asherah may have existed, although she has no specific heavenly connections. Nonetheless, it seems more likely that the Queen of Heaven is a goddess whose worship is known in Judea, and therefore that she is Asherah.[15]

Nature of the *Asherah*

What exactly were the asherah? They seem to be made of wood since, according to the biblical texts, they could be cut down and burned. They could be planted or erected and uprooted or removed. A few of the asherah, those associated with the Temple, might have been images of the goddess Asherah, but the majority were not. They were wooden objects, perhaps in the shape of a stylized tree. They may have been actual trees, the interpretation suggested in the Mishnah, the rabbinic commentary on the Bible made in the second and third centuries CE. Most modern scholars find this unlikely, but Taylor suggests that they were living trees of small varieties such as willow or almond (rather than large varieties such as oak or terebinth), extensively pruned and shaped.[16]

The asherah were widespread, being present "on every high hill and under every green tree." This phrase occurs in the Bible several times (for instance 1 Kings 14:23). Though this phrase is rhetorical, not to be taken literally, it does indicate the presence of the asherah in many local and family shrines.[17] Presumably they were symbols of the goddess

Asherah, used in her worship. But they were more than symbols. "In the ancient Near East, the idol was the god. . . . But what was the stylized tree or the hypostasis of the female side of Yahweh to the average worshipper? Nothing other than Asherah, the goddess."[18]

Evidence from Nonbiblical texts

The site at Kuntillet Ajrud, occupied around 800 BCE in northern Sinai, was probably a way station for caravans. Fragments of inscribed pottery from broken storage jars were found there. Translations of parts of the inscriptions read, "I bless you by Yahweh of Samaria and by his Asherah," and "I bless you by Yahweh of Teman and by his Asherah." A further inscription on plaster may also refer to Asherah/asherah. Another text, dating from the second half of the eighth century BCE, was chiseled from a pillar in a burial cave at Khirbet-el-Qom, near Hebron in Judah. Part of this text is translated as "Blessed be Uriyahu by Yahweh for from his enemies by his [YHWH's] Asherah he [YHWH] has saved him." Other fragmentary lines also appear to mention asherah.[19]

It is unclear whether these texts refer to "Yahweh and his Asherah" or "Yahweh and his asherah." The former would pair the goddess directly with Yahweh as his consort. The latter has Yahweh using symbols of the goddess as a tool in blessing, which still implies a close connection. Even if the asherah now belong to the cult of Yahweh (since they are "his"), this simply puts the presence of the goddess further back in time. The use of "his" with a proper name is not found elsewhere in Hebrew, so many scholars prefer "his asherah."[20] As against that, a blessing by two deities is more likely than a blessing by one deity and objects belonging to him, which suggests that one should read "his Asherah." Freedman prefers the reading, "his Asherah," and provides an ingenious argument to deal with the grammatical difficulty.[21] He suggests that "his Asherah" is used to indicate that Asherah is associated with Yahweh and not with any other deity, and finds a similar use of words in Shakespeare's "For never was a story of more woe / Than this of Juliet and her Romeo."[22]

Images of Ashera

Further information about deities is gained by looking at images such as plaques and seal-rings.[23] Certain symbols identify an image as that of a deity, and specific symbols are associated with specific deities.[24] The problem with looking at Asherah in this way is that there are no images that unambiguously name her. Edwards discusses a very important relief image from Egypt showing a goddess with three names, Qudshu, Anath, Astarte.[25] The latter two are prominent West Syrian deities, so it is generally considered that the third name must also be that of a major West Syrian goddess, the three being regarded as merged into one. Specifically, Qudshu must be Asherah, one of whose epithets is *qudshu* ("holiness"). There are over a dozen similar images, several of which bear the name Qudshu, all of which show a goddess standing on a lion. The association of goddesses with lions is common, and one such goddess is Asherah.

Various drawings were found on other fragments of the jars at Kuntillet Ajrud. Some depict anthropomorphic figures, possibly deities, but have no clear connection with Asherah. However, one drawing shows a stylized tree on the back of a lion, with ibexes on either side feeding from it. A figure standing on a lion is usually a deity, and goddesses are often depicted as trees. It seems likely that the goddess Asherah is represented by this image. Similar images of a tree with ibexes occur in a 13th-century BCE ewer from Lachish, and a 10th-century cult stand from Taanach, the latter also containing a naked female figure between two lions. It seems that all these images represent a goddess, presumably Asherah.[26]

The "pillar figurines" found in Judah, dating from the eighth and seventh centuries BCE, must have played a significant part in local society, as over 800 of them have been found in many different locations.[27] These fired clay figurines have an undifferentiated lower body, without any legs, feet, or sexual organs, the upper body consisting of a woman's breasts and arms, with her hands under the breasts, and a head. The construction, with the base wider than the body, provides an easy way of making them so that they stand safely. Though there is a superficial resemblance to asherah poles, this is probably just a result of their simple construction.

What is the purpose of these figurines? They are not likely to be toys, given their locations, conditions of wear, and material. Nor are they likely to represent mortal women, as they are too uniform and almost certainly represent the same figure. Magical or religious use seems most likely. Distinction between the two is not always clear, and a purely magical use would require the figure to represent a being not known from other sources.[28]

Kletter argues that terms such as "mother goddess" and "fertility goddess" are too vague to be of any use. He says, "The main question is do the JPFs [Judaic pillar figurines] represent a goddess? If not, then all these terms ["mother goddess," "fertility goddess"] are groundless. If the JPFs do represent a goddess, then there is no escape from trying to identify a specific goddess." He holds that it seems most likely that they represent a goddess known to the people of Judah at that time. This indicates that they represent Asherah. These small figurines would seem to represent the goddess in private houses or local shrines. They are probably not connected with major temples, where images of Asherah are likely to be large statues.[29]

Hochma and Shekinah: Vestigal Goddesess?

The removal of any goddess from the Hebrew religion did not remove the need for a female aspect of deity. This surfaced in the forms of Hochma and Shekhinah.[30] Although Hochma is not a direct replacement for Asherah, some of the language and imagery of Asherah, notably references to trees and the Tree of Life, became part of the figure of Hochma.[31] Also, the menorah, the seven-branched candlestick used originally in the Temple at Jerusalem, seems to be based on the stylized tree that is an image of Asherah.[32]

The Hebrew word *hochma* ("wisdom") is feminine in gender. Hochma appears in various Biblical texts personified as female.[33] In Prov. 8:22–30, "The Lord created me the beginning of his works, before all else that he made, long ago," and "When he set the heavens in their place I was there, when he girdled the ocean with the horizon." Another term, *Shekhinah*, denotes the presence of God, especially when located in a particular place; the word comes from the Hebrew word meaning "to dwell." The word is feminine grammatically, but Shekhinah is not thought of as female in mainstream Judaism. However, in the mystical tradition of the Kabbalah, she is a female being, a partner to God.

Hochma and Shekinah should not be regarded as goddesses, since there is no specific worship of them or related cult. But they are both female aspects of deity and can help to restore female presence to Judaism and Christianity. Shekinah is an aspect particularly relevant to Judaism. By contrast, Hochma—especially under her Greek name, Sophia—was easily assimilated into Christianity. Her role was largely taken over by Christ and by the male Logos, whose description parallels many of the descriptions of her, but she has always been present in the Orthodox tradition, especially its mystical side.[34] Modern Jews and Christians who want to include a female aspect of deity often connect with Shekinah and Sophia.

Conclusions about Hebrew Religion and a Goddess

The most important point about the Hebrew goddess is that she was present. She is particularly clearly seen in popular religion, the religious behavior of the majority of the population, but she is even present to some extent in the formal religion of the temple and priests. She was known as Asherah. She seems to be the consort of Yahweh, though the evidence is not conclusive. The Khirbet el-Qom and Kuntillet Ajrud inscriptions, if read as "Yahweh and his Asherah," lead to this conclusion. Also, Asherah was the consort of El in Ugarit, and El was the original god of Israel with Yahweh becoming Israel's god, either replacing El or becoming identified with El.[35] This also points to Asherah as consort of Yahweh. Dever's recent discussion of an intriguing house shrine adds support to this view.[36] Finally, a primary goddess and a primary god, such as Asherah and Yahweh, are likely to be consorts.

There is no evidence to suggest that she was more significant or fundamental than him, and this seems highly unlikely for this context. However Binger, working in a wider context, makes a point of referring to the primary goddess as a "female counterpart" of the primary god. One cannot say anything about her characteristics, other than that she was associated with trees. Nor is the form of her worship ascertained, except that it took place "on every high hill and under every green tree." Her nature or the forms of her worship cannot be deduced by comparison with similar goddesses elsewhere; although such comparison may be relevant, they may also be unreliable. It will be even less reliable if, as Binger suggests, Asherah is not a name but a title, the title of the primary local goddess.[37]

Yahwist monotheism, as in Judaism, is capable of including both female and male equally.[38] But all too often it emphasizes the male and devalues the female, denying women their place as of equal value to men. Remembering Asherah and her place in the religion whose sacred texts have been so influential helps emphasize that the sacred is both female and male, and that women and men are both created in the image of god. Ackerman points out that the monotheistic minority won and the majority, whose worship includes other gods along with Yahweh, was suppressed.[39] She is a reminder that "we should be just as concerned with those who failed as with those who succeeded. . . . We must recall for those whom the Bible has rendered mute the utter diversity which characterized the ancient Israelite cult."

Appendix: Biblical Verses Referring to Asherah/Asherah

The biblical verses that contain the word *asherah* or *Asherah* are as follows: Exod. 34:13; Deut. 7:5, 12:3, 16:21; Judg. 3:7, 6:25–30; 1 Kings

14:15, 14:23, 15:13 (2 Chron. 15:16), 16:33, 18:19; 2 Kings 13:6, 17:10, 17:16, 18:4, 21:3, 21:7, 23:4–15; 2 Chron. 14:3 (or 14:2, depending on the translation), 15:16, 17:6, 19:3, 24:18, 31:1, 33:3, 33:19, 34:3, 34:4, 34:7; Isa. 17:8, 27:9; Jer. 17:2; Micah 5:14 (or 5:13).

There are also verses that do not use the word *asherah* but may nonetheless be making a reference to her or it. As one example, Hosea 14:9 (or 8, depending on the translation) reads

Ephraim, what has he still to do with idols?
It is I who answer and look after him.
I am like a luxuriant cypress,
From me comes your fruit.

Some scholars have suggested that this is a condemnation of Asherah and her worship, and that the second line should read "I am his Anath and his Asherah." This is unlikely, as it requires that the Hebrew text be emended unnecessarily. However, Hebrew is full of puns, partly because the lack of vowels in writing allows for various choices for the exact words. Such a pun is very possible in this case since it only requires the change of one consonant, from *ani aniti wa'asurennu* to *ani anato wa'asserato*.[40]

Notes

1. The items in the bibliography are only a few of many on this subject. For the general reader, the most accessible materials are William G. Dever, *Did God Have a Wife?* (Grand Rapids, MI: Eerdmans, 2005), and the following articles: Asphodel P. Long, "Asherah, the Tree of Life and the Menorah: Continuity of a Goddess Symbol in Judaism?" in *Patriarchs, Prophets and Other Villains*, ed. Lisa Isherwood (Oakville, CT: Equinox Publishing, 2007), originally given as the First Sophia Fellowship Feminist Theology Lecture at the College of St. Mark and St. John, Plymouth, England, December 4, 1996, and published in 1997 by the Britain and Ireland School of Feminist Theology (available online at http://www.asphodel-long.com); Johanna H. Stuckey, "Asherah, Supreme Goddess of the Levant," *Matrifocus* 3, no. 3 (Beltane/May 2004), http://www.matrifocus.com/BEL04/spotlight.htm; and Johanna H. Stuckey, "Asherah and the God of the Early Israelites," *Matrifocus* 3, no. 4 (Lammas 2004), http://www.matrifocus.com/LAM04/spotlight.htm.

2. BCE and CE, standing for "Before the Common Era" and "Common Era," are used by many scholars to avoid the Christian-centered BC and AD. For the same reason, "Hebrew Bible" is used instead of "Old Testament."

3. Original text with translation can be found in J. C. L. Gibson, *Canaanite Myths and Legends*, 2nd ed., (Edinburgh: T. & T. Clark, 1978), and a slightly

different translation with commentary in Simon B. Parker, ed., *Ugaritic Narrative Poetry* (Atlanta: Scholars Press, 1997). For a discussion with emphasis on Asherah see Steven A. Wiggins, *A Reassessment of Asherah with Further Considerations of the Goddess* (Piscataway, NJ: Gorgias Press, 2007).

4. Mark S. Smith, *The Early History of God*, 2nd ed. (Grand Rapids, MI: Eerdmans, 2002), 19–31, discusses the relationship of Israel and Canaan.

5. Compare "god" and "God" in English.

6. Adele Berlin and Marc Zvi Brettler, "Historical and Geographical Background to the Bible," in *The Jewish Study Bible*, ed. Adele Berlin and Marc Zvi Brettler (New York: Oxford University Press, 2004), 2048.

7. Berlin and Brettler (ibid., 2052), say, "Whether the extent of the territory controlled by David and Solomon is as large as biblical sources suggest is questionable. Clearly the biblical historians have magnified the period of the United Monarchy, the reign of David and Solomon."

8. Israel Finkelstein and Neil Asher Silberman, *The Bible Unearthed* (New York: Free Press, 2001).

9. Michael D. Coogan, ed., *The Oxford History of the Biblical World* (Oxford: Oxford University Press, 1998), and Berlin and Brettler, "Historical and Geographical Background to the Bible" are good historical sources.

10. Stephen A. Geller, "The Religion of the Bible," in *The Jewish Study Bible*, ed. Berlin and Brettler, 2021.

11. The name of the god of the ancient Hebrews and modern Judaism is written with four Hebrew consonants, *yod, he, vau, he*—there are no vowels in the original written Hebrew, but vowels were added in later texts. This used to be rendered in English as "Jehovah," but modern scholars use the form "Yahweh."

12. Oddly, *asherim* is a masculine plural of a feminine singular.

13. I use the Revised Standard Version (RSV) for biblical quotations unless otherwise noted. However, it is often valuable to compare translations, as readings may differ considerably. For a discussion of different translations, and other useful information about the writing of the Bible, see Sarah S. Forth, *Eve's Bible: a Woman's Guide to the Old Testament* (New York: St. Martin's Griffin, 2009).

14. Latest thinking is that there was no such thing as cult prostitution, either male or female, and that the word means a temple functionary. See, for example, Meindert Dijkstra. "El, the God of Israel," in *Only One God?*, ed. Bob Becking et al. (Sheffield: Continuum, 2001), 119. The weaving might refer to making clothing for an image of Asherah, in which the goddess was regarded as being present; compare with the presentation of a robe to Athene as part of a major festival in classical Athens, the Panathenaia.

15. Othmar Keel and Christoph Uehlinger, *Gods, Goddesses, and Images of God in Ancient Israel* (Minneapolis: Fortress Press, 1998), 338–341, but John Day, in *Yahweh and the Gods and Goddesses of Canaan* (Sheffield: Sheffield Academic Press, 2000), concludes that she is Astarte (144–150).

16. Joan E. Taylor, "The Asherah, the Menorah, and the Sacred Tree," *Journal for the Study of the Old Testament* 66 (1995): 29–54.

17. See the discussion of folk religion in Dever. *Did God Have a Wife?*

18. Susan Ackerman, *Under Every Green Tree: Popular Religion in Sixth-Century Judah* (Atlanta: Scholars Press, 1992), 65–66.

19. Judith M. Hadley. *Evidence for a Hebrew Goddess: The Cult of Asherah in Ancient Israel and Judah.* (Cambridge: Cambridge University Press, 2000), 84–105, 106–155.

20. John Day, "Asherah in the Hebrew Bible and Northwest Semitic Literature," *Journal of Biblical Literature* 105, no. 3 (1986): 392.

21. David Noel Freedman, "Yahweh of Samaria and His Asherah," *Biblical Archaeologist* (December 1987): 249.

22. The same English usage also occurs in 19th-century British popular songs, such as "Villikins and His Dinah" and "Burns and His Highland Mary."

23. These rings have a design set into a stone or a flattened piece of metal. When pressed into moist clay, the design is transferred to the clay and acts as a signature when the clay is dry. Cylinder seals are similar, with the design around the cylinder, which is rolled across the clay.

24. A similar use of symbols is found in Christianity, where an image of a saint holding a bunch of keys would identify it as Saint Peter, while a saint fighting a dragon will be Saint George or Saint Michael.

25. I. E. S. Edwards, "A Relief of Qudshu-Astarte-Anath in the Winchester College Collection," *Journal of Near Eastern Studies* 14 (1955): 49–51.

26. Hadley, *Evidence for a Hebrew Goddess*, 152–155, 156–176; Othmar Keel, *Goddesses and Trees, New Moon and Yahweh: Ancient Near Eastern Art and the Hebrew Bible* (Sheffield: Sheffield Academic Press, 1998); Keel and Uehlinger, *Gods, Goddesses, and Images of God.*

27. Raz Kletter, *The Judaean Pillar-Figurines and the Archaeology of Asherah* (Oxford: Tempus Reparatum, 1996).

28. Ibid., 81.

29. Ibid., 74–75, 81.

30. Asphodel P. Long, *In a Chariot Drawn by Lions* (London: The Women's Press, 1992), and Asphodel P. Long, "The Goddess in Judaism—An Historical Perspective," in *The Absent Mother: Restoring the Goddess to Judaism and Christianity*, ed. Alix Pirani (London: Mandala, 1991).

31. Judith M. Hadley, "Wisdom and the Goddess," in *Wisdom in Ancient Israel*, ed. John Day, R. P. Gordon and H. G. M. Williamson (Cambridge: Cambridge University Press, 1995); Mark S. Smith, "God Male and Female in the Old Testament: Yahweh and His 'Asherah,'" *Theological Studies* 48 (1987): 337.

32. Joan E. Taylor, "The Asherah, the Menorah, and the Sacred Tree," *Journal for the Study of the Old Testament* 66 (1995): 29–54; Long, "Asherah, the Tree of Life, and the Menorah."

33. However, the kabbalistic texts, written later, treat Hochma as male.

34. Long, "The Goddess in Judaism," and Long, *In a Chariot Drawn by Lions.*

35. Gen. 17.1, 28.3; Exod. 6.3, and elsewhere in Hebrew, but often lost in translations. The name "Israel" refers to El. Day, *Yahweh and the Gods and Goddesses of Canaan*, 13–14.

36. William G. Dever, "A Temple Built for Two. Did Yahweh Share a Throne with His Consort Asherah?" *Biblical Archaeology Review* 24, no. 5 (March/April 2008): 55–62.

37. Tilde Binger, *Asherah: The Goddesses in Ugarit, Israel, and the Old Testament* (Sheffield: Sheffield Academic Press, 2007), 145–148.

38. Gen. 1:27 has often been interpreted as implying that God is both male and female. Also some of the biblical attributes of God are female ones. See Phyllis Trible, *God and the Rhetoric of Sexuality* (Philadelphia: Fortress Press, 1978).

39. Ackerman, *Under Every Green Tree*, 217.

40. Day, "Asherah in the Hebrew Bible," 404–405, and Day, *Yahweh and the Gods and Goddesses of Canaan*, 57–58.

Bibliography

Ackerman, Susan. *Under Every Green Tree: Popular Religion in Sixth-Century Judah.* Atlanta: Scholars Press, 1992.

Becking, Bob, et al. *Only One God?: Monotheism in Ancient Israel and the Veneration of the Goddess Asherah.* Sheffield: Continuum, 2001.

Berlin, Adele, and Marc Zvi Brettler. "Historical and Geographical Background to the Bible." In *The Jewish Study Bible*, ed. Adele Berlin and Marc Zvi Brettler, 2048–2062. New York: Oxford University Press, 2004.

Binger, Tilde. *Asherah: The Goddesses in Ugarit, Israel, and the Old Testament.* Sheffield: Sheffield Academic Press, 2007.

Coogan, Michael D., ed. *The Oxford History of the Biblical World.* Oxford: Oxford University Press, 1998.

Cornelius, Izak. *The Many Faces of the Goddess: The Iconography of the Syro-Palestinian Goddesses Anat, Astarte, Qedeshet and Asherah c. 1500–1000 BCE.* Fribourg: Academic Press, 2004.

Day, John. "Asherah in the Hebrew Bible and Northwest Semitic Literature." *Journal of Biblical Literature* 105, no. 3 (1986): 385–408.

Day, John. *Yahweh and the Gods and Goddesses of Canaan.* Sheffield: Sheffield Academic Press, 2000.

Dever, William G. *Did God Have a Wife?* Grand Rapids, MI: Eerdmans, 2005.

Dever, William G. "A Temple Built for Two: Did Yahweh Share a Throne with His Consort Asherah?" *Biblical Archaeology Review* 24. no. 5 (March/April 2008): 55–62.

Dijkstra, Meindert. "El, the God of Israel." In *Only One God?*, ed. Bob Becking et al., 81–126. Sheffield: Continuum, 2001.

Edwards, I. E. S. "A Relief of Qudshu-Astarte-Anath in the Winchester College Collection." *Journal of Near Eastern Studies* 14 (1955): 49–51.

Finkelstein, Israel, and Neil Asher Silberman. *The Bible Unearthed.* New York: Free Press, 2001.

Forth, Sarah S. *Eve's Bible: A Woman's Guide to the Old Testament.* New York: St. Martin's Griffin, 2009.

Freedman, David Noel. "Yahweh of Samaria and His Asherah." *Biblical Archaeologist* (December 1987): 241–249.

Geller, Stephen A. "The Religion of the Bible." In *The Jewish Study Bible,* ed. Adele Berlin and Marc Zvi Brettler, 2021–2041. New York: Oxford University Press, 2004.

Gibson, J. C. L. *Canaanite Myths and Legends.* 2nd ed. Edinburgh: T. & T. Clark, 1978.

Hadley, Judith M. *Evidence for a Hebrew Goddess: The Cult of Asherah in Ancient Israel and Judah.* Cambridge: Cambridge University Press, 2000.

Hadley, Judith M. "Wisdom and the Goddess." In *Wisdom in Ancient Israel,* ed. John Day, R. P. Gordon, and H. G. M. Williamson, 234–243. Cambridge: Cambridge University Press, 1995.

Hestrin, Ruth. "Understanding Asherah: Exploring Semitic Iconography." *Biblical Archaeologist Review* 17 (1991): 50–59.

Keel, Othmar. *Goddesses and Trees, New Moon and Yahweh: Ancient Near Eastern Art and the Hebrew Bible.* Sheffield: Sheffield Academic Press, 1998.

Keel, Othmar, and Christoph Uehlinger. *Gods, Goddesses, and Images of God in Ancient Israel.* Minneapolis: Fortress Press, 1998.

Kletter, Raz. *The Judaean Pillar-Figurines and the Archaeology of Asherah.* Oxford: Tempus Reparatum, 1996.

Long, Asphodel P. "Asherah, the Tree of Life and the Menorah: Continuity of a Goddess Symbol in Judaism?" In *Patriarchs, Prophets and Other Villains,* ed. Lisa Isherwood. Oakville, CT: Equinox Publishing Ltd., 2007.

Long, Asphodel P. "The Goddess in Judaism—An Historical Perspective." In *The Absent Mother: Restoring the Goddess to Judaism and Christianity,* ed. Alix Pirani, 27–65. London: Mandala, 1991.

Long, Asphodel P. *In a Chariot Drawn by Lions.* London: Women's Press, 1992.

Margalit, Baruch. "The Meaning and Significance of Asherah." *Vetus Testamentum* 40, no. 3 (1990): 264–297.

Meshel, Ze'ev. "Did Yahweh Have a Consort? New Religious Inscription from the Sinai." *Biblical Archaeology Review* 5 (1979): 24–35.

Miller, Patrick D., Jr. *The Religion of Ancient Israel.* London: SPCK, 2000.

Olyan, Saul M. *Asherah and the Cult of Yahweh in Israel.* Atlanta: Scholars Press, 1988.

Parker, Simon B., ed. *Ugaritic Narrative Poetry.* Atlanta: Scholars Press, 1997.

Patai, Raphael. *The Hebrew Goddess.* New York: Ktav, 1967.

Pettey, Richard J. *Asherah, Goddess of Israel.* New York: Peter Lang, 1990.

Reed, W. L. *The Asherah in the Old Testament.* Fort Worth: Texas Christian University Press, 1949.

Smith, Mark S. *The Early History of God.* 2nd ed. Grand Rapids, MI: Eerdmans, 2002.

Smith, Mark S. "God Male and Female in the Old Testament: Yahweh and His 'Asherah.'" *Theological Studies* 48 (1987): 333–340.

Stuckey, Johanna H. "Asherah and the God of the Early Israelites." *Matrifocus* 3, no. 4 (Lammas/August 2004), http://www.matrifocus.com/LAM04/spot light.htm, accessed June 30, 2010.

Stuckey, Johanna H. "Asherah, Supreme Goddess of the Levant." *Matrifocus* 3, no. 3 (Beltane/May 2004), http://www.matrifocus.com/BEL04/spotlight .htm, accessed June 30, 2010.

Stuckey, Johanna H. "The Great Goddesses of the Levant." *Journal of the Society for the Study of Egyptian Antiquities* 30 (2003): 127–157.

Stuckey, Johanna H. "Sacred Repositories and Goddess Figurines." *Matrifocus* 7, no. 3 (Beltane 2008), http://www.matrifocus.com/BEL08/spotlight.htm.

Taylor, Joan E. "The Asherah, the Menorah, and the Sacred Tree." *Journal for the Study of the Old Testament* 66 (1995): 29–54.

Trible, Phyllis. *God and the Rhetoric of Sexuality.* Philadelphia: Fortress Press, 1978.

Wiggins, Steven A. *A Reassessment of Asherah with Further Considerations of the Goddess.* Piscataway, NJ: Gorgias Press, 2007.

4

Lilith: The Primordial Feminine

M. Kelley Hunter

Ancient yet totally contemporary, this particularly shady female image is mentioned in ancient literature and has continued to fascinate through the ages. With an ambiguous reputation, ranging from seductive vampire to cosmic goddess, Lilith offers a daring revision of the magical, mystical, and transformative power of the feminine, today and through history. Her name now a rallying call for feminists, the power of Lilith goes beyond politics and social change, back deep into the primordial wilderness of human nature. She intimately touches sensitive psychological edges of personal experience, while also flaunting herself on the world stage, dramatizing collective fears and desires. Any story that features Lilith is full of shadows, highly subjective, and open to a wide range of interpretation.

The same musical lilt is heard in the names of other related ladies of the dark, such as Lily, Layla, Lola, Lolita, Lila, Leela, Lillian, Loralei, and Delilah, even in the Hindu Kali and Lalita. Her name derives from various Sumerian spirits and demons. *Lil* is a wind spirit. The hairy *lilin* were a class of demons, of which the *lilits* were the females. The *ardat lili* were restless female ghosts seeking sexual satisfaction. The *lamashtu* and *labartu* kept vigil near pregnant women, waiting to snatch their newborns. The demonic *lilitu* were mentioned in the book of Isaiah (34:14), translated as "screech owl" and sometimes spelled Lilith. The father of the Sumerian hero Gilgamesh was said to be a *lillu* demon, a vampirish succubus which could mate and produce human children. The *lil-la-ke*

Figure 4.1 Adam and Eve with Lilith as the serpent on the north portal of the west facade of Notre Dame Cathedral in Paris. (Lilith at Notre Dame, photography by M. Kelley Hunter.)

were said to dwell in the primordial tree, a "tree of light" at the beginning of the world where it meets the sea at dawn. This last image echoes Lilith's role in the myth of Inanna.[1]

Lilith in the Tree

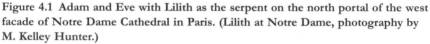

> Then a serpent who could not be charmed
> Made its nest in the roots of the huluppu tree.
> The Anzu-bird set his young in the branches of the tree.
> And the dark maid Lilith built her home in the trunk.
> The young woman who loved to laugh wept.
> How Inanna wept![2]

Lilith appears in one of the oldest extant myths, the story of Inanna, queen of heaven, written in cuneiform during the third millennium BCE on clay tablets unearthed as recently as the late 19th century during excavations in southern Iraq. Samuel N. Kramer, one of the original translators, popularized this story of Inanna in *Sumerian Mythology* and, with storyteller Diane Wolkstein, in *Inanna, Queen of Heaven and Earth*.

Before time began, a great storm in the deep of the deep uprooted a tree during the tempestuous mating of two primordial gods. Young Inanna pulls this huluppu (willow) tree from the water and plants it in her garden, the original Garden of Eden. She intends to use its wood to carve her throne of power and her bed of marriage. Unwelcome creatures take over the tree—a snake (or dragon), the wild anzu bird, and the dark maid Lilith. The serpent and the bird are regularly associated with Lilith and other goddesses of wisdom and power. At the base of the tree it represents earth-gnosis, oracular powers. In her study, *Lilith: The Edge of Forever*, Filomena Maria Pereira confirms that:

> The association of goddess, tree, bird and serpent are ancient and enduring. . . . Certain themes seem to emerge from these stories. For example, the tree as the "embodiment" of the divinity, housing the potential power of Life giving energy. It is also the axis mundi connecting the three realms of heaven, earth and the underworld.[3]

Pereira's reference to the anzu bird as "the personification of the thundercloud, imaged as an enormous vulture floating with outstretched wings in the sky."[4] Images of animal-human hybrids and bird-faced women date back millennia BCE to late Paleolithic times, reports cultural historian Elinor Gadon, suggesting shamanistic roots. "The myths and legends about woman-animal hybrids reflect a fascination with the possibility of the animal nature of the female—still potent, raw, primal, fierce, instinctual, bodily, unrepressed."[5] The particular feathered familiar of Lilith is the screech owl, which sees in the dark of the night and is often considered a harbinger of death. Nicknamed a feathered wildcat, the common screech owl sings songs and duets described as both tremulous and lugubrious. One song is a mellow whistle that ends in a shrill whining or screech, thus its name.

Lilith, connected to serpent and bird, is the anthropomorphic conduit from one to the other, from the instinctive wisdom at the roots to the spiritual enlightenment in the branches. In order to harvest the tree, Inanna must contend with the untamed nature of these creatures. She calls in her brother Gilgamesh, a hero-king who stars in his own myth, to cut down the tree. The serpent is killed, the bird flies off to the mountains, and Lilith flees into the wilderness. Later, after ascending her throne and consummating her marriage, Inanna will heed an inner call and descend to the underworld.

A sculpted terracotta plaque known as the Burney Relief from around 1800 BCE is generally considered a depiction of Lilith. This piece was acquired by the British Museum in 2003 and renamed "The Queen of Night." Winged with clawed feet, flanked by owls and standing on lions, the image seems to suggest this beastly demon of the night wind. Yet she is crowned with the triple-horned royal headdress and holds the rod and ring of power, so she may be Inanna herself. Perhaps it is Inanna in a Lilith aspect, as Lilith-Inanna.

In the fluid cultural interplay of the early eastern Mediterranean, Inanna's garden became the biblical Garden of Eden. Lilith again appeared in the tree, this time as the serpent who offered Eve the apple. This scene is embedded in the left west "Portal of the Virgin" in Notre Dame Cathedral in Paris. Christian artists continued to depict this serpentine woman in paintings, woodcuts, and sculptures in the 15th and 16th centuries. Michelangelo's Renaissance version is viewed on the ceiling of the Sistine Chapel in Vatican City. This artistic tradition of the snake woman was carried on enthusiastically in the 19th century.

Lilith as the First Woman

"So God created man in his own image, in the image of God created he him; male and female created he them," the first verse of Genesis in the Bible says. Meanwhile an esoteric rumor persisted that Lilith was the first wife of Adam, created at the same time by God. But in the first chapter of Genesis, there is no mention of Eve or of a taboo tree. The more familiar story appears in the second chapter of Genesis, in which God creates Eve from Adam's rib and forbids them, on pain of death, from eating of the tree of the knowledge of good and evil.

Lilith is mentioned in several passages in the Talmud, third- to sixth-century rabbinical discussions, and in the Zohar, 13th-century kabalistic commentaries in the midrash tradition of amplifying the mystic meaning of the Hebrew Bible. Often cited, the anonymous medieval text called *The Alphabet of Ben-Sira* offers an alternate, possibly tongue-in-cheek creation story. Yahweh shapes both Adam and Lilith from earth. Considering himself superior, made of clean dirt rather than dirty dirt, Adam expects Lilith to be submissive to him. Claiming equality, she will not be put beneath him, sexually or any other way.

I will not be put beneath you as a serving maid.
I am his who dares to pay my price.

I ask too much, you say? Yet I give all. Why do you hold back?
I warn you. If you send me away, you will fall asleep,
And your rib will be taken out for your mate.
You banish me,
But you will be cast out from the garden and struggle to be reborn.
I will return to remind you of what you really want.[6]

Lilith utters the ineffable name of God, which only she knows, and flies away. The name is a sequence of vowels ultimately unutterable because it is impossible to pronounce, according to artist and Jewish scholar Allyson Grey.[7] Such secret names of God, in the form of sacred syllables, mantras, or chants are used to evoke cosmic power in healing or magic the world over. How does Lilith know this sound of power? It is one of her mysteries.

In self-exile near the Red Sea, Lilith cavorts and consorts with evil spirits. Yahweh sends three angels to bring her back. Though threatened with the death of a hundred of her demonic children daily, she refuses. She begins to haunt humans as a succubus, stealing male seed in the night, and as an infant killer, a crib-death hag. She pledged to the three angels that she would not invade any home or child under their protection. Amulets marked with incantations were made to ward off her presence, especially during pregnancy, at birth and in the first weeks of life. The use of such magical amulets, bowls, knives, plaques, and other objects was widespread in Jewish and Muslim cultures across the eastern Mediterranean and continues among some peoples today, a 5000-year-old tradition of protection against the Liliths.

When Lilith refused to return to her designated spouse, Yahweh carved Eve from Adam's rib. Lilith then came back as the serpent to give Eve some advice, along with the apple.

Duality of the Feminine

I am dark, daughters of Jerusalem, and I am beautiful![8]

In elevating the masculine aspect of divinity, Jewish and Christian traditions began to despiritualize the earthy, sensual side of human nature as unclean and unholy, and thus devalued the goddesses associated with the earth and the senses. In Sumeria and Babylonia, goddesses such as Inanna and Ishtar had been celebrated as the embodiment of love and honored in sacred sexual rituals. The religious transition to masculine gods judged such rites as blasphemous, yet they did not disappear completely. The sacred marriage rite, the "conjunctio" of heaven and earth as well as of female and male, appears in the Old Testament, as the beautifully sensual "Song of Songs, which is Solomon's," slipped in between Ecclesiastes and Isaiah. "Kiss me, make me drunk with your kisses! Your sweet loving is better than wine," invites the dark-skinned beauty in the first lines.[9]

The early bird-footed image of Lilith is recalled by a story of the Queen of Sheba, who travels to meet Solomon, wisest of kings. When she arrives at his palace, she lifts her skirts to cross a floor of reflecting glass. Her hairy legs and clawed feet expose her demonic underside (see Miri Hunter Haruach in volume 1 of this set). The evocative story of Solomon and Sheba is one of seduction and wisdom. This tale and the biblical "Song of Solomon" have been interpreted as mystical love allegories.

In his classic work *The Hebrew Goddess* Raphael Patai compares Lilith with the Matronit (or Shekhinah), a Kabalistic female divinity, and notes the enduring significance of both extending from fourth-millennium BCE Sumer into 19th-century Hasidic Jewish beliefs. Her dual nature, from she-demon to goddess or consort of God, reflects ambivalence of religious as opposed to sexual experience. Archetypal Lilith evokes primal human fears of the imminence of death and the inherently complex nature of male-female relationships as a reflection of a relationship to the creator. Any step can take one closer or further from God. Lilith, with her assertive sexuality, challenges intentions, questions moral beliefs, and pushes beyond judgments and taboos. She has been identified with the angel who wields the revolving flame of the sword, guarding the gate to the garden of paradise lost.[10]

Lilith in the Arts

Lilith may be 5000 years old, yet she is as fresh as modern mythofeminism. Today, numerous Web sites are dedicated to Lilith: academic, artistic, and mythic studies; "heavy metal" images; sexy products and services. *Lilith* is the name of a Jewish feminist magazine. Lilith has continued to intrigue artists, musicians, writers, and dramatists from Faust to the 2001 opera *Lilith* by the New York Opera Company, one of the latest and boldest artistic expressions.

Several artists have taken the name Lilith. Marie Juliette "Lili" Boulanger (1893–1918) was a French musical prodigy, the first woman to win the prestigious Prix de Rome for her cantata, *Faust et Helene*, at age nineteen. She died just five years later, leaving a generous repertoire of innovative music. Asteroid 1181, discovered in 1927, was named "Lilith" in her honor. Mary Maud Dunn (1894–1967), award-winning poet and science fiction writer, took the pen name of Lilith Lorraine. A few lines from her poem, "She," proves her acquaintance with Lilith:

> There is a tideless ocean in her eyes,
> There is a serpent soul that sways and swoons.[11]

Continuing the tradition, Lilith Saintcrow adopted that pen name as the prolific author of several series in the popular contemporary literary genre of vampire hunters and dark night stalkers with special powers.

Lilith is often associated with worlds outside this one, be they the dark astral worlds of the night demons and vampire hunters or the magical worlds of faerie. In Elizabeth Cunningham's *The Wild Mother* (1993), Lilith comes from the otherworld over the border into faerie, trailing foliage and flowers in her footsteps when an obsessed Adam compels her into the "real" world against her will. Lilith appears as a mysterious central character in Sharon Shinn's *The Shape-Changer's Wife* (1995), set in the misty days of Druid magic. Lilith is a solemn woman with a unique, impersonal, still presence, subtly alluring and autonomous:

> I am not like other women," she said sharply. "I do not like the things they like or feel the things they feel. And it is better so. I do not want to be like them. I do not want to turn into one of them.[12]

As the story unfolds, a fascinated sorcerer's apprentice guesses the secret, that her magician husband had shape-shifted her into a woman in order to possess her. Her true form is a willow tree that lives in the king's sacred grove, referring back to Inanna's garden and the Garden of Eden. Eventually the apprentice overpowers the magician and returns Lilith to her true form as a Tree of Life. "It was the most beautiful, the most awful thing he had ever seen, this transformation of a woman to a tree.[13]

On television, Lilith appeared as the neurotic psychiatrist wife of Frasier on the American television shows *Cheers* and *Frasier*, and as the queen witch in an episode of Britain's popular science-fiction show *Doctor Who*. For her innovative music festival featuring only female singers, Sarah McLachlan chose the name "Lilith Fair" to represent the voice of women's autonomy, creativity, and power. This hugely successful traveling show was considered a risky venture by the music world when it began in 1997. Women who live their Lilithian autonomy are often reviled, but many men, both heterosexual and gay, appreciate Lilith. Musician Peter Gabriel wrote a song called "Lilywhite Lilith," who will "take you through the tunnel of night." The Radical Gay Faerie gatherings honor Lilith in dramatic fashion.

How did Lilith become so prominent in modern imagination? When this feared storm demon and baby-snatcher was transformed into the first wife of Adam, she maintained a place in esoteric Kabbalistic literature and was picked up by Goethe in the 19th century. Lilith's popularity today stems from a brief appearance in *Faust*. Johann Wolfgang von Goethe writes a scene in which Mephistopheles warns Faust about Adam's first wife, a dangerous beauty who ensnares men by binding them with her hair. From this mention onward, Lilith became a highly ambivalent image for artists in the 1800s as the Victorian era progressed with its self-conscious distrust of the feminine. In his "Lamia" (1819), John Keats writes somewhat sympathetically of this Lilith-related shape-shifter from Greek mythology, a serpent who takes a woman's form to seduce and destroy men. Lamia is the name of a Libyan queen seduced by Zeus. When his jealous wife Hera took away her children, Lamia took revenge by stealing others' children, following in Lilith's footsteps. A century later, John William Waterhouse clearly indicated inspiration from Keats in "A Mermaid," and two paintings of "Lamia" (1909). In one she holds her snakeskin on her lap, reconnecting her image with the serpent.

Pre-Raphaelite painter Dante Gabriel Rossetti brought Lilith into full view. His now-iconic painting "Lady Lilith" (1868) came to popularize and epitomize an increasingly modern view of Lilith as an independent *femme fatale*. Seated languorously in a flowered boudoir, a voluptuous Lilith is pictured brushing her long golden hair while looking coolly in a mirror. Rossetti wrote a short poem called "Lilith" (or "Body's Beauty") to amplify the painting, speaking of her dangerous beauty and shining hair that binds and strangles (as in Faust). Continuing the theme in an extended erotic ballad, "Eden's Bower" (1869), Rossetti imagines a sexual deal Lilith made with the serpent for aid in her revenge against Adam and Eve, still living happily in Eden. The identity of Lilith and the serpent becomes entwined:

In the ear of the Snake said Lilith:—
(Eden bower's in flower.)
"To thee I come when the rest is over;
A snake was I when thou wast my lover."[14]

As the ballad continues, Lilith tells her own version of the fall and elicits sympathy along with revulsion. Amy Scerba (1999), among other scholars, has pointed out the cultural impact of Rossetti's vision of Lilith as a turning point that opened the way to eventual feminist embrace of this powerful female figure.[15]

As the century began to turn along with the age, Lilith became a key archetypal female figure, and the alternate creation story of the Garden of Eden became a rich field of exploration for the complexities of sexuality in human nature and relationship. Robert Browning offered a radically different re-visioning of Lilith in "Adam, Lilith and Eve" (1883). In this poetic vignette, Lilith reveals her eternal love for Adam, while Eve confesses she never loved him at all. In his 1885 occult-fiction novel *Lilith*, George MacDonald, master fairytale writer and Christian minister, is more traditional and cautionary. He portrays Lilith as destructive and willful, claiming the sole power of creation based on her ability to give birth. When Adam refuses to worship her, she deserts him and takes up with the Shadow, who makes her Queen of Hell. At night she turns into a leopardess who hunts children, living on their blood like a vampire. As Adam and Eve awaken Lilith to her true self, she is horrified and blames god for making her the way she is.

The year 1892 was a big one for Lilith. Artists Kenyon Cox and John Collier both painted Lilith as a beautiful woman embracing a large snake. Cox added a bottom panel of Lilith as the women-headed serpent in the tree watching as Adam and Eve are expelled from Eden. Today Collier's painting has a large presence on the Internet. That same year, Marie Corelli published an esoteric novel, *The Soul of Lilith*, in which a cold and willful magician has revived a young girl named Lilith from death. He keeps her in a death-like trance, commanding her spirit to travel into other realms to seek knowledge of the universe, signs of the death and sorrow he believes underlie life. She brings back reports of other worlds and distant stars, eternal life, light, and the omnipresence of Love, but no sorrow. Reluctantly he realizes he is in love with her and her ethereal beauty. "Love me, not my shadow!" she pleads. When she comes to him in her true self, he is overcome by her angelic light and experiences a mental breakdown. He finishes his days humbled in sorrow and devotion to the love of Lilith: "Beautiful, indestructible, terrible Lilith! She permeates the world, she pervades the atmosphere, she shapes and unshapes herself at pleasure. . . . She is the essence of God."[16]

This positive, spiritual view of Lilith by a woman was soon followed by another. In her 1907 dramatization *Die Kinder der Lilith* (*The Children of Lilith*), German playwright Isolde Kurz offers a reversal of the usual myth, blaming the woes of mankind on Adam's betrayal of Lilith, the first woman, who embodied heaven on earth. Lilith becomes the guardian angel at the entrance to the Garden, wielding her flaming sword of truth.

George Bernard Shaw honors Lilith as the primordial woman in the Garden of Eden, the first and only God-created human. In his 1921 play *Back to Methuselah*, the serpent talks to Eve in a "strange seductively musical whisper" of Lilith, the first one in the garden. It was she, confides the serpent, who embodied the feminine power of conception and rebirth.

> She had a mighty will: she strove and strove and willed and willed for more moons than there are leaves on all the trees of the garden. Her pangs were terrible: her groans drove sleep from Eden. She said it must never be again: that the burden of renewing life was past bearing: that it was too much for one. And when she cast the skin, lo! there was not one new Lilith but two: one like herself, the other like Adam.[17]

More recently, in her 1999 novel *Leaving Eden*, Ann Chamberlin continues the theme of Lilith's primordial motherhood of the many human clans. This author attributes the ageless power, wisdom, and attraction of Lilith to her ancient pre-Adamic heritage and her estrus-driven sexual magnetism. Things change when Adam has become attracted to Eve, the new woman with lunar-based sexual cycles. He resists Lilith, leading to disharmony with natural law, the increasing domination of Man over Nature, and the ongoing struggle for survival. Lilith dies and transfers her power in a shamanic rebirth rite to her daughter, who then leaves the dying Eden to Adam and Eve.

On stage, Martha Graham seems to have drawn from Rossetti's "Eden's Bower" for her dance called "Embattled Garden," which premiered in 1958. Lilith and The Stranger (the serpent) return to the garden to seductively undermine the peaceful coexistence of Adam and Eve. A half-century later, in November 2001, the New York City Opera produced three performances of *Lilith*, Deborah Drattell's provocative dance-opera, giving a modern interpretation of this ancient, unresolved story. At the funeral of Adam, Eve encounters Lilith, her dark twin. If their souls could be joined, Lilith would find the mortality she seeks and Eve her faith. In a withered Garden of Eden, Eve and Lilith seek union until distrustful Lilith accuses Eve of treachery. Eve is thrown back to Adam's grave to disappear into the night, while her daughter inherits her veil of sorrow and continues the unfinished story of woman at odds with herself.

In the visual arts, among countless images of Lilith by modern artists, a 1994 sculpture of Lilith by Kiki Shuth was placed climbing down a wall in the Metropolitan Museum of Art in New York. Jan Collins Selman in "The Garden Series" and Lilian Broca in her extensive exploration both offer rich interpretations of Lilith's story and the love triangle in Eden. Many of Broca's images are published in *A Song of Lilith*, illustrating a poem by Joy Kogawa. Lilith's "mystery and subtlety was—and continues to be—a revelation for me," writes Broca, who clearly articulates the modern view: "Lilith is the archetype for the intelligent, independent, spiritual, decisive woman of action with sensitivity to the need for change in the world."[18]

As if unveiling a lost ancient text, physicist Robert G. Brown wrote an inventive version of Lilith's origins as told by herself in the alleged lost scrolls of *The Book of Lilith* (2006). She tells the story of what happened in the Garden, of her rape by Adam and how she split herself into two. As Eve, the obedient wife, she stayed with Adam; as Lilith, exiled and footloose, she went off with Cain to civilize the ancient world. She ended her life as a cave-dwelling yogini and died in samadhi after her eventual reunion with a wiser and wizened Adam.

Not surprisingly, the modern Lilith has undergone psychoanalysis. She appears in several stories by Anais Nin. In "The Voice" (1948), Lilith is the girl-child alter ego of a woman in psychoanalysis, whom Lilith finally sees and resolves the psychological pattern that swings back and forth from emotional neediness to control. She can then merge with her "other" to experience herself as whole. J. R. Salamanca's *Lilith* was made into a 1962 movie of the same title that has become a cult classic. A study of the Lilith archetype informed by Jungian psychology, the film's character of Lilith is the beautiful inmate in a sanitarium, assigned to a young intern who is seduced into her secret world. In the film, Lilith challenges him: "You think loving me is sinful? You think I have a talent for love? If my talent were greater than you think, would you stop loving me?" After she starts an affair with another female inmate, a male patient, also in love with Lilith, challenges the intern:

Do you think they can cure Lilith . . . Think they can cure this fire? . . . She wants to leave the mark of her desire on every living creature in the world. If she were Caesar she'd do it with her sword. If she were a poet she'd do it with words. She's Lilith. She has to do it with her body.[19]

Lilith: Vital Image for the Ages

This mythic, cultural, and artistic overview has demonstrated the ambiguous nature and enduring fascination of this primordial goddess. Stories and images of Lilith tend to be provocative and shadowy like herself, full of paradox, psychological complexity, and transformational potential. Lilith is associated again and again with astral magic and fearsome demons, with sexuality, creativity, power, desire, and will—and with nature, especially trees and certain animals, particularly owl, serpent, cat. Yet she is not abstract or to be taken for granted in any way. The allure of Lilith becomes personal and subjective, as she stimulates both deep desires and fears, erasing easy boundaries of reality and morality.

This dark goddess is erotic and consciousness-altering. The source of her wisdom is hidden, subtle, and sacred. She sings the "Song of Solomon" and whispers secret mysteries to Eve as she offers the apple from the Tree of Life. From the roots of the Tree, she taps into the core of Earth and stretches up and out toward the heart of the galaxy, the below and above both sources of her deep wisdom. Goddess of earth and heaven, her uncompromising sword of truth cuts to the bare soul. She represents the deepest desires of the soul that brook no denial. She insists again and yet again on clear-sightedness, intention, and action; otherwise she turns negative.

Emerging from origins lost in preliterary oral tradition, Lilith has evolved over the course of human culture as an archetype that mirrors deep instinctive experiences regarding feminine power. The image of Lilith is highly attractive during this time of the renewed awareness of the goddess and the various facets of the divine feminine, an awakening naturally accompanied by a cultural re-empowerment of women.

Notes

1. Barbara Koltuv, *The Book of Lilith* (York Beach, ME: Nicolas-Hays, 1986), introduction; Siegmund Hurwitz, *Lilith, the First Eve* (Einsiedeln, Switzerland: Daimon-Verlag, 1999), 36; R. Campbell Thompson, *Devils and Evil Spirits of Babylonia* (Whitefish, MT: Kessinger, 2003), xxxvi–xxxvii; Raphael Patai, *The Hebrew Goddess*, 3rd ed. (Detroit: Wayne State University Press, 1990), 221; Filomena Maria Pereira, *Lilith: The Edge of Forever* (Las Colinas, TX: Ide House, 1998), 36–37.

2. Diane Wolkstein and Samuel N. Kramer, *Inanna, Queen of Heaven and Earth* (New York: Harper and Row, 1983), 6. Reprinted with permission.

3. Pereira, *Lilith*, 38.

4. Ibid., 25.

5. Elinor Gadon, "Probing the Mysteries of the Nirapur Yoginis," *ReVision* 25, no. 1 (2002): 38.

6. Kelley Hunter, *Black Moon Lilith* (San Diego, CA: AstroCommunication Services, 2000), 25.

7. Personal communication, October 2008.

8. Ariel Bloch and Chana Bloch, *The Song of Songs: A New Translation* (Berkeley: University of California Press, 1995), 47.

9. Ibid., 45.

10. Patai, *The Hebrew Goddess*, 253.

11. Lilith Lorraine, *Let the Patterns Break* (Rogers, AR: Avalon Press, 1947), 103.

12. Sharon Schinn, *The Shape-Changer's Wife* (New York: Ace Books, 1995), 65.

13. Ibid., 196.

14. Dante Gabriel Rossetti, "Eden Bower," in *Poems: A New Edition* (London: F. S. Ellis, 1881). Reproduced at http://www.rossettiarchive.org/docs/20-1869 .blms.radheader.html.

15. Amy Scerba, *Changing Literary Representations of Lilith and the Evolution of a Mythical Heroine* (Pittsburgh: Carnegie Mellon University, 1999), 2–3.

16. Marie Corelli, *Inspired Novels: The Soul of Lilith* (Mundelein, IL: Palmer, 1962).

17. George Bernard Shaw, *Back to Methuselah: A Metabiological Pentateuch* (New York: Brentano's, 1921), 5, 8–9.

18. Joy Kogawa and Lilian Broca, *A Song of Lilith* (Toronto: Polestar, 2000), viii–ix.

19. Robert G. Brown, *The Book of Lilith* (lulu.com, 2006).

Bibliography

Bloch, Ariel, and Chana Bloch. *The Song of Songs: A New Translation.* Berkeley: University of California Press, 1995.

Chamberlin, Ann. *Leaving Eden.* New York: Tom Doherty, 1999.

Cohen, Deborah Bodin. *Lilith's Ark: Teenage Tales of Biblical Women.* Philadelphia: Jewish Publication Society, 2006.

Corelli, Marie. *Inspired Novels: The Soul of Lilith.* Mundelein, IL: Palmer, 1962.

Cunningham, Elizabeth. *The Wild Mother.* Barrytown, NY: Station Hill Press, 1993.

Gadon, Elinor. "Probing the Mysteries of the Nirapur Yoginis." *ReVision* 25, no. 1 (2002): 33–41.

George, Demetra. *Mysteries of the Dark Moon.* San Francisco: Harper, 1992.

Grenn-Scott, Deborah J. *Lilith's Fire: Reclaiming Our Sacred Lifeforce.* San Mateo, CA: Universal Publishers, 2000.

Hunter, M. Kelley. *Black Moon Lilith.* San Diego, CA: AstroCommunication Services, 2000.

Hunter, M. Kelley. *Living Lilith: Four Dimensions of the Cosmic Feminine.* Bournemouth: The Wessex Astrologer, 2009.

Hurwitz, Siegmund. *Lilith, the First Eve.* Einsiedeln, Switzerland: Daimon-Verlag, 1999.

Kogawa, Joy, and Lilian Broca. *A Song of Lilith*. Toronto: Polestar, 2000.

Koltuv, Barbara. *The Book of Lilith*. York Beach, ME: Nicolas-Hays, 1986.

Kramer, Samuel N. *Gilgamesh and the Huluppu-tree: A Reconstructed Sumerian Text*. Chicago: University of Chicago Press, 1983.

Lorraine, Lilith. *Let the Patterns Break*. Rogers, AR: Avalon Press, 1947.

Mac Donald, George. *Phantastes and Lilith*. Grand Rapids, MI: Eerdmans, 1964.

Nin, Anais. *Winter of Artifice*. Athens, OH: Swallow Press, 1960.

Patai, Raphael. *The Hebrew Goddess*. 3rd ed. Detroit: Wayne State University Press, 1990.

Pereira, Filomena Maria. *Lilith: The Edge of Forever*. Las Colinas, TX: Ide House, 1998.

Plaidy, Jean. *Lilith*. New York: Ballantine Books, 1967.

Rossen, Robert, director. *Lilith*. Culver City, CA: Columbia Pictures, 1965.

Salamanca, J. R. *Lilith*. New York: Simon and Schuster, 1961.

Scerba, Amy. *Changing Literary Representations of Lilith and the Evolution of a Mythical Heroine*. Pittsburgh: Carnegie Mellon University, 1999.

Schinn, Sharon. *The Shape-Changer's Wife*. New York: Ace Books, 1995.

Schwartz, Howard. *Lilith's Cave: Jewish Tales of the Supernatural*. New York: Oxford University Press, 1998.

Shaw, George Bernard. *Back to Methuselah: A Metabiological Pentateuch*. London: Constable, 1927.

Sterling, George. *Lilith: A Dramatic Poem*. New York: Macmillan, 1926.

Thompson, R. Campbell. *Devils and Evil Spirits of Babylonia*. Whitefish, MT: Kessinger, 2003.

Wolkstein, Diane, and Samuel N. Kramer. *Inanna, Queen of Heaven and Earth*. New York: Harper and Row, 1983.

5

Mary Magdalene: Tradition, Myth, and the Search for Meaning

Susan Little

If Mary Magdalene is not a goddess in the usual sense, she is surely an embodiment of the feminine divine. As it is with goddesses in many cultures, her story and her power have been distorted to fit conventional societal norms. And like other personifications of goddess energy, the force of Mary's life is resurfacing today. Women and men alike are rediscovering her as an exemplar through which to nurture the divine in their own lives.

Apostle of the Apostles

In the first century, the eastern Mediterranean was fractured by cultural and religious conflicts. In such a world and time, when women were generally considered to be the property of men, the biblical Mary Magdalene may have been a woman of means with the freedom to travel where she would, with whom she would. Remarkably, she chose an itinerant rabbi, whose message of peace was welcomed at the margins of society among the poor and outcast but regarded with suspicion by political and religious establishments. There are many indications in ancient texts that she was Jesus' close disciple and favored companion. But when Jesus died, a struggle for leadership ensued among his followers. The privilege of place that Mary had enjoyed vanished into the fault line that opened between "orthodox" and

Figure 5.1 Christian scripture describes a woman named Mary Magdalene who was a companion of the savior, Jesus. Many legends have grown up around this powerful, enigmatic figure. (Mary Magdalene Icon, © 2009 Christine Lamb, Used by permission.)

"gnostic" Christian believers. Elaine Pagels describes this definitive phase of early church history in detail in her book, *The Gnostic Gospels*.

After the initial conflict, Mary Magdalene continued to be covered by a shroud of distortion, her importance undermined as she lay buried under the early church fathers' portrait of her as a repentant prostitute. Recent scholarship shines a revealing light on Mary Magdalene and confirms how wrong the conventional portrait had been. It also leads to a question: Who was she?

Even her name adds to the confusion. Almost one-fourth of Jewish women in her area in that era bore the name Mary and, in the Christian Testament, almost half. In all probability, they were namesakes of the prophet Miriam, sister of Moses, or Mariamme, revered murdered wife of Herod the Great. As many as five Marys are associated with Jesus: it is easy to confuse them and their roles. The result of this confusion is the conflation of Mary Magdalene with several other women, especially Mary of Bethany—the sister of Martha and Lazarus—and an unnamed "sinner" in the Gospel of Luke who washes Jesus' feet with her tears, wipes them with her hair, kisses them, and anoints them with oil. The process of conflation is traced by elaborate analysis through centuries of art history by Susan Haskins where she states: "Mary Magdalen, chief female disciple, first apostle and beloved friend of Christ, would become transformed into a penitent whore."[1] She was thus wrongly labeled for hundreds of years.

Above and beyond the confusion about her identity, there is a murky silence through which Mary's powerful voice may, with careful listening, still be heard. The best-known source of information about Mary Magdalene is the Christian Testament where she is the primary witness to the birth of the Christian faith. The Gospel of Luke shows her taking part in Jesus' ministry in Galilee. Matthew, Mark, and Luke have her following him to Jerusalem. In all four gospels, she stands near at his crucifixion and burial and discovers his empty tomb. In three gospels she is told by an angel (or a young man dressed in white, or two men in clothes that gleamed like lightning) why the tomb is empty. Three texts report that Mary received a commission to deliver the explanation of the empty tomb to Jesus' disciples, a responsibility that led to her being called *apostola apostolorum*, "apostle of the apostles." Three other texts say that she was the first person to see the resurrected Jesus. Nowhere do the gospels say anything about her being a prostitute.

The Gospel of Luke mentions that Jesus drove seven demons out of Mary Magdalene, probably referring to a spiritual or physical sickness. Esther de Boer points out that the number seven, being "the full count of perfection," means that Mary was overwhelmed by her disease.[2] Some scholars think that Luke may have added the account of Mary's healing, and that of other women, as evidence that she chose to follow Jesus out of gratitude. This could be a way of saying that she did not receive a special call by Jesus, a way of belittling her importance in comparison to the twelve male apostles.

Even taken together, the Bible's references to Mary Magdalene are brief. And still their very existence signifies her importance. Elisabeth

Schüssler Fiorenza explains that all early Christian writings were meant to deal with actual problems in the nascent church and to resolve them in a manner consistent with the theological objectives of the writers. She concludes that the androcentric nature of their largely patriarchal world shaped the writers' ideas about women and yielded what they wrote, and did not write, about women. For this reason, much information about women in early Christianity may be irretrievably lost.

Best-beloved of Jesus

A second source of information about Mary Magdalene is an assortment of noncanonical Christian texts. In 1945 there was a stunning archeological discovery at Nag Hammadi in Egypt: Coptic translations of older Greek manuscripts, fifty-two Gnostic texts from early centuries of the Christian era. Among these were previously unknown Christian gospels and even writings attributed to Jesus' followers. Within the Nag Hammadi texts are revealing references to Mary Magdalene. Other texts from different discoveries contain stories of her as well, among them the *Pistis Sophia*, *Gospel of Peter*, and *Gospel of Mary*.

Gnostic and apocryphal writings reveal what Pagels calls "the complexity of the early Christian movement."[3] In spite of that original complexity, within 200 years of Jesus' death, the church had instituted doctrine that all believers must adhere to. Christianity is generally defined by a few writings selected from among many of that early period. Many were lost. Countless others were excluded, labeled as heresy, suppressed, or buried. The Mary Magdalene of these writings was buried along with them. And therein lies the challenge: to hear the voice within the silence.

The stream of Gnostic thought within early Christianity incorporated a belief that divinity is inherent in all persons and that escape from the evils of the world can be achieved by knowledge (*gnosis*) of one's own divine self. In the Gnostic gospels, Mary reports visions of Christ in which he reveals to her, and her alone, certain sacred mysteries. The mystical content of these texts is integral to understanding the Gnostic Mary Magdalene.

Holly Hearon says that, in the "oral storytelling environment of the first century," narratives about Mary would have been more often heard than read.[4] Although the oral tradition is lost, knowledge of it invites reading of the texts with first-century listeners in mind—their communities and their diversity. This way of reading, combined with excellent scholarship by feminist theologians and historians, provides provocative insights about Mary Magdalene and her formative role in those first-century communities.

Examination of the earliest years of Christianity is an elusive undertaking. The central point concerning Mary Magdalene is that, in the Christian Testament, Peter is portrayed as the leader of the community, while Mary is generally demeaned. In many noncanonical gospels, a very different Mary emerges. Schüssler Fiorenza states that the Christian Testament identifies Mary Magdalene as the leader of Jesus' women disciples, but that some Gnostic groups went much farther, claiming apostolic authority for not only her but for other women as well. Antagonism between Peter and Mary Magdalene exemplifies the larger dispute over apostolic authority, a theme developed in several Gnostic writings.

The *Gospel of Philip* contains a scene in which Mary Magdalene is described as the esteemed companion of Jesus. In one of their gatherings, the rest of the disciples, offended by Mary's favored rank, ask of Jesus, "Why do you love her more than all of us?" It is easy to imagine that there was sarcasm in his answer: "Why do I not love you as her?"[5] She was the one who understood completely.

In the *Gospel of Mary* the disciples are assembled, grieving for the dead Jesus and terrified for themselves, worried that the authorities would find them and place them under arrest. Very much as Jesus often did, Mary Magdalene rises to address the disciples, offers words of encouragement, and reminds them of his promise to be with them always. Peter says, "Sister, we know that the Savior loved you more than any other woman. Tell us the words of the Savior that you know but which we haven't heard."[6] But she does not.

Instead, she tells them of a vision in which the Lord appeared to her. She goes on to introduce new teachings he revealed to her. Andrew and Peter dismiss the idea that the Lord actually appeared to her in a vision. Then, moved to tears, Mary confronts Peter:

> "Do you think that I've made all this up secretly by myself or that I am telling lies about the Savior?" Levi said to Peter, ". . . If the Savior considered her to be worthy, who are you to disregard her? For he knew her completely . . . loved her devotedly."[7]

After that, Mary went out to preach with the apostles. But Peter always took the orthodox view that it was the *historical events* in the life of

Jesus that were important. Mary represented the Gnostic opinion that Jesus' *continuing presence* revealed mysteries of the kingdom of heaven through the minds of those elect disciples who were capable of comprehending.

Dislodged Disciple

From the available literature, canonical and noncanonical, Jane Schaberg explores a possible profile of Mary Magdalene. The profile includes some eminent and unique roles: leader not just of the women, but of male disciples as well; intimate companion of Jesus who praises her for her superior understanding; visionary and seer; one who speaks boldly. If the attributes are correct, what happened to this Mary?

In his own ministry Jesus set the stage for women's equality. He violated religious and social conventions by talking openly with women and welcoming them as companions. Marcus Borg points out that Jesus not only challenged the conventional wisdom of his own day but also continues to challenge the conventional wisdom of the church today. Throughout the Hebrew Bible and in postbiblical Judaism, it was expected that a man would welcome a good wife, but women collectively were not regarded favorably. In synagogue services, this prayer of thanksgiving was recited routinely: "Blessed art thou, O Lord, who hast not made me a woman." Rigid rules were laid down for separation of the sexes. Women were excluded from religious, political, and social life. A first-century mishnah says, "If any man teach his daughter Torah, it is as though he taught her lechery."[8] Jesus' behavior toward women was, therefore, quite extraordinary. Among his close associates were women identified as Joanna, Susanna, and, of course, Mary Magdalene.

Within two decades after Jesus' death, women were leaders in local Christian groups. They were prophets, teachers, and evangelists. Wherever the apostle Paul preached the gospel he made the declaration that male/female differences no longer applied in Christ. He sanctioned women as deacons and associates in the churches he founded. In his letter to the Romans Paul greets Junia(s) as an exceptional apostle who was in Christ before he himself was. But Paul did not promote women's social and political equality.

What were the political implications of women's leadership in the church? Pagels points out that if anyone, man or woman, who was not one of the original twelve male disciples could lay claim to divine inspiration for unconventional ideas, the authority of priests succeeding Peter would be weakened. In going up against Peter, Mary Magdalene became the standard-bearer for Gnostic teachers who challenged orthodox thinking.

Ultimately, the orthodox won out. In a story told in *Pistis Sophia*, Peter and Mary have an argument, and, when Peter complains to Jesus that he has grown weary of Mary's commentaries and can no longer tolerate her domination of their group discussions, Jesus rebukes Peter and defends her right to speak.

In the Eastern Orthodox tradition, where Mary Magdalene has always been more revered than in Roman Catholicism, there is a story in which she travels to Rome and has an audience with Emperor Tiberius. Mary shows Tiberius an egg, which represents new life through the resurrection of Christ. The emperor replies that it is no more possible for a man to rise from the dead than for the egg she is holding to turn red. And the egg immediately turns to bright red. Despite such recorded miracles, Mary's exalted position in the Eastern Church did nothing to confer apostolic authority upon women in their ecclesiastical hierarchy.

The debate about whether women were legitimate transmitters of apostolic revelation was intense; that is, who had spiritual authority to preach the gospel of Christ? By the end of the second century, the answer was "not women." By 200 CE most local churches, swept up in the tide of social opposition, forbade women's participation in worship, and those groups that did retain women as leaders were labeled heretical. The controversy raged among orthodox and Gnostic circles. Reports in Gnostic gospels about Mary Magdalene's collaborative relationship with Jesus were countered by so-called apostolic letters from the orthodox side. Some letters attributed to Paul spoke of women's subordination and submission to men. The orthodox community settled firmly into the idea that men's dominion over women was *divinely* ordained, at home and in the church. It is important to be aware that, although this was the general view, some orthodox Christians opposed it openly, notably the revered church father Clement of Alexandria. At the same time, though Gnostic Christians tended to describe God as both masculine and feminine and to build their communities as human reflections of that image of God, some Gnostic sources were contemptuous of women.

The question of the status of women was not the only struggle within the early church. The nature of God and the nature of Christ were certainly at the center of debates about fundamental issues such as human sin, the feminine aspect of the divine, and bodily resurrection. A blistering disagreement swirled around the crucifixion of Jesus that would have a strong influence on how Mary Magdalene was viewed in later centuries. The Gnostic text called *Acts of John* describes Jesus as a spiritual being, not human. John says of Jesus,

> I will tell you another glory, brethren; sometimes when I meant to touch him I encountered a material, solid body; but at other times again when I felt him, his substance was immaterial and incorporeal . . . as if it did not exist at all.[9]

And Jesus of himself,

> I have suffered none of the things which they will say of me; even that suffering which I showed to you and to the rest in my dance, I will that it be called a mystery.[10]

Objections to the text grew until, in the fifth century, Pope Leo ordered all copies destroyed. And even though heretical groups continued to copy and hide the *Acts of John*, thus preserving the dispute about whether Jesus was really crucified, the orthodox Christian leadership insisted that the suffering and death of Jesus become utterly fixed as the foundation upon which the faith would stand.

Pagels argues that the root of this inflexible attitude can be found in the appalling realities of early Christian life. Jesus' disciples had witnessed the agony of his last hours on earth. Soon their foremost leaders, Peter and James, had followed in his footsteps to be tortured and murdered. In those first 200 years, many thousands of Christians were slain throughout the Roman empire. In the time of widespread torture and slaughter of Christians, to suffer as a martyr was to unite a believer to Christ as no other act could do. Early martyrs, and those who have suffered for their Christian faith in subsequent centuries, found their personal experience confirmed in the physical life and death of Jesus.

Beleaguered churches throughout the Mediterranean world corresponded with each other, sharing horrific experiences and finding common comfort. Simultaneously, the biblical canon was being assembled, and decisions about which books to include provided another driver toward standardization. Pagels makes the point that local churches came to see their diversity of thought as an impediment to unity with the larger church. Uniformity in all matters became the goal. Every Christian was required to confess the persecution, crucifixion, death, and burial of Jesus.

In a way, martyrdom had become a supreme force behind the establishment of the institutional church. The view of Jesus as a spiritual being was overtaken by belief in the primacy of his bodily experience, especially his crucifixion and death. Gnostics were called atheists and blasphemers for proposing that Jesus was a spiritual being who only *appeared* to suffer and die or that his spiritual nature enabled him to transcend his human suffering. Again, it is important to note that both orthodox and Gnostic believers were arrayed on a continuum of interpretations of the crucifixion. But in general, to orthodox believers, a suffering Lord was far superior to one who somehow eluded suffering.

Conformity to church doctrine and submission to the authority of governing bishops became litmus tests of true believers. Many Gnostic groups, finding themselves outsiders, scattered and disappeared. The model of women and men together as disciples of Jesus, both with him and after his death, sharing leadership and wisdom, was for the most part finished. And Mary Magdalene's importance in early Christianity with it.

Reinstated Radical

Efforts to extinguish Mary's fire persisted, but the systematic institutional desire to silence her created intriguing erasures and gaps in the scriptural record. The open spaces gave birth to a spectacular mystique. And from the mystique arose the myths.

There are fascinating stories: Mary Magdalene was once betrothed to John the Evangelist, who abandoned her. She was put out to sea in a rudderless boat with Martha, Martha's brother Lazarus (who had been raised from the dead by Jesus), and others in the hope that they would all drown. Variant stories say that she went to Egypt and then on to France with her friends and Sara, her twelve-year-old daughter by Jesus. Sara then became the first of a still-surviving bloodline of European royalty.

Legends about Mary Magdalene's life in southern France are robust and fervent. It is said that when she landed in Marseilles, she preached the gospel to the pagans who soon replaced their temples with Christian churches. Two of her male disciples were elected bishops, in Marseilles and in Aix. Finally Mary's great hunger for Christ overtook her, and she went into the desert to live in a cave so she might never look upon any other man. There she fasted for thirty years, sustained by angels who took her up to heaven every day for spiritual food. When she died and was buried, miracles took place at her grave. Accounts of Mary's life in southern France led to special veneration in the area, a phenomenon that spread throughout western Europe. By the 13th century, dozens of churches bore her name. Hundreds of her relics were housed in shrines, and Magdalene cults flourished around the shrines.

The love that Mary Magdalene and Jesus had for each other, and the possibility of sex between them, embellishes the legends. Michael Baigent, Richard Leigh, and Henry Lincoln claim to have decoded secret writings that had been sheltered by societies such as Knights Templar, Cathars, Rosicrucians, and Masons. The bloodline resulting from the marriage of Mary and Jesus is called the "Holy Grail dynasty." Margaret Starbird pursues the story with the deep conviction that her book is not only meant to explore the Holy Grail heresy but is also "an argument for the restoration of the wife of Jesus based on important circumstantial evidence. It is also a quest for the meaning of the Lost Bride in the human psyche in the hope that her return will help to heal the wasteland."[11]

As is common with many iconographic figures, Mary Magdalene has been appropriated by many people for many reasons. Captivity and detention unleash imagination. Books and movies abound. A lively Magdalene community thrives on the Internet. And why not? What is wrong with being fascinated, enthralled, inspired? Sometimes devotion to mistaken images of Mary has positive results; for example, charities benefiting marginalized women and their children that have been established in the name of Mary Magdalene. Mary's misidentification as a prostitute has led, sometimes, to a constructive feminine spirituality, otherwise suppressed in church tradition. Women of faith have looked to her as a role model in a paternalistic church, an accessible woman, a woman more like them in their real lives than a holy virgin. They cry out, "If she is a sinner and can be saved, there is hope for me."

Mary Magdalene embodies what has been hushed, but not completely silenced—the feminine voice of God. The inexorable search for her continues. Speaking not just of Mary Magdalene, Schüssler Fiorenza says that "a reconstruction of early Christian communal self-understanding" is a process "moving toward greater equality, freedom and responsibility, as well as toward communal relations free of domination."[12]

Revived scholarly interest in Mary Magdalene has brought to bear the use of historical analysis in the quest for her truth. Jane Schaberg provides compelling scriptural and historical evidence that Mary was present at Jesus' tomb and that Jesus empowered her with God's spirit. Most important, though, is what Schaberg says about the enigma of the ongoing search. She contends that even if Mary Magdalene and the stories about were her pure legend, Mary could still be a spiritual resource for people of faith. "We can read the Gospels any way we want and need to, as every previous generation has done; we can seek to grasp what the texts once meant and mean, and to participate in their seemingly inexhaustible capacity to bear many meanings."[13] Schaberg and others like her remain committed to both history and literature as instruments of social transformation.

She Lives!

In modern Israel, a slim strip of a country where the remains of civilization after civilization throb underground, old worlds sometimes reveal their stony bones. On the northwest shore of a freshwater lake known as the Sea of Galilee, near the town now called Migdal, lie the obscure ruins of an ancient archeological site, teeming with private untold stories. It is here that many people search for Mary Magdalene.

The old town's various names through the millennia are magnets pulling pilgrims into the past—Migdal Nunya, Migdal Seb'iya, Taricheae, Magadan, Dalmanutha—forgotten names that refer to commercial activities that probably took place there, "Tower of Fish" or "Place of Salted Fish" or "Tower of Dyers." But there was one name that still calls irresistibly from a distance of 2000 years—Magdala. This name is recognizable to modern readers because of its identification with Jesus of Nazareth. It was in Magdala that Jesus is said to have found a particular friend, a companion whose legend blossomed into a mythology of her own, the woman celebrated from that day to this as Mary Magdalene. Fascinating as archeology is, people do not go to the ruins of Magdala only to examine them; many people go there in search of a living Mary Magdalene, the real woman, the woman behind the mystery.

In the space of the seventy-mile drive from Jerusalem north to the Sea of Galilee, the landscape turns from dry desert to green and moist farming country. Acres of squared-off sections display a variety of crops, including, in full, leafy grandeur, miles of bananas. The ruins of ancient Magdala can be found on the lakeshore a mile south of the town of Migdal. A gravelly road runs through what was once an amusement park now scarred with rusted, abandoned rides. The site of the dig is protected by a brick and chain-link fence, topped in places by concertina wire, a locked gate, and a sign announcing in Hebrew that entry is forbidden.

Ordinary visitors can only walk around the perimeter of the fence, scampering over rock piles and climbing partway up the fence by balancing on precarious toeholds. They can pick out the crumbling footprint of a thirty-foot-square building that may have been the synagogue frequented by Mary. Or it might have been a springhouse where she went with friends to draw fresh water each day. Visitors can squint and stare through the fence with longing. Then they can walk away from the site and take a few steps toward the Sea of Galilee to gaze out across the water where it is cool in the shade of broad-leaf trees and palms that line the shore. They can see the tiniest of streams flowing through the undergrowth to where the lapping of the lake takes the stream into itself. They can dream their dreams of Mary Magdalene. They can listen for her voice. They can call out her name.

Jane Schaberg reflects on the ruins at Magdala, which she has visited often and knows very well. Years ago she made the acquaintance of Marwan Assadi, head of an Arab family who lived as caretakers for many years in a corrugated metal shack on the property. She tells of a visit with Mr. Assadi during which he served her refreshments in the shade beside his home: "There is something haunting about the site. Surprised by my own question, I asked if there were any ghosts here. 'Yes,' said Marwan, pointing, 'she sits over there.'"[14]

Notes

1. Susan Haskins, *Mary Magdalen: Myth and Metaphor* (London: HarperCollins, 1993), 15.

2. Esther De Boer, *The Mary Magdalene Cover-Up: The Sources behind the Myth* (New York: T. & T. Clark, 2006), 23.

3. Elaine Pagels, *The Gnostic Gospels* (New York: Random House, 1979), xxxviii.

4. Holly Hearon, *The Mary Magdalene Tradition: Witness and Counter-Witness in Early Christian Communities* (Collegeville, MN: Liturgical Press, 2004), 193.

5. Pagels, *Gnostic Gospels*, 77.

6. Jane Schaberg, *The Resurrection of Mary Magdalene: Legends, Apocrypha, and the Christian Testament* (New York: Continuum, 2002), 169.

7. Ibid., 170.

8. Marcus Borg, *Jesus: A New Vision—Spirit, Culture and the Life of Discipleship* (New York: HarperCollins, 1987), 133, 146.

9. Pagels, *Gnostic Gospels*, 88.

10. Ibid., 89–90.

11. Margaret Starbird, *The Woman with the Alabaster Jar: Mary Magdalen and the Holy Grail* (Santa Fe, NM: Bear and Co, 1993), xxiii.

12. Elisabeth Schüssler Fiorenza, *In Memory of Her* (New York: Crossroad, 1983), xxxv.

13. Schaberg, *Resurrection of Mary Magdalene*, 350–351.

14. Ibid., 49.

Bibliography

Borg, Marcus. *Jesus: A New Vision—Spirit, Culture and the Life of Discipleship.* New York: HarperCollins, 1987.

De Boer, Esther. *The Mary Magdalene Cover-Up: The Sources behind the Myth.* New York: T. and T. Clark, 2006.

Fiorenza, Elisabeth Schüssler. *In Memory of Her.* New York: Crossroad, 1983.

Haskins, Susan. *Mary Magdalen: Myth and Metaphor.* London: HarperCollins, 1993.

Hearon, Holly. *The Mary Magdalene Tradition: Witness and Counter-Witness in Early Christian Communities.* Collegeville, MN: Liturgical Press, 2004.

Pagels, Elaine. *The Gnostic Gospels.* New York: Random House, 1979.

Schaberg, Jane. *The Resurrection of Mary Magdalene: Legends, Apocrypha, and the Christian Testament.* New York: Continuum, 2002.

Schüssler Fiorenza, Elisabeth. *In Memory of Her.* New York: Crossroad, 1983.

Starbird, Margaret. *The Woman with the Alabaster Jar: Mary Magdalen and the Holy Grail.* Santa Fe, NM: Bear and Co., 1993.

6

The Fat Lady of Malta: Interpreting Her Obesity, Nudity, and Sexuality

Cristina Biaggi

The Maltese goddess figurines from the late Neolithic (3500–2500 BCE) stand out as unique expressions of their creators' conceptions of the numinous.[1] They represent the continuation of a philosophical idea given visual form by a long line of female deity figurines originating in the Paleolithic (30,000 BCE). Because of their particular characteristics— some figures are nude, others clothed, some do not show primary sexual traits, and all are obese—there have been considerable and diverging speculations about their significance.

Although there has been abundant research and writing on the Maltese archaeological material since the beginning of the last century resulting in a variety of different interpretations, no new comprehensive examination of the specific morphology and meaning of the figures has been made in the recent past. The purpose of this chapter is to focus on the morphology, archaeological context, and derivations of these images; to discuss various interpretations concerning the significance of their nudity, obesity, and sexuality; and to offer additional explanations concerning their form and meaning.

Over forty of these figures ranging in size from seven inches to seven feet have been found in the late Maltese temples, in the Hypogeum, and in the newly excavated Xaghra Circle. Most of them were carved from

Figure 6.1 On the Mediterranean island of Malta, dozens of gigantic sculptures have been found representing robust or even obese women. Because the culture that produced them left no record, interpretation of these statues offers a complex set of questions for the scholar. (Photograph by Cristina Biaggi.)

Globigerina limestone, a soft limestone found in Malta, and then painted with red ochre. They seem to be a product of local development since there is nothing else like them in the Mediterranean. The prototypes for these figures reside in the Paleolithic (e.g., the Venus of Willendorf, the Venus of Lespugue, and the Savignano Venus) via the Mediterranean early Neolithic (e.g., the Anatolian figures at Hacılar and Çatalhöyük, the early Neolithic figures of Greece and the Balkans, the Seated Fat Lady of Saliagos, the Predynastic figures of Egypt, and many others). All of these figurines are fat and depicted in a frontal stance.

Two Basic Varieties of Goddess Images

There are basically two varieties of figures from the Late Maltese Temple period (3150–2500 BCE): nude and clothed. The nude figures share certain characteristics. They are enormously fat, with large buttocks, bulbous thighs, legs, arms, and forearms, a corpulent chest, and tiny hands and feet. A further feature is that they lack all sexual characteristics, either male or female. They appear in various positions and stylized poses. There are standing figures and squatting or seated figures with legs folded to the left or right.

The seated figures average nine inches in height. Hands are placed gracefully either at the sides or on the folded legs. Some figures lack affixed heads but have a hollow socket between the shoulders for a separate head. Small holes around the neck area indicate that a head was attached by means of a dowel or string that could be used to make the head move.[2] "It has been suggested that the sockets in the necks of some figurines were to take interchangeable heads, male or female as appropriate to immediate circumstance," according to archaeologist David Trump.[3] The separate carved heads are small in proportion to the bodies. The face is oval, the hair close to the head, the eyes small and set horizontally, the nose wide with a definite ridge, the mouth small with full lips, and the chin barely indicated. Prototypes for the poses of the seated figures were found among Predynastic Egyptian figures and in the Balkans; figures with small separate heads were discovered in Hacılar in Turkey.[4]

The standing figures are less numerous, but much larger—twenty inches in height. Usually three rolls of fat appear at the abdomen, and the legs are so stylized that sometimes the figurines seem to be wearing shorts. Some figures stand on pedestals that have carved motifs on the sides. Some clothed figures are represented sitting on stools or couches. These figures are dressed in bell-shaped skirts that reach halfway down the legs. Some display a necklace or décolleté that is reminiscent of earlier deity figures along the Mediterranean. One fragment from Tarxien shows part of the calf and fringed skirt of a draped figure seated on a stool. Four small figurines of the nude fat variety are represented below the figure's skirt. The largest seated goddess figure, which when complete must have been about nine feet high, belongs to this variety. She wears a full pleated skirt and is supported by small feet. She stands on a pedestal that is decorated by a relief reminiscent of the Classical Greek "egg and dart" pattern, an ornamental architectural device consisting of an egg-shaped object alternating with a dart-shaped element. Trump claims that this figure and others like it strongly imply that this is a cult figure, and that the most reasonable interpretation is that "she is a Mother Goddess" and she "stands, sits, or lies at the very heart of the religion of the temples."[5]

The Significance of the Double Figure

A very important new find is the Double Fat Lady from the Xaghra Circle. This sculpture consists of a beautifully carved and painted pair of obese figures. They are seated on an intricately carved bed daubed with red ochre and revealing wooden struts on the underside and curvilinear designs on the upper. The fat figures are not explicitly male or female. They wear the familiar pleated skirts, painted black, of the finest Maltese cult figures. The head of one figure features a haircut that includes a pig-tail at the back. The other's head is missing. Both figures hold objects on their laps: one, a tiny dressed person "who may be a baby, the other a cup."[6] Vicki Noble writes of such figures,

> The long and rich heritage of Double Goddess figurines . . . reflects the organic cycles of nature that informed the ancient Goddess religion archetypically expressed through the body of every woman as the repeating alternation between ovulation and menstruation. These two aspects of the feminine are iconographi-cally depicted in the multivalent and widespread image of two divine women, expressing the dual poles of nature: death and life, dark and light.[7]

Archaeologist Simon Stoddart agrees with this view and suggests that this could symbolize the cycle of life: The figure on the right symbolizes birth and that on the left, death.[8]

Relating to the dual nature of this image, Noble continues, "the cumulative effect of the repetition of images intensifies the efficacy of the protection granted by the image is reminiscent of the power of repeated mantras . . . used in Eastern religion and clearly understood to be magical spells." Concerning what the figures are holding in their laps, which clearly suggests their ritual purpose, Noble writes, "One [figure] appears to be holding a smaller version of herself, and the other seems to hold a ritual cup or vessel."[9] The author contends that the figures represent an early incarnation of the cult of Demeter and Persephone. The ceiling of the oracle chamber in the Maltese Hypogeum, which dates from a similar period of time, was painted with red, spiraling, plantlike designs suggestive of pomegranates and which could be linked to the mystery religion of Demeter and Persephone in Greece, indubit-ably an early fertility cult.[10]

Nude or Clothed: The Same Divinity?

It is significant that the Maltese goddess is depicted both nude and clothed. Clothing and adornment are and always have been symbolic of rank and status; nudity has been used symbolically in art to elicit emotions and to express ideas. That some of the figures are nude and others clothed might signify that they were meant for different functions in Maltese religion. Perhaps their special sanctity and magical power were increased by their nudity. Perhaps they represented different aspects of the same deity to be invoked on different occasions and for different reasons. Perhaps they even represented different deities.

That the clothed and nude figures represented a similar divine being is suggested by their similarities: Both are fat, are approximately the same size, show traces of red ochre, are made of stone, had moveable heads, stand on pedestals, and come from the same period; neither shows sexual characteristics. The moveable heads could have been made to move in ritual to assent or dissent a particular request made by a worshiper. Trump writes, "Cult activities seem to have reached a feverish pitch in the final phases of the Tarxien Period (2500 BCE)."[11] The difference in the figurines suggests that they represented different numinous aspects of the goddess: The clothed figures are often seated on a stool decorated with sacred symbols, wear a bell-shaped skirt, and are shown with much smaller figures crowding below (possibly worshipers), while the nude figures stand or squat and are always alone. These trappings of rank—the sacred stool, the bell-shaped skirt, and the necklace—are found in other recognized deity figures around the Mediterranean, for example, the enthroned goddess of Çatalhöyük or the Minoan snake goddess. The clothed goddess or her priestesses had to be approached and addressed in a certain manner after certain preliminary rituals had been completed.

The clothed and nude figures could represent two aspects of the goddess, perhaps invoked at different times and for different reasons. The seated figure could be the great mother of all, much like the *Potnia* of the Mediterranean, a seated or standing sacred female figure wearing a crown or diadem, while the nude figures could be the quintessential and fecund fertility goddess. The clothed figures might be the goddess, shown sometimes with her votaries or acolytes depicted much smaller than she and seated under her skirt. She could represent the goddess as queen, sitting properly gowned and adorned on her earthly throne. The queen may have been considered to be the human manifestation of the goddess, her divine representation on earth, while the nude figure might simply depict the goddess in her extreme opulence. Perhaps the nude figures, representing the opulent sensual goddess, were ritually clothed during certain sacred periods of the year. Finally, the nude and clothed figures could have represented two aspects of one deity worshiped by different groups in Maltese society.

The sometime claim that the purpose of the nudity of the figures was to "excite the senses of males," is unwarranted given the fact that the figures were found in the sacred areas of the temples and that they were covered with red ochre, the sacred anointment of death and rebirth since the Paleolithic.[12] The nude figures could have evoked erotic-mystical emotions in both sexes in the early Maltese society, which was unencumbered by later patriarchal sexual codes that objectify and preclude the mystical in the female body.

Obesity: Symbolic or Actual?

The significance of the figures' obesity is based on a long tradition dating from the Paleolithic period (30,000 BCE). According to archaeologist Marija Gimbutas,

> [T]he "Monstrous Venus" of prehistory was one manifestation of a long enduring tradition of cosmogonic myth as old . . . as human culture. Its evolution can be seen in later form, even in historic times. The "Monstrous Venus" is a religious representation—the reification of the Life Genetrix[13]

The obesity of the Maltese figures may have been a measure of their sanctity. Maltese archaeologist Themistocles Zammit believes that obesity was associated with power, wealth, and fertility, and that it was related to sanctity and was considered a desirable and beautiful condition. Italian archaeologist Luigi Ugolini thinks that it symbolized prosperity. Trump believes that "[b]oth form and findspot strongly imply that we are looking at cult figures."[14]

Although these scholars believe that the obesity of the Maltese sculptures was symbolic, Italian anthropologist Raffaello Battaglia thinks that it was inspired by obese living models who were considered special in their society.[15] Further, he sees that there are two problems to solve: (1) the nature of this obesity and (2) the reasons for reproducing obese female figures.

Battaglia divides the figures into several groups according to geographical and chronological distribution: Mediterranean-Balkanic (Malta, Crete, Aegena, the Balkans), Egyptian-Ethiopian (Egypt and Ethiopia, and Berber, West Sahara, the Grand Canaries). In each group the figures are dealt with in slightly different ways. In some cases (Grand Canaries), neither the breasts nor the pubic region is shown. In others (Balkans), the breasts are not emphasized, but the pubic triangle is slightly visible. Still others (Bulgaria), which are very stylized, stress the pubic triangle, but not the breasts. Breasts are not a necessary component in the representation of females—they are not emphasized or may even be lacking in prehistoric or early

Neolithic figures, for example, the Paleolithic Venus of Lespugue and some of the Çatalhöyük figures. Obesity in Neolithic representations can take several forms. In some cases, specific parts of the body are enlarged (the legs and hips, as in the Canary Islands); in others, the entire body is obese (Malta, Rumania).

To support his contention about living models, Battaglia draws evidence from a number of writers, both ancient (Xenophon) and more recent (Jaos dos Barros, John Speke, Mehmed Emin Pasa), who witnessed actual examples of extreme artificially produced obesity around the Mediterranean and in Africa. Artificially induced obesity was still practiced in Tunisia, Algeria, and Morocco at the time of Battaglia's writing, around 1920. Obesity in women could have had a magical function, to favor fecundity. According to Neolithic and even Paleolithic peoples, a woman is endowed with magical powers that, among other things, influence the growth of vegetation. "Therefore, according to the law of mimetic magic, to increase the volume of her body by fattening is to increase the intensity of the magic powers which emanate from her."[16] Although natural obesity in women may have been thought to favor fecundity in ancient times, the author believes that artificially produced obesity is a product of a patriarchal culture because it presupposes the loss of a woman's control over her own body, which is not a characteristic of early goddess worshiping cultures.

Sexuality of the Maltese Figures

There are diverging opinions concerning the sexuality of the goddess figurines, for they lack primary sexual characteristics. The nude figures do not have apparent breasts nor do they have evident vulvas. However, a roll of fat appears on the chest. The fact that there is no central division within this mass of fat to separate the breasts in a naturalistic fashion has caused scholars to claim that the figures represent males. "These figures were almost certainly female because of the distribution of the fat on the buttocks."[17] And if one examines the seated or standing figures from the back, one will notice that the furrow of the buttocks is not delineated; in fact the buttocks appear as a continuous surface. The stylized departure from realism was obviously adopted in the depiction of the breasts.[18] Furthermore, the vulvas of the figures are *not* visible in the seated or standing figures because they are obfuscated by the fat.

Zammit claims that the sexless figures are male, even though there is never any indication of a phallus or a beard.[19] The lack of sexual characteristics can be discerned in other Neolithic representations thought to be female, such as the goddess image of Çatalhöyük. In these, the reproductive organs are not shown.[20] Evans states that the sexless quality of these figures, probably the result of a gradual evolution, had become incidental and did not detract from their power as deities.[21]

Prehistorian Christopher Kininmonth thinks that the figures might have represented eunuchs.[22] After lengthy examination of the figures, this author concludes that, despite the lack of clearly defined sexual characteristics, the statues appear more female than male. Their lack of sexual characteristics might be due to extreme stylization and to a change in ideology. The lack of sexual characteristics is prevalent in the Paleolithic and early Neolithic female figures, which far outnumber male figures. The femaleness of a figure is gleaned from other characteristics such as morphology, context, or its similarity and derivation from other female figures. At Hacılar, the "absence of marked breasts . . . suggests a possible indication of youth, contrasts with marked opulence."[23] The wide hips and narrow shoulders of the Maltese figures certainly are more female than male; no male figures in early art look like the Maltese figures. Red ochre, with which the figures were painted and which may have been menstrual blood in its earliest manifestation, is the color of fertility, death, and rebirth—and the color of the goddess.

The lack of sexual characteristics might represent the result of a process of evolution from figures whose power as sacred images lay in well-defined sexual characteristics to figures whose power lay in their opulence. The sex of the figures may have been deliberately left out to concentrate on the most important thing: the fatness and therefore the opulence and sanctity of the figures. The lack of sexual delineation in the late figures might also be interpreted as recognition of the similarities between the sexes, as in medieval angels, whose sexuality was not apparent. But, because they are the product of Maltese religion, which was female oriented, these nude figures were more female than male. The medieval angel, by contrast, is assumed to be male because he is the product of the patriarchal Christian religion. The Maltese figures seem to embody cosmic power and overflowing fullness on a superhuman scale that is beyond dualism, beyond sex.

Other Maltese Figures

These very fat sexless goddess figures contrast with the earlier Skorba figures and other contemporary figures, including the Sleeping Priestess and the Venus of Malta, all of which have strongly emphasized pubic regions. All of these figures are made of clay and are much smaller than the later figures. The attributes of the earlier Skorba figures could be the result of the newly established religion brought to Malta by the first colonists and influenced by the prevailing artistic depiction of the numinous, which at that point emphasized sexual characteristics. The form of the later fat figures could have been increasingly equated with their numinous quality. "[T]he worship of corpulent images gradually blossomed into a consuming passion." "The prehistoric Maltese society seems to have let a fixation on sculpture and art replace contact with the world beyond the islands' rocky coasts."[24]

The Sleeping Priestess figure may not be a goddess, but rather a priestess engaged in dream incubation, adept in giving oracles, interpreting dreams, or suggesting cures for illness. The Venus of Malta is very different from the larger stone goddess figures because of her size and her naturalistic proportions and stance. Her slightly voluminous yet natural form recalls Paleolithic figurines such as the Savignano figure. The faint traces of red ochre on her body suggest that she must have been important, either as another aspect of the great goddess who had her roots in the Paleolithic, as a priestess, or a fetish figure. The position of her arms might be significant in identifying her as a fetish figure, created to insure the fertility of a particular woman.

From the evidence assembled, it is clear that the worship of the great goddess was commonplace from the Upper Paleolithic to the late Neolithic in Europe and the Near East. Evidence in the form of archaeological remains, including an overwhelming amount of female figures as opposed to male figures in the early Neolithic, suggests that a numinous female power existed in prehistoric times in other parts of the world, such as South America, China, and Japan. The Maltese goddess figures represented the very stylized visual manifestation of that worship in Malta. The nude and clothed figures represented two aspects of the goddess: their obesity was important because it implied power, abundance, sanctity, and fecundity, and because it strengthened their symbolic connection with the temples they represented in shape; and their sexlessness signified their universal quality—female in identification, but beyond the dualism of male and female.

The Maltese scenario may have gone like this: The Maltese had a female-centered culture and worshiped a great goddess. Priestesses guided in temporal as well as religious matters. But perhaps contacts from abroad put the Maltese, especially a dissatisfied contingent dominated by men, in touch with new ideas. Men became increasingly more active in the religious practices, evidenced by the prevalence of phallic altars during the late Tarxien period.

> The society was becoming increasingly dominated by a religious hierarchy in which cult specialists . . . controlled much of the industry of the people. Vast amounts of human time and energy were invested in temple-building, artistic endeavors and ritual feasts. The people seem to have expended relatively little effort on the building of villages or domestic structures, on terracing or on farming methods. The obsession with the cults of the temples seems to have been complete.[25]

In the meantime, the economy of Malta was failing. Overpopulation and soil exhaustion caused disease and famine.[26] A political crisis ensued and a large part of the population migrated to the mainland. The balance of power was thus upset, the priestesses lost their credibility, and the remaining Maltese were weakened, making it easy for the bronze-wielding people to assume power without a struggle. The demise of the Tarxien temple builders after 2500 BCE marked the end of the creation of "Fat Ladies" of Malta.

Notes

1. The Maltese archipelago is in the Mediterranean, approximately 90 miles south of Sicily and 288 miles north of North Africa.

2. John Davies Evans, *Malta* (London: Thames and Hudson, 1959), 142.

3. David Trump, "Summing Up and the Way Forward," *Exploring the Maltese Prehistoric Temple Culture*, http://www.otsf.org/emptc.htm (accessed December 31, 2008).

4. Saul S. Weinberg, "Neolithic Figurines and Aegean Interrelations," *American Journal of Archaeology* 55, no. 2 (1951): 132; Colin Renfrew, "The Development and Chronology of Early Cycladic Figurines," *American Journal of Archaeology* 73, no. 1 (1969): 28–29; James Mellaart, *Excavations at Hacilar* (Edinburgh: The University Press, 1970), 1:168–178.

5. David Trump and Daniel Cilia, *Malta: Prehistory and Temples* (Malta: Midsea Books, 2002), 95, 98, 112.

6. Caroline Malone et al., "The Death Cults of Prehistoric Malta," *Scientific American* (December 1993): 116.

7. Vicki Noble, *The Double Goddess: Women Sharing Power* (Rochester, VT: Bear and Company, 2003), 1–2.

8. Simon Stoddart, "The Maltese Death Cult in Context," in *Cult in Context: Reconsidering Ritual in Archaeology*, ed. David A. Barrowclough and Caroline Malone (Oxford: Oxbow Books, 2007), 58.

9. Noble, *Double Goddess*, 65, 69–70.

10. Cristina Biaggi, *Habitations of the Great Goddess* (Manchester, CT: Knowledge, Ideas and Trends, 1994), 30.

11. Malone et al., "Death Cults of Prehistoric Malta," 117.

12. Raffaello Battaglia, "Le statue neolitiche di Malta e l'ingrassamento muliebre presso I Mediterranei," *IPEK* 2 (1927): 141.

13. Marija Gimbutas, "The 'Monstrous Venus' of Prehistory or Goddess Creatrix," *The Comparative Civilization Review* 7 (1981): 18.

14. Themistocles Zammit, "Neolithic Representations of the Human Form from the Islands of Malta and Gozo," *Journal of the Royal Anthropological Institute of Great Britain and Ireland* 54 (1924): 77; Luigi Maria Ugolini, *Malta: Origine della Civilta Mediterranea* (Roma: La Libreria dello Stato, 1934), 124; Trump and Cilia, *Malta*, 98.

15. Battaglia, "Le statue neolitiche di Malta," 159.

16. Ibid., 151, 159

17. Trump and Cilia, *Malta*, 115.

18. Battaglia, "Le statue neolitiche di Malta," 143.

19. Zammit, "Neolithic Representations of the Human Form," 74.

20. James Mellaart, *Çatal Hüyük* (London: Thames and Hudson, 1967), 202.

21. Evans, *Malta*, 142.

22. Christopher Kininmonth, *Malta and Gozo* (London: Jonathan Cape, 1979), 54.

23. Mellaart, *Çatal Hüyük*, 178.

24. Malone et al., "Death Cults of Prehistoric Malta," 111, 117.

25. Ibid., 117.

26. David Trump, *Skorba* (London: Thames and Hudson, 1966), 51.

Bibliography

Barrowclough, David A., and Caroline Malone, eds. *Cult in Context: Reconsidering Ritual in Archaeology.* Oxford: Oxbow Books, 2007.

Battaglia, Raffaello. "Le statue neolitiche di Malta e l'ingrassamento muliebre presso I Mediterranei." *IPEK* 2 (1927): 131–160.

Biaggi, Cristina. *Habitations of the Great Goddess.* Manchester, CT: Knowledge, Ideas and Trends, 1994.

Evans, John Davies. *Malta.* London: Thames and Hudson, 1959.

Gimbutas, Marija. "The 'Monstrous Venus' of Prehistory or Goddess Creatrix." *Comparative Civilization Review* 7 (1981): 1–25.

Kininmonth, Christopher. *Malta and Gozo.* London: Jonathan Cape, 1979.

Malone, Caroline, Anthony Bonanno, Tancred Gouder, Simon Stoddart, and David Trump. "The Death Cults of Prehistoric Malta." *Scientific American* (December 1993): 110–117.

Malone, Caroline, Simon Stoddart, Anthony Bonanno, Tancred Gouder, and David Trump. "Mortuary Ritual of the 4th Millennium B.C. Malta: The Zebbug Period Chambered Tomb from the Brochtorff Circle at Xaghra (Gozo)." *Proceedings of the Prehistoric Society* 61 (1995): 303–345.

Mellaart, James. *Çatal Hüyük*. London: Thames and Hudson, 1967.

Mellaart, James. *Excavations at Hacilar.* Vol 1. Edinburgh: The University Press, 1970.

Mifsud, Anton, and Charles Savona-Ventura, eds. *Facets of Maltese Prehistory.* Valletta, Malta; Prehistoric Society of Malta, 1999.

Noble, Vicki. *The Double Goddess: Women Sharing Power.* Rochester, VT: Bear and Company, 2003.

Pessina, Andrea, and Nicholas C. Vella. *Un Archeologo Italiano a Malta: Luigi Maria Ugolini, An Italian Archaeologist in Malta.* Malta: Midsea Books, 2005.

Renfrew, Colin. "The Development and Chronology of Early Cycladic Figurines." *American Journal of Archaeology* 73, no. 1 (1969): 1–31.

Stoddart, Simon. *The Maltese Death Cult in Context: Reconsidering Ritual in Archaeology,* ed. David A. Barrowclough and Caroline Malone. Oxford: Oxbow Books, 2007.

Stoddart, Simon, Anthony Bonanno, Tancred Gouder, Caroline Malone, and David Trump. "Cult in an Island Society: Prehistoric Malta in the Tarxien Period." *Cambridge Archaeological Journal 3* (1993): 3–19.

Trump, David. *Skorba*. London: Thames and Hudson, 1966.

Trump, David. "Summing Up and the Way Forward." *Exploring the Maltese Prehistoric Temple Culture.* 2003. http://www.otsf.org/emptc.htm (accessed December 31, 2008).

Trump, David, and Daniel Cilia. *Malta: Prehistory and Temples.* Malta: Midsea Books, 2002.

Ugolini, Luigi Maria. *Malta: Origine della Civilta Mediterranea.* Roma: La Libreria dello Stato, 1934.

Weinberg, Saul S. "Neolithic Figurines and Aegean Interrelations." *American Journal of Archaeology* 55, no. 2 (1951): 121–133.

Zammit, Themistocles. "Neolithic Representations of the Human Form from the Islands of Malta and Gozo." *Journal of the Royal Anthropological Institute of Great Britain and Ireland LIV* (1924): 67–100.

7

The Goddess Tanit and Her Revenants in Sicily: Demeter, Persephone, Anne, and Mary

Dolores DeLuise

Tanit was the most important deity in the Carthaginian pantheon from the sixth through first centuries BCE. Sicily, standing at the crossroads of Africa and Europe, rich with archeological remains, and possessing right up to the present time a tenacious feminine spirituality, is a primary site from which to understand the breadth and scope of the worship of Tanit in the ancient world and to identify the matriarchal legacy she bequeathed. Tanit's identity evolved from those of predecessor goddesses like Atirat and Asherah of the Middle East and eventually merged with that of Demeter and Persephone—mother and daughter, harvest and death—of the Greek pantheon. After the firm establishment of Christianity in the Middle Ages, the Virgin Mother and her mother, Saint Anne, carried along with their Christian identities those of the goddesses who had formerly inhabited the land. Because Tanit melded with her predecessors and successors, traces of her worship can still be discerned today, particularly in remote areas, where what may look like Christian ritual is actually goddess worship.[1]

In preliterate times, the acquisition and transmission of knowledge were intuitive and therefore fragmented; one piece of information could overlap in meaning or contradict another, yet they could both contain recognizable, undeniable truths. One of the typical outcomes of this way of knowing was Tanit's dual role; while called Queen of Heaven, she was also the goddess of the underworld, and these polar opposites existed without contradiction. Likewise, she was not only the fertility goddess but also the virgin goddess of war. She was brought to a temple in Rome because the Romans equated her with Juno and called her Dea Caelestis, the goddess of heaven, despite the fact that the Romans and the Carthaginians were enemies. In the Carthaginian culture, ongoing human life was insured by human sacrifice, over which Tanit, the mother, ruled.

This blurring of boundaries occurs as well in the sacred texts of many present-day religions, such as the Torah, the Christian Bible, and the Quran, which had their origins in the oral traditions of antiquity and therefore share some common elements with respect to the seemingly contradictory logic of preliterate religious culture. The Christian Gospels, for example, contain four narratives of the same events, yet in many places they contradict, omit, transpose, or reverse information, very much as in dreams.

Sicily: A Land Rich in Myth

The largest island in the Mediterranean, Sicily, roughly triangular and located off the southwest coast of Italy, has a long history of colonization because of its location and the riches of the land itself. It was first settled by various non-Indo-European tribes—Sicanians, Sicels, and Elymians—traces of whom can still be found. The Greeks undertook the most significant colonization of Sicily, beginning at about 800 BCE, and the eastern part of Sicily became part of *Magna Graecia*, or "Greater Greece." At roughly the same time, inroads were made on the western or African coast by the Carthaginians, who claimed the western third of the island for themselves. Lilybaeum (present-day Marsala) on the western shore and the nearby island of Motya were the two most important Carthaginian strongholds.

The conquest and colonization of Sicily continued for millennia. The Romans of the Western Empire eventually drove out both Carthaginians and Greeks, and they were succeeded by the Byzantine empire of the east, which ruled Sicily until 827 CE. Sicily was then ruled by three successive Arab dynasties until about 1200, when Christianity was restored by the Normans. Because of its Arab/Muslim period and official status as an emirate—that is, a politically defined territory ruled by a hereditary Muslim monarch—which did not end until the ninth century CE, Sicily was not thought of as part of Europe until quite late in western history, and was therefore culturally isolated from greater Christian Europe, having more in common with the Middle East and North Africa, lands of the dark-skinned, non-European "other."[2] The story of Sicily's otherness continues to be related in the story of its goddesses.

No written stories of Tanit are extant; if any had existed, they would have been destroyed when the Romans sacked Carthage in 146 BCE. What remains as a record of her work are references from biblical and classical sources and archeological evidence: objects dug from the ground and scattered all over the world in the form of shrines, images, words on pottery, and grave markers. It is through these disparate elements that her significance can be reconstructed. Because of its geography, epigraphic and iconographic remains, and proximity to Carthage, Sicily is a primary site from which to understand why and how Tanit was worshiped.

The details of Tanit's life are nowhere, yet her image was everywhere in the Carthaginian world. Her function was to preside over the passage from this life to the next. Her image as goddess of the underworld has been discovered on thousands of stelae, or grave markers. What follows are some historical and cultural strands that must be woven together in order to visualize the culture over which Tanit held sway.

The Carthaginian empire, the longest-lasting culture of the classical world, flourished in the western Mediterranean from 814 BCE (according to tradition) to 143 BCE. Their culture existed before 814, however, because the forbears of the Carthaginians were the Canaanites of the Hebrew Bible, whose earliest elements date back to the tenth through sixth centuries BCE. The capital city, Carthage, is located near present-day Tunis in North Africa, and its influence spread throughout the western coastal area of North Africa, Spain, Corsica, Sardinia, and the western section of Sicily. At the height of its power and influence, it dominated the economic infrastructure of the ancient Mediterranean.

Carthage was originally a colony of Phoenicia, the great seafaring culture of the Middle East, where Lebanon and Syria are presently located. The African colony eventually became rich and powerful on its own, and, after the fall of Phoenicia's capital city, Tyre, in 575 BCE, the Carthaginians conquered and settled other lands on their own behalf. "Punic," derived from Latin for "Phoenicia," shall refer to that which is related to or derived from Phoenician/Carthaginian culture.[3]

Phoenicia, the once-powerful homeland, became a nostalgic memory, growing fainter with time as the Carthaginians took up their own position in the world theater on the stages of commerce, war, politics, and religion. Although the Phoenician deities were distant in time and space, the Carthaginians never forsook that hereditary pantheon, and Tanit acceded to her mightiest position of power in Carthage, becoming their patron goddess, much like Athena in Athens.

The Phoenician alphabet, first to represent letters phonetically, was in wide use throughout the Mediterranean; it is directly through the Punic alphabet that many present-day systems have been developed, including Cyrillic, Greek, and Roman.[4] The Carthaginians, the premier mercantile culture in the ancient Mediterranean, used the Punic writing system mainly for their wide-ranging commerce. Since the written portion of their civilization was destroyed by the Romans in the Sack of Carthage in 143 BCE, scholars can learn nothing about their wars and culture, including the stories of their deities, from the Carthaginians themselves but must rely instead on Greek and Roman historical commentators—their enemies. Relying on such sources for knowledge of the Carthaginians means truth must be carefully sorted out from propaganda.

The term *chthonic* refers to the realm of the earth and the worship of gods who are situated inside the earth, in the underworld. The ancient view of the environment was strongly driven by a need to adapt to these natural forces. Religion needed to be a means through which people could obtain reassurance that the cold, hard earth of the winter months would yield once more to the life-giving and nourishing earth of the following season, and, like the earth, women needed to be fruitful. As a consequence, the perspective through which the Punic peoples viewed the world was focused on natural occurrences and the cycle of natural events that took place over the course of the agricultural year: birth, death, rebirth. Given these conditions, it follows that the goddess of fertility needs to be in close touch with the earth itself, even when it seems to be dead, and especially when interring the dead.

Death was a prominent feature in the religions of the Punic sphere because people applied to themselves the model of the yearly demise and rebirth of nature. Many places where the deities were worshiped were located near springs, lakes, and faults in the earth. Such sites were perceived as having literal access to the underworld where the chthonic deities were located.[5] Just as nature is reborn, so must be people, and natural events dictated the progression of their lives in a form of sympathetic magic.

Sympathetic Magic

Two mysterious, potent forces—the sun and women, with the power both had to give life and take it away—had to be somehow regulated; both had to be appeased and appear to remain under control. One way the ancients thought they could control their world was through the intuitive system of thinking called sympathetic magic, wherein mimesis, the imitation of an object, action, or idea, produces like results.

By using this kind of thinking, it may seem as though humans can control the sun. Thus at the celebration of the winter solstice, bonfires were lit, approximating the light and warmth of the sun, and festivities of all kinds took place. This ancient practice, and its satisfying results, is still carried on in various guises: the lighting of Christmas trees, Yule logs, and Chanukah menorahs; homecoming bonfires; and neopagan rites that attempt to resuscitate ancient solstice rituals.

Another element essential is the feeling of attaining control of the life-giving power of women who, in their own way, are as powerful as the sun but less constant. Figures depicting women as the earth goddess, such as the Venus of Willendorf, are approximately 24,000 years old. In preliterate cultures all over the world, a woman's size was a revered indication of power—the power to give life.

Henotheistic Religion

Before he was regarded as the creator of the universe, the Hebrew god Yahweh was a local divinity; this is called henotheism, or monotheistic worship that exists in a framework of polytheism. Each people had its own god(s) whom they considered better than other gods. The Hebrew Bible discusses Yahweh's relationship to other gods in this sense.[6] Monotheistic worshipers today cannot imagine worshiping a deity not of their religion, but such worship was possible through henotheistic thinking. Ancient cultures often borrowed the gods of neighboring cultures, renaming them and refashioning their functions to fit their particular needs; thus the Canaanite goddess Atirat eventually became Asherah in Phoenicia and finally the Carthaginian goddess Tanit.

This point was elucidated by an important discovery made in the 1970s. An ancient temple was uncovered in the city of Sarepta in Phoenicia and inscribed "Asherah Tanit," showing how the identities of the two goddesses may have merged. This inscription also demonstrates Tanit as an ancient Middle Eastern deity and not one newly imported to Carthage from another culture.[7] Before this discovery was made, it had been suggested that Tanit may have been a local Libyan deity who was incorporated into the Carthaginian pantheon, but when her name was found on the temple inscription in the Phoenician homeland, it became certain that she had been worshiped there and subsequently brought to Carthage. In addition, a fifth-century BCE shipwreck off the coast of Haifa, Israel, revealed terracotta figurines stamped with Tanit's distinctive emblem.[8] She had a definite presence in the Middle East and gained ascendance in the western Mediterranean with the blossoming of the Carthaginian empire.

The Carthaginian Pantheon

Ba'al was one of the major deities of the Carthaginian pantheon, brought there from Phoenicia via their forebears, the Canaanites. The religions of the Canaanites and Hebrews are linked by the worship of the predecessor of Tanit, the Phoenician goddess Asherah, whom was worshiped in the Temple in Jerusalem.[9] When the Phoenicians settled in the western Mediterranean at Carthage, their gods traveled with them. Ba'al Hammon, god of the sun, a direct descendent of the Canaanite Ba'al, was the most important. He was represented with his arms outstretched toward the sacrificial fire, in which he received the offering of sacrificial victims who could appease him so that his ongoing protection would be assured. Mot, the god of death, and Melquarth, the god of the underworld and the vegetation cycle, were also prominent. As time went on, the mother goddess Tanit ruled equally with Ba'al, but became ultimately the primary deity of the Carthaginian empire.

The idea that moral and ethical beliefs are associated with religious beliefs does not inform ancient religions of the Middle East, with the exception of Judaism, which adopted the Ten Commandments, mandated by an authoritative father god. Monotheism, therefore, became associated with positive morality and its opposite, "idol worship," was regarded as anathema. Child sacrifice of the cultures surrounding the Hebrews was considered an "abomination" by the divine lawgiver and was associated with idol worship. Since Christianity inherited Hebrew monotheism, it also inherited its ethical connotations. This is not to say that the Hebrews themselves did not, at some time, practice child sacrifice. Most notably, Abraham was prepared to sacrifice his son, Isaac, when Yahweh commanded him to sacrifice a ram instead. One must question why this substitution was an issue of such importance, and the most probable answer is that sacrificing children was not unknown among the Hebrews. Because of Yahweh's directive to Abraham, animal, not human, sacrifice became the standard until the destruction of the Second Temple in 72 CE, and brought with it the ethics of monotheism, which it passed on to Christianity. The figure of Jesus continues to replace humans and animals as the ritual sacrifice.

Elsewhere in the Bible, the Israelites are commanded to "consecrate" their first-born to God and, in a required ceremony, formally purchase the child away from god's service; this ceremony is still performed among Jews in a symbolic sense. The term *consecrate* meant "dedicate" and used for both children and animals.[10] It is easy to imply that at some preliterate time the buying back of a child and/or the substitution of an animal may have been literal. The cult of Tanit revolved around child sacrifice where, in some instances, animals or purchased children could be substituted for one's own child, paralleling the concerns taken up in the Bible.

The Sign of Tanit

One way to determine the extent of the worship of Tanit is through the Sign of Tanit, which can be found on the majority of stelae (stone grave markers) in the Carthaginian tophets, places where sacrifices were burned. There is uncertainty regarding the significance and origin of this symbol, which arose in the sixth century BCE at the time Tanit eclipsed Ba'al as the most important Carthaginian deity. What it meant to the Carthaginians may not be precisely known, but possibilities suggest themselves.[11] The Sign of Tanit gained popularity and overtook all other symbols at a particular time in the development of Carthaginian culture. It may be the representation of a person with hands crossed over the chest in the Egyptian position in which royalty was buried. In such case, it may have been that the victim became heroic by "passing through MLK" (*Moloch*, the term used in the Semitic languages to indicate the recipient of sacrificed victims) and that the stelae upon which they are inscribed indicate the interment of a hero of the people who made the ultimate sacrifice for the good of all.[12]

In some places, where the figure does seem representational or iconic, the Sign of Tanit has been interpreted as a female with raised arms crossed over her breasts in what seems to be a ritual gesture. In an alternative view, the disc on the top may be the sun and the crossbar beneath may be a flattened-out crescent moon, signifying the celestial bodies, masculine and feminine, life and fertility. In this line of thinking, the bottom of the symbol beneath the crossbar resembles the shape of a sacrificial altar.

The symbol is divided by the crossbar, and that brings all these interpretations of the Sign of Tanit directly into context—the mind divided from the body, the heavens divided from the earth, this life divided from the next. But all these are also inextricably joined to form the entire symbol, yielding its essence. While it meant death, it also meant the totality of the life cycle as seen with a chthonic outlook. Rebirth can only be effected from previous birth and death, and death of the recently born seems to have been the most efficacious.

Tanit is also associated with other symbols. On coins and stelae, she is often represented near a palm tree, which is a symbol of fertility and good luck. The other sign with which she is associated is the caduceus, two snakes twining up a staff. The snake is a symbol with chthonic overtones, and it often represents female deities.

Child Sacrifice

Child sacrifice is probably the most difficult aspect of Punic culture and religion to understand, but it was an important exercise of sympathetic magic. The reasoning of sympathetic magic insists that like produces like. So to insure the life-giving properties and return of the sun, Ba'al, the sun god, required life as the fuel for his bonfire. The more valuable a sacrifice, the more powerful it was. Thus, it was common in Punic cultures to offer children of prominent individuals as sacrifices, for the good of all, the logic of which stated, "We give you this valuable life so that you will return life of equal value to us." Through indirect sources it has been related that the child might have been the oldest or the best-loved. Some commentators indicate that the child was purchased by the votaries to offer in place of their own child. It was also reported that music and tambourines were played to drown out the sound of weeping parents; conversely, another source claims that if the parents made any response, the sacrifice was invalid. Most important, however, Diodorus of Sicily says that in times of war and danger, the number of sacrifices was increased so that the gods would favor Carthaginian endeavors. His assertion has been recently borne out by dated archaeological evidence.[13]

The first 20th-century excavation of a tophet took place in Moyta, the last Carthaginian stronghold in Sicily. Found there were the cremated remains of infants and animals in urns buried under a field of stelae, and the proximity of the two seemed unremarkable at the time. Similar discoveries were made two years later in Carthage, however, at which time the inscriptions were re-evaluated, and it was only then realized that these were ritual, sacrificial burials.

Now that Sicily is fully established as part of Western Europe, the issue of child sacrifice is in question. Scholars living in areas that had been settled by Carthaginians do not wish to envision themselves as descendents of child-sacrificing savages. Both sides are adamant in their arguments. Some

Italian and Tunisian scholars claim that because of frequent miscarriage and death in childbirth, the tophets contain only the remains of well-developed fetuses and children who had died naturally. Other scholars analyze a number of elements. First, they explain that the external written evidence, biased though it may be, is consistent and comes from a number of different sources over many hundreds of years. Next, they cite the presence in Carthaginian cities of ordinary Punic burial sites, which are different in character than the tophets. The strongest evidence comes from the sheer number of the remains and the fact that in some places animals, clearly sacrificed, were buried alongside the infants. In addition, in the cities where tophets were discovered, there is only one tophet while there are a number of other burial places, containing both adults and infants. Ordinary burial sites contain both cremated and inhumated remains, whereas in the tophets the infants were interred only after being burned.[14]

Since a great many stelae bore the Sign of Tanit or other likeness of her, the question is raised about her specific role in the sacrifice. The sacrifices were clearly made to appease the god Ba'al Hammon, and Tanit, as "The Face of Ba'al," seems to have facilitated these sacrifices. Other goddesses of the eastern Mediterranean, whose stories are preserved in writing, also seemed to have been the active partners in a female/male relationship, like Inanna and Isis who, with great energy and force of personality, brought their male partners, Damuzi and Osiris, back from the realm of the dead. Tanit may have played a similar role in the life of Ba'al who, like Osiris, was able to rule over the land of the dead with Tanit as his helpmeet on earth.

What is clear is that Tanit was important in Carthaginian culture because of her ability to travel to the Underworld and return and to communicate with the heavens with equal ease. She was a familiar figure who could alleviate anxiety about what might happen after death. Selecting a child for sacrifice and putting it in Tanit's care might have helped people suppress fears of their own deaths.

Sicily was the home of another goddess who communicated with this world and also the next: Persephone. There is strong evidence that their cults overlapped in at least one location in Sicily, and taking a look at her story will shed light on the significance of and the persistence of the cult of Tanit.[15]

The Story of Demeter and Persephone

Unlike Tanit, Persephone has a particular story in a number of variations in both Greek and Roman cultures. Persephone's extraordinary beauty reflected the divinity of her parents, brother, and sister: Demeter the mother goddess on earth, and Zeus in Olympus, father god of the heavens. In their home in Sicily, the most fertile land in the Mediterranean, Demeter and Persephone had been attending a feast near Lake Pergusa. Persephone and the other young girls were walking on the lakeshore picking wildflowers, laughing and talking as they went. She was lost in the beauty of the place, and, intoxicated by the scent, was seduced by each successive bloom, just out of reach, one more beautiful than the next, and she slowly made her way closer and closer into the nearby forest, farther and farther away from her friends.

She did not hear the thunderous noise of horses' hooves until she felt herself in the grasp of large hands, firmly encircling her in a death grip. She looked up and saw the stern, awful countenance of the God of Hell: Hades, her uncle. From inside an open, massive, black carriage, and with the air rushing by like a hurricane, she looked out, and the last thing she saw by the light of day was her beautiful purple sash flying away, carried in the air. It got smaller and smaller, writhing like a loosed snake, as the distance between them increased.

"Mother . . . Mother," she called, but the rushing wind pushed her words back down inside her. Then no words would come at all. The chariot, which had been skimming along the top of the water, was now going down, down, under the water, into a cave and under the earth. Her mind's eye held the image of her purple scarf, and that was all she could see in the darkness under the earth.

Demeter felt a slight chill as evening began to approach, and, taking it as a sign, decided that it was time to collect Persephone and return home after their lovely day. She and the other mothers walked down to the lakeside to gather up the children, but none of them had remembered seeing Persephone for a while. Everyone thought she had gone back to her mother, whose side she rarely left. They searched and searched, calling her name at the lakeside and near the forest, but by the time it was completely dark, they had not yet found her. Demeter ran around the lake, calling frantically but receiving no answer. She entered the woods, running through it with the strength and endurance only a mother can have when her child's life is at stake. She couldn't find Persephone and was stricken with grief and panic.

Demeter searched without rest throughout Sicily for her daughter. Her clothes torn, her hair, once braided and crowned with strands of wheat, had become disheveled, and streamed behind her as she ran. When it became truly dark, she ran to the top of Mount Etna, dipped two pine torches into the flame, and they burst up in a shower of light. She held one in each hand and they guided her through the darkest places in the countryside and the mountains. The volcano sent up red flames throughout the night, lighting up all of Sicily so that Demeter could find her way to her beloved only child.

Her search was fruitless. Demeter, wailing now in grief, tearing her clothes, beating her breast, returned home and took up her chariot drawn by twin snakes. She traveled the world searching for her lost daughter, imagining her all the while fallen and hurt, alone, calling out, receiving no response. All to no avail; Persephone had disappeared.

Demeter returned to Lake Pergusa and rested at the shore, finally defeated, pondering the reality of her great loss. A water nymph had caused Persephone's fallen sash to rise up out of the water and float to the shoreline where Demeter sat. Here was an ominous sight, Demeter thought, as she saw the swathe of purple approach the shore. The nymph arose from the water and told Demeter that her own brother, Hades, had kidnapped her child and, violating the water of the sacred lake itself, descended with Persephone to his realm in the underworld through a cave at the bottom of the water.

"I have seen her," said the nymph. "And although she is young and frightened, she is yet a queen, ruling the underworld at the side of Hades."

Demeter, horror-stricken, immediately boarded her chariot and went to Olympus to Zeus, father of her child.

"There is nothing I can do," Zeus told his sister. "Our power and authority is divided three ways; I rule the heavens, Hades the underworld, and Poseidon, the sea. There is nothing I can do," he repeated.

"But I've come to you because she's your child too!"

"And she's quite beautiful. I can well understand why Hades loves her and wants her to be his queen."

"Never!"

"I'm sorry. It is already done."

Demeter left Zeus and returned home to Sicily. Her mourning continued, as did her rage, which she took out on humankind, particularly in Sicily, her home, which, having had that honor, had been the most fertile land on earth. She destroyed the plows she had taught the people to make, spoiled the seeds, and turned the land against them, and they began to die of starvation.

When Zeus learned of Demeter's actions, he sent for her, and when she appeared before him he told her that he was aggrieved.

"No one is more grieved than I," Demeter responded.

"Let us have a compromise. If I could restore Persephone to the living, I would, but no one can return from the dead if they have eaten in the underworld. Those are the rules of the Fates. Persephone has eaten seeds of the pomegranate.

"I have been able to convince the Fates, however, to permit her to spend half the year with you. The rest of the time, she shall rule with Hades in the underworld."

Demeter, frantic to have her child back by any means, accepted these terms, and at the end of six months the Fates accompanied Persephone from the underworld to her waiting arms.

The Cult of Malophoros

Syncretism, or blending together of religious elements and deities, is visible in Sicily in the cult of Malophoros in Selinus, site of present-day Selinunte.[16] The city was founded by the Greeks in the seventh century BCE near the southwestern shore of the island. In 250 BCE Selinus was sacked by the Carthaginians, perennially at war with the Greeks in Sicily, and both buildings and populace were destroyed. The few survivors faced a marginal existence on the outposts of Carthaginian civilization, perhaps receiving charity or perhaps left to fend for themselves. Although they had no formal settlement, their numbers were sufficient enough to maintain temple worship of Demeter and Persephone, as uncovered archeological evidence clearly shows.

This discovery reveals that worship of Tanit was concurrent with worship of Demeter and Persephone. Holy places remain holy throughout millennia, and pass from one religious observance to the next.[17] Many Christian churches sit on the sites of former pagan places of worship and mosques, and the sanctuary of Malophoros shows how this occurred. Originally constructed by the Greeks for the worship of Demeter and Persephone, it was refurbished in the third century BCE as a Carthaginian temple with an adjacent tophet. The reconstruction altered the original Greek temple. It was set into the earth itself, so that its interior resembled a Phoenician place of burial, the atmosphere necessary for worship of chthonic deities. This makes the temple significantly unlike the atmosphere of Greek temples in Sicily, constructed in the open air on sites whose natural beauty cause contemplation of the possibility of heaven on earth. The artifacts discovered at the temple of Malophoros demonstrate a syncretic adaptation of worship of both Demeter and Tanit and that the worshipers were primarily women.

This religious overlapping offers an interpretation of the story of Perse-phone as a sacrifice made not *by means of* the mother but *in spite of* the mother. Conversely, the sacrifice may have been Persephone's. It has been suggested that Demeter's love for her daughter seems at first the idealized version of a mother's selfless love for her child but when examined more closely reveals a mother who cannot let her child go, therefore depriving her of her own life and loves. This story was markedly different from infant sacrifice made to appease the deities, but it may have resonated, nevertheless, as a kind of response to it in a country that continues to be matrifocal but that has a proverb, "Better to lose your daughter than your money." The contradictions posed by these two truths parallel the irrationalities contained in religious belief.

Child sacrifice under the auspices of the mother goddess Tanit was final and irreversible, but child sacrifice in the mother/daughter story of Demeter and Persephone was incomplete and reversible, and the next mother that succeeded in the land, Saint Anne, provided a great contrast in that she only gave life. When considered along with the two previous mothers, her story seems as though it may be an overcompensated response.

The Story of St. Anne

Southwest of Palermo rise the Madonie Mountains, named after and dedicated to the Madonna, but atop the hill that overlooks the small mountain town of Castelbuono, a spirit of a different sort haunts the precincts. In the church there is a holy relic: the head of Saint Anne. Townspeople claim that it was brought back from the Holy Land during the crusades, originally to France, but, they say proudly, the Castelbuonese stole it from them. The head of Saint Anne is a religious symbol whose meaning transcends reality and is based in the human need for the reassurance of rebirth, much like the Sign of Tanit. A noncanonical but officially recognized Catholic saint, Anne continues to be honored with undiminished fervor, in one of those religious contradictions for which there is no explanation.

Saint Anne, patron of genealogy, fertility, and matrilineal descent, began her existence in an apocryphal gospel.[18] Although Catholic sources say that Anne and her husband, Joachim, both saints, were the parents of the Virgin Mary and thus the grandparents of Jesus, the myth of her life was added gradually into medieval church history. Her biography states she had outlived three husbands, mothered two more daughters, and was the matriarch of a large extended holy family. For various theological reasons, the details of Anne's life became important in the Middle Ages, when religious observance was no longer overseen by the tolerant Arab Emirate but replaced by the Christianizing Norman conquerors. It was easy to take up worship of the earth mother of antiquity in her new guise as Saint Anne. According to folk legend, her head arrived in Sicily during the period of time between the Norman Conquest, 1061, and the end of the First Crusade, 1099, an auspicious moment to have brought out an old artifact and surreptitiously install it in the new religion.[19]

Every year on July 26 Castelbuono celebrates the Feast of Saint Anne. Every other day of the year she rests in the permanent twilight of a church inside a Norman castle. The most important representation of her in the town is a larger-than-life silver bust. Set into a cave-like opening at the heart is a black, shriveled-up skull. This artifact resides in a sophisticated illustration of an advanced civilization, and they contradict each other. This religious symbol is the literal embodiment of ancient goddess worship in Sicily existing within a Christian institution, a fact reinforced during the drama of the procession on the feast day of Saint Anne.

The procession originates at the Norman fortress, just outside the town gates atop the hill. There is a cobbled ramp leading down from the main castle doors to the courtyard. In the opposite direction, from within the town, spectators first hear silver bells ringing to the cadence of a gait. Traveling to the town gates is a statue of the Virgin Mary, Our Lady of the Rosary, who stands on a crescent moon. She rides atop a *carrozza*, a Sicilian carriage covered with a fringed canopy, a silver bell between each knot, which ring in near unison with each step the bearers take.

At first it seems that Saint Anne's daughter is leaving the town, heading toward the castle, going the wrong way, but her entourage makes a turn. The Virgin faces the town in the direction from which she had come, the direction Saint Anne will take when she emerges from the castle through the gates. The Virgin waits.

The drama opens with the flicker of candles. Many candles. They weave their way down the castle ramp and through the courtyard in a serpentine path, growing slowly, slowly, longer, longer. The lights thin out, become diffuse, as they seem to take a slow step forward, but then, like a living thing, a drawn-in breath, they contract like a caterpillar making its way along the branch of a tree. Slowly, the glimmering, undulating throng approaches the town gates, slowly, descending the steep ramp, traversing from side to side, and a distant outline begins to form in the candlelight.

High above the people, seemingly disembodied at a distance, is the larger-than-life silver reliquary of Saint Anne. Her approach is majestic, her gaze steady, regal, austere, the black skull nestling in the place where her heart should have been. Her silver skin is agleam from the candles that surround her on her position atop a huge, beautiful renaissance *carrozza*, painted, gilded, and garlanded with what seem like a thousand stargazer lilies, their scent piercing the air with a ferocious sweetness.

Saint Anne enters the town and slowly passes the Virgin. The people are silent, gazing up at her in awe and insatiable longing. Around her silver shoulders rests a mantle of jewels, radiating a light of its own. Drummers and priests precede her, and she is surrounded by altar-children as she is carried forward by a dozen strong men. A large contingent of barefoot pilgrims holding candles, what had been in the distance the mass of breathing lights, follows, and many others follow them.

After Saint Anne enters the town, the Virgin and her worshipers, who had been waiting where they had turned, follow her in the procession back into the town, the way they had come. The chilling noise of snare drums and church bells sounds variously as the procession makes its way through the town.

Later in the night, after she has traveled throughout the town, Saint Anne returns to the castle. Her virgin daughter, who had followed her through the town, turns back toward the town and returns to her church inside the town. When the townspeople are questioned about why the Virgin came to the gate, waited for her mother, followed her mother through the town, and then returned to her own church, they say that the daughter cannot go to the mother's space inside the castle; she must remain within the walls of the town. Why? It would be a "violation." The only times she can leave the town and seek refuge in her mother's space are in cases of war, pestilence, or plague. It is just a matter of separate space, they say; just that and nothing more.

This Sicilian town acts out the Demeter and Persephone story under cover of Christianity. The silver representation of Saint Anne in Castelbuono is a metaphoric mirror of goddesses. On the one hand, it is a sophisticated piece of art, and on the other it is a leftover artifact of a lost culture. Although the representations of the goddesses are opposite in appearance and cultural origin, they are housed together harmoniously: Tanit and Demeter come together in the figure of Saint Anne, a kind of matriarchal trinity. Literally, it is as though the new religion and culture had made room within the symbol of its very identity to accommodate the ancient religion, since the actual skull alone could not survive in the new religion. And just as the new had carved out a place for the old, it had also permitted it to survive through metaphoric depictions of the blackness of the skull, the metaphoric Black Madonna, as Christianity, forcing the issue of idol worship, subsumed the old gods into the hagiographic pantheon.

Significantly, this reenactment of the Demeter/Persephone story of division of space—the reunion followed by the return of the mother to the higher ground and the daughter to the lower, occurs at the precise moment the land begins its downward spiral in the agricultural year, marking the beginning of Demeter's annual period of mourning. This mirrors as well the separation symbolized by the Sign of Tanit, life, death, and rebirth, tangled together with the Virgin Mother and her mother, who, like Tanit, could be more than one thing at a time, namely, the genealogy of the savior whose death resulted in life.

There is something unique about the mother-daughter relationship in Sicily. Mothers and daughters either live for or very much against each other. On the one hand, there is that Sicilian proverb, "Better to lose your daughter than your money." On the other hand, a daughter is *figghiuzza mia* ("my little daughter") or *mammuzza mia* ("my little mommy"), one's very self, the visible part of the soul, the spirit making its way in the world.

Although Tanit's rule there is long over, her mark remains on Sicily in another interpretation of the Sign of Tanit: the enigmatic *trinacria*, the symbol of Sicily. It is a three-legged figure surrounding a feminine head from which snakes emanate. The figure is a merging of the Greek goddess Medusa with the triangular shape, extended limbs, and head of the Carthaginian symbol representing Tanit. The triangle, integral to its structure, is the ancient universal symbol of the vulva, source of women's power, and even the shape of Sicily itself.

Notes

1. See Jean Markale, *Courtly Love: The Path of Sexual Initiation* (Rochester, VT: Inner Traditions, 2000), and Merlin Stone, *When God Was a Woman* (San Diego: Harvest Books, 1978), for discussions of the relationships between goddess worship and subsequent religious worship and contemporary life. For an overview of goddess worship in Europe and Asia Minor see Marija Gimbutas's works, *The Living Goddesses* (Berkeley: University of California Press, 2001); *The Goddesses and Gods of Old Europe: Myths and Cult Images* (Berkeley: University of California Press, 2007), and (with Joseph Campbell) *The Language of the Goddess* (London: Thames and Hudson, 2001).

2. Some reading about Sicily might begin with one or more of these books: Joseph F. Privitera, *Sicily: An Illustrated History* (New York: Hippocrene Books, 2002); Giovanni Francesio, *Sicily: Art, History and Culture* (San Giovanni Lupatoto, Italy: Arsenale Editrice, 2006); Ross Holloway, *Archaeology of Ancient Sicily*

(New York: Routledge, 2000). On the diverse peoples of Sicily, see M. I. Finley, *A History of Sicily: Ancient Sicily to the Arab Conquest* (New York: Viking, 1968); Denis Mack Smith, *History of Sicily, 800–1713: Medieval Sicily* (New York: Dorset Press, 1989); Donald Matthew, *The Norman Kingdom of Sicily*, Cambridge Medieval Textbooks (Cambridge: Cambridge University Press, 1992); and Aziz Ahmad, *History of Islamic Sicily* (Cambridge: Harvard University Press, 2000).

3. Phoenician and Carthaginian cultures are best understood as part of a single story and they are often considered together: Maria Eugenia Aubet, *The Phoenicians and the West* (London: Cambridge University Press, 2001); Sanford Holst, *Phoenicians: Lebanon's Epic Heritage* (Cambridge: Cambridge and Boston Press, 2005); Glen E. Markow, *Phoenicians* (Berkeley: University of California Press, 2000); Ella Marston, *The Phoenicians* (Tarrytown, NY: Marshal Cavendish, 2000); Sabatino Moscati, *The Phoenicians* (New York: Rizzoli International Publications, 2000); George Rawlinson, *Phoenicia: History of a Civilization* (London: I. B. Tauris, 2005); Gilbert Charles Picard,, *Carthage: A Survey of Punic History and Culture from Its Birth to the Final Tragedy*, Great Civilizations Series, trans. Dominique Collon (Basingstoke: Palgrave Macmillan, 1991).

4. See Steven R. Fischer, *A History of Writing* (London: Reaktion Books, 2003).

5. Much of the Carthaginian fascination with the earth, the deities of the earth, and the underworld was due to the influence of Egyptian religion.

6. Jonah 1:14–16; 1 Sam. 26:19, for example.

7. James B. Pritchard, *Recovering Sarepta, a Phoenician City* (Princeton, NJ: Princeton University Press, 1978).

8. Explained in M. Dothan, "A Sign of Tanit from Tal Akko," *Israel Exploration Journal* 24 (1974): 44–49.

9. See Judith M. Hadley, *The Cult of Asherah in Ancient Israel and Judah: Evidence for a Hebrew Goddess* (London: Cambridge University Press, 2000).

10. Exod. 13:2; Deut. 15:19, for example.

11. Image of the Sign of Tanit can be found in Sabatino Moscati, *The World of the Phoenicians*, trans. Alastair Hamilton (New York: Praeger, 1968).

12. See Philip J. King and Lawrence E. Stager, *Life in Biblical Israel*, Library of Ancient Israel (Louisville, KY: Westminster John Knox Press, 2002), particularly 359–361, and Lawrence E. Stager and Samuel R. Wolff, "Child Sacrifice at Carthage: Religious Rite or Population Control?" *Biblical Archeology Review* (January/February 1984): 31–51.

13. Ancient commentators on Carthaginian child sacrifice include Plutarch, Tertullian, Orosius, Philo of Byblos, and Diodorus Siculus.

14. In an article that appeared in the *Wall Street Journal* on May 26, 2005, "Carthage Tries to Live Down Image as Site of Infanticide," Andrew Higgins explains clearly the details of the "whitewashing" of the practice of child sacrifice being attempted by Arabic and Italian scholars of archeology. On one side of the controversy is Lawrence Stager, Harvard professor of archeology, and on the other is Mhamed Hassine Fantar, a Tunisian archeologist who has attached himself to the

opinion of the late Italian archeologist Sabatino Moscati. Moscati denied the allegations of ancient Roman historians that the Carthaginians sacrificed children to their gods chiefly on the grounds that they were enemies; Stager conducted extensive excavations of Carthage in the 1970s and has published widely on his findings. Fantar and Stager, with Joseph A. Greene, published a debate on Fantar's Web site, Phoenicia.org, where the two points of view are listed side by side. Fantar takes up Moscati's arguments that question the reliability of classical sources, while Stager and Greene's presentation provides positive, wider-ranging evidence.

15. The primary classical sources for the story of Demeter and Persephone include the *Homeric Hymns* (2 and 13); the *Orphic Hymns* (40 and 41); Callimachus's *Hymn to Demeter* (6); Ovid's *Metamorphoses* (5); Ovid's *Fasti* (4); and *Dionysiaca* of Nonnus (5). See Marguerite Rigoglioso's article, "Persephone's Sacred Lake and the Ancient Female Mystery Religion in the Womb of Sicily," *Feminist Studies in Religion* 21 (Fall 2005): 6–29, which explains the geographic significance of Lake Pergusa in the Demeter/Persephone story.

16. The history of the site and the evidence leading to this story are related in Donald White, "The Post-Classical Cult of Malophoros at Selinus," *American Journal of Archeology* 71, no. 4 (1967): 335–352.

17. See Karen Tate, *Sacred Places of Goddess: 108 Destinations* (San Francisco: Consortium of Collective Consciousness, 2006).

18. *Protevangelium of James*, 1–6, c. 150 CE.

19. See Kathleen Ashley and Pamela Sheingorn, *Interpreting Cultural Symbols: Saint Anne in Late Medieval Society* (Athens: University of Georgia Press, 1990), for the evolution and importance of the role played by St. Anne in medieval Catholic worship.

Bibliography

Ahmad, Aziz. *History of Islamic Sicily.* Cambridge: Harvard University Press, 2000.

Ashley, Kathleen, and Pamela Sheingorn. *Interpreting Cultural Symbols: Saint Anne in Late Medieval Socity.* Athens: University of Georgia Press, 1990.

Aubet, Maria Eugenia. *The Phoenicians and the West.* London: Cambridge University Press, 2001.

Dothan, M. "A Sign of Tanit from Tal Akko." *Israel Exploration Journal* 24 (1974): 44–49.

Finley, M. I. *A History of Sicily: Ancient Sicily to the Arab Conquest.* New York: Viking, 1968.

Fischer, Steven R. *A History of Writing.* London: Reaktion Books, 2003.

Francesio, Giovanni. *Sicily: Art, History, and Culture.* San Giovanni Lupatoto, Italy: Arsenale Editrice, 2006.

Gimbutas, Marija. The *Goddesses and Gods of Old Europe: Myths and Cult Images.* Berkeley: University of California Press, 2007.

Gimbutas, Marija. *The Living Goddesses*. Berkeley: University of California Press, 2001.

Gimbutas, Marija, and Joseph Campbell. *The Language of the Goddess*. London: Thames and Hudson, 2001.

Hadley, Judith M. *The Cult of Asherah in Ancient Israel and Judah: Evidence for a Hebrew Goddess*. London: Cambridge University Press, 2000.

Higgins, Andrew. "Carthage Tries to Live Down Image as Site of Infanticide." *Wall Street Journal*, May 26, 2005.

Holloway, Ross. *Archaeology of Ancient Sicily*. New York: Routledge, 2000.

Holst, Sanford. *Phoenicians: Lebanon's Epic Heritage*. Cambridge: Cambridge and Boston Press, 2005.

King, Philip J., and Lawrence E. Stager. *Life in Biblical Israel*. Library of Ancient Israel. Louisville, KY: Westminster John Knox Press, 2002.

Markale, Jean. *Courtly Love: The Path of Sexual Initiation*. Rochester, VT: Inner Traditions, 2000.

Markow, Glen E. *Phoenicians*. Berkeley: University of California Press, 2000.

Marston, Ella. *The Phoenicians*. Tarrytown, NY: Marshal Cavendish Press, 2000.

Matthew, Donald. *The Norman Kingdom of Sicily*. Cambridge Medieval Textbooks. Cambridge: Cambridge University Press, 1992.

Moscati, Sabatino. *The Phoenicians*. New York: Rizzoli International Publications, 2000.

Moscati, Sabatino. *The World of the Phoenicians*, trans. Alastair Hamilton. New York: Praeger, 1968.

Picard, Gilbert Charles. *Carthage: A Survey of Punic History and Culture from Its Birth to the Final Tragedy*. Great Civilizations Series. Translated by Dominique Collon. Basingstoke: Palgrave Macmillan, 1991.

Pritchard, James B. *Recovering Sarepta, a Phoenician City*. Princeton, NJ: Princeton University Press, 1978.

Privitera, Joseph F. *Sicily: An Illustrated History*. New York: Hippocrene Books, 2002.

Rawlinson, George. *Phoenicia: History of a Civilization*. London: I. B. Tauris, 2005.

Rigoglioso, Marguerite. "Persephone's Sacred Lake and the Ancient Female Mystery Religion in the Womb of Sicily." *Feminist Studies in Religion* 21 (Fall 2005): 6–29.

Smith, Denis Mack. *History of Sicily, 800–1713: Medieval Sicily*. New York: Dorset Press, 1989.

Stager, Lawrence E., and Samuel R. Wolff. "Child Sacrifice at Carthage: Religious Rite or Population Control?" *Biblical Archeology Review* (January/February 1984): 31–51.

Stone, Merlin. *When God Was a Woman*. San Diego: Harvest Books, 1978.

Tate, Karen. *Sacred Places of Goddess: 108 Destinations*. San Francisco: Consortium of Collective Consciousness, 2006.

White, Donald. "The Post-Classical Cult of Malophoros at Selinus." *American Journal of Archeology* 71, no. 4 (1967): 335–352.

8

The Anatolian Mother: Kybele

Zühre Indirkas

The human body has been perceived as having symbolic value in every society. In the same vein, it is thought that the ability of a woman to nourish a life born of her own body, with milk also produced by her own body, has inspired profound interest and respect at least since the Late Paleolithic era (30,000–8000 BCE). Figures of women in a variety of materials, ranging from bone and ivory to limestone and terra cotta, have been found across a broad region extending from Western Europe to Siberia. Despite the widespread dispersion of these examples, they have a number of features in common, suggesting that they are symbols of the female power of fertility. These features are in the main broad hips, huge breasts, and exaggerated vulvas.

Early human beings made sense of the cyclical order of nature, consisting of the birth and death of living things, by believing in the sanctity of nature itself, while a parallel was also drawn between the cosmic rhythm of nature and a woman's fertility.[1] Some researchers, taking this relationship of women's fertility as a model of the cosmos as their point of departure, have created a school of thought that identifies such female figures as representatives of a universal mother goddess.

Although the evidence of the existence of such a cult in prehistoric periods is disputed, it does seem that humanity's first image of life was the mother.[2] Among the earliest-known examples of such cult figures that have been found, mention may be made of the Venus of Willendorf, a carved limestone 11-centimeter figure of an exaggeratedly female body grasping her breasts, which is dated to about 30,000 to 25,000 BCE and was

Figure 8.1 Kyebele, sixth century BCE. Büyükkale near Boğazköy. (Reprinted with permission from the Museum of Anatolian Civilizations, Ankara.)

discovered in Austria; the Venus of Dolní Vestonice, an 11.5-centimeter fired clay figure, which is dated from 25,000 to 24,000 BCE and was discovered in Moravia; the Venus of Laussel, a 43-centimeter nude female figure carved of limestone and holding what is thought to be a bison's horn, which is dated from about 25,000 to 20,000 BCE and was discovered in France.

Kybele in Anatolia

Turning to Anatolia, the peninsula once known as Asia Minor that now makes up 97 percent of the territory of the Republic of Turkey, the mother goddess theory is explored in the context of the region's own historical processes. Examples of large-breasted, rotund women such as those discovered in Neolithic settlements dated 8000 to 5500 BCE have been unearthed—and continue to be unearthed—in the course of excavations at sites all over Anatolia where there is evidence of permanent settlement and the beginnings of agriculture. These figures of women, which are frequently accompanied by various wild animals, are the earliest predecessors of the mother goddess concept even if only as religious or magical symbols. Worship of the sacred female symbolizing the fertility and abundance of nature was to continue among the subsequent inhabitants of Anatolia as well.[3]

The most important centers of such worship in prehistoric Anatolia that have been identified are Çatalhöyük (first half 7000s BCE), Çayönü (all Neolithic phases), Caferhöyük (first half 7000s BCE), Hacılar (6000s BCE), and Kızların Mağarası ("The Cave of the Maidens," 7000s BCE, a cavern discovered at Mt. Başet near Van in eastern Turkey). Nevertheless the first goddess to be identified in inscriptions as "mother" who is truly an Anatolian mother goddess is Kybele. In Phrygian inscriptions dated to the seventh century BCE she is invoked as "Matar"—"Mother."[4] She is frequently identified as "Matar Kubileya," the latter word usually being interpreted as a Phrygian adjective meaning "of the mountain." Thus "mother of the mountain" became the mother goddess of the Phrygians.

The Phrygians, who entered Anatolia from the Balkans, appear as a distinct political group after 750 BCE. During the reign of King Midas (725–675 BCE), they became a powerful kingdom that controlled all of central and southwestern Anatolia. In the process of absorbing the cultures of their Anatolian predecessors, the Phrygians developed a cult centered on Kybele that very likely was an amalgam of the religious iconography of the region. Although this cult is recognized as being originally Phrygian, it clearly incorporates elements of older Anatolian cults. During the reign of Midas, the Phrygian city Pessinus became an important cult center.[5] Its places of worship in most cases consisted of a few steps that were either carved into a rock face or were freestanding amid the greenery of a forest. These temples have but a single facade, a triangular roof above a stone wall in which there is usually a niche.[6]

Figures of the goddess in a standing position have been found in some of these niches. In the majority of cases, the figure is accompanied by a pair of lions whose forepaws are braced against the goddess. This association with predatory animals was likely intended to symbolize the goddess's power to control nature. Of the outdoor temples that were created for Kybele cult worship, probably the most famous is Yazılıkaya (seventh century BCE) located between Eskişehir and Afyon. A relief of the Phrygian mother goddess at Gordion (seventh–sixth centuries BCE), a

Phrygian mother goddess at Bahçelievler (seventh century BCE), and a goddess at Büyükkale near Boğazköy (mid-sixth century BCE) are believed to be among the earliest examples of Anatolian Kybele figures. In the later examples, Kybele is depicted holding apples or pomegranates in her hands over her breasts and is accompanied by a pair of musicians, one playing an aulos (a double pipe) and the other a timbalos (tambourine). It is believed that music played an important role in her rituals.

Mythology of Kybele

Although sources differ in the exact details of their accounts of the mythology of Kybele, in their essence they are all the story of the mother goddess Kybele's passion for a youth named Attis (in some accounts "Attes"), who dwelt in the forests of Phrygia. Although many legends concerning Kybele and Attis are known to exist, all of them are essentially expressions of a belief dominated by the motifs of earth/abundance and death/resurrection. One of these is the legend of Agdistis. As related by Pausanias, a second-century CE traveler and geographer, Zeus "let fall in his sleep seed upon the ground, which in course of time sent up a demon, with two sexual organs, male and female." The demon, which they named Agdistis, was feared by the gods, who had its male organ cut off. From the amputated organ sprouted an almond-tree with its fruit already ripe. A daughter of the river Sangarios took one of the fruits and laid it in her bosom. The fruit immediately disappeared and she became pregnant. The baby born of this union was exposed, but he was discovered, named Attis, and reared by a he-goat. The boy's beauty was more than human, and Agdistis fell in love with him. As a young man, Attis was sent by his relatives to Pessinus to wed the king's daughter. As the marriage-song was being sung, Agdistis appeared. Attis went mad and cut off his genitals, "as also did he who was giving him his daughter in marriage." Repenting what he had done to Attis, Agdistis persuaded Zeus to grant that the body of Attis should neither rot nor decay.

According to another version, there was a sacred rock called "Agdos" in a wild place in Phrygia.[7] This rock was worshiped as a symbol of Kybele. Zeus fell in love with the goddess but she refused him. Unable to penetrate her, he impregnated the rock instead. From this union was born Agdistis, a hermaphrodite. Dionysus drugged Agdistis and by means of a ruse the latter was deprived of his male organs. An almond tree grew from the severed genitals of Agdistis. Nana, daughter of the river-god Sangarios, concealed some of the fruit of this tree in her bosom, thereby becoming pregnant with Attis, to whom she gave birth. Sangarios ordered daughter Nana to abandon the baby in the wilderness. The infant was found and tended by a he-goat. For this reason, the child is associated with the word "attagus," which means "he-goat" in Phrygia; from this, the name "Attis" may be derived. "Attagus" also means "beautiful," however, and the name "Attis" may also have been given for that reason as well.

Agdistis was now a woman, having been castrated by Dionysos. Kybele and Attis both fell in love with this handsome creature. Attis however went to Pessinus to marry the daughter of its king, Midas. Enraged with jealousy, Agdistis drove Attis and everyone in the wedding party insane. Attis took refuge beneath a pine tree and in his madness castrated himself and perished. Distraught, Kybele buried him. Violets sprang up in the soil nourished by his blood and covered the ground beneath the same tree.

Deprived of her betrothed, Midas's daughter fell into despondency and committed suicide. Kybele buried her, too. Violets grew over her grave, and an almond tree sprouted from it. Feeling remorse, Agdistis begged Zeus that the body of Attis would never decay. Zeus consented, saying that Attis's hair would continue to grow and his little finger would continue to move. Thereupon Agdistis took the body of her beloved to Pessinus, where it was buried. In Attis's memory a feast was held and a priesthood formed.

A feature of all the accounts is a considerable amount of syncretism involving Agdistis and the mother goddess Kybele. Symbolic of earth's abundance and of the rebirth of plant life, these legends are allegorical in their meaning. The tales related by Pausanias and others are an attempt to explain the reasons and origins of the practice of ceremonial self-castration by the priests of the Kybele cult in Pessinus.

The Kybele Myth According to Ovid

The Roman poet Ovid's account of the Kybele/Attis myth starts with Attis as a beautiful youth dwelling in the Phrygian forest, where Kybele becomes infatuated with him. Wishing to bind him to her forever, she decides to make Attis the guardian of her temple, but she makes this conditional upon his remaining chaste. Attis however falls in love with the nymph Sagaritis. Enraged by the betrayal, Kybele cuts down the tree in which the nymph's soul resides and drives Attis insane. In his madness, Attis castrates himself.

Concerning the death of this handsome youth beloved by Kybele, two different stories are related. According to one, he was killed by a wild boar in a manner resembling the death of Adonis. The myth of Adonis, beloved of the Greek goddess Aphrodite, can be traced back to the Mesopotamia Mediterranean and bears many similarities to the story of Attis and Kybele. A vindictive divinity set a wild boar on Adonis. The handsome youth was wounded in the groin by the animal's tusks and bled to death.

According to the other story, Attis bled to death beneath the pine tree after castrating himself. Both versions are said to have been local tales related by the people of Pessinus, a city that contained a great temple that served as a center of the Kybele cult. This legend of ritual self-destruction is infused with a degree of violence and savagery suggesting that it may have been handed down from very early times. Indeed it was criticized on those grounds among the Romans, who banned the cult for that reason. According to Frazer, the validity of the version in which Attis is killed by a wild boar is confirmed by the people of Pessinus's refusal to eat pork.[8]

According to legend, Attis was transformed into a pine tree after his death. While the ceremonies associated with Attis festivals are not fully known, the general tenor of accounts is that Attis was a vegetation deity and that the ceremonies, which were held every spring, were a time for mourning his death and celebrating his rebirth. In that respect, Attis's roots are similar to those of Adonis. Although the stories are different, in every legend about Kybele there is also a figure that resembles Attis. The origins of the self-castration practiced by priests of the mother goddess Kybele cult are linked to the Kybele-Attis cult.

Kybele in Greece

Although the Phrygian kingdom was overthrown by the Cimmerians (686–676 BCE), belief in the mother goddess survived the invaders. Pessinus remained a cult center, and the Kybele cult continued to spread throughout Anatolia. Eventually the belief transcended the boundaries of the peninsula, first into Greece and then into Rome.

The Kybele cult reached Greece from Anatolia by way of Athens in the fifth century BCE. This was a time when Athens was embroiled in the Peloponnesian Wars, the second of which ended in 404 BCE with the complete victory of Sparta. In response to their crushing defeat, the Athenians may have embraced the alien Anatolian cult and incorporated its elements into their own beliefs in the hope of gaining the aid and support of Kybele. In the event, they welcomed Phrygia's Kybele into their own city and built a great temple for her there. In this endeavor they also had the support of the sibyls or prophetesses of the Pythian Apollo at Delphi.

In Sophocles' *Philoctetes*, the Chorus addresses her as "All-nourishing mountain mother Earth"; in Euripides' *The Bacchae*, she is "the great mother."[9] As her reputation grew, her name, appearance, and myth all became Hellenized, but while she was syncretized with goddesses such as Demeter and Rhea, she always retained an element of foreignness. Thus although the Ionians revered her, they also criticized her as well. In Greece, the mother goddess was often known as Meter Oreie ("Mountain-Mother"), and there she continued to symbolize abundance and the power that invigorated seed. In one Homeric Hymn, Kybele is celebrated thus:

> Chant your hymn for me
> this time,
> Muse,
> clearly,
> daughter of great Zeus,
> to the mother of all the gods
> the mother of all men
> She loves the sound
> of castanets
> the sound of kettle-drums
> and on top of this noise
> she loves the shouts
> of flutes
> and the clamor of wolves
> and the cries of bright-eyed lions
> and hill echoes
> and wood hollows
> she loves them
> And that's
> how I greet you, goddess,
> and all the other goddess
> with this song[10]

Kybele in Rome

With the spread of Roman power beyond Italy, Kybele (now spelled Cybele) reached Rome in late third century BCE as Magna Mater, the "Great Mother." The Roman historian Livy gives an interesting account of how this arrival took place. As he relates it, at the time that the Romans were engaged in the Second Punic War with Hannibal (204 BCE), the prophetic Sibylline Books were consulted and it was discovered that "if a foreign foe should carry war into Italy, that foe could be driven out and conquered if the Mater Magna were brought from Pessinus to Rome."[11] This prophecy was confirmed by other oracles. Acting upon this advice, the Romans sent an embassy to the king of Pergamon with a request for permission to take a black stone in one of the goddess's temples back to Rome. This was not actually a statue of the goddess but rather a venerated object deemed to be a physical manifestation of her.

It is not known for certain which of the goddess's temples this sacred stone was taken from. The two possibilities that were identified in antiquity are the temple in Pessinus and a temple on Mount Ida, which at the time was part of the Pergamon kingdom. It is most probable that the object brought to Rome was a meteorite that had fallen near the site of the Pessinus temple, which had become increasingly identified with Kybele among the Romans. The image of the goddess was received with a splendid ceremony upon its arrival and Kybele's reputation was further enhanced by the subsequent defeat of Hannibal a year later.

Nevertheless the Romans were not very comfortable with the cult and its outlandish costumes, alien-sounding flutes and tambourines, and ecstatically dancing effeminate priests, and they became increasingly more leery of it. Although the cult continued to enjoy imperial approval, Roman citizens were forbidden to serve as Kybele cult priests. The temple built to the goddess and housing the sacred black stone remained standing although it suffered from destructive fires on several occasions. The ultimate fate of the sacred stone is unknown.

Kybele Today

Traces of the Kybele myth persist even today in symbolic form at the popular level in Anatolia. For example in Çorum, a city quite near an ancient Kybele cult center, there is a large, cube-shaped, marble plinth. According to a local belief, a woman suffering from infertility will be able to conceive if she leaps over it. Other such superstitions remain active in Anatolia.

Modern and contemporary Turkish artists have taken an interest in Kybele as a symbol of procreation and the power of nature, and they make this ancient goddess a central theme of their work. These artists interpret the goddess and her legends in line with their own worldviews and styles. One of them is the contemporary artist Canan Şenol, who identified herself with Kybele during the late stages of her pregnancy and expressed the sanctity embodied in the concepts of the goddess's procreativity and fertility in terms of her own body. Thus the mysterious power of Kybele continues to persist today both in natural symbols at the popular level in Anatolia as well as in contemporary Turkish art.

Notes

1. Fatma Oz, "Ana Tanrıça'nın Değişen Bedeni," *Varlık* 1074 (1997): 28.

2. Lynn E. Roller, *In Search of God the Mother: The Cult of Anatolian Cybele* (Berkeley: University of California Press, 1999), 27; Anne Baring and Jules Cashford, *The Myth of the Goddess: Evolution of an Image* (London: Penguin Books, 1991), and Marija Gimbutas, *The Language of the Goddess* (London: Thames and Hudson, 2001).

3. E. Akurgal, *Anadolu Kültür Tarihi* (Ankara: Tübitak Publications, 1998), 121.

4. For ancient Phrygian inscriptions in which the word "matar" / "mater" compilation: M-01c, M-01d I, M-01d II, M-01e, W-01a, W-01b, W-03, W-04, W-06, B-01.

For "Kubileya" / "Kubeleya": W-04, B-01, in C. Brixhe and M. Lejeune, *Corpus des Inscriptions Paleo-Phrygiennes* (Paris: Institut Français d'Etudes Anatoliennes, 1984).

5. Walter Burkert, *Structure and History in Greek Mythology and Ritual* (Berkeley: University of California Press, 1979), 103.

6. For the temples, see Naumann Friedrike, *Die İkonographie der Kybele in der Phrygischen und der Griechischen Kunst* (Wasmut: Tubingen Press, 1983), and Oktay Belli, *Anadolu Tanrıçaları* (Istanbul: Promete Publications, 2001).

7. According to the story the Mother of the gods is a stone from the same rock from which Deucalion and Pyrrha took the stones that gave birth to postdiluvian humanity. The original rock named Agdos is located in Phrygia. In Philippe Borgeaud, *Mother of the Gods from Cybele to the Virgin Mary*, trans. Lysa Hochroth (Baltimore: Johns Hopkins University Press, 2004), 44–45.

8. G. James Frazer, *The Golden Bough: A Study in Magic and Religion: A New Abridgement from the Second and Third Editions* (New York: Oxford University Press, 1998), 348.

9. *Philoctetes by Sophocles*, trans. Ian Johnston (Arlington: Richer Resources Publication, 2008), 22; *Bacchae by Euripides*, trans. Ian Johnston (Arlington: Richer Resources Publication, 2008), 10.

10. *The Homeric Hymns*, trans. Charles Boer (Woodstock, CT: Spring Publications, 1996), 8. Reprinted with permission.

11. J. Maarten Vermaseren, *Cybele and Attis*, trans. A. M. H. Lemmers (London: Thames and Hudson Press, 1997), 39.

Bibliography

Akurgal, Ekrem. *Anadolu Kültür Tarihi*. Ankara: Tübitak Publications, 1998.

Akurgal, Ekrem. *Anadolu Uygarlıkları*. Istanbul: Net Turistik Publications, 1989.

Akurgal, Ekrem. *Hatti ve Hitit Uygarlıkları*. İzmir: Yaşar Eğitim ve Kültür Vakfı Publications, 1995.

Akurgal, Ekrem. *Die Kunst Anatoliens.* Berlin: Walter de Gruyter, 1961.

Alban, Gillian M. E. "Melusine the Serpent Goddess." In A. S. Byatt, *Possession and in Mythology.* Lanham, MD: Lexington Books, 2003.

Bachofen, Johann Jacob. *Myth, Religion, and Mother Right.* Princeton, NJ: Princeton University Press, 1992.

Baring, Anne, and Jules Cashford. *The Myth of the Goddess: Evolution of an Image.* London: Penguin Books, 1991.

Belli, Oktay. *Anadolu Tanrıçaları.* Istanbul: Promete Publications, 2001.

Berger, Pamela. *The Goddess Obscured: Transformation of the Grain Protectress from Goddess to Saint.* Boston: Beacon Press, 1985.

Bøgh, Birgitte. "The Phrygian Background of Kybele." *Numen* 54 (2007): 304–339.

Borgeaud, Philippe. *Mother of the Gods from Cybele to the Virgin Mary,* trans. Lysa Hochroth. Baltimore: Johns Hopkins University Press, 2004.

Brixhe, C., and M. Lejeune. *Corpus des Inscriptions Paleo-Phrygiennes.* Paris: Institut Français d'Etudes Anatoliennes, 1984.

Burkert, Walter. *Ancient Mystery Cults.* Cambridge, MA: Harvard University Press, 2001.

Burkert, Walter. *Structure and History in Greek Mythology and Ritual.* Berkeley: University of California Press, 1979.

Campbell, Joseph. *Creative Mythology.* New York: Penguin Books, 1991.

Cemal, Ahmet. "Kybele'den Günümüze Uygarlık Arayışı." *Cumhuriyet,* May 28, 1998, 28.

Dürüşken, Çiğdem. *Roma'nın Gizem Dinleri; Antik Çağda Yaşamın ve Ölümün Bilinmesine Yolculuk.* Istanbul: Arkeoloji ve Sanat Publications, 2000.

Ergener, Reşit. *Anatanrıçalar Diyarı Anadolu.* Istanbul: Yalçın Publications, 1988.

Erhat, Azra. *Mitoloji Sözlüğü.* Istanbul: Remzi Publications, 1989.

Euripides. *Bacchae,* trans. Ian Johnston. Arlington: Richer Resources Publication, 2008.

Frazer, James G. *The Golden Bough: A Study in Magic and Religion: A New Abridgement from the Second and Third Editions.* New York: Oxford University Press, 1998.

Friedrike, Naumann. *Die İkonographie der Kybele in der Phrygischen und der Griechischen Kunst.* Wasmut: Tubingen Press, 1983.

Gimbutas, Marija. *The Living Goddesses.* Berkeley: University of California Press, 2001.

Gimbutas, Marija. *The Language of the Goddess.* London: Thames and Hudson, 2001.

Halikarnas Balıkçısı. *Merhaba Anadolu.* Ankara: Bilgi Publications, 1997.

The Homeric Hymns, trans. Charles Boer. Woodstock, CT: Spring Publications, 1996.

İndirkaş, Zühre. *Ana Tanrıçalar, Kybele ve Çağdaş Türk Resmindeki İzdüşümleri.* Ankara: Ministry of Culture Publications, 2001.

THE ANATOLIAN MOTHER   125

İndirkaş, Zühre. *Die Alttürkischen Mythen in Mittelasien Und Ihr Weiterbeben in Anatolien* [Ancient Turkish Myths in Central Asia and their Impact in Anatolia]. Zürich: Spur Verlag, 2003.

Işık, Fahri. *Doğa Ana Kubaba*. Istanbul: Suna-İnan Kıraç Akdeniz Medeniyetleri Araştırma Enstitüsü Publications, 1999.

James, Edwin Oliver. *The Cult of Mother Goddess*. London: Thames and Hudson, 1959.

Marler, Joan. "The Body of Woman as Sacred Metaphor." In *Il Mito e il Culto della Grande Dea: Transiti, Metamorfosi, Permanenze*, 9–24. Bolgona: Associazione Armonie, 2003.

Mellaart, J. *Çatalhöyük: A Neolithic Town in Anatolia*. London: Thames and Hudson, 1967.

Mellaart, J. *Earliest Civilizations of the Near East*. London: Thames and Hudson, 1965.

Neumann, Erich. *The Great Mother*. Princeton, NJ: Princeton University Press, 1955.

Oz, Fatma. "Ana Tanrıça'nın Değişen Bedeni," *Varlık* 1074 (1997): 28.

Pausanias. *Guide to Greece*, trans. Peter Levi. Middlesex: Penguin Books, 19857.17.8.

Roller, Lynn E. *In Search of God the Mother: The Cult of Anatolian Cybele*. Berkeley: University of California Press, 1999.

Sophocles. *Philoctetes*, trans. Ian Johnston. Arlington: Richer Resources Publication, 2008.

Uzunoğlu, Edibe. "Tarih Öncesinden Demir Çağ'a Anadolu'da Kadın." In *Çağlarboyu Anadolu'da Kadın. Anadolu Kadınının 9000 yılı*, 16–25. Istanbul: T. C. Kültür Bakanlığı, Anıtlar ve Müzeler Genel Müdürlüğü Publications, 1993.

Vermaseren, J. Maarten. *Cybele and Attis*, trans. A. M. H. Lemmers. London: Thames and Hudson, 1997.

Yaman, Zeynep Y. "Anadolu Uygarlıklarının Görsel Tarihi." In *Anadolu'nun Görsel Tarihi Fasiküller* (I-II-III), 43–51. Istanbul: Örsa Holding Publications, 1995.

Zeytinoğlu, Emre. "Anadolu'nun Görsel Tarihi Üzerine." In *Anadolu'nun Görsel Tarihi Fasiküller* (I-II-III), 7–42. Istanbul: Örsa Holding Publications, 1995.

9

Heroine of Troy: The Many Faces of Helen

Judith Roche

Many stories are told about Helen of Sparta and her several fates. In the most famous of these, she is the most beautiful woman the world has ever seen and the cause of the Trojan War, which has become an archetype for all wars in European cultural imagination. But there are variations on that theme. Helen is a goddess, a bitch, a witch, a faithful though much-maligned wife, or the thoughtless cause of much suffering. She is a mortal stand-in for the goddess Aphrodite, a divine variant of Ariadne or Pandora, a sun goddess, a moon goddess, the spiritual leader of the dance for young women.

In the beginning, if one reads history through art, humanity honored a primary goddess. The beginning, in this case, was the revolutionary period of the Upper Paleolithic (ca. 35,000 BCE) in the Mediterranean and Near East, which saw the beginning of symbolic behavior, and of art, which produced the first symbolic relationships with the divine. The great goddess was the source of life on earth, and her images from this era in bone, stone, ivory, and clay have been found throughout the ancient world. There are, by contrast, no representations of father gods. Deity appears to have been female, perhaps an idealized representation of women as creative force. As time went on, this great goddess's multiple aspects became differentiated into many goddesses.

Early 20th-century poet Ezra Pound was fond of saying, "The gods are real . . . they are states of mind."[1] A young woman in the height of her sexual power is a different state of mind from a mother watching her children grow and suffering their painful maturation. Each would be described as embodying a different goddess. Helen may be a state of mind as well as a goddess, but Helen is also a pivotal character in one of the fundamental stories of classical literature, the cause of what became the very paradigm of war. However, both during the Bronze Age, the time of the Trojan War (ca. 1500 BCE), and later, eighth century BCE, the time of Homer and Hesiod, the gods were very real to people, not just states of mind, as the modern point of view would have it.

Helen of Troy: Her Story

Helen, half-mortal and half-immortal, was born to Leda. Her father was, in many stories, the high god Zeus, who took the form of a swan in order to rape the beautiful Leda, who conceived as a result. In other stories her father was Tyndareus, mortal husband of the mortal Leda. Alternatively, her mother was Nemesis, an older goddess, and her birth came as the result of a rape by Zeus, again in the form of a swan, which would make Helen fully divine. Most accounts of her beginnings claim that Helen hatched from an egg. In the first and most common story, Leda, the mortal queen of Sparta, births twin eggs. In one are Helen and Clytemnestra, her twin. The other egg produces the Dioscouri, twin brothers Castor and Polydeuces. Of the two sets of twins, Helen and Polydeuces are the progeny of Zeus, Clytemnestra and Castor are the children of Tyndareus, who lay with Leda on the same night as swan-formed Zeus. In an alternative story, Nemesis laid the egg, which had been fathered by Zeus in the form of a swan, and gave it to Leda to hatch and rise.

Euripides has Helen speak of her own birth. "As for me, glorious Sparta is my homeland. Tyndareus is my father (though there is a story that Zeus flew to my mother Leda in the shape of a swan who was fleeing from an eagle and had his way with her by treachery, if that story is reliable), and Helen is my name."[2]

Helen herself has a dual nature, a "twinning," throughout classical literature: either she is a shallow, self-centered *femme fatale*, and the cause of many deaths and much suffering, or she is a much-maligned and faithful wife to Menelaus, her husband and the king of Sparta. Another interpretation holds that Helen contains both a "good twin" and an "evil twin." Classical writers, including Stesichorus, Hesiod, Euripides, and Herodotus, tell of Helen, the woman of epic poetry, and a phantom Helen. The first waited out the war in Egypt while the phantom, indistinguishable from the real, went to Troy—meaning the war was fought for an illusion. Moreover, the twin sisters, Helen and Clytemnestra, marry the brothers Menelaus and Agamemnon, respectively. And Helen's twin brothers, the Dioscouri, play an important role in the stories of Helen.

The beginnings of the Trojan War are traced to a contest over the golden apple tossed at the wedding of the mortal Peleus and the goddess Thetis. Only one goddess was not invited to the party: Ate (strife). She revenged this slight by throwing a golden apple inscribed with the words *For the Fairest* into the celebratory crowd. Three goddesses—Aphrodite, Athena, and Hera—claimed the apple, each believing she was the fairest. Wishing to avoid trouble, Zeus gave the task of deciding who should claim it to Paris, the world's handsomest man. Paris was tending sheep on Mount Ida near Troy when Hermes, messenger for the gods, led the three goddesses to him. Hera promised to make Paris ruler of the world if he choose her, Athena offered victory in battle, and Aphrodite offered the love of the most beautiful woman in the world. Paris chose the last prize and gave the apple to Aphrodite. But when Paris came to claim his prize, the beautiful Helen was already married to Menelaus, the king of Sparta.

When the time had come for Helen to marry, all of the eligible and powerful princes of Greece came to court her, for her beauty was already legendary. Odysseus, ever clever, came up with a plan to forestall battles among them: they would all swear a solemn oath to defend Helen and her chosen husband from harm. Helen's father, King Tyndareus, let Helen make the choice, and she chose Menelaus, brother of mighty Agamemnon, who was already married to her twin sister Clytemnestra. Helen and Menelaus married, and he became king of Sparta through Helen's inheritance—which suggests an ancient matrilineal succession. This meant that Helen and her twin sister were now married to the two most powerful kings in Greece, though as king of Mycenae Agamemnon was the most powerful. But that solemn oath sworn by the suitors would come back later to haunt them.

After settling the beauty contest, Paris (also called Alexandros throughout Homer's *Iliad,* eighth century BCE), made plans to sail to Sparta to pick up his prize, although Cassandra, his prophetic sister in Troy, gave dire warnings against it, as did Oenone, the wife Paris already had. King Menelaus welcomed Paris to the Spartan court with characteristic Greek hospitality, but soon after his arrival Menelaus's grandfather died in Crete and Menelaus sailed away to the funeral. Helen promptly fell in love with Paris, for no one in the ancient world (or possibly this) could resist the will of Aphrodite. The pair escaped in Paris's ship, along with substantial

Spartan treasure, also presumably Helen's birthright, heading to Troy. Helen left behind a daughter, Hermione, and perhaps a son, Nicostratus. Again, the stories conflict—perhaps Nicostratus was born to Helen and Menelaus after they returned from the war, or perhaps to Menelaus and a slave woman.

Paris had committed a great sin for the ancient Greek world, grievously abusing the hospitality of a host. When Menelaus returned from Crete to find Helen and the treasures gone, he gathered Greek royalty, which included Helen's former suitors who were bound by oath to assist him. The leader of the force was Menelaus's brother Agamemnon. As the warriors prepared their ships for the trip, however, the winds died away. Thousands of men at the shoreline, fretting to be under way, grumbled and threatened to go back home until a prophecy announced that Agamemnon had offended the goddess Artemis by a careless boast.

There was nothing to be done but to sacrifice his and Clytemnestra's eldest daughter, Iphigenia, to Artemis for favorable winds. The girl was told that she was to be married to Achilles. She was taken to Aulis, expecting to be the bride of the most celebrated hero of the time, but her throat was slit on the spot. Some say Artemis substituted a deer at the last moment, spiriting away Iphigenia to Taurus to become a priestess. Favorable winds arose, and the fleet set sail for Troy. The famous face of Helen had launched a thousand ships and already claimed a life.

In the *Iliad,* the story of the ten-year Trojan War is long and torturous, fraught with political maneuvering, treachery, bravery, and sacrifice. Homer's account is a warrior's tale, but in it Helen walks the walls of the city at dusk, picking out the men she knows from her home in Sparta, possibly looking for her erstwhile husband Menelaus on the battlefield below her. She is largely resented in Troy, as the cause of the long, cruel war. Women hate her and so do men, except when they get a glimpse of her famous beauty behind a veiled scarf, and they sigh in manly understanding of how this could happen. "No wonder Achaeans and Trojan have been fighting all these years for such a woman! I do declare she is like some divine creature come down from heaven. Well, all the same, I wish she would sail away, and not stay here to be the ruin of us and our children."[3]

Helen's Divided Loyalties

Helen almost comes to hate herself and what she has wrought. Homer tells of an exchange between Helen and Aphrodite late in the war. It is right as Menelaus and Paris fight hand-to-hand as a strategy to end the war: The winner would take Helen and the killing would be over. From the walls of the city, Helen watches her two husbands fight. Being the better warrior, Menelaus is on the point of winning, pinning Paris down by his head. But Aphrodite, invisible to the warriors, breaks Paris's helmet strap and spirits her favorite away, leaving an astonished Menelaus with an empty helmet in his hands. Aphrodite deposits Paris in the couple's shared bedchamber, Paris being more of a lover than a fighter.

Then Aphrodite, disguised as a trusted old wool-carder, comes to Helen, who is weaving in another part of the palace. The goddess of love tells Helen that her man is waiting for her and that she must go to him, telling her that Paris is flushed with beauty and looks like he has just come from a dance. But Helen, recognizing the beautiful breast and throat of the goddess, refuses. She rudely tells Aphrodite to go sleep with him herself if she wants him to have a woman. For a mortal to speak to a goddess with such irreverence is remarkable in the ancient world. Aphrodite rises to her full glory and says, "Don't try me too far, hard-hearted woman! Or I may be angry and leave you and hate you as much as I love you now!"[4]

Helen succumbs to the glory of the goddess and to her fear of losing divine protection in her already precarious position. She wraps her bright cloak around her and follows Aphrodite in silence to the bedchamber where Paris awaits her. She berates Paris and tells him she wishes he had been killed in the battle, but he softens her mood. They make love, while Menelaus is striding around the battlefield like a charging bull, still trying to find Paris.

To this point in Homer, Helen is understood to be the *cause* of the war, but everyone in the Bronze Age world also understands that the power of the gods is not to be questioned. Helen can hardly be *faulted*, though many bitterly resent her in light of the suffering the war begets. The word for "blame" is *nemesis*, specifically, the fault of *hubris* or overweening pride, but nemesis—the name of one of the goddesses described as Helen's mother—is also translated as "indignation." In Homer there is no nemesis or moral offense in Helen's deeds. Once a god has decided a course of human action, the human must play it out. Jack Lindsey notes, "Aphrodite embodies not only Helen's beauty but also its social effects, its total meaning and action. Helen must play out her entangled role to the bitter end; she has no choice, herself as much swayed by her fatal beauty as the men who desire her."[5] Even Priam, the king of Troy, watching his men and even his sons fall around him, comforts Helen by telling her it is not her fault. Later, at the fall of Troy, they will blame Helen, but for now, she must embody the will of golden Aphrodite on earth.

Menelaus finally kills Paris. The city falls to the Greeks, with the resulting murder and mayhem and rape everywhere. Helen is left with the wrath of the Trojan women, who have lost their husbands and their sons and are about to be raped and taken in slavery. Euripides' *The Trojan Women* picks up the story just after the fall of the city. Hecuba, queen of Troy and wife of Priam, berates Helen: "What sufferings have I met with, what sufferings lie in store for me—and all because of one marriage and one woman!" Later Andromache, wife of the slain Hector, says, "You daughter of Tyndareus, you were never born from Zeus. I say that you are the child of many fathers, first of all the avenging Spirit, then of Envy and Murder and all the evils that the Earth breeds!"[6]

Andromache and Hecuba urge Menelaus to kill Helen on the spot, in the ruins of Troy. He says he will certainly kill her, but later, back in Greece. But sometime on the long sailing trip back to Sparta, Helen's charm and beauty must have worked its magic on Menelaus. The *Odyssey* shows them a comfortably married couple at home again long after the end of the war.

In Homer's accounts, Helen had pangs of loyalty toward the Greeks. But book 4 of *The Odyssey* shows Helen and Menelaus at home in Sparta, entertaining Telemachus, son of Odysseus. Helen has concocted a potion for Telemachus, who is grieving for his lost father, to ease his heart's suffering and stop him from weeping, furthering her reputation as either a witch or a healer, depending on one's perspective. "Whoever drank this mixture in the wine bowl would be incapable of tears that day. . . . It has been supplied her by Polydamma, mistress of Lord Thon in Egypt, where the rich plantations grow herbs of all kinds, maleficent and healthful."[7]

Helen and Menelaus both describe the fall of Troy to Telemachus. She tells how Odysseus disguised himself as a filthy beggar and came into the city. She recognized him but did not betray him to the Trojans. Instead she bathed him, gave him a fresh cloak, and swore not give him away. Menelaus picks up the story. He tells of being inside the Trojan Horse when Helen circled it with Deiphobus, another son of King Priam and thus brother to Paris, who became her husband after the death of Paris. The horse was a novelty in the city and people milled around, curious. Helen seemed to know that secret soldiers were hidden in its belly and called out to the inhabitants in the voice of their wives. The weary men inside, having not heard their wives' voices in the ten years of the war, were powerfully tempted to answer, but Odysseus, also inside the horse, stopped them from doing so. Helen knew the soldiers were inside but did not pass that information on to the Trojans. So which side was she on?

Helen in Egypt

Some sources claim that Helen was never in Troy. Stesichorus, a poet of Sicily from the first half of the sixth century BCE, was the first to claim that Helen never made it there. Apparently, Stesichorus wrote an unflattering poem about Helen, now lost, and was blinded for it, presumably by Helen herself. He then wrote his *Pallinode*, an apology, also lost except for fragments quoted by other writers, and his sight was miraculously restored. In the second poem, Stesichorus describes how Helen was spirited to Egypt while Paris sailed to Troy with a phantom, an illusion indistinguishable from the real woman. The messenger-god Hermes abducted the real Helen while she was picking flowers, which connects her with the death-queen Persephone, also abducted while picking flowers.

This is the story Euripides takes up in his *Helen* play. The phantom is made by the goddess Hera who, as the patron of marriage, acts to keep Helen's marriage safe. Helen waits out the war in Egypt, remaining faithful to Menelaus and under the protection of Proteus, king of Egypt. Euripides, writing in fifth-century BCE Greece, a time of waning belief in the Olympians, is freer to entertain psychological interpretations than earlier writers and, seemingly, has less respect for the older stories. As Meagher notes, "The *Helen* is, surely, Euripides' statement on the politics of erotic fantasy; for Helen—the epitome of woman in the Greek tradition—is indeed the ultimate fantasy." Euripides presents a confusion of myth and reality throughout, showing the conflation of Helen's paternity, the fate of Helen's two brothers, the phantom Helen and the "real" Helen, and the duel nature of Helen as the faithful and the unfaithful wife, which Meagher sees as a "de-mythologization, in this case the myth of empire and of woman."[8]

The play opens after the war's end. Proteus has died, and Helen is at his tomb, claiming the protection of the sanctity of the tomb. Now that honorable Proteus is dead, his son, the less-than-honorable Theoclymenus, is trying to force Helen into marriage. As long as she has a hand on the tomb, she is safe from his demands. Menelaus washes up on the nearby shore with the phantom Helen, after suffering shipwreck on his way home from sacking Troy. Encountering the real Helen, the king does not believe she is his wife, for he has just left the phantom Helen in a cave for safety. Though Helen tries to convince him of her reality, he does not believe her until he gets word that the phantom Helen has vanished, claiming that her work on earth is now finished and she can fly back up to the heavens.

The lovers embrace and plot an elaborate ruse to allow them to escape Theoclymenus. Helen comes up with the details of the trick (in Euripides, the women are often the cleverest characters). The couple escapes with the help of Helen's brothers, the Dioscouri, who descend from the heavens via the *mechane*, a crane of wooden beams and pulleys used in ancient theater to lower gods onto the stage when they needed to appear miraculously. They stop Theoclymenus from pursuing the lovers and from killing their sister. The Dioscouri also predict that when Helen dies she will become a goddess and receive gifts from mortals. Castor, one of the brothers, has the final line, to explain the suffering Helen and all involved have gone through. "The gods do not hate the nobly born. But they endure more hardship than do men of no account."[9]

Herodotus (fifth century BCE) offers a different version of the Egyptian Helen. He says that Paris and Helen were blown off course to Egypt. Proteus, on hearing how they came to be there, is outraged at Paris's violation of the rules of hospitality. He tells Paris, "To be welcomed as a guest, and to repay that kindness by so foul a deed! You are a villain."[10] Proteus takes the treasure to send back to Menelaus, and Helen stays in the Egyptian court before returning to her husband. Paris goes to Troy without Helen. Further, Herodotus, who had traveled to Egypt, says he visited a sacred temple there at Memphis dedicated to the "foreign Aphrodite." Herodotus reasons it must be a temple to Helen because she passed some time there, and Aphrodite is never called a "foreigner" anywhere else.

Helen as Goddess

But long before these stories were told and subsequently written in ink on goatskin, Helen was a fertility and vegetation goddess, with temples and festivals that honored her. Some were in Sparta, where one temple was named the Menelaeion by a 19th-century archeologist who believed it to be a site at which Helen and Menelaus were worshiped jointly; although as the site dates to the eighth or ninth century BCE, it is possible that Helen was the primary deity there. Sites have been found at Therapne, southwest of Sparta, and one not far from Platanistas, where a grove of plane trees was dedicated to Helen Dendrites ("Helen of the Trees"), for Helen was associated with that specific tree.

As goddess, Helen was celebrated in the Helenophoria, a festival centered near Sparta. Isokrates, a Greek rhetoritician (436–338 BCE) says that Spartans sacrificed to her and to Menelaus, and maidens rode in a special chariot to her shrine for the festival. At the Helenophoria baskets called *helenai* were carried in Helen's honor. Ritual objects carried in procession or placed at altars were important in early Greek religious ceremonies, and this one was named for Helen, or she for it. Helen was also the presiding goddess at the Spartan girls' ceremonial dances. In her cult at Sparta, young girls took part in running competitions. The girls dedicated wreaths to her, danced, and made a libation of oil at a plane tree in a plane grove nearby the shrine. Lindsey quotes a fragment of a marriage-song by Theokrites in Helen's honor, "we'll cut letters in the bark [of the plane tree], in Dorian Style, so that the wayfarer may read: Worship me, I'm the Tree of Helen."[11] In Athens girls were married shortly after the onset of puberty, but in Sparta girls enjoyed the games and contests until the age of eighteen before they married.

Helen was especially associated with beauty. Herodotus tells that once a highborn Spartan family had a daughter of surpassing ugliness. Seeing how sad the parents were at the baby's ugliness, the nurse carried her every day to the temple of Helen at Therapne. There she placed the baby before the image and beseeched the goddess to change the baby's looks. One day as nurse and baby were leaving the temple an old woman came up and asked to see the baby. She stroked her head and blessed the child, and the child was thereafter beautiful. It was believed that the old woman was really the goddess Helen, especially since this took place at Helen's temple.

The threads of Helen's goddess connections weave from many spindles. Tradition has it that the first cups were modeled after Helen's breasts, in her role as nourishment-giving "nurse mother." She is connected to several goddesses, most significantly Aphrodite, but also Ariadne, Persephone, Artemis, and Pandora. Some of these connections are revealed in the myth that the abduction by Paris was not Helen's first. When she was but twelve she was abducted by Theseus while performing a ritual dance to Artemis. Theseus and his good friend Peirithous decided they both wanted to marry daughters of Zeus. Theseus abducted Helen, and his friend decided to take Persephone. They left Helen a captive and descended to Hades for Persephone. While they were gone the Dioscouri rescued Helen and brought her back to Sparta. According to some stories, Iphigenia was the result of that rape, but Helen gave the child to her sister Clytemnestra to raise.

Helen is said to have had five husbands: Theseus, Menelaus, Paris, Diophobus, and finally Achilles. Philostratus (first century BCE) asserts that Helen and Achilles were married on the island of Leuke in the Black Sea. Poseidon himself created Leuke ("white island") for the two to live on. Then he attended the wedding along with all of the Nereids and water nymphs.[12] As Helen was the embodiment of Aphrodite and was herself a fertility goddess, it was quite fitting that she have multiple husbands.

The motif of the abducted goddess connects Helen both to Ariadne and to Persephone. Both Helen and Ariadne were abducted by Theseus, but neither stayed with him. Both were associated with birds, and both were hanged from trees. The cult of Ariadne, possibly older than that of Helen, was preserved on Crete well into the Bronze Age, leading to cross-fertilization with the cult of Helen. The cult of the goddesses survived in Crete and the Cycladic islands after that of the Olympians replaced it in mainland Greece. Both Ariadne and Helen cults become subsumed into the Aphrodite cult, Aphrodite being the more prominent goddess. Helen carried on as a "faded goddess" and a mortal woman in the literature. Ariadne carried on in myth, largely as the heroine of the labyrinth story.

According to Pausanias, in Rhodes it was claimed that Helen returned to Sparta after the war and lived peaceably with Menelaus for several years. On the death of Menelaus, his sons by a slave woman drove Helen from Sparta. She took refuge in Rhodes with Polyxo, widow of the king of Rhodes, who had died at Troy. Though Polyxo pretended to welcome Helen, she secretly determined to avenge her husband's death. Polyxo had her maids dress as Erinyes ("furies") and hang Helen from a plane tree. Thereafter, the people built a temple in Helen's honor and worshiped her as Helen Dendrites.

This motif connects Helen to other hanged goddesses, notably Artemis and Ariadne. Pausanias tells a story of children hanging an effigy of Artemis. The children were killed for their sin, but afterward Artemis was worshiped with effigies hung in trees. The strong element of tree and vegetation in Helen's cult brings out her affinity with Artemis. In Arkadia, Artemis was the walnut tree, while at Boitai she was worshiped as a myrtle. At Syracuse, where she was *Phakelites* (from *phakelos*, "bundle" or "faggot"), Artemis's image was wrapped and bound with boughs or withies, branches of flexible willow bound into a rope. A consideration of the hanged goddess points out the strength of tree-cults and the way in which legends arose around tree *daimons,* spirits or supernatural beings that fall between living creatures and deities. As Lindsay says, "The idea of the Hanged Goddess substantially derived from the custom of hanging images or masks in trees, and ritual fillets helped create the idea of the rope—though behind the custom lay the belief in the tree as a form or image of the earth-mother."[13]

There are many black-and red figure vases and jugs from Bronze Age times showing masks and puppets hanging from trees, as a demonstration of the "hanging motif" in ancient Greek religious ritual. Helen is often depicted with ritual fillets, narrow strips of ribbon or similar material, hanging from her wrists, which suggest the fillets could be used to hang her, or figures depicting her, from trees. Lindsey notes, "We see the magical use of fillets far back in the Minoan world. The Greeks had a custom of regularly attaching garlands and fillets to graves to establish contact with the dead. The thread, ribbon, rag, or fillet was a powerful way of communicating with the dead. It is also the path, or way, through the intricacies of one's life."[14]

In the *Iliad* Helen is shown weaving when Iris (the rainbow goddess, Hera's messenger) comes to summon her to watch the duel between Menelaus, her husband, and Paris, her lover. Helen is working a length of doublewide purple material, weaving the battle scenes. The subject of her artistry is both aesthetic and deadly. Weaving is a symbol for poetic composition in the Indo-European tradition (weaving or spinning a tale), while spinning is a symbol for the Moirai ("fates"). These fates—Clotho, Lachesis, and Atropos—spin out a thread for every human life and when the thread is cut, the person dies. In the fourth book of *The Odyssey*, Homer gives precise details about Helen's threadwork. She is shown at home in Sparta with Menelaus, spinning from a silver workbasket that runs on castors and using a golden spindle. Her workbasket is full of fine spun yarn, and she is working from deep-blue dyed wool.

Ariadne, too, is associated with thread, most famously that she gives her lover Theseus to untwist as he moves through the labyrinth in search of the monstrous Minotaur. Ariadne also leads the dance in the moonlight through the labyrinth. Daedalus, the magical master-builder, was said to have constructed the "dancing floor" in the form of the labyrinth for her dance, for which reasons Ariadne was the "Lady of the Labyrinth." To dance in the labyrinth's tangled turns was considered the proper way to approach the sacred. There are numerous examples of labyrinth-patterned maze dances in ancient times. The labyrinth, whether expressed as a laid-out maze pattern or a winding dance, was felt to provide the correct ritual approach to the underworld. Theseus is said to have danced the *gernos*, or crane dance, around a horned altar.[15] And Helen was the goddess of initiation and marriage preparation, presiding over dances performed by the young girls of Sparta. She is depicted with a spiral meander imprinted on her skirt or robe, a pattern that dates from at least the Late

Paleolithic and was connected to the birth-death-rebirth cycle. Sacred dances imitated the movement.

This custom is also followed today in the spiral pattern of folk dances and in labyrinth patterns put on church floors. Many are modeled after the pattern of the 12th-century labyrinth at the Cathedral of Chartres in France. During the Middle Ages pilgrims walked the Chartres labyrinth as part of a spiritual quest. More recently the tradition became revived in Europe and America, and today many walk the labyrinth in churches and public spaces as a meditation.

Helen and Misogyny

Helen's famous fickleness runs as a contrapuntal melody to her famous beauty. She leaves her husband on a caprice and starts the war, she tries to betray the Greeks when she circles the Trojan horse, she recognizes Odysseus in disguise but does not tell the Trojans. Though she calls herself "bitch" in the *Iliad*, she in fact behaves like a goddess.[16] History may play through her but when she does intervene it is as a goddess, not as a mortal with moral constraints.

The literary Helen was much hated as the cause of the archetypal paradigmatic war. This hatred connects her to Pandora, the first woman according to Hesiod's account in the *Theogony* (late seventh or early eighth century BCE). This text, perhaps the earliest Greek literature, shows an increasingly misogynist culture. The first woman made by Zeus is called *kalon kakon*, "beautiful evil." This represents a shift in consciousness from the time of the great goddess, revered and honored, to a new cosmology. In the first Greek writing the shift has already occurred. In this new world order, "Thunderous Zeus made women to be a *kakon* for mortal men."[17] By the time Hesiod wrote his *Works and Days*, the *kalon kakon* had a name: Pandora, who released all evils and suffering to the world of humans. Zeus asks Hephaestus, god of fire and metalworking, to create this creature out of earth and water, Athena to teach her to weave, Aphrodite to give her charm and beauty, and "painful yearning and consuming obsession; to put in a bitch's mind and a knavish nature. . . . The Graces and the lady Temptation put necklaces of gold about her body."[18] Hesiod describes how Zeus laughed at the evil he has unleashed on men with this beguiling creature, Pandora, this "unmanageable trap," baited with beauty and charm meant to snare men.[19] Pandora has a *pithos* or jar (which often has been mistranslated) that, like her, is fashioned from earth and water, is womb-shaped, and contains all the evils of the world, including disease, toil, pain, care, old age. Pandora opens the *pithos* to let all escape, but closes it before hope can escape. This "beautiful evil" designation connects Helen, the beguiling beautiful woman whose love brings war and suffering, to Pandora, whose name means "all gifts," though most of the gifts she brings create grief.

Helen and Aphrodite

The mortal Helen, as the world's most beautiful woman and the inspiration of sexual desire in all men, is a mortal reflection of the divine, golden Aphrodite, the inspiration of sexual desire in all creatures. Both have many lovers. And, famously, Aphrodite, goddess of love, lies down with Ares, god of war, just as Helen is known for both love and war. As representatives of sexual passion and war, both have connections with war-like Sumerian Inanna and the Semitic Ishtar (see Johanna Stuckey's chapter in this volume), historical prototypes of Aphrodite; both goddesses are known for strong appetites for both love and war. Unlike their earlier incarnations, neither Aphrodite nor Helen intends violence, but their actions set it in motion.

Both are associated with birds, sexual love, and fertility. Aphrodite is especially connected with doves, geese, and swans. Helen, born from a swan's egg, can read the future in the flight of birds. Aphrodite is the most beautiful of the goddesses, as Helen is the most beautiful of mortal women, and both ignite passion that cannot be denied.

In the beginning was the great goddess, she who loved, gave life, and claimed it again. As time went on and the great goddess differentiated into various qualities, her character changed from the sacred life force to "the most beautiful woman," a projected male fantasy. So Helen—the bountiful vegetation and fertility goddess, a bird and tree goddess, the path in and out of the life cycle—becomes the most hated woman of all time, the cause of war and great suffering. "My beauty is my Hell," she says in Euripides' *Helen* and "while other women are made happy by their beauty, mine is the very thing that has destroyed me."[20] But here she is speaking with a double-consciousness: she is the unobtainable object of male fantasy, desired then vilified for the passion she evokes. She is aware of this fantasy as a role she has been given to play. Hesiod calls her an inhabitant of his Fourth Age of human life, one of "the godly race of the heroes who are called demigods" and descended from a union of gods and mortals and the heroes of epic myth.[21] The path back to her life as a goddess is a murkier meandering, fragments and snatches obscured by time.

Notes

1. Poet Robert Duncan, lecture, New College of California, 1985.

2. Euripides, *Helen*, trans. David Kovacs (Cambridge, MA: Loeb Classical Library, 2002), 20–25.

3. Homer, *The Iliad*, trans. W. H. D. Rouse (New York: New American Library, 1938); 3:155.

4. Ibid., 410.

5. Jack Lindsay, *Helen of Troy* (Totowa, NJ: Rowman and Littlefield, 1974), 25.

6. Euripides, *The Trojan Woman*, trans. James Morwood (New York: Oxford World Classics, 2000), 499–500, 765–770.

7. Homer, *The Odyssey*, trans. Robert Fitzgerald (New York: Farrar, Straus, and Giroux, 1998), 4:238–250.

8. Robert Emmet Meagher, *Helen: Myth, Legend, and the Culture of Misogyny* (New York: Continuum, 2005), 105.

9. Euripides, *Helen*, 1675.

10. Herodotus, *The Histories*, trans. Aubrey De Selincourt (New York: Penguin Books, 1972), 2:115.

11. Lindsay, *Helen of Troy*, 213.

12. Philostratus, *On Heroes*, trans. Jennifer K. Berenson Maclean, Ellen Bradshaw, and Case Dué (Atlanta: Society of Biblical Literature, 2003), 54.2–55.6.

13. Lindsey, *Helen of Troy*, 225.

14. Ibid

15. Ibid., 276.

16. Friedrich notes Helen is the only classical hero who ever calls herself or himself "bitch," though Hesiod uses that epithet for Pandora's qualities.

17. Hesiod, *Theogony* 585, in Meagher, *Helen*, 50.

18. Hesiod, *Theogony* and *Works and Days*, trans. M. L. West (New York: Oxford University Press, 1988), 66–97.

19. Meagher's *Helen* has a thorough discussion of the role of Pandora in connection with Helen and I am indebted him for some of these points.

20. Euripides, *Helen*, 305.

21. Hesiod, *Works and Days*, 160.

Bibliography

Briffault, Robert. *The Mothers*. Abridged by Gordon Rattray Taylor. New York: Atheneum, 1959.

Dalby, Andrew. *Rediscovering Homer*. New York: W. W. Norton, 2006.

Dillon, Matthew. *Girls and Women in Classical Greek Religion*. New York: Routledge, 2002.

Euripides. *Helen*. Translated by David Kovacs. Cambridge, MA: Loeb Classical Library, 2002.

Euripides. *Orestes.* Translated by David Kovacs. Loeb Classical Library, 2002.

Euripides. *The Trojan Woman.* Translated by James Morwood. New York: Oxford World Classics, 2000.

Friedrich, Paul. *The Meaning of Aphrodite.* Chicago: University of Chicago Press, 1978.

Gimbutas, Marija. *The Goddesses and Gods of Old Europe.* Berkeley: University of California Press, 1982.

Harrison, Jane Ellen. *Prolegomena to the Study of Greek Religion.* New York: Arno Press, 1975.

Herodotus. *The Histories.* Translated by Aubrey De Selincourt. New York: Penguin Books, 1972.

Hesiod. *Theogany* and *Works* and *Days.* Translated by M. L. West. New York: Oxford University Press, 1988.

Homer. *The Iliad.* Translated by A. T. Murray. Cambridge, MA: Loeb Classical Library, 1990.

Homer. *The Iliad.* Translated by W. H. D. Rouse. New York: New American Library 1938.

Homer. *The Odyssey.* Translated by Robert Fitzgerald. New York: Farrar, Straus, and Giroux, 1998

Lindsay, Jack. *Helen of Troy.* Totowa, NJ: Rowman and Littlefield, 1974.

Meagher, Robert Emmet. *Helen: Myth, Legend, and the Culture of Misogyny.* New York: Continuum, 2005.

Monaghan, Patricia. *The Encyclopedia of Goddesses and Heroines.* Santa Barbara, CA: Greenwood, 2009.

Neumann, Eric. *The Great Mother.* Princeton, NJ: Princeton University Press, 1972.

Ovid. *Metamorphoses.* Translated by Rolfe Humphries. Bloomington: Indiana University Press, 1955.

Philostratus. *On Heroes.* Translated by Jennifer K. Berenson Maclean, Ellen Bradshaw, and Case Dué. Atlanta: Society of Biblical Literature, 2003.

Pomeroy, Sarah B. *Goddesses, Whores, Wives, and Slaves.* New York: Schocken Books, 1975.

Virgil. *The Aeneid.* Translated by Robert Fitzgerald. New York: Random House, 1981.

10

Gaia: Dynamic, Diverse, Source and Place of Being

Glenys Livingstone

In Earth's earliest times, before there was any creature to observe the light and the dark, there was only one continent, Pangaea. Over millions of years Pangaea broke up, at first into two supercontinents, Gondwana and Laurasia, and these subdivided until the present configuration of the continents was reached. The earliest humans observed the light and the dark as a measure of time, and sensed their ground and place of being as their mother and caves as her belly/womb. These early humans were drawn to caves where they often found springs of fresh water. They could be sheltered and sustained there, and with their imaginative minds they could converse with their divine mother, frequently leaving art expressing their connection with her.

Gaia (sometimes Gaea or Ge) is an ancient name from the region now known as Greece for the planet now commonly named Earth.[1] Gaia/Ge personified the source of being and embraced both birth and death, a miracle of renewal manifest in life cycles everywhere, in female and male alike, in the wild and the cultivated, in animals and plants. Earth's power for these peoples was identified as moist, fertile, black, and strong, but it was yet not separate from the heavens and the cosmos itself.[2]

Everything issued forth from her. In the earliest stories, Gaia conceived and gave birth to all parthenogenetically, solely from within her own substance and powers. Gaia was not creator in the sense of being a *maker* and thus separate from her creation, but Gaia was creator in the sense of birthing all. Thus she was of the same material as her creations, all of whom remained seamlessly imbued with her life-force. In Gaia *matter* and *mater* were one, and she was eternal: that is, her capacity for renewal felt as never-ending. Marija Gimbutas notes a depiction wherein a younger aspect of Gaia rises up from the ground, which is Gaia herself; the image conveys that Gaia gives birth even to herself.[3]

Jane Ellen Harrison describes Gaia, the whole planet, as not separate from each and every local mother goddess nor from the lesser deities known as nymphs. In the ancient Greek mind, as Harrison describes it, the "many were not so sharply and strenuously divided" as in the later Olympian pantheon of classical deities of Greece. Rather, there was a state of unitary consciousness, a "protoplasmic fullness and forcefulness not yet articulate into the diverse forms of its ultimate birth." Thus some other goddesses of Greece are often strongly associated with Gaia; some are well known, such as Hera, Demeter, and Rhea, while others are lesser known such as Melaina, "black" whose name apparently refers to the black fertile soil. It was understood that the goddesses were all Gaia's daughters, each unique but at once the "All-Mother Ge."[4]

By the time of the earliest writings about her, Gaia was named as only one of four deities who were original or "autogenetic" to the area.[5] Yet Homer, who wrote in approximately 800–700 BCE and who was influenced by the earlier oracular tradition of the priestess-poets of Gaia, speaks of her as "mother of the gods," the foundation of all, the oldest one. His near-contemporary Hesiod speaks of a time "told for generations, as it were, at the mother's knee," when "earth and sky were once one form." Gaia had brought forth the heavens, and as the primary creator she was always remembered, as Homer expresses in his "Hymn to Gaia":

Now
And in my other songs
I shall remember you.[6]

Human and deities alike "had been born of the Great Mother."[7] Gaia and her laws—"Nature, as we might say"—stood beneath all the dramas and "immoral behaviour" of anthropomorphic deities, that prevailed, and her moral order was invoked and oaths sworn to her well into the classical period.[8] This kind of power and law of the land is not unlike that of other earth mothers of other places: as Gimbutas notes in many Old European cultures Earth was called upon as witness to disputes.[9] She was social conscience and could not be deceived.

Gaia's First and Ongoing Creations

Gaia's first creations—heaven (Ouranos), the hills (Urea), and the sea (Pontus)—were conceived by parthenogenetic means. She then went on to create further offspring by mating with her creations, firstly with Ouranos, by whom she gave birth to a race called the Titans. It was against the Titans that the later ruling deity Zeus—himself a child of Gaia's lineage—waged combat to establish his new order. Gaia sometimes helped Zeus in his quest for sovereignty, yet in his final battle against Gaia's dragon-son Typhon, she opposed him.[10] The stories reveal an apparent maternal conflict of interest. There is also an earlier conflict between Gaia and Ouranos, when he attempted to block or claim her creativity, in which Gaia's son Kronos (brother-son to Ouranos) assisted her by castrating his father. From the spilled blood, Gaia proceeded to create more great entities: the Erinyes ("furies"), the giants, and the nymphs named the Meliai; the myth expresses Gaia's rich and sacred fertility that could not be thwarted.

Gaia also mates with Pontus and brings forth many more children, who in turn become parents. One interpretation of Gaia's later method of procreation by sexual means has been that she had a desire for love;[11] yet perhaps the stories of Gaia's mating is a memory of the evolutionary point when meiotic sex unfolded as a favored procreative process over that of mitosis. The advent of meiotic sex, at about one and a half billion years ago, made the web of life more complex by enabling the development of multicellularity:[12] it was a deepening of creativity and could be interpreted as a deepening of love or at least a deepening of the potential for communion. Gaia's nature is a multiplicity of forms, and she achieves this with meiotic sex, albeit with the resultant ensuing conflicts between the multiple beings, all agents in their own right.

Another deeper analysis of the conflicts between the deities in Greek mythology by Nanos Valaoritis presents them as a cosmic conflict of female and male, "deciphering a gender-based duality" that permeates other cultures of the world but is "intensively expressed in Greek myths," the pattern being particularly evident in the beginning conflict between Gaia and Ouranos. When this analysis is applied, "the conflict between generations of gods, titans and giants can be viewed within a more general conflict between earth/sky (Ouranos/Gaia), male/female, celestials and chthonians."[13]

This was essentially a conflict of worldviews: an early cultural stratum in which the earth-goddess was central, and another emerging one in which male celestial deities held sway. The analysis postulates that the myths themselves preserve the conflict between what Valaoritis calls "seemingly opposite social structures and ideologies" and the complexities of allegiances that humans experienced within the hybrid societies of the transitional phases.[14]

Sacred Sites for Hearing Gaia's Wisdom

In earliest times, Gaia was understood as alive and sentient. Gaia was thus understood to be the primeval source for guidance. She was the primary oracle. People sought places where she might be heard most clearly, where they might receive Gaia's portents to guide their actions and thoughts. Much evidence suggests that the earliest such popular site was Dodona. The earth mother spoke there in early times, though later Dodona became a sanctuary and oracle of Zeus. Although the earliest name of a goddess associated with that site is Dione, Gaia "may have been the first goddess venerated at the site" as Dione belonged to her lineage, and T. Dempsey also describes Dione as characteristically chthonic. Charlene Spretnak notes that the common means of listening for earth-mother's wisdom at Dodona was for the priestess or consultant to sleep in a holy shrine with an ear upon the ground.[15]

But Delphi, the city of the tribe Delphoi, ultimately prevailed as the site of Gaia's oracle. The name of the place and of the settling tribe is significant. It is a poetically rich Greek term with connections to *womb, dolphin*, and even *brother* (in the sense of "born of the same womb").[16] Delphi, as a womb-temple, was said to be the center of sacred knowledge, and was the navel of the world, the Omphalos. Delphi was inhabited initially sometime between the 14th and 11th centuries BCE by goddess-focused peoples. Gaia's sacred shrine was apparently at first located in the Corycian Cave, high up on the shoulder of Mount Parnassus near Lykoreia. The shrine was later moved to Pytho at the foot of the mountain; perhaps there were shrines in both locations for a period.[17]

At the same time there was a change in the method of receiving Gaia's wisdom, as the Pytho site was above a crevice issuing forth vapors. Her priestesses spoke while in trance, perhaps sitting on a tripod over the crevice. This tripod has been called a mantic tripod; it was a shamanic tool, a three-legged stool imbued with power by the actions of its occupant and imbuing her with power to speak the words of the deity, to prophesy. The priestess was required to sit astride such a chair, with receptive womb open to the energies of Gaia.[18] This physical inclusion and capacity was felt as essential to hearing Gaia and uttering her portents. The vapors may have been the original cause of the trance, and perhaps one reason for the ultimate location of Gaia's oracle at the lower site.

The spring in the Corycian Cave was home to a triad of nymphs or naiads, one of whom was named Corycia. Different sources give various names for her sisters, but often they are called Kleodora and Melaina, sometimes Daphnus and Thiua. Together the three sisters have been known as the Thriae or Thriai, and recognized as the "the triple muse of divination at Delphi."[19] Delphos is also the name of the son of one of the Corycian nymphs; his mother, sometimes named as Thyia or Thuia and sometimes as Melaina, was often identified with Gaia. The Thriae are said to have invented the art of prophecy. Their name has been translated as "little stones," because of the story that tells how they threw stones into an urn of water to observe their movements. At Dodona the priestesses interpreted the rustling of leaves in the sacred tree or drew lots from pitchers. The Thriae are said to have taught the later gods the prophetic arts.

These three of Delphi were also associated with the bee and known as bee-maidens. Thus they can be seen as precursors to the later oracular priestesses at Delphi who were called Delphic bees. The omphalos at Delphi was shaped as a beehive. Such an association of goddess and bee is an ancient one found within many other cultures and generally represents regenerative qualities.[20] Because the bee was a parthenogenetic symbol and Gaia's nymph figures were patterned after her in this capacity, her priestesshoods at Delphi were at some point believed to be parthenogenetic. Rigoglioso proposes that the early priestesshood of Gaia was a college of women "who at the very least *attempted* parthenogenetic birth as a spiritual discipline *and who were believed to have been successful.*"[21]

The Delphic Oracle

The oracular priestess of Delphi was commonly named Pythia ("female serpent"), because the first oracle there was felt to be the snake. Divination was performed by means of interaction with the snakes at Delphi. The primal snake was called the Python, a dragon-snake that guarded the sanctuary. Apollo slew Python to establish his shrine at Delphi, the shrine being rededicated to him sometime between the 11th and ninth centuries BCE.[22] There are at least five versions of the story depending on the time period of its writing, with the serpent sometimes being male.[23] But as Marija Gimbutas's research points out, the snake is more frequently associated with goddesses and earth powers than with male divinities. Early stories and artistic images show the snake as an emanation of earth, born of her. Gimbutas notes that the *omphalos* was understood as "both the Earth Mother in her young aspect and the snake."[24] And like the bee, the python may have represented Gaia's parthenogenetic powers.[25] So Apollo's act may be interpreted as a statement related to the cosmic conflict that continued in Greek literature and art. Jane Ellen Harrison is clear:

> when we remember that the omphalos is the very seat and symbol of the Earth Mother, that hers was the oracle and hers the holy oracular snake that Apollo slew, the intrusion is hard to bear.[26]

and further:

> Apollo may seat himself on the omphalos, but he is still forced to utter his oracles through the mouth of the priestesses of Gaia.[27]

Among Apollo's follow-up actions was the establishing of the Pythian Games, a forerunner to the Olympic Games. Some say it was as a penance for his sacrilege, others that it was in celebration of his victory.

The Pythias at Delphi were evidently women of accomplishment: Phemonoe, first priestess of the Apollo era, invented the poetic meter, the hexameter in which she delivered her prophecies. The famous words "know thyself" at the entrance to the Delphi temple have also been attributed to her. Some of her poetry was later ascribed to Orpheus and others. Another early priestess, Herophile, was a visiting poet at Delphi around the 13th century BCE.[28] Even later, in the classical period, a priestess of Delphi named Themistoclea was the teacher of the mathematician and philosopher Pythagoras. Over time it seems that the priestesshood was compromised; the cultural worldview was shifting to favoring male lineage and authority. Marguerite Rigoglioso describes how over centuries a transition was being made "from a female-exclusive, Ge-serving priestesshood to a male-controlled, Apollo-serving clergy."[29] The earliest priestesses were clearly Gaia's, yet over centuries some willingly became "wives" of Apollo, while others resisted.

Whereas in the beginning one priestess served as the oracle once a year, and only for local people of the region, as Delphi's reputation grew more priestesses were added and the consultations were given more frequently. Huge sums of money came to be involved, and heads of state and dignitaries claimed priority for consultation. The holy shrine succumbed to political and economic considerations. By the first century BCE, Rigoglioso notes that the Pythia was described by a Roman historian, Plutarch, as "inexperienced and uninformed about everything," a peasant who "brings nothing with her as the result of technical skill or of any other expertness or faculty as she goes down in the shrine (to prophesy)."[30]

Whence Gaia Now?

Gaia's Delphic shrine was closed late in the fourth century CE by Roman emperor Theodosius, who imposed Christianity as the official religion throughout the lands he controlled. Whereas even under Apollo's rule, Gaia's body gave forth the sacred teachings attributed to him, Gaia was now denied. Theologian Rosemary Radford Reuther describes how the new god "sacralized domination" of the Earth.[31] The new regime claimed transcendence of matter.

On the surface, for this period the celestial appeared to be winning the cosmic conflict with the chthonic, as the work of many scholars such as Reuther documents. Though the name of the goddess remained threaded into language ("geology," "geometry," "geography"), she was increasingly understood as a passive dead ball of dirt upon which humans travailed and from which they extracted sustenance. She was no longer subjective and sentient, graciously giving forth. Evolutionary biologist Elisabet Sahtouris observes that the "organic" philosophies of Thales, Anaximander, and Heraclitus no longer held sway, but rather the "mechanical" cosmos of Pythagoras, Parmenides, and Plato, which suited the new god.[32]

Over ensuing centuries, as humans increasingly mechanized their relationship with their planet, new instruments were used to confirm a "celestial mechanics" rather than an organic evolution. Sahtouris reflects that humans became objective observers of Gaia, becoming "eye/I," noting that *ego* is the Greek word for *I*.[33] Sahtouris suggests that as a young species, humans were like adolescents leaving home, sometimes rebelliously or ungraciously. Gaia, as ground of being, was no longer held sacred or felt to be alive. Whereas once she may have at least been considered monstrous, she could now be placed as mere backdrop to human activities.

Yet the desire for knowledge of her, for the physical world of which humanity is a part, could not be put to sleep. The scientific stepping away from Gaia became paradoxically a return to her, when it separated itself from religion. Scientists then entered, many unwittingly, into a journey of return to the chthonic, deeper and deeper into the nature of matter, the planet, and the cosmos. At times this was a further desecration of her, expressed openly as an invasion of her, yet for many it was a pathway into her wonders and beauty. By the late 18th century CE, some 1400 years after the closure of Delphi, geologist James Hutton described Earth as a "living organism" and announced that "its proper study should be by physiology." He went on "to compare the cycling of the nutritious elements in the soil and the movement of water from the oceans to the land, with the circulation of blood."[34] The concept of the planet being alive did not die away.

By the late 20th century CE in the context of a convergence of many strands of science that had developed around the globe, Gaia's name was reinvoked with the work of James Lovelock and Lynn Margulis for a hypothesis that became increasingly acceptable as a scientific theory and that was embraced by the larger global community.[35] Many were people who expressed a hunger for mother deity, while others were distressed by the toxification of the earth. The Gaia Hypothesis, which envisions the planet as a connected self-regulating body, put Gaia's name back on the lips of her offspring. Humans also ventured into her heavens, from which perspective all her children could now see her as one whole body. Was this further objectification or was it a coming home?[36]

As Gaia's oceans are now quantified, her atmosphere analyzed, her lithosphere prodded and excavated for earlier stories, her biospheric methods more deeply known, is this a deepening of relationship with her or further interrogation? As Gaia's name is now invoked around the globe, even to promote commodities, is this a further compromise of her, or is it where she wants to go? Is it a diluting of her essence or is it a homeopathic cure? Some hope that the renewed invoking of her in this era will serve to heal this seamlessly connected body-planet.

Gaia's story will only continue to be told in the hearts and minds of her maturing creations, many of whom are naming and redeveloping their religious practices as Gaian or PaGaian[37]—coining new poetry, re-creating sanctuaries as sacred ritual spaces, reinventing womb-temples or new Delphis, for the creative expression of Gaia, and for again listening for her portents, guidance for their thoughts and actions. Might this be a "Ge-ology," a term used by Christine Downing to speak of coming to know Gaia in a complete sense?[38]

Gaia's name is a point of connection across a great diversity of beings, surely more so than most deities. It seems this is her very nature, holding all within her arms, both "uranium and the rose" as poet Claudia L'Amoreaux has described.[39] Earth as goddess is awesome and dynamic, a butterfly not to be pinned, a power not to be owned.

Notes

1. The name "Earth" is derived from a Nordic goddess's name, Erde. Elisabet Sahtouris, *Gaia: The Human Journey from Chaos to Cosmos* (New York: Simon and Schuster, 1989), 5–6.

2. This sense and imagery of "Earth power" is taken from Marija Gimbutas's *The Living Goddesses*, ed. Miriam Robbins Dexter (Berkeley: University of California Press 1999), 208, and *The Language of the Goddess* (San Francisco: HarperCollins, 1991), 159.

3. Gimbutas, *Language of the Goddess*, 159.

4. Jane Ellen Harrison, *Prolegomena to the Study of Greek Religion* (1903; New York: Meridian Books, 1957), 263–264 and 164 as cited by Christine Downing, *The Goddess: Mythological Images of the Feminine* (New York: Crossroad, 1984), 131–136.

5. Marguerite Rigoglioso, "Bearing the Holy Ones: A Study of the Cult of Divine Birth in Ancient Greece," PhD diss., California Institute of Integral Studies, 2007, 127.

6. Anne Baring and Jules Cashford, *The Myth of the Goddess: Evolution of an Image* (Hammondsworth: Arkana, 1991), 303–305.

7. Joseph Campbell, *The Masks of God: Occidental Mythology* (New York: Arkana, 1991), 237.

8. Baring and Cashford, *Myth of the Goddess*, 309; Charlene Spretnak, *Lost Goddesses of Early Greece* (Boston: Beacon Press, 1992), 45.

9. Gimbutas, *The Language of the Goddess* (San Francisco: HarperCollins, 1991), 159.

10. Baring and Cashford, *Myth of the Goddess*, 318.

11. Patricia Monaghan, *The Encyclopedia of Goddesses and Heroines* (Santa Barbara, CA: Greenwood, 2010), 404–405.

12. Elisabet Sahtouris and James Lovelock, *Earthdance* (Lincoln, NE: iUniverse, 2000), 126–131, for this story of the "invention of sex" added to "Gaia's dance"; and Brian Swimme and Thomas Berry, *The Universe Story: From the Primordial Flaring Forth to the Ecozoic Era* (New York: HarperCollins, 1992), 105–109.

13. Nanos Valaoritis, "The Cosmic Conflict of Male and Female in Greek Mythology," in *From the Realm of the Ancestors: An Anthology in Honor of Marija Gimbutas*, ed. Joan Marler (Manchester, CT: Knowledge, Ideas, and Trends, 1997), 247, 251.

14. Ibid., 248.

15. Marguerite Rigoglioso, *The Cult of Divine Birth in Ancient Greece* (New York: Palgrave Macmillan, 2009), 140; T. Dempsey, *Delphic Oracle: Its Early History, Influence, and Fall* (Whitefish, MT: Kessinger Publishing, 2003), 19–20; Spretnak, *Lost Goddesses of Early Greece*, 45.

16. Adrian Poruciuc, "The Romanian Dolf and the Greek Delphis-Delphys-Delphoi Problem," in *From the Realm of the Ancestors*, 132.

17. Joseph Fontenrose, *Python: A Study of Delphic Myth* (New York: Biblo and Tannen, 1974), 406–433, particularly 416.

18. Rigoglioso, *Cult of Divine Birth,* 180–185.

19. Adam McLean, *The Triple Goddess* (Grand Rapids, MI: Phanes Press, 1989), 79.

20. Baring and Cashford, *Myth of the Goddess,* 73 and 118–120.

21. Rigoglioso, *Cult of Divine Birth,* 3 and chap. 7; Rigoglioso, "Bearing the Holy Ones," p. iv. For more description of the bee as a parthenogenetic symbol, see Rigoglioso, *Cult of Divine Birth,* 192–204.

22. Rigoglioso suggests earlier dates; *The Cult of the Divine Birth,* 177–178.

23. See Fontenrose, *Python,* 13–22; and also Merlin Stone's bardic telling of some of the many versions in *Ancient Mirrors of Womanhood: A Treasury of Goddess and Heroine Lore from around the World* (Boston: Beacon Press, 1984), 364–365.

24. Gimbutas, *Language of the Goddess,* 121–133, 149.

25. Rigoglioso, *Cult of Divine Birth,* 188.

26. Jane Ellen Harrison, *Prolegomena to the Study of Greek Religion* (New York: Meridian Books, 1957), 320–321.

27. Ibid., 338–339.

28. Rigoglioso, *Cult of Divine Birth,* 176–180.

29. Ibid., 178.

30. Ibid., citing Plutarch's moralia.

31. Rosemary Radford Reuther, *Gaia and God* (New York: HarperCollins, 1992), 3.

32. Sahtouris and Lovelock, *Earthdance,* 2–3.

33. Ibid., 3, 8.

34. James Lovelock, *The Ages of Gaia: A Biography of Our Living Earth* (Oxford: Oxford University Press, 2000), 9.

35. James Lovelock, *Gaia: A New Look at Life on Earth* (New York: Oxford University Press, 1979). Gaia's name was reinvoked with the work of James Lovelock and Lynn Margulis for a hypothesis that became increasingly acceptable as a scientific theory and that was embraced by the larger global community.

36. See Yaakov Jerome Garb, "Perspective or Escape?" in *Reweaving the World: The Emergence of Ecofeminism,* ed. Irene Diamond and Gloria Feman Orenstein (San Francisco: Sierra Club Books, 1990), 264–278.

37. Glenys Livingstone, *PaGaian Cosmology: Re-inventing Earth-based Goddess Religion* (Lincoln, NE: iUniverse, 2008).

38. Christine Downing, *The Goddess: Mythological Images of the Feminine* (New York: Crossroad, 1984), 139, 155.

39. Claudia L'Amoreaux, "Invocation to the Goddess," in *Celebrating Women's Spirituality 1995* calendar (Freedom, CA: The Crossing Press, 1995).

Bibliography

Baring, Anne, and Jules Cashford. *The Myth of the Goddess: Evolution of an Image.* Hammondsworth: Arkana, 1991.

Campbell, Joseph. *The Masks of God: Occidental Mythology.* New York: Arkana, 1991.

Dempsey, T. *Delphic Oracle: Its Early History, Influence, and Fall.* 1918. Reprint, Whitefish, MT: Kessinger Publishing, 2003.

Downing, Christine. *The Goddess: Mythological Images of the Feminine.* New York: Crossroad, 1984.

Farnell, Lewis R. *The Cults of the Greek States,* Vol. 3. Oxford: Oxford University Press, 1907.

Fontenrose, Joseph. *Python: A Study of Delphic Myth.* New York: Biblo and Tannen, 1974.

Garb, Yaakov Jerome. "Perspective or Escape?" In *Reweaving the World: The Emergence of Ecofeminism,* ed. Irene Diamond and Gloria Feman Orenstein, 264–278. San Francisco: Sierra Club Books, 1990.

Gimbutas, Marija. *The Language of the Goddess.* San Francisco: HarperCollins, 1991.

Gimbutas, Marija. *The Living Goddesses.* Edited by Miriam Robbins Dexter. Berkeley: University of California Press, 1999.

Harrison, Jane Ellen. *Prolegomena to the Study of Greek Religion.* 1903. Reprint, New York: Meridian Books, 1957.

L'Amoreaux, Claudia. "Invocation to the Goddess." In *Celebrating Women's Spirituality 1995* (calendar). Freedom, CA: The Crossing Press, 1995.

Livingstone, Glenys. *PaGaian Cosmology: Re-inventing Earth-based Goddess Religion.* Lincoln, NE: iUniverse, 2008.

Lovelock, James. *The Ages of Gaia: A Biography of Our Living Earth.* Oxford: Oxford University Press, 2000.

Lovelock, James. *Gaia: A New Look at Life on Earth.* New York: Oxford University Press, 1979.

McLean, Adam. *The Triple Goddess.* Grand Rapids, MI: Phanes Press, 1989.

Monaghan, Patricia. *The Encyclopedia of Goddesses and Heroines.* Santa Barbara, CA: Greenwood, 2010.

Plutarch's Moralia. Translated by Frank Cole Babbitt. 14 vols. New York: G. P. Putnam, 1927–6919.

Poruciuc, Adrian. "The Romanian Dolf and the Greek Delphis-Delphys-Delphoi Problem." In *From the Realm of the Ancestors: An Anthology in Honor of Marija Gimbutas,* ed. Joan Marler, 130–134. Manchester, CT: Knowledge, Ideas, and Trends, 1997.

Reuther, Rosemary Radford. *Gaia and God.* New York: HarperCollins, 1992.

Rigoglioso, Marguerite. "Bearing the Holy Ones: A Study of the Cult of Divine Birth in Ancient Greece." PhD diss., California Institute of Integral Studies, 2007.

Rigoglioso, Marguerite. *The Cult of Divine Birth in Ancient Greece.* New York: Palgrave Macmillan, 2009.

Sahtouris, Elisabet. *Gaia: The Human Journey from Chaos to Cosmos* New York: Simon and Schuster, 1989.

Sahtouris, Elisabet, and James Lovelock. *Earthdance.* Lincoln, NE: iUniverse, 2000.

Spretnak, Charlene. *Lost Goddesses of Early Greece.* Boston: Beacon Press, 1992.

Stone, Merlin. *Ancient Mirrors of Womanhood: A Treasury of Goddess and Heroine Lore from around the World.* Boston: Beacon Press, 1984.

Swimme, Brian, and Thomas Berry. *The Universe Story: From the Primordial Flaring Forth to the Ecozoic Era.* New York: HarperCollins, 1992.

Valaoritis, Nanos. "The Cosmic Conflict of Male and Female in Greek Mythology." In *From the Realm of the Ancestors: An Anthology in Honor of Marija Gimbutas,* ed. Joan Marler, 247–261. Manchester, CT: Knowledge, Ideas, and Trends, 1997.

11

The Deer Mother: Earth's Nurturing Epicenter of Life and Death

Kathryn Henderson

The nurturing creator Deer Mother has been—and in certain remote locations across the arctic regions of Siberia, from China to Finland, Lapland, Sweden, Russia, and Norway, continues to be—revered as source of life, death, and rebirth by those who live closely with the reindeer. The nomadic Scythians carried reverence for the regenerative Deer Mother from the east, across the steppes, and into Europe from around the eighth to the fourth millennium BCE. Evidence of the spirituality of Scythian culture is found in awe-inspiring art that bears witness to the sacred centrality of a doe image, first in petroglyphs and later in skilled renderings in gold, bronze, iron, wood, leather, cloth, and tattoo. Over millennia her image shifted from monumental antlerless elk to antlered deer, then to an antlered human image, until her animal aspect was ultimately supplanted by the image of a goddess in human form to whom her people offered libations in recent centuries.

In this artistic lineage from Deer Mother who was the source of life and death rose a female figure, enthroned and honored. While that final image disappeared with the coming of patriarchy, reverence for the Deer Mother, who resides at the base of the cosmic world tree where souls go to be reborn, remains central among certain peoples of the far north who live closely with the reindeer despite efforts to stamp out their

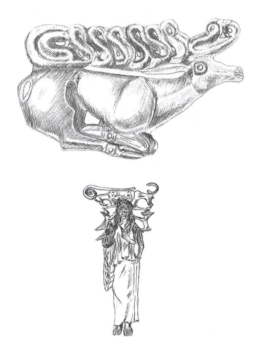

Figure 11.1 Across the northern part of Europe and Asia, a great Deer Mother was worshiped as an ancestor of humanity. The top image shows a seventh–sixth century BCE shield with a recumbent deer; the lower one, a bronze mirror handle depicting the mistress of animals, wearing antlers of Scythian-style animals. (Art by Kathryn Henderson. Reprinted with permission.)

belief by Christian missionaries on the one hand and the communist state on the other.

The animal mother is one of the most ancient images of birth-giving goddess, spanning continents, millennia, and cultures. Marija Gimbutas notes that the image of the goddess as doe is widespread in historical sources and folk memories and that the deer is one of the primary forms of the birth-giving goddess from the Paleolithic. The reindeer goddess as creator of life, guardian of birth-giving, and protector of the herds is so powerful that she sets the sun in motion for the cycle of seasons, melting the ice in the spring so the reindeer can travel to give birth. She is a transforming and protecting deity. Gimbutas's research reveals that the earliest traces of deer cults are found in the Magdalenian level, dating about to 14,000 years ago. Evidence from Cantabrian Spain, east of the well-known Altamira cave-painting site, consists of ritual burial of deer remains in an egg-shaped depression decorated with colored clay and carved deer antlers; another site reveals sandstone plaquettes with engravings of deer, reindeer, and other animals.[1]

Other evidence of ancient deer cults are the beautifully crafted cult vases in the shape of deer from Central Anatolia in the Neolithic and from Muldava, central Bulgaria (ca. 5800 BCE), the latter decorated with spirals, crescents, and triple bands, white on red. Antler cult staffs and figurines or heads of elk-doe carved of antler, bone, and amber have also been found at several sites in Latvia and Lithuania dating from the fourth millennium BCE, as well as similar evidence from the Neolithic as far south as northern Italy. The pictorial representations on late Cucuteni bowls from the Western Ukraine schematically portray the bodies of deer transformed into crescents, suggesting a crescent moon to emphasize cyclical lunar characteristics. These images are associated with snake and egg images, making clear the theme of goddess of regeneration.[2]

Scythian Deer Goddess

The Scythians, also known as the Scytho-Siberians, occupied the Eurasian steppe between the eighth and first centuries BCE. The larger group included semi-nomadic peoples whose territory abutted Greece, Persia, and Zhou China. The western Scythians inhabited the Crimea, the steppes, and forest-steppes north of the Black Sea and the Kuban River basin. Description of the functional art of the Scythians offers a rich source of information for understanding the significance of the deer in a mythic belief system. Art historian Esther Jacobson has traced the deer image forward and backward in time across South Siberia, Central Asia, the southern Ukraine, and Russia, noting that it is part of a symbolic system that "retraced in imagistic form the shifting outlines of a tradition of myth and belief" and within which the image of the deer is key.[3] This symbol set is made up of antlered deer, horned caprids (goats, sheep, antelope, bovines), and horses, panthers and tigers, wolves and bears, birds of prey and waterfowl, all rendered in both fantastic and realistic forms and frequently intertwined as predator and prey.

These images occur again and again in the art of the nomadic Sytho-Siberian culture that held sway across the Eurasian steppe and forests in the first millennium BCE. Such images functioned as a complex system of signs carried on the bodies of humans and their horses. The material items (cloth, leather, fur, wood, and a tattooed mummy) that have survived, preserved in the permafrost from burial sites, are the embellished items of a nomadic people. These burial finds include small metal plates,

often gold, that would have been sewn all over clothing, gold shield plaques, or strips of embellished gold that would have been assembled over
cloth to become a crown, together with gold earrings, bracelets, necklaces,
torques, and mirrors. They also include pole tops, quivers, shields and
sword shafts, urns and amphora, utilitarian household objects and orna-
mentation on horse trappings, and in some cases ceremonial masks for
horses.

Examination of key Scythian artworks allows tracing of the changing
form of the Deer Mother through time. The earliest record are petroglyphs of a giant cow elk and the deer stones, erected at Neolithic burial
sites, inscribed with groups of running deer embellished with elaborately
looped and extended antlers that became a hallmark of later Scythian
style. The monumental recumbent deer shield plaque, incorporating such
undulating antlers, is the most significant representation of the Deer
Mother revered by early Scythians (late seventh or early sixth century
BCE). That such figures are does rather than stags is attested to by a pecto-
ral depicting an elaborately antlered doe, nursing a fawn, clearly an image
of birth and nurturance.[4]

Jacobson maintains that it is unmistakable that Scythian antlered images
are female.[5] Scythian ancestors came out of the north. The reindeer of the
north is one of the few caprids in which the female bears horns most of
the year, while the males shed theirs. Moreover, the mythology, shamanic
traditions, and spiritual practices of reindeer herders who now reside in the
arctic show a similar reverence for the Deer Mother. Jacobson notes that
even though the Scythians may have remained in one general location for
some time, migrating between seasonal locations with their herds, over
longer periods of time the deer image was enclosed in the signs of change
perpetuated by nomadic excursions further afield. So deer images represent
a variety of species, rendered so articulately that one can identify elk or
moose, reindeer, and variation of the Red Deer, Noble Deer, or Maral. As
the early nomads moved out of reindeer habitat and further south and
west, horses and other caprids became more central in their economy,
hence the prevalence of those images in their art and sacrificed horses in
burials that echo the sacrifice of a herder's personal reindeer to serve as
guide to the other world.[6]

The reindeer creator represents the complete cycle of life: birth, death,
and rebirth. That the deer in Scythian art is indeed the birth-giving Deer
Mother is shown first by the prevalence of the image. A second hallmark
in Scythian art is the consistent depiction of predator and prey in mortal
combat. Again the deer images convey the complete cycle. Not only is the

deer the paramount prey depicted in the jaws of death, she is also the vehicle of rebirth, for her antlers transform and blossom into birds at their tips.

One of the best-preserved artifacts representing this cycle is a carved wood and leather horse crest in the shape of a transforming deer's head in the mouth of an eagle-griffin. Another example of such imagery is the incredibly articulated animal tattoos on the body of a male mummy. Both are from the large burials of Pazyryk, northern Altay. The deer-griffin sculpture is finely rendered in articulate three-dimensional detail, capturing the voracious griffin jaws about to engulf the entranced deer as her antlers blossom into delicate bird heads. The two-dimensional tattoo images are equally painstakingly detailed.

The majority of the tattooed body is covered in animal figures in the process of transforming into one another. One of the most striking is a deer figure with a beaked head, its body skewed so the front quarters are erect and appear to be running while its hind quarters, resembling those of a horse, are turned 180 degrees, feet in the air as if in the throes of death. The elaborate antlers, again, blossom into a bouquet of bird heads. A gold beak-headed deer with bird-blossom antlers used as a human head ornament, also from Pazyryk, continues the theme. Clearly these images represent rebirth through death, inscribed onto the body of the deer.

The Deer Mother Assumes Human Form

Subsequently the Deer Mother begins to take female form, at first retaining some of her animal qualities, especially as antlers. A most significant transitional image is found on a felt tapestry depicting a part-human, part-animal figure confronting the griffin nemesis from another Pazyryk burrow. The animated scene shows a figure with female head and torso, adorned with flowering stylized antlers and embodying the legs of a deer or caprid. A more Hellenized image from Kherson is an artfully rendered mirror handle in the shape of a woman in Greek-style attire, adorned with an elaborate headdress that suggests antlers in its curvilinear framing. These antlers simultaneously encompass two felines engaged in consuming an ox, atop two wolves that stand on the figure's shoulders. A raven perches on the right hand of this mistress of animals.

It is interesting to note that some of the animals depicted are those that make up the ecosystem of the reindeer and caribou migrations: the wolves who follow the herd, thinning out the weak, and the birds who feed on the rich droppings.[7] The animal predators/prey connection and the antlered female are typically Scythian motifs while the human figure is rendered in the Greek naturalistic style and wears Greek clothing. Scholars suggest that in renderings of a later date the goddess as well as other figures become increasingly realistic in style.[8] Such influence is seen throughout Scythian art as they engaged in trade with the Greeks and were exposed to Greek art, craft, ideas, and culture. Nevertheless, both of these works document a middle period in which the Deer Mother takes a form that is both human and animal.

Still within the decorative Scythian style, images on the large Pazyryk felt hanging (ca. fourth century BCE) depict a seated woman with a blocky crown, similar in shape to the crown found with the body of the woman buried in the fifth burial chamber at Pazyryk. A gold-worked crown of similar shape, depicting Scythian-garbed Amazons fighting griffins, was found in burial in the Krasnoday Territory. Jacobson notes that Greek historian Herodotus, who first recounted tales of Amazons, though he is known for sensationalism and ethnocentrism, got some things right. Excavations in recent decades have unearthed a large number of burials of women laid out with spears, bows, arrows, quivers, and swords. Though relatively uncommon, such burials have been found in sufficient number to support the conclusion that there was a place in Scythian society for women to take up a warrior role.[9]

Repeated eight times on the wall hanging, the seated woman is greeted by a man on horseback, half her size. The woman is clearly the superior figure who conveys a power and sense of solemn purpose to the composition. Her hand nearest the viewer is raised, as if in a gesture of speech. With the other she grasps a large branch with fanciful foliage, stylistically reminiscent of the antlers in the other Pazyryk felt tapestry with griffin, discussed above. The antlers may represent the cosmic world tree or tree of life.

A similar grouping occurs in a solemn depiction on two identical gold plaques from the Siberian Treasure of Peter the Great, a late Scythian burial. One male figure reclines, his head in the lap of the woman seated under the tree. She is twice his size, her face in profile, her visage bearing a serene smile. Another male, seated at the feet of the deceased, holds the reins of two horses. A Scythian shield or quiver, presumably belonging to the deceased, hangs in the tree. A braid of hair from the base of the neck of the woman coils upward and becomes one with the tree, as does her headdress. Jacobson reads the scene as conveying the "impression that death has called one of the riders and that the moment of death is somehow bound to the figure of the woman under the tree."[10] She notes further that the felt hanging is associated with death by its placement outside the north wall of the burial chamber and its imagery joining the female figure and tree.

Similarly, the gold plaques from Chertomlyk, Merdzhana, and Karago-deuashkh suggest that representations of seated women, addressed by males carrying rhytons or cups in association with altars or branches, were appropriate to the rituals accompanying death, representing honor and libations offered to a female deity. Another set of images conveying this message is embossed on an elongated triangular gold plaque from the Chertomlyk burial, Dnepropetrovsk region, which would have adorned a similarly shaped headdress. The triangle is divided into three sections, one above the other, depicting scenes in which a female deity is honored. In the bottom one, flanked by female attendants, celebrants surround her with libations. She wears a very tall cone-shaped headdress adorned with the self-same triangular plaque on which she is depicted. In the next scene, she stands behind two horses, driving them from a chariot. In the top triangle, she confronts the viewer, standing, frontally at her location at the top of the world, worthy of worship and adoration. Over time, just as they did with the antlered-woman mirror handle, Scythian artists chose to represent their deepest spiritual ideas in a less stylized manner, moving to more realistic depiction. The change in style paralleled their transformation of the image of the Deer Mother from animal form to a goddess in human form, honored with appropriate reverence and libations.

Jacobson observes two important themes in the rendition of the deer image in Scythian representations. One is the ubiquitous depiction of animal predators and prey entwined in struggle (discussed above). Equally important is the structural placement of the image. The deer image was usually placed at the center of an axis or arranged in mirror imagery on either side of that center, whether on a horse, a utilitarian item, or the human body. The deer image could be the victim of attack from a feline, wolf, or a great bird of prey, or its body could be in transformation from deer to bird, deer to horse, or from horse/deer to tree, yet the symmetry of pattern in which the images are arranged remains strikingly consistent within the Early Nomadic and Scythian traditions. She notes that clearly these patterns were not merely ornamental but functioned as systems of related images that carried complex symbolic relationships of which the deer was key. She posits that this axial symmetry represents the cosmic tree, or the world tree or mountain, turning to Siberian ethnographic sources for reconstruction of archaic mythic and ritual systems that involve deer, drawing them together to understand the truly Siberian cosmic life source—the animal mother, the source of life and death.[11]

Mythic Traditions of the Siberian Evenk

The mythic traditions of the Evenk, reindeer herders who are found across the whole of Siberia, lend important insights about beliefs and practices connected to the Deer Mother. Evenk forerunners are believed to have originated in the forested lands west of Lake Baykal, moving to the north and west into the Siberian tundra. They were characterized by an economy dependent on hunting and reindeer herding. These Evenk conceptualized their spatial universe, *buga*, as tripartite: (1) an upper world of tundra, animals, and people, inhabited by deities of natural phenomena, similar in all aspects to the world of people, (2) the middle world, realm of living people, (3) a lower world, identical to the middle world except that everything is reversed, with what is alive above being dead below while what is dead above is alive below. These worlds, in turn, also have layers reserved for different groups: the living, the dead, the rulers of the worlds, the spirits, and so on. Various terms incorporating the term *buga* designate homeland, weather, firmament, heaven, universe, and world. A central term in Evenk cosmology is *bugady* ("of or belonging to the buga") that is, the sacred clan rocks and trees that belong to the clan land (buga), sacred because they mark the originating places of the clan, the place from whence the clan's spirit ancestors emerged from their totemic source.[12]

This important kin relationship is expressed in the Evenk concept of the Bugady Mushunin, the mistress-mother of the clan who is not only the clan's spirit mistress but also the mistress of nature and of the world, conceived as a woman and also as a wild female reindeer or elk. A second female figure, Bugady Enintyn, contains in her name *enin,* which means both cow elk and mother. Together these two mythic figures combine clan mistress and mistress-mother of the clan, pointing to the ancient totemic aspect of the cow elk or reindeer doe in the Evenk belief system. The Evenk concept of Bugady Enintyn as mother of animals and people as well as mistress of the universe confirms her merged human and animal aspects. Invoked as "Grandmother Bugady," this goddess is called upon by the Evenk people to provide animals and fish as sustenance.[13]

The shamanic tradition, emerging later than the clan-based animal mother, reveals the transformation of the ancient totemic Deer Mother into a half-animal, half-human figure, her subsequent demotion into a cult object, and finally, subordination to the shaman's power and functions. In the ritual of *shingkelevun*, performed to ensure success in the hunt, the shaman must travel to the dwelling of the mistress of the clan lands, who lives under a rock or under the roots of the sacred clan tree. There the shaman seeks to learn whether she may release the animals into the tundra, but only if Bugady Enintyn agrees. The clan mistress instructs the supplicant how to travel there. Bugady Enintyn, conceived as giant doe, permits the shaman to lasso animals that are turned into magic woolen threads. These the shaman carries home in a drum, exhibiting them to Bugady Mushunin for passage through her *bugady* and back to the homeland, where the animals are released for the people to hunt. The shaman's journey for the clan's sustenance leads to a place, marked sacred by a sacred tree or sacred rock—a space controlled by a female being, conceptualized as a woman. This female figure serves as guardian of the gateway to the path that must be followed to arrive at the sacred space of the giant doe, the maternal source of human and animal life.[14] That the shaman's tent pole has come to be construed as the world tree Jacobson sees as a loss of the centrality of the Deer Mother in the people's consciousness.

Deer Mother and Shamanic Worldview

The Evenk shaman's drum is made from the skin of a deer born at the base of the cosmic tree, a deer born specifically for that purpose. A spirit ancestor would have taken the soul of the would-be shaman to the underworld of shamans where the soul is led to the *turu*, the tree that is at once the clan's sacred tree and the sacred tree of the clan's shamans. Among its roots lies the great animal mother, the reindeer doe or elk. She eats the shaman's anthropomorphic soul and gives birth to an animal double that is hung by spirit ancestors in a cradle in the cosmic tree's branches. This double, the *khargi*, half-human/half-animal or half-human/half-bird (still represented by human-bird figures on Evenk shaman's cloaks today) functions as the chief soul of the shaman and can assume any human or animal form. The transformation and reconstitution of the shaman, accomplished through the doubling of his or her being and through the power of the Deer Mother, echoes the transformative power of the shaman's deerskin drum.[15]

Another related object found in many burials of both men and women is the mirror, a tool symbolic of doubling. Artamonov, former director of the Hermitage Museum in Leningrad, noted that shamans still use copper mirrors to catch souls and to light the path to the lower world.[16] Jacobson notes that mirrors appear regularly in the burials of Scythian females and males, rich and poor, from the seventh through the late fourth century BCE.[17] This suggests that mirrors may have been regarded as possessing magical properties, useful to the soul on its journey to the next world.[18] It is also consistent with the representation of the Deer Mother as mirror handle.

Jacobson notes that the compression of historical stages within a belief system such as this one and the complementary tension between human and animal, male and female, which accompanies it are reflected in another Evenk concept, that of the cosmic elk. Kheglen the cosmic elk is identified with the Big Dipper constellation, while the Little Dipper is regarded as her calf. The two are said to go into tundra thickets by day and to reappear at night when the movements of the constellations enact the great hunt.

An older version of the myth casts the hunter as the bear, Mangi, who nightly chases and devours the sun-elk of the Great Dipper. Anisimov notes that in Evenk, *mangi*, as well as meaning "bear," designates "spirit of the ancestors," "master of the lower world," and "devil." Here the elk and bear appear as quintessentially important cosmic animals while the bear conveys a complex duality in the role of challenger to the primary animal, the cosmic elk.

In a later version of the myth, the cosmic elk Kheglen ran out of the heavenly taiga and caught the sun on its antlers, then plunged back into the thicket, bringing darkness to the world. The hunter-hero, Main, pursued and killed the elk at midnight, returning light to the middle world, but then could not leave the upper world and was fated to repeat the cycle every night. Jacobson reads the antlers as referring to the tension between an archaic female-centered cosmos and an evolving emphasis on a male-centered social order, represented by the hero so that in the perpetual hunt the conflict between human hero and animal female for control of the sun remains unresolved.[19] In recent versions of the tale, the Milky Way represents the hunters' tracks while the hunters, represented by the three stars of the Dipper's handle, are said to be a Russian, a Ket (another people of the tundra), and an Evenk. Every night the Evenk hunter kills the elk, to be replaced night after night by her calf who becomes her, in a myth reflecting current political tensions.

The Evenk, like many Siberian peoples who live along great rivers, believed that the shaman would transport the soul of the deceased down the river to the land of the dead, protected as always by a female guardian, mistress of the land of the dead, a ubiquitous figure in arctic belief systems. The Evenk beliefs are not singular; Siberian myth and folklore insistently references ancient traditions of a female progenitor animal, animal-woman, or being with aspects of both. A Nganasan shamanic tale finds at the end of shaman's journey a tent on a high precipice. Inside the tent are two antlered women, naked but for a covering of reindeer hair. Their hearth fire resembles the intensity of the rays of the sun. From these reindeer-women the shaman obtains wild and domestic deer along with the reindeer hair that will form his cloak.[20] The generative force here is clearly human-animal, while the association of these animal mothers with the hearth-sun echoes the association of the cosmic Kheglen with the sun she carries on her antlers. It also parallels the pan-Siberian association of the sun and fire with female deities. These animal-women are the "successors to more ancient concepts embodied in the Evenk Bugady Enintyn, the giant elk who devours and gives birth, who lies at the base of the clan tree and whose antlers become the tree itself."[21]

A Creation Myth of the Sami People

Leonard notes that peoples of the Arctic still worship the reindeer goddess, known by many names.[22] Leonard's research reveals that the Kola Sámi people of Siberia revere a hairy reindeer goddess, known as Lady of the Reindeer, as supernatural mistress of wild animals.[23] Not unlike the Evenk, the Sámi people of Lapland see the reindeer goddess as linked with the sun goddess, Geijen-neite, who came to earth to remind people of the need for reverence for the reindeer and to teach them how to care for their beloved animals. Reindeer-herding peoples, some still practicing their ancient ways, have succeeded in celebrating the unity of the mystical and practical aspects of life, sustained by the belief that everything that moves is alive and that a spirit dwells in every living thing. Deer are killed for food but with reverence and thanksgiving for the gift, never for sport or ego. As a Chukchi shaman put it: "All of life, including death, is sacred, and the task for humans is to bear witness to the world's wonders through an attitude of respect, reverence, and awe."[24]

The Sámi word for "rein" which makes up *reindeer* means "the way" to the four cosmic corners. This meaning is quite different from the meanings of "rein" in English: the straps used to control an animal, or a restraining or controlling influence. In keeping with their quite different concept, the Arctic Sámi regard reindeer as messengers of the spirit world who can travel back and forth between heaven and earth, especially at death. The reindeer helps people make their final journey through death by carrying their souls to the other world. In early times, great stone and antler altars called *seite* were erected on sacred sites such as along the ridges of rounded fells, the mountains frequented by reindeer. Here sacrifices were made annually at the first milking of the reindeer.

Leonard recounts a creation myth from the Swedish part of Lapland describing the forming of the earth from the body of the sacred doe. One day, while walking alone near the eternal waters, the creator Jubmel was suddenly shocked by harsh voices and mocking shrieks. The chants of ill-intentioned spirits disturbed the peace and tranquility of the eternal void. Jubmel, upset by this offensive interruption, vowed to create another world abounding of such peace and harmony that abiding love, compassion, and joy would permeate everywhere and the evil spirits would not dare remain. Jubmel chose the beautiful body of the gentle reindeer doe to shape the new world, her loving heart to form the basis for the new creation. He called the lovely Vaja, the reindeer doe, away from Passevaari, the holy mountain where she grazed. The radiant reindeer doe came running, gladdening the creator's heart, shafts of sunlight reflecting from her golden hooves.

Looking into the Vaja's tender eyes Jubmel said, "You my little Vaja, with the infinity sadness in your eyes; from your body I will form the world to set apart the home of holiness." Taking a tiny bone from the body of the reindeer doe the creator built a bridge spanning the abyss between the light world and the nether regions. From the Vaja's bones the new earth's structure was fashioned: rocks, boulders, and mountain peaks and ridges. Her flesh became the rich, dark soil. Her blood and veins became the abundant rivers, flowing through the valleys. Forests sprang from her hair, and her skull rose to become the sky, shielding the earth from the heaven's blazing light. The reindeer's mysterious dark eyes transformed themselves into the morning and the evening stars, guides for the songmakers, poets, dreamers, and lovers, giving them hope and inspiration.

All this accomplished, Jubmel hid the Vaja's beating heart in the deepest center of the earth to remind lost wanderers, lonely mountaineers, and those in sorrow that aid would always be forthcoming. The Vaja's heart became the earth's heartbeat. When peace and love reign, the reindeer doe's heart beats with joy. But if hatred and greed threaten the earth's harmony, her heart convulses in pain, causing tremors that shake the earth from top to bottom.[25]

This is just a portion of the myth, which tells how people forgot their earth-deer-mother and fought among themselves, and a flood destroyed the world. Then the Deer Mother, known as Beijen-neite, returned to earth to be near them, sometimes allowing herself to be seen in human form and sometimes in the form of a reindeer. She taught them the ways of goodness and humility, and how to tame the wild deer and to make clothes and shelter from it. Warmed by the loving care of the sun who is also the deer-mother, Beijen-neite, they became the Sámi people who learned the tales of the hidden treasures from the songs and the drums of the shaman and who journey searching for the peace and harmony that is safeguarded by the heartbeat of the sacred reindeer doe.[26]

Patricia Monaghan, in her study of sun goddesses, noted that Beiwe is the goddess of the Sámi people who travels with her daughter, Beiwe-Neida, through the sky in an enclosure of reindeer antlers and brings back the green season, making plants grow to nurture the reindeer and aid their reproduction. She reports that at the solstice Beiwe's worshipers sacrificed white female deer, threading the meat on a bough that was then formed into a ring and tied with bright ribbons. When the first rays of light appeared after the dark winter the Sami smeared their doors with butter so Beiwe could eat it with her hot beams and begin her yearly recovery.[27]

Leonard adds that the Sámi people regarded the sun as mother to all living creatures. The reindeer were seen as the children of the sun-mother who preserved her reindeer children, which she offered as gifts to humans, bringing both deer and humans natural warmth so they could prosper. The Evenk people have created a lovely poem about the reindeer as the child of the sun.[28]

Reemergence of the Deer Mother

The birth-giving Deer Mother spans Paleolithic to contemporary times. With the coming of Perestroika, which brought a loosening of communist dogma and consequently an end to persecution of shamanic beliefs and practices by native peoples, herding people of the Siberian Arctic no longer have to hide the old ways and are once again teaching them. From their mythic traditions, better understanding emerges of the cosmic Scythian deer goddess, half-human, half-deer who is one with the cosmic tree where death is transformed to birth as a bouquet of hatching birds and the cosmos is understood as a loving mother doe who brings the sun, images relevant today, when the planet needs to be resacrilized to protect all her children.

Notes

1. Marija Gimbutas, *The Language of the Goddess* (San Francisco: Harper and Row, 1989).

2. Marija Gimbutas, *The Goddesses and Gods of Old Europe, 6500–3500 BC: Myths and Cult Images* (Berkeley: University of California Press, 1974).

3. Esther Jacobson, *The Deer Goddess of Ancient Siberia: A Study in the Ecology of Belief* (Leiden: E. J. Brill, 1993), 1.

4. Depicted in, Mikhail Illarionovich Artamanov, *The Splendor of Scythian Art: Treasures from Scythian Tombs* (New York: Praeger, 1969).

5. Jacobson, *Deer Goddess of Ancient Siberia.*

6. Nils Stora, *Burial Customs of the Skolt Lapps* (Helsinki: Academia Scientiarum Fennica, 1971).

7. George Calef, *Caribou and the Barren-lands* (Ottawa: Canadian Arctic Resource Committee, Firefly Books, 1981).

8. Esther Jacobson, *The Art of the Scythians: The Interpenetration of Cultures at the Edge of the Hellenic World* (Leiden: E. J. Brill, 1995).

9. Jacobson. *Deer Goddess of Ancient Siberia.*

10. Ibid., 80.

11. Ibid.

12. Artamanov, *Splendor of Scythian Art,* 181–182.

13. Jacobson. *Deer Goddess of Ancient Siberia.*

14. N. V. Anisimov, "Cosmological Concepts of the Peoples of the North," in *Studies in Siberian Shamanism,* ed. H. N. Michael (Toronto: Arctic Institute of the North, University of Toronto, 1963), 84–123.

15. N. V. Anisimov, *Evenk Religion from the Perspective of History and Origins, and the Problem of the Source of Primitive Belief* (Moscow: Leningrad, 1958), 156.

16. Artamanov. *Splendor of Scythian Art,* 93.

17. Jacobson. *Deer Goddess of Ancient Siberia.*

18. Anisimov, *Evenk Religion,* 156.

19. Jacobson. *Deer Goddess of Ancient Siberia,* 197.

20. Anisimov. "Cosmological Concepts," 186.

21. Jacobson, *Deer Goddess of Ancient Siberia,* 197.

22. Linda Schierse Leonard, *Creation's Heartbeat: Following the Reindeer Spirit* (New York: Bantam Books, 1995).

23. While many different spellings of Sámi have been used in texts written by Sámi and non-Sámi when the spelling was not standardized, the usage *Sámi* is their own name for themselves as it is written in their own language and they encourage others to use it. To do so shows respect. From translators note in Veli-Pekka Lehtola, *The Sámi People: Traditions in Transition,* trans. Linna Weber Muller-Wille (Fairbanks: University of Alaska Press, 2004).

24. Leonard, *Creation's Heartbeat.*

25. Ibid.

26. Ibid.

27. William Billson, "Some Mythical Tales of the Lapps," *Folklore* 29, no. 3 (September 1918): 178–192; Bo Lundmark, "They Consider Sun to Be a Mother to All Living Creatures: The Sun Cult of the Saamis," in *Saami Pre-Christian Religion,* ed. Louise Backman and Åke Hultkrantz (Stockholm: Universitet Stockholms, 1985), 179–188; Rafael Karsten, *The Religion of the Sameks* (Leiden: E. J. Brill, 1955), 32–33; and Patricia Monaghan, *O Mother Sun! A New View of the Cosmic Feminine.* (Freedom, CA: The Crossing Press, 1994).

28. Leonard, *Creation's Heartbeat.*

Bibliography

Anisimov, N. V. "Cosmological Concepts of the Peoples of the North." In *Studies in Siberian Shamanism,* ed. H. N. Michael, 157–229. Toronto: Arctic Institute of the North, University of Toronto, 1963.

Anisimov, N. V. *Evenk Religion from the Perspective of History and Origins, and the Problem of the Source of Primitive Belief.* Moscow: Leningrad, 1958.

Artamanov, Mikhail Illarionovich. *The Splendor of Scythian Art: Treasures from Scythian Tombs.* New York: Praeger, 1969.

Billson, William. "Some Mythical Tales of the Lapps." *Folklore* 29, no. 3 (September 1918): 178–192.

Calef, George. *Caribou and the Barren-lands.* Ottawa: Canadian Arctic Resource Committee, Firefly Books, 1981.

Gimbutas, Marija. *The Goddesses and Gods of Old Europe, 6500–3500 BC: Myths and Cult Images.* Berkeley: University of California Press, 1974.

Gimbutas, Marija. *The Language of the Goddess.* San Francisco: Harper and Row, 1989.

Jacobson, Esther. *The Art of the Scythians: The Interpenetration of Cultures at the Edge of the Hellenic World.* Leiden: E. J. Brill, 1995.

Jacobson, Esther. *The Deer Goddess of Ancient Siberia: A Study in the Ecology of Belief.* Leiden: E. J. Brill, 1993.

Karsten, Rafael. *The Religion of the Sameks.* Leiden: E. J. Brill, 1955.

Lehtola, Veli-Pekka. *The Sámi People: Traditions in Transition.* Translated by Linna Weber Muller-Wille. Fairbanks: University of Alaska Press, 2004.

Leonard, Linda Schierse. *Creation's Heartbeat: Following the Reindeer Spirit.* New York: Bantam Books, 1995.

Lundmark, Bo. "They Consider Sun to Be a Mother to All Living Creatures: The Sun Cult of the Saamis." In *Saami Pre-Christian Religion,* ed. Louise Backman and Åke Hultkrantz, 179–188. Stockholm: Universitet Stockholms, 1985.

Monaghan, Patricia. *O Mother Sun! A New View of the Cosmic Feminine.* Freedom, CA: The Crossing Press, 1994.

Stora, Nils. *Burial Customs of the Skolt Lapps.* Helsinki: Academia Scientiarum Fennica, 1971.

12

Silkies: An Interspecies Love Story in Legend, Song, and Story

Brenda Peterson

When she slips ashore, the silkie woman hides her secret: dense, sleek sealskin. It is silver and speckled like beach stones and moonlit sand. It is as luxurious as an embrace. Only the slight scent of salt stays with the slender woman as she meets her lover in their hideaway, a shelter of stone that villagers call Silkie's Cove. He is a young sailor, a fisherman who has fallen under her seaspell. He brings her clothes and on this night he asks her the questions that every silkie woman dreads. Will she stay in his shore world with him? Will she bear their child on land, as all seals do? But instead of returning her newborn to the sea that is mother to us all, will she promise to stay on land with him forever?

As they lie together on the cool sand, the silkie woman's eyes reflect moonlight and sorrow. Those eyes—fathomless, unblinking—are easy to mistake for human. When she speaks, her voice is a little hoarse for she has been at sea for days, sleeping underwater in kelp forests, dreaming of her human, but forswearing the shore they share for fear that he will ask just this question.

"Will you marry me, my Kate?" the young sailor says softly. "Will you never more go away from me?" When she does not answer but gazes at him with eyes deep as their ocean, he pleads, "For the child's sake."

Figure 12.1 Magical beings who are half-woman, half-seal, silkies inhabit the lore of Ireland, Scotland, and the surrounding islands. (Copyright Hrana Janto.)

The silkie woman listens to the pulsing shush of the surf and is still silent. Nearby she can hear the snores of other seals, asleep, drifting just below the surface of the sea. For seals, like humans and many other animals, also dream. They can also sing, some sailors swear, hearing the low lull and lament of the seal folk far out at sea.

Tears stream from the silkie woman's huge eyes as she lays her silver webbed hand on her sailor's head. His curls and skin are wonderfully darkened from days in the sun on the open ocean. He is handsome and tender—for a human. His body has a sleek, aerodynamic slope from broad shoulder to strong flanks. He is almost as strong as a seal. His legs twine around hers and he pulls her close against his chest.

Oh, these human legs. She shape-shifted the moment she eased out of her elegant sealskin. How thin and painful these appendages are so she must adapt to a hesitant walk, instead of a glide and spiral and pirouette in the sea. How gravity weighs her down, like sinking into shifting sand. And how the villagers frown at her as she tries to pass unseen among them. "She's a dark one, she is," they whisper so she will not hear. But her hidden ears are just as good as a human's. "You can see plain—she's not one of us."

It is high tide, time for the silkie woman to let the waves lift her back to her water world. So easy to let the sea pull her back to her fluid grace, her rookery of cliff rocks where other seals rest their heads on one another's back, nurse their young on rich milk fat, and nap with the sunlight warming their fur. This is usually the time she leaves her sailor, right before dawn. He tries not to hold her too tightly. He kisses her tenderly, as always, and then he lets her go. "You will always be my silkie," he whispers.

Because her sailor eases his embrace, she can reach out to him and say at last, "Yes . . . I will try to stay. But you must never hide my sealskin from me. I must always be free to go back to the sea."

With a smile as clear as the new sun rising over their island, the sailor promises. Will he keep his promise? Ah, that is the story.

An interspecies romance between seal and shore folk could be happening even now on any beach, any sea—from the misty Orkney or Hebrides Islands to the mysterious Shetland isles of Scotland, to Swedish fjords, to the subarctic coasts of Norway and Greenland, and even to the lands of Chinook Indians in North America. The great sea story-cycle of silkies finds its folkloric origins in Norse and Celtic traditions and in Native traditions of seal-people shape-shifters off America's northwest coast. There are even some Japanese legends of undersea folk in the famous story of "The Palace Under the Sea."

The word "silkie" probably comes from the Norse word *selch* ("seal"). The female changelings are also known as selchies or selkies, selies, Silly Wychtis, or Silly Witches, the latter name possibly connected to Sele, the Celtic harvest goddess. These silkies could take either human or seal form. According to Monaghan,

> On the Orkney islands, people with slight webbing between toes or fingers were called descendents of the noblewoman Brita (or Ursilla), who grew bored with her human mate and made off with a virile male seal; this is an unusual motif, for typically the ancestral mother, not the father, was a seal. Brita's children were born with webbed feet and hands, which had to be clipped into fingers and toes.[1]

Certain Celtic names are associated with seal ancestry. In the Hebrides Islands, descendents of seal women are called by the names MacCondrum and MacPhees, while in Ireland the family names of Coneely (Connelly, Conley), MacNamara, O'Flaherty, and O'Sullivan (and sometimes Lee) indicate descent from seal women.[2] Such traditions enforce the connections between seals and humans.

Silkie Legends

According to legend, silkies can be either male or female. Most classic silkie legends feature beautiful seal-women who can shift between their sleek seal and human bodies. With their mesmerizing eyes, their haunting songs, and their mysterious powers, these silkie women seduce men as surely as does the sea. Often, the seal-women bear children from these passionate liaisons—"the dark ones" they are called—and these silkies pass among villagers who both revere and fear them. A silkie's possessive husband might hide her sealskin so she cannot return to the sea but must stay onshore with him and their children. Since seals travel far in the wide oceans foraging and fishing and finding their own communities, to be land-locked is a sorrow that even human love cannot completely ease. Thus a trapped silkie woman may be discovered on a rocky cliff or sitting on a spit gazing out into the waves that sing to her. But without her sealskin she is bound to her husband, family, and the land dwellers.

That is, until the day one of her children finds her sealskin. Sometimes it is an ocean spirit who inspires the child to search and discover his mother's radiant skin. With a cry of joy mixed with heartache, the silkie slips back into her silver fur and returns to the welcoming waves. Sometimes she calls to her child who shape-shifts and dives with her. The husband who has stolen her true nature is left alone. And what does this say about loved ones who have their independence, the sanctuary of their own skins, the expansive embrace of the sea, which in most all cultures feminine?

Silkies are goddesses of this blue planet first before they are seducers or wives of the land folk. Silkies belong fathoms deep in the vast and fluid subconscious world. Those who fall in love with them follow other animals who inhabit a world others must only imagine. Like guides to any underworld, silkies teach mysteries that cannot be controlled, even through love. And what may be a tragic loss for humans—the return of the seal-wife to the sea—may be a happy ending for a silkie.

One silkie story stands out for its more hopeful ending. Off the rocks of Loch Duich, silkie folk come ashore to dance and celebrate together. The silkies have set aside their beautiful sealskins to dance jubilant jigs on land. Three fishermen cannot simply witness this ecstasy; they must steal the sealskins of three maidens. In return for what they have stolen, the two older brothers promise the silkie girls gowns made of silk, feather beds, and many children. Their lust and possessiveness lead to loss. One man is deserted by his silkie when she finds her stolen skin. Another burns the sealskin to keep his silkie on land; in doing so, he burns his silkie love alive.

But the youngest brother makes no promises of material reward for a life enslaved onshore. Instead, on his wedding night, he makes a gift of his silkie maiden's sealskin. He returns her birthright to her, leaving her free to come and go as she likes. In gratitude and true love, the silkie comes back to this youngest brother every ninth night. Great is their happiness.

The People of the Sea: A Journey in Search of the Seal Legend by David Thomson is a motherlode of seal folklore. First published in 1954 and reissued in 2000 with an introduction by the celebrated Irish poet Seamus Heaney, this book traces Celtic silkie myths. Raised with Scottish fishermen and storytellers, Thomson sets out to interview people who sing and tell stories of the "dream-like hold" the seals have upon people. One Irish storyteller sums up interspecies fascination with seals: "But what is in the mind of them, I don't know—the creatures."[3]

An Orkney crofter tells Thomson, "There was supposed to be a creature in the water for every one on land."[4] These mirror images, these other animals living alongside humanity, represent a parallel universe sometimes just as mysterious and engaging as dark matter. In the way that astronomers study the stars to find out how Earth fits into the universe's scheme of things, folklorists study myths of all cultures to figure out truths to live by. Astronomers have discovered that all life on earth is literally made of stardust falling from space. Humans are also made of stories.

Silkie Stories and Songs

For millennia, songs and stories of silkies mingling with seafaring humans have woven an interspecies tapestry. Any library or Internet search reveals the depth of this romantic alliance and its consequences. Unlike Hans Christian Andersen's social-climbing and assimilating "Little Mermaid" tale, legends of silkies are more sanguine and intriguing. The romance is less weighted toward satisfying only the human heart and more toward exploring the animal nature of all beings.

From the haunting Welsh myth retold in *The Seal Children* by British writer Jackie Morris, in which a silkie woman helps her changeling children escape poverty and travel to the New World, to the famous Joan Baez song "Silkie" wherein a silkie predicts the tragic death of his only son, the silkie legends continue to have resonance. Jane Yolen's poem, "The Selchie's Midnight Song," speaks of the seal's first and final bond with the sea.[5]

In general, the silkie woman is not a happy homemaker. Some folklorists suggest that the silkie myths express human longing for another world. Stewart Hendrickson writes:

> These stories may be used to explain why a woman might leave her husband ("She was quite unlike the island women and some of her ways were so strange. Why, she'd go out on the rocks when the tide was low to talk to the seabirds and seals") or why a man might leave his family. These people of the sea were always different, and came and disappeared in mysterious ways.[6]

In some silkie myths, the shape-shifter is male who seduces an island girl and forever haunts her. One of the most famous traditional silkie ballads, attributed to James Waters of Columbia University, is "The Great Silkie of Sule Skerry." In a lonely island in the Scottish Orkneys a woman is entranced by a mysterious man she meets on land. The evocative refrain of both song and story is:

> I am a man upon the land,
> I am a selchie in the sea.[7]

Jane Yolen adapts this familiar tale in "Sule Serry." As Yolen updates the tale, a young girl named Mairi is removed from home in London during the World War II bombing raids to an isolated Scottish isle were she grudgingly stays with relatives. Lonely for her beau Harry back in London, Mairi bemoans the fact that she cannot help in the war effort.

One day while rowing her coracle, or skiff, she runs aground on rocks and explores them more out of defiance than interest. Inside a blue-green incandescent cave she hears an eerie "moan-song." Following the musical voice, she discovers a wounded man with gray hair and powerful shoulders sleeping under a sealskin coat. He is beautiful, but alien. He is also the first naked man she has ever seen; and yet she summons her courage to help him, believing he must be a fisherman or Royal Air Force pilot shot down from his plane.

When he speaks to her, his tone is almost a chant, and she is compelled to bend to him, to seek his arms, to let his silver, webbed fingers trace her lips. Then, she is kissing him and "all the sea was in that kiss, cold and vast and perilous . . . he was strong as the tide." Mairi feels only "the briefest of pain, and a kind of drowning, and she let the land go."[8] The young girl awakens as if from a reverie to find her young man still and moaning. She rows back to her village for help but the fishermen are skeptical and afraid. Maybe Mairi has stumbled upon the Great Selchie man? Or maybe the man wounded in the grotto "might be one of ours . . . it's hard to say which side he's on."[9]

They go to rescue him and discover a German pilot still entwined with his white silk parachute. When they parade him through the street as a "Bloody Hun," the enemy, Mairi protests that this is not the same man she saw in the cave. But they pay her no mind. Only then does Mairi reach into her pocket to find an ancient green and gold coin, "crusted, as if it had lain on the ocean bottom for some time."[10] Hand on her belly, she remembers the song, the prophecy of Sule Serry, that the son begotten by the Great Selchie man would live with her on land only seven years, then the seal father would return to take his son back to the sea with him. The mother would then marry a gunner—someone like Harry back in London who would one day hunt seals and who would one day kill his wife's firstborn, as well as her lover, the Great Selchie.

No wonder Yolen's story ends with reminding humans that she felt "safe and lonely at once." And finishes: "The sound of the sea followed her all the way home, part melody and part unending moan."[11]

There is often sadness to interspecies love, a longing to know the Other while one is still trapped in one's own experience, culture, or species. There is also an alien and detached nature particular to the silkie myths. Also, the haunt of abandonment. In Yolen's poem "Ballad of the White Seal Maid," the silkie proclaims: "But never a thought to the man left on shore,/ for selchie's my nature and name."[12]

Silkies in Contemporary Film

There are other bonds remerging with the silkies and new stories being told on the shores. One of the most moving and magical of these modern legends is by John Sayles in *The Secret of Roan Inish*, filmed in Ireland but drawn from the Rosalie K. Fry novel *Secret of Mor Skerry*, set in Scotland. This film reveals the fate of those who sacrifice their interspecies bond with the seal folk. The story is told from the viewpoint of a young girl, Fiona. She learns from her grandfather about her family's silkie ancestors and the loss of her baby brother, Jamie, now being raised by seals on their old island home. When Fiona finds Jamie, she also uncovers the secret of the island: Why the villagers left the island and why they must return.

The Secret of Roan Inish teaches that humans must acknowledge common ancestry with other animals, from whom shape-shifting stories are drawn. The dark eyes of seal folk show just how much like seals humans are—and how soulful the interconnection between the species. One traditional Orcadian legends states that some angels fell on the land and some on the sea. The former were the fairies, and the latter were said to be the seals.

Real Seals: Natural History Meets Legend

Throughout the silkie stories and songs, these mesmerizing seal folk may live with humans out of love or obligation, but they do not linger. Are there any tales of silkies being buried alongside their mates or families in the earth? Interestingly, the stories differ from actual seal behavior in this regard. Actual seals may come ashore to die when they are injured or ill, because like other marine mammals, they fear drowning. But humans do not spin tales about silkies resting peacefully in human cemeteries, contained by the earth. In folklore, seals always return to the sea, the primal ocean that spawned all life. They go back to the source.

Shore dwellers who tell these interspecies love stories between mammal kin are including other animals in humanity's extended families. Silkie tales are drawn from real bonds of natural history and interdependence. Like humans, seals give birth on land; they nurse their newborns on milk and often rest day and night onshore seeking safety and community. It is a common sight to see seals napping on beaches, stretching their supple bodies in the "banana position" to regulate their temperature and to stretch their weary bodies after hours foraging at sea.

At night, seals often come ashore to mate; this land-lust might have first inspired human stories. Scientists have discovered that seals dream; like humans, seals experience REM sleep. Harbor seals' newborns can molt their skin (called the *lanugo*) while still in the womb. Many types of seals molt their dense fur while on land, sloughing the skin off with the help of rocks and gravel. Imagine coming upon one of these luxurious fur skins while combing the beach. What a discovery—and what a story to be made of such skin.

Seals are among the most amphibious of all marine mammals because they spend almost as much time on land as they do at sea. Like other marine mammals, such as dolphins, seals have been known to save human lives at sea—guiding fishermen through storms or, in some documented cases, swimming a human who is lost at sea back to land again.

Seals enjoy a liminal—in-between the worlds—life between shore and sea. This blurs the boundaries between them and humans. As such, they are coastal companions and teachers. Early hominids may have learned to fish from seals. Indigenous coastal peoples depended upon seals for food and clothing. But do seals also have something to teach about love and spiritual survival?

If the old silkie stories were still respected today, humans would allow more awe and even reverence to other animals, those beings that indigenous storytellers often call the First People. Once seals shared all the shores, and subsistence hunters felt a sacred sense of interdependence. But as humans have developed and dominated the coastlines, few shores remain where humans can fall in love with silkies and learn their mysteries. And the species has become less human for this loss.

The great silkie legends have given way to the cynical and self-centered idea that seals are "nuisance animals" to be driven off beaches. In Europe, seal populations are crashing. There have been alarming epidemics in seals of pneumonia and viral encephalitis that could be caused by pollution. Climate change and ocean acidification has drastically crashed fish populations, affecting the migration paths and hunting grounds of marine mammals. The film *A Sea Change: Imagine a World Without Fish* chillingly documents this "darkening of our oceans."[13] In Canada a brutal harvest of baby harp seals has long drawn international condemnation, and in 2009 the European Union at last voted for a total ban on commercial trade in seal products. Off the coast of North America, while there is a healthy seal population, 50 percent of seal pups do not survive their first year. Predators such as orcas do not account for this death rate, which is due to pollution and human predation.

Once humans felt reverence for seals. To this day in Scottish islands, many families trace their ancestry to seal folk, and because of this totemic taboo they will not eat seal meat. The Inuit taught their hunters to drop seawater gratefully into the mouths of slain seals. Now, fishermen routinely use sharp gaffes to kill seals, scapegoating these other mammals for overfishing. Seals get caught in driftnets left unattended by fishermen, despite laws that require tribal and commercial fishermen to watch any nets they set, especially near rookeries. Weaned pups and juvenile seals are not yet savvy about nets and often follow fish into these death traps.

In the 21st century silkie myths are even more vital to human survival than in the past, for seals actually show the health of earth's shared oceans and the futures of its species. Now more than ever, it is a cautionary tale full of romance and loss and loyalty.

Notes

1. Gwen Benwell and Arthur Waugh, *Sea Enchantress: The Tale of the Mermaid and Her Kin* (New York: Citadel Press, 1965), 17–20.

2. Alpin MacGregor, *In the Peat Fire Flame: Folk Tales and Traditions of the Highlands and Islands* (Edinburgh: The Moray Press, 1937).

3. David Thompson, *The People of the Sea: A Journey in Search of the Seal Legend* (New York: Counterpoint, 2000).

4. Ibid., x.

5. Jane Yolen, *Neptune Rising: Songs and Tales of the Undersea Folk* (New York: Philomel Books, 1982).

6. Rosalie K. Fry, *The Secret of Ron Mor Skerry* (New York: Dutton, 1959).

7. Joan Baez, "Silkie," on *Joan Baez*, vol. 2, Vanguard Records, 1961.

8. Yolen, *Neptune Rising*, 53.

9. Ibid., 56–57.

10. Ibid., 59.

11. Ibid., 54.

12. Ibid., 43

Bibliography

Baez, Joan. "Silkie." On *Joan Baez*, Vol. 2. Vanguard Records, 1961.

Bastian, Dawn E., and Judy K. Mitchell. *Handbook of Native American Mythology.* Santa Barbara, CA: ABC-CLIO, 2004.

Beck, Mary. *Shamans and Kushtakas: North Coast Tales of the Supernatural.* Anchorage: Alaska Northwest Books, 1991.

Benwell, Gwen, and Arthur Waugh. *Sea Enchantress: The Tale of the Mermaid and Her Kin.* New York: Citadel Press, 1965.

Crossley-Holland, Kevin. *Folk-Tales of the British Isles.* New York: Pantheon Books, 1985.

Griff, Dorsey, ed. *Silkie: Seal Folk Tales, Ballads, and Songs.* Netarts, OR: Griffin Press, 1985.

Hogan, Linda, and Brenda Peterson. *Sightings: The Gray Whale's Mysterious Journey.* Washington, DC: National Geographic Books, 2002.

Kolbert, Elizabeth. "The Darkening Sea." *New Yorker*, November 20, 2006, 66.

MacGregor, Alasdair Alpin. *The Peat-Fire Flame: Folk Tales and Traditions of the Highlands and Islands*. Edinburgh: The Moray Press, 1937.

Martin, Rafe. *The Boy Who Lived with the Seals*. New York: G. P. Putnam's Sons, 1993.

McLaughlin, Mary. "Sealwoman/Yundah" (song). *Celtic Voices: Women of Song*. Narada Media, 1995.

Monaghan, Patricia. *The Red-Haired Girl from the Bog: The Landscape of Celtic Myth and Spirit*. New York: New World Library, 2004.

Morris, Jackie. *Seal Children*. London: Francis Lincoln Children's Books, 2004.

Reeves, Randall R., Brent S. Stewart, Phillip J. Clapham, and James A. Powell. *National Audubon Society Guide to Marine Mammals of the World*. New York: Knopf, 2002.

Ni Mhaolchatha, Meav. "You Brought Me Up" (song). *Silver Sea* CD. Valley, 2002.

Peterson, Brenda. *Animal Heart*. San Francisco: Sierra Club Books, 2004.

Rys, John. *Celtic Folklore: Welsh and Manx*. Oxford: Clarendon Press, 1941.

Scheffer, Victor B. *The Year of the Seal*. New York: Scribner's, 1970.

A Sea Change. Directed by Barbara Ettinger. Niijii Films, 2009.

The Secret of Roan Inish. Directed by John Sayles. Sony Pictures, 1995.

Solas. "The Grey Selchie" (song). *The Words That Remain*. Sanachie, 1998.

Swan, Brian, ed. *Coming to Light: Contemporary Translations of the Native Literatures of North America*. New York: Random House, 1994.

Swire, Otta F. *The Highlands and Their Legends*. Edinburgh: Oliver and Boyd, 1963.

Thompson, David. *The People of the Sea: A Journey in Search of the Seal Legend*. New York: Counterpoint, 2000.

Williamson, Duncan. *Tales of the Seal People: Scottish Folk Tales*. Northhampton, MA: Interlink Publishing Group, 1998.

Yolen, Jane. *Neptune Rising: Songs and Tales of the Undersea Folk*. New York: Philomel Books, 1982.

13

Swan Maiden: The Animal That Adam Could Not Name

Boria Sax

"I would that we were, my beloved, white birds on the foam of the sea!"[1] Those words by the young W. B. Yeats contain in essence the swan maiden tale, a story of enormous cultural variation and psychological complexity. Behind the many textual and thematic variations is a fairly simple experience: "the thrill of identification in which the boundary between people and animals momentarily seems to disappear."[2]

A swan becomes a woman by casting off an enchanted skin, after which she bathes in a pond. A man sees her, falls madly in love, and hides the skin. Unable to resume her bird form and fly away, she agrees to marry the man. They have children, and for many years they live together in apparent happiness. Then one day she finds the skin, puts it on to become a bird again, and flies away. The husband then goes in search of her, and perhaps they are reunited in the end. That is the basic swan maiden tale, variants of which have been recorded throughout the world.

Folklorists generally divide the swan maiden tale into two sections: first, there is the "swan maiden" or tale type 400*, where the asterisk indicates that the tale is intimately related to material that follows directly; second, there is tale type 400, which is "the search for the lost wife." This is not a scientific taxonomy but a practical one, designed to help researchers and storytellers find related tales.[3] Every detail of the story may vary. The maiden, for example, is a bride from an alien world, but she need not necessarily be a swan. She may be a crane, vixen, seal, snake, or any other sort of beast. She may also be a goddess, a fairy, or a demon. The tale may also be told with genders reversed, in which case the story usually becomes type 425 or "the search for the lost husband." Those who wish to tell or simply enjoy the tale will find that swan maiden stories usually seem easy to recognize, though hard to define precisely.

In addition to these tales, countless others seem related to swan maiden stories by virtue of shared themes, motifs, or structures. They might be corrupted, undeveloped, or fragmentary variants of the tale. Is the "Cinderella" of Charles Perrault a swan maiden story?[4] Like a swan maiden, Cinderella is transformed by putting on a dress. Also like a swan maiden, she flees her prince to reassume her old identity, and the prince begins a quest for his missing bride. Or is Eve in the Bible a sort of swan maiden, who once left her husband Adam to consort with snakes? Such comparisons illustrate how the story of the swan maiden seems to pervade human culture, suggesting new variants and analogues.

The tale of the swan maiden has been recorded hundreds of times in widely separated cultures and on every continent, which suggests that it is extremely ancient. Still another indication of the story's antiquity is that the events seem to emerge from a world where the boundaries among human beings, deities, animals, and even plants are relatively fluid. The story has both the pathos of an ancient myth and the emotional complexity of a modern novel. It may seem "romantic," in the sense of being an idealized tale of love—except that the bride is captured by trickery and violence. At the same time, if not equal, the relation between bride and groom is certainly balanced. The tale preserves, like many marriages, a precarious harmony, with perpetual tension below the surface. The true nature of the wife remains a mystery to her husband and perhaps even to herself as well.

It is this mystery that gives the swan maiden tale a religious dimension. Even when she is temporarily subordinate to her husband, there is little doubt that the swan maiden is ultimately more knowing and more powerful than he is. The animal wife has been associated with several images of feminine divinity, from the Valkyries in Germanic cultures to snake deities of Mesopotamia. Alan Miller has written in reference to variants of the tale, "The bird form strongly tends in North Asia to be seen as feminine. Bird figures are goddesses here. Further, as female they are the originators of life and hence the means whereby significant life, that is, life touched by the sacred, is produced. They are the foundresses of dynasties, of cults, of races, of priesthoods."[5] Although the connections lie much too far back in prehistory to be traced with any confidence, these diverse female divinities may be variants of a primeval mother goddess.

The Origin of the Swan Maiden

A. T. Hatto has argued that the story came from Central Asia and was inspired by attempts to domesticate migratory waterfowl, which would fly away at the onset of winter. In an effort to demonstrate this, he looked at the migratory routes of swans and related birds and tried to link these with the locations in which the tale had been recorded.[6] The theory is elegant, but it also has many problems. To begin with, what correlations between the migratory routes of waterfowl and the prevalence of swan maiden tales Hatto managed to uncover were loose at best, perhaps only imagined. Furthermore, the theory does not account for the variants of the tale where the bride is an animal other than a migratory bird—a fox or seal, for example. Finally, as any suburbanite today knows, swans and other migratory waterfowl will not necessarily fly south for the winter if offered an adequate supply of food.

Still another theory is that the swan maiden tale derives ultimately from the story of Urvasí and Purūravas from the Rig Veda, which is based on oral traditions that may go back to the first or second millennium. Urvasí is a goddess who is banished from heaven and becomes the wife of King Purūravas, who loses her through violation of taboos. After a series of adventures, the king becomes a demigod, and they are reunited. There is no complete version of the story, which must be reconstructed from several fragmentary references.[7] Though the story has many of the themes and perhaps the ambiance of a swan maiden tale, any claim that it is the original story involves a great deal of conjecture.

The most distinctive and memorable motif found in a great many, though by no means all, swan maiden tales is the detachable skin that, when put on, changes the wearer from a human being to another creature. The feature seems fanciful with a swan, but far less so with a snake, which does cast off and discard its skin. This suggests that the original story was not about a swan or other bird but about a snake, but the motif of the detachable skin was retained as it was retold about many creatures from swans to seals. Further evidence for this is the association of many archaic goddesses, especially from the Near East, with serpents. Snakes and birds, especially water birds, are often paired in mythology, and both are found near bodies of water.[8]

An episode in the Epic of Gilgamesh, a story far older than even the Rig Veda, that features the motif of a detachable skin is likely a version of the swan maiden story. It comes near the end of the Mesopotamian epic, which is best known from the copy found in the library of the seventh-century BCE Assyrian king Ashurbanipal but probably originated early in the third millennium. After Gilgamesh spurns the sexual advances of the goddess Ishtar and his companion Enkidu insults her, the infuriated deity brings suit before the council of the immortals and demands that the two heroes be punished with death. Other deities object and, as a compromise, Enkidu is killed by disease but Gilgamesh is allowed to live. Shattered by the loss of his companion, Gilgamesh undertakes a journey to the under-world. After many adventures, he is returning with little to show, when he finds the plant of immortality growing at the bottom of the sea. He picks it, planning to cultivate the plant and bring eternal life to his people. Returning home, he sees a well of cool water and stops to bathe. A serpent rises from the depths of the water and eats the plant, sloughs off its skin, and returns to the well. Gilgamesh sits and weeps, saying, "was it for this that I toiled with my hands? Is it this I have wrung out my heart's blood?"[9] Gilgamesh's old nemesis the goddess Ishtar was, like many other Near Eastern goddesses, often associated with serpents. The one that eats the plant of immortality is likely either sent by her or else a form of the god-dess herself.

A further indication that this episode is the origin of the swan maiden tale, or at least a very early version, is that the Epic of Gilgamesh seems to contain the central motifs of that story, albeit not in the form they generally take. While it is not at all clear whether the relationship of Gilgamesh to Enkidu is what would now be called homosexual, it is compared to a mar-riage many times, so Gilgamesh's journey to the underworld is close to being "the search for the lost bride." The more familiar swan maiden tales change the story of Gilgamesh by rather imperfectly fusing the figures of Enkidu, Ishtar, and the snake (or swan). All three are, in various ways, used to symbolize the natural world, with Enkidu as a wild man, Ishtar as the power of the elements, and the snake as inexorable destiny. Perhaps this is the reason for the unusual emotional complexity of the animal-bride story. In most versions of the story, the bride still seems to implicitly retain a tri-part identity as woman, goddess, and animal.

In earlier rejecting the advances of Ishtar, Gilgamesh had accused her of often taking mortal lovers whom she would later transform into ani-mals and destroy. Ishtar has none of the pathos or lyricism generally asso-ciated with the swan maiden herself, but comes across in the Epic of

Gilgamesh as almost entirely malevolent. It is possible that the swan maiden tale may be even older than the stories of Gilgamesh or Ishtar. It may lie at the start of civilization and commemorate the rupture between ourselves and the natural world. In her ambiguity, the animal bride reflects intense yet contradictory feelings for nature, which has variously seemed to be a source of ceaseless violence and peace, an implacable adversary, and a refuge from distress.

The Sumerian tablets telling of the marriage of Inanna and the shepherd-king Dumuzi are to an extent an even earlier version of the Epic of Gilgamesh. The goddess Inanna (see Johanna Stuckey's chapter in this volume) is a still more archaic form of Ishtar. Dumuzi, like Gilgamesh, is an early king of Uruk, and both kings are sons of the sheep-goddess Sirtur/Ninsun, so they seem to be versions, or incarnations, of a single hero.[10] Inanna takes Dumuzi as her consort, but after they have had a child he takes leave of her in order to fulfill his duties as a king. Inanna later descends into the underworld. After much humiliation, she is rescued by her father, the god of wisdom Enki, and she forces Dumuzi to take her place below the earth.[11] The alternating descent and resurrection of the married pair probably represent stages in the agricultural cycle. The two, in alternating stages of their story, become to one another swan maiden and animal groom. But the tale takes place in an archaic shadow-world, where the distinctions among animals, deities, and human beings are far from clear.

The Medieval and Early Modern Swan Maiden

The medieval era brought many retellings of the swan maiden story, yet the most influential has certainly been that of Melusine, a fairy who, for imprisoning her father in a mountain, has been punished by being changed into a serpent from the waist down every Saturday. She can only be released from the spell by marrying a man who promises faithfully never to look at her during her transformation. One day a young count named Raymond kills his hunting companion by accident and wanders through the woods in fear of retribution. Melusine finds and befriends him next to a pond, and the two are soon married. Melusine builds a palace for their home at Lusignan, and they have nine sons. All are exceptionally strong and capable but deformed in one way or another. The first, Urian, has a flat face, protruding ears, one red eye and one green eye. Anthony is covered with hair and has long claws. Geoffrey the Tooth has a tusk like that of a boar.

After the couple has many years of happiness, acquaintances suggest to Raymond that Melusine has been unfaithful. Raymond spies on his wife through a hole in the door one Saturday, and he sees that she had been transformed into a serpent from the waist down. Later, during a quarrel, he calls her "odious serpent," thus revealing what he has seen. As soon as these words are out, Melusine begins to assume her serpentine form and flies three times around the castle crying out in a tearful farewell, then vanishes. Like a tribal totem, Melusine continues to watch over her descendants. There are many reports of her being seen near the castle of Lusignan, especially in times of crisis.

Melusine is a primal mother, source of all life. The deformities of the various sons recall the large and powerful animals that were identified with noble families in heraldry such as the lion, boar, and wolf. Her fertility joins her with many archaic earth-mother goddesses, from the Greek Gaia (see Glenys Livingstone's chapter in this volume) to the Babylonian Tiamat. Behind this story, there is a pattern of the agricultural year, with its pattern of sowing, fertility, and departure. The way Raymond spies on her and uncovers her secrets suggests a man intruding on women's mysteries. In the perspective of archaic thought, these are close to the mysteries of the earth. The story was written down by Jean D'Arras for the Duke of Berry in the early 14th century. Though known primarily as the founder of the powerful house of Lusignan, Melusine was also claimed as an ancestress by many houses of France and Luxembourg, and similar stories were told of noble houses in Germany. It influenced many important literary works, including "Undine" by Friederich de la Motte Fouqé, "Lamia" by John Keats, and "The Little Mermaid" by Hans Christian Andersen.[12]

The Swan Maiden Tale in Modern Times

The Victorians were fascinated with the tale of the swan maiden, which addressed their preoccupation with the sanctity of marriage and motherhood. It also, however, appealed to their fascination with enchantments and with exotic creatures. Like previous tellers, they thought of the tale primarily from the perspective of the husband, whose desertion by the bride seemed the most tragic of fates. By the late 19th century, however, a rebellion against bourgeois domesticity was becoming a dominant intellectual trend.

Henrik Ibsen's drama *A Doll's House*, first staged in 1879, was loosely based on the swan maiden story, which is widely known in his native

Norway.[13] The heroine Nora is a young lady seduced by the domestic idyll of her society and apparently controlled by her husband Helmer. She pretends to be a silly child but secretly works behind his back to pay off a loan and support their family. Before a Christmas party, a maid finds Nora's old dancing dress, representing the skin of the swan maiden.[14] In a crisis, Helmer reveals himself as petty, selfish, and concerned only with maintaining the appearance of social respectability, so Nora abruptly decides to leave him and her children. The tensions that run through the swan maiden tale build through scenes of densely written dialogue to a finale, as Helmer, still hoping that Nora will change her mind, is emotionally shattered by the sound of a slamming door. The theme of divorce was still taboo in the final quarter of the 19th century, and audiences were both shocked and elated to see the hypocrisies of middle-class society so ruthlessly exposed.

In the spirit of archaic folktales, Ibsen tells the story but refuses to take sides. In the middle to late 20th century, many feminists took the play as a manifesto of rebellion against social hypocrisy. Yet one may wonder if Nora is far less changed at the end of the play than many observers thought. Just before leaving him, Nora tells her husband, "There has to be absolute freedom for us both." But freedom, like domestic bliss, is never absolute. Nora's romantic veneration of marriage is replaced by an equally romantic veneration of liberty, yet her refusal to confront hard realities has remained.

The swan maiden tale has, from its inception to the present, remained the story of the troubled love between mother nature and father culture. Their children may feel pressured to take sides and still love them both. Today scientific discoveries such as mapping the genome seem to challenge traditional distinctions including those among human beings, animals, and plants, since they uncover a structural unity in all forms of life. Artificial intelligence, meanwhile, is breaking down the differentiation between mind and matter. And yet the opposition between nature and culture is probably intensifying. Many people today have hardly any contact with the natural world apart from pets and the trees along city streets, plus an ever-diminishing number of common birds.

The word "Nature" originally comes from the Latin *nasci*, meaning "to be born," so a feminine gender lies not simply in the grammar of romance languages but in its very origin. Nature is no longer primarily a place, since human beings and their technologies now penetrate the remotest parts of the globe.[15] Yet, elusive as definitions may be, nature is not a phantom to be banished by some sophisticated new means of analysis. It remains the Other to humanity's collective self, all things beyond the reach of human beings, human concepts, and human technologies. It is as much an experience as a concept, something that perhaps may be best grasped through stories. Nature, a bit like the Judeo-Christian God, has now withdrawn, yet the longing for her remains. The tale of the swan maiden has mirrored changes in the relationship between human beings and the natural world at least since the start of civilization, and, in the midst of an almost unprecedented environmental crisis, may now be more pertinent than ever before.

Notes

1. William Butler Yeats, "The White Birds," in *The Poems, a New Edition*, ed. Richard J. Finneran (New York: Macmillan, 1983), 41–42.

2. Boria Sax, *The Serpent and the Swan: Animal Brides in Folklore and Literature* (Knoxville: McDonald and Woodward/University of Tennessee Press, 1998), 221.

3. For the standard classification of tales used by folklorists, see Aanti Aarne and Stith Thompson, *The Types of Folktale: A Classification and Bibliography* (Helsinki: Academia Scientiarum Fennica, 1964).

4. Charles Perrault, "Cinderella," in *The Classic Fairy Tales*, ed. Iona Opie and Peter Opie (New York: Oxford University Press, 1974), 152–166.

5. Alan L. Miller, "The Swan Maiden Revisited: Religious Significance of 'Divine-Wife' Folktales with Special Reference to Japan," *Asian Folklore Studies* 46 (1987): 81.

6. A. T. Hatto, "The Swan Maidens: A Tale of North Eurasian Origins," *Bulletin of the School of Oriental and African Studies* 24 (1961): 326–352.

7. Barbara Fass Levy, *In Search of the Swan Maiden: A Narrative on Folklore and Gender* (New York: New York University Press, 1994), 33–63.

8. Sax, *Serpent and the Swan*, 57–76.

9. *The Epic of Gilgamesh*, trans. N. K. Sandars (New York: Penguin, 1970), 114.

10. Diane Wolkstein and Samuel Noah Kramer, *Inanna, Queen of Heaven and Earth: Her Stories and Hymns from Sumer* (New York: Harper and Row, 1983), 151, 189.

11. Ibid., 11–90, 136–173.

12. For the development of the Melusine cycle in both folklore and literature, see Sax, *Serpent and the Swan*.

13. Henrik Ibsen, "A Doll House," trans. Rolf Fjelde, in *The Complete Major Prose Plays* (New York: Penguin, 1978), 119–196.

14. Levy, *In Search of the Swan Maiden*, 294–302.

15. Bill McKibben, *The End of Nature* (New York: Random House, 1989).

Bibliography

Aarne, Aanti, and Stith Thompson. *The Types of Folktale: A Classification and Bibliography.* Helsinki: Academia Scientiarum Fennica, 1964.

The Epic of Gilgamesh. Trans. N. K. Sandars. New York: Penguin, 1970.

Hatto, A. T. "The Swan Maidens: A Tale of North Eurasian Origins." *Bulletin of the School of Oriental and African Studies* 24 (1961): 326–352.

Ibsen, Henrik. "A Doll House." In *The Complete Major Prose Plays*, trans. Rolf Fjelde, 119–196. New York: Penguin, 1978.

Levy, Barbara Fass. *In Search of the Swan Maiden: A Narrative on Folklore and Gender.* New York: New York University Press, 1994.

McKibben, Bill. *The End of Nature.* New York: Random House, 1989.

Miller, Alan L. "The Swan Maiden Revisited: Religious Significance of 'Divine-Wife' Folktales with Special Reference to Japan." *Asian Folklore Studies* 46 (1987): 81.

Perrault, Charles. "Cinderella." In *The Classic Fairy Tales*, ed. Iona Opie and Peter Opie, 152–166. New York: Oxford University Press, 1974.

Sax, Boria. *The Serpent and the Swan: Animal Brides in Folklore and Literature.* Knoxville: McDonald and Woodward/University of Tennessee Press, 1998.

Wolkstein, Diane, and Samuel Noah Kramer, *Inanna, Queen of Heaven and Earth: Her Stories and Hymns from Sumer.* New York: Harper and Row, 1983.

Yeats, William Butler. *The Poems, a New Edition.* Edited by Richard J. Finneran. New York: Macmillan, 1983.

14

A Walk with Berehinia: Goddess of Ukraine and Russia

Mary B. Kelly

"An outstanding young girl was selected to be the Perehinia [Berehinia]. She was wrapped in red scarves and led around the village. The villagers would walk behind her and softly sing or talk to her. In her upraised arms the Perehinia carried wooden spoons with which she made various movements . . . a wreath of flowers was placed on her head." The curator of the Ukrainian Museum in New York, Lubow Wolynetz, noted that though this cult had otherwise been all but forgotten, the custom of leading Perehinia (an alternative spelling for the goddess Berehinia) remained an old harvest ritual until the early 20th century, documented by ethnographers.[1] Thus, the name of the oldest goddess in the Ukrainian/Russian pantheon was remembered in 1920s Ukraine and was connected with both ritual and textiles.

The Goddess in Prehistory

In the lands that border the Black Sea coasts, and along the rivers that run toward the White and Baltic seas, female deities have frequently been represented on cloth and overwhelmingly associated with ritual and cult activities. In this black earth area where seeds need no fertilizer to ripen, the goddesses have stood for fertility of both the grain crops and of human births. Prior to the arrival of the Slavs, Neolithic settlements

Figure 14.1 The Russian spring goddess, Berehinia, is still depicted in ornate cross-stitch embroideries in Slavic countries. (Copyright Hrana Janto.)

existed at Tripiliye, south of Kiev. Here, small clay shrines showed interiors that included ovens for baking the sacred grain into ritual bread, looms for creating ritual textiles, a horned throne for the priestess and an altar on which clay statuettes female deities were set up. On some, actual wheat grains were impressed into their bodies. On others, the ancient fertile field ideogram—a diamond divided in four parts with a round "seed" or dot in each—was incised on their pregnant abdomens. Thus, even at this early date, goddesses represented the double blessing of fertility for the fields and fertility for families. On the torsos of other deities, a simple tree of life, also a fertility symbol, was incised from neck to navel.

The Tripiliyan population at this time "lived in large matriarchal villages united by a woman (mother, grandmother, ancestress)." The representations of their deities show mostly females, adorned with headdresses, necklaces, and tattoos. Representing the mother/ancestress and her gift of fertility, they stood in each home on a raised platform near the oven.[2] Thus goddess reverence goes back a long way in this area and "whether one chooses to accept the primacy of Goddess worship and matriarchal rule or not, one thing is clear; among ancient ritual artifacts . . . the female form predominates," comments Ukrainian scholar Natalie Moyle.[3]

In this land of rich harvests, grain fields were the first sight many Asian migrants saw of settled agriculture. Over the centuries, tribes moving west gave up their nomadic ways and learned to plow and reap. The first to do this were Scythians, arriving from the mountains of the Altai and Siberia in the seventh century BCE. Sarmatians arrived in the fourth century, and as the Migration Period began in earnest, these lands were flooded with new Asian migrants. Slavs living along the rivers that flowed into the Black Sea are first mentioned in Greek sources in the first century, and it is soon after Berehinia's first historical appearance.

Naming Berehinia

In the first mention of this deity, the sixth-century Byzantine historian Procopius gave an account in Greek of Slavs who worshiped trees and female spirits of the lake and riverbanks called "Beregini." In a Greek lexicon of gods and goddesses who were supposed to be taboo for Christians, whose dogma held that all pagan deities were evil, the god Perun is mentioned as one to avoid as well as "the Berehinia." This work was translated into Russian in the 12th century. One might therefore deduce that the goddess still had active influence in cult practice 600 years later, although by then the Slavs were nominally Christian. Roman Jacobson translates the goddess's name as Perehinia and sees her as the female counterpart to Perun. The names come from words for oak trees, whose followers were termed *perehynyi* ("those who worshiped oaks").[4]

Berehinia, the oldest named goddess of Ukrainians and later Russians, was known as Bogina Berehinia ("goddess Berehinia"). In Russia, where she became a fertility deity connected with water, her name comes from *bereg* ("riverbank"). Her name in Ukrainian may be connected to *berech* ("to protect"), and she is considered a protective goddess. In Ukraine until the 19th century, Berehynia represented both the fertility of agricultural harvests and the protection and continuance of the family clan.

In later centuries Russians used different names for her two aspects. As mother of many children, she was called Rozhanitza, the birth goddess, while as goddess of agricultural fertility she was the grain mother, Mokosh. The image of Rozhanitza, with a large deer-headed crown and outspread legs from which a stylized child emerges, derives from the Deer Mother of the Siberian Ugrians (see Kathryn Henderson's chapter in this volume), memorialized on Paleolithic "deer stones."[5] As such, she is probably the oldest image from a hunting culture before the advent of agriculture. Mokosh, the grain goddess, arose with Neolithic deities in

Tripilian times but was not named until much later by Russians. Often associated in the 19th century with riverbanks, mists, and water in general, Berehinia was demoted to the status of a less powerful *rusalka*, a kind of female soul who lived in trees or in water. In this guise, she was depicted on 19th-century wooden houses in the Nizhni Novgorod area, carved on lintels and windowsills as a single or double-tailed mermaid. An example found at the Folk Art Museum in Moscow displays a central motif, the Berehinia mermaid with a double tail. The carving over the window is compelling. Berehinia's intense and searching eyes gaze hypnotically at the viewer. This is intentional, according to Victor M. Vasilenko. "The girl who looked from this window would incarnate the Berehinia and become for a moment, the goddess," he commented.[6]

By the 10th century, Slavs had established Kiev in Ukraine as their capital. Its importance was heightened by trade routes, one on land, the other by rivers that crossed at the city center and extended southwards as far as Byzantium and the Caspian Sea, and to the White and Baltic seas to the north. Trade with Byzantium initiated the Christianization of Slavs, under Princess Olha (Olga/Helga), later canonized as St. Olga. These efforts came to a halt as the Tatar invasions from the east laid waste to much of Ukraine, and from that time, the region was dominated by Polish/Lithuanian interests as well as local Hetmen who continued looting until the 19th and 20th centuries, when the Soviets took over.

But much precious material survived, and it was from Kiev State Museum of Art that Vasilenko pointed out sixth-century examples of bronze fibulae on which Berehinia is depicted. The deity is holding birds, whose beaks seem to be "whispering to her in her ears," as Vasilenko explained.[7] Other fibulae depicted her with water creatures, such as ducks, snakes, and frogs. Invariably the fibulae had the goddess's figure at one end with bird symbols and that of a water creature (dragon, snake head, and so on) at the other. Both symbols functioned as good luck motifs, not symbols of evil. Boris Rybakov states that from the earliest times, snakes were depicted as bearers of good, and protectors of everything valuable.[8] This combination bird/snake repeats on the iconography of Russian/ Ukrainian embroidered ritual towels, so numerous in the textile collections of Kiev and other Ukrainian cities, as well as those in Russia from the 18th and 19th centuries.

Berehinia and Ritual Cloth

The goddess Berehinia was frequently depicted on ritual cloths. Whether in Russia or Ukraine, these long woven or embroidered linen towels, decorated at each end, had a vital part in rituals of both rites of the seasons and rites of passage. Decorated with symbols of sun, tree, and birds, their central and most prominent motif was a large Berehinia with upraised arms. Her figure and the accompanying fertility symbols were thought necessary for the growth and development of the fields, the flocks, and of the family.

One of the first collectors of ritual cloth in Russia, Natalia Shabelsky, found them being made on her estates by peasants in the 1850s and began to study and collect them. She also asked questions about them and ultimately established schools for embroidery in Russia. Her huge collections of textiles and other folk objects are now in Russian museums, as well as some in America. When Shabelsky's daughters published material about the ritual cloths in 1910, they included the following comments:

> In addition to their ordinary use, the towels were still used as in the most ancient times, as accessories to religious cults for solemn ceremonies and family holidays. They served also to decorate the temples of the idols, they hung them in the guise of sacrifices on sacred trees.[9]

Thus, it becomes evident that the worship of trees mentioned in the earliest references to Berehinia was still a powerful force for belief in the 19th century when ritual cloths were being made and used outdoors. Shabelsky thought that Russian embroidery patterns dated from remotest times, and it was in large part thanks to the ingenious work of women that these symbols had been preserved. Each ornament has a particular significance and its special purpose, somewhat erased and lost with time, but with the forms still preserved through tradition. It was clear that Shabelsky was collecting specific pieces, ones that related to fertility rituals such as spring plowing, cult worship, and those with motifs relating to women and their work. Without her pioneering efforts, most of this material would not be preserved, exhibited, or understood.

The ritual cloths were also used in each home. One need only open a large marriage chest to see beautiful specimens of the embroideries of the women of the house and of the earlier generations. Here, in an array of color and meaning, were the clothing and textiles for all the special occasions of the woman's life: white linen shirts made for the first day of the haying season, shifts embroidered with fertility designs all around the hems, wrists, and neck were ready for the day of marriage. Many ritual towels were six feet long, embroidered on each edge and carefully folded until the day they would be used to ritually bind a couple in marriage, to wrap the trees in spring, or to decorate graves on the day of memory. They were hung on beams overhead for the woman to pull on when she was in labor and later swaddled her baby. Long ritual cloths overhung every icon; on them the pagan goddess looked out, protecting the worshiper who venerated the icon. Bed hangings also had rows of protective goddesses along their edges, to keep harm from the sleepers. These ritual fabrics would follow the woman throughout her life, each piece marked with time-honored symbols. At her death, her shroud was ready in the chest, which also stored the work of other female family members. A ritual towel was tied to her grave.

The long cloths show the rites of the seasons: Berehinia holding birds as she welcomes the sun in the spring; the goddess, her hands upraised, overseeing the Midsummer Night festivities and fires; the mother goddess giving birth to children as the harvests ripen and winter returns. Lubow Wolynetz observes, "The ritual cloth was used as a sacred item, a talisman or an amulet, in all important rituals connected with life, marriage and death. Although customs and traditions varied according to region, *rushnyky* performed a ritual function in all of them.[10]

A Secret Language?

To know more about the Berehinia image, attention must be paid to textiles, which formed women's way of writing. Through most of the time when the ritual textiles were being made, most women and many men were illiterate. Thus most written references were recorded by literate men, sometimes in languages other than Russian/Ukrainian, far away from where they were used. This was made clear by Raisa Zaharchuk-Chuhai at the Ethnographic Museum in Lviv, Ukraine. When looking at Bukovinian embroideries, she pointed out that fabric had a spiritual function as a talisman. Cloth became a protective device; each mother made cloth to protect her children and her family.

It was also a remembrance of tradition, a kind of history. The fabric record told the woman's point of view, her view of the universe, her version of history, and her philosophy. The decorated fabric was thus a kind of ancient language. It communicated ideas in visual terms that could be read and understood by others. Of course, women in folk cultures had different ways to communicate. They used words to speak or sing. But they could also communicate by symbols on their cloth. This was by no means unique to the region, as many women throughout the north of Asia and Europe echoed these ideas. So the fabrics bearing the many images of Berehinia embodied the very essence of culture, heritage, and the history of women, their remembrance of things long ago and their hopes for future blessing. "The embroidery is a beautiful blend of the material and spiritual culture of the people. It truly carries a spiritual function," Zaharchuk-Chuhai concluded.[11]

Elements of Pre-Christian Worship in 19th-Century Folk Belief

Before the advent of Christianity in the 10th century, each tribal group in Central Europe worshiped its own gods and goddesses. Those of Balto-Slavic origin worshiped Perun (god of oak trees and thunder), the goddess Berehinia, and minor deities of the sun, the forests, and water. Rites were conducted in small outdoor temples with priests officiating. Once Christianity was firmly established by the aristocracy, "higher" paganism was rooted out in the upper classes, but the lower mythologies and deities "have been preserved to our own time."[12] This situation is referred to as "double faith."

In Ukraine, this "double faith" was carried out with the help of family cults and clans. At seasonal festivals, images made of straw, wood, or branches were dressed in human garb and carried in processions, marking the spring planting, the harvesting of grain, and the conjuring for the future in the new year. In some, as mentioned earlier, a living girl personified the deities honored. Many rites were family-based, organized by the head of the house or by groups of women or young girls. Larger community activities were held in connection with agricultural work. In spring, the Rusalii festival welcomed the sun; the summer wheat harvests at midsummer in June featured the Kupalo rites. Walking with Berehinia was the feature of the completion of the harvest; Kolaida on Christmas Eve honored the ancestors and looked to the spirits to predict good harvests of the coming year.

Berehinia on Ukrainian Textiles and Folk Art

Like Ukrainian symbols, symbols on 19th-century cloth from both Russia and Ukraine tend to be much more abstract and geometric; they were used for both protection and to promote fertility. This is particularly true of the long red and white ritual towels from the northern area of Krolevets. Woven in successive bands, each tells the story of the arrival of the sun, the growth of the sacred tree, and at the center is the Berehinia, with her upraised arms. Wolynetz describes them thus:

> One of the most prominent ornaments on the ritual cloths from Krolevets was the image of the woman goddess or the mother goddess of earth, Berehinia. Berehinia is the goddess of wealth, harvest and fertility . . . there are ritual cloths that show a series of pictures of Berehinia; one figure overlapping the other.[13]

On ritual cloths she is portrayed with her arms upraised. She usually holds two flowers on which roosters or other birds perch. Sometimes Berehinia is shown with three flowers: two in her hands and one above her head. Other examples include those on which large suns fill the upper border, Berehinia is shown in the center, and sheaves of wheat line the lower border. All these symbols reinforce each other and create a very powerful effect in strong red and white. The towels are still being made today and can be collected in markets in Ukraine.

Also contemporary and still being made today are decorated eggs, famous throughout the world for their brilliance and detail. Ukrainian women make them each Easter with dyes and wax, in ritual silence, using traditional designs. One design is the Berehinia, a red egg on which the goddess, with large crowned head and upraised arms, spreads her legs wide in the birth position. This archaic figure is echoed occasionally on embroideries. On Bukovinan embroidery from southern Ukraine, the ancient frog-like Berehinia is shown in multicolored embroidery enhanced with gold thread. On other samples, the goddess spreads her legs to reveal her small daughter inside her womb-like skirt. This Berehinia has large claw-like feet. These archaic designs, in the collections of the Ethnographic Museum in Lviv, are examples of the finest embroidery techniques— meticulous, highly colored, and outlined in black and gold to make them shine.

From the western Carpathian mountains of Ukraine come the geometric embroideries of the Hutzuls. Long separated from the lowlands of Ukraine by distance, this tribe from the high mountains close to the Romanian border retains its distinctive motifs, color ways, and dress. During Soviet times nearby lowland peoples were prohibited from wearing traditional folk dress. Here, in addition to the traditional red, black, and white embroidery, women weave the archaic front and back aprons and knit socks in orange and green. They wear folk dress every day but for festive occasions they add the *vinok*, a sparkling gold headdress that makes them look sun-headed.

Grommets, pompoms, and colorful embroidery decorate their sheepskin vests, which also show the mother goddess and her daughter with sun-like headdresses in distinctive leather appliqué.

Besides fertility, Berehinia has a protective function. Sheila Paine remarks about these images that in the heartland of Russia and Ukraine the ritual embroideries were retained until early in this century; their pagan origins are clear, both in their uses and in their motifs. She further notes that the Russian ceremonial towels, "hung at the crossroads and on birch trees, are decorated with archaic motifs, the most common of which is the goddess, arms upraised in supplication and often with huge hands to avert evil."[14] Ever conscious of their amuletic properties, she points out that these same motifs on Ukrainian towels called *rushnyky* also hung around icons or on the walls of houses to fend off evil. Small rows of these upraised-hand figures are used around the neck opening, the sleeve openings, and the hem, preventing evil from attacking the body. Similarly, they line the sides of ritual cloth, their zigzag skirts creating a barrier to destructive forces. A Hutzul shift, purchased in the village of Kosmach, has such motifs as do socks zigzagged around the ankles.

Lubow Wolynetz, herself a Hutzul, has written about the conservation of the symbols, saying that many of the individual motifs are ancient symbols, magical signs dating back as far as the Neolithic Age and primeval humanity's language and writing. "Preservation of these ancient motifs to the present time in Hutzul embroidery, textiles, wood and *pysanky* (eggs) points to the deeply intuitive perceptions the Hutzuls had of these items and the necessity of guarding them," she writes.[15]

Traveling throughout the United States and Canada to see Ukrainian collections brought here by immigrants, and speaking with egg decorators and embroiderers, it is possible to hear these symbols still referred to by their ancient names. While in Russia it is rare for researchers to identify them this way, using instead the words Mother or Maiden to describe the motifs, in Ukraine and in North America not only the learned but also the ordinary people identify "the Berehinia" quite readily.

Berehinia in Russia

When Ukraine and Russia separated and Ukraine became "Little Russia," each developed separate ways of creating folk art and the image of female deity. The attributes of the Russian Berehinia were also separated: those connected with crop fertility were given the name Mokosh, while the fertility of humans became the province of Rozhanitza. Soviet and Russian researchers in the last century began to examine these motifs in folk embroidery, to classify them and to explain their meaning. Ethnographers Gorotzov and Rybakov looked at material in cultural contexts while textile specialists Boguslavskaia and Maslova accumulated valuable data on techniques and materials. Their theories helped to explain the meaning of the motifs. Other researchers, such as Kalmykova, linked the motifs to various rituals of folk culture.

Boris Rybakov classified the names and attributes of the various goddesses known in Russia.[16] In his view, Rozhanitza was the most important goddess in the Paleolithic period; her image was associated with hunting, the deer, and childbearing. She is usually shown horned, between two deer, and in the birth position. Mokosh arose in the Neolithic period, when agricultural fertility was paramount and is shown with upraised hands, trees of life, and grain sheaves. Berehinia was associated with spring rituals, water signs, and birds.

These deities were honored at seasonal festivals throughout the year and, since Russia is such a large and varied place, this chapter will only touch on them briefly. Berehinia retained her place as the spring goddess. She is shown on ritual cloth facing forward, her hands upraised. Often crowned with flowers, she holds flowers, birds, or small sprouting branches in her hands. As fertility bringer, she may also have branches growing from her body or her skirt.

The early spring ceremonies called for the sun's return, to begin the process of the agricultural year. The goddess is shown holding suns or wearing a sun-like crown, similar to those worn by Hutzul girls. Because in myth the sun was thought to ride across the heavens on a horse or cart, the goddess may also be portrayed in this manner. On Russian ritual cloths, Berehinia rides a double-headed horse, her hands upraised and her head rayed like the sun and embroidered in shining yellow silk. On other cloths made for the spring planting, the goddess stands at the center, holding the reins of two horses on which her daughters ride. Beside her are sprouting seeds and the horses pull plows. Several examples of these embroideries from the Shabelsky collection are in the United States.[17]

To reinforce the idea of fertility, the image of Berehinia is often overlaid with another ancient fertility motif, the tree of life. On Russian embroideries, Berehinia has a tree growing from her head, holds trees, stands between two trees, or has branches growing out of her body. These motifs combine or overlay two powerful symbols, making their doubled power more effective. *Rusallii*, the spring festival, brought girls out into the forests to gather herbs, to conjure their fortunes, and to revitalize themselves. They wove wreaths of flowers and herbs and girded themselves with rye belts, also twisted. The circular and twisting motions encouraged the circular sun to return. As early as the medieval period (11th to 13th century CE), these festivals were held in the center of villages. Young girls at that time wore long sleeves, which whirled around them as they danced, encouraging the sun and fertility. Medieval Russian bracelets, made to hold up these sleeves, were engraved with images of the girls dancing these spiral dances. The festivals varied across Russia, but all had human fertility as well as crop fertility in mind. Ludmila Kalymkova described a springtime ritual in which women brought their fertility to the newly plowed fields, by picking up their skirts and rolling naked in the furrows, thus making the connection between human and crop fertility.[18]

The Rusallii festival, a kind of fertility inducer for crops and people, was held during Trinity week. Originally it had the intent of drawing the rusalkii out of their watery home in order to bring rain and mist to newly growing crops. Lascivious dances (mentioned above) enlivened the participants. On Midsummer Night, a large festive boat decorated with ribbons and flowers and two female figures affixed to the mast was sent downstream as devotees swam in rivers by torchlight. Photographs of these events can be seen in the Russian Museum, St. Petersburg, and in the Russian film *Andrei Rubliev*.

Rusalkii had varied interpretations over time, many created by Christian writers who wished to discourage these festivities. They were variously described as dead ancestresses, women who died in childbirth, or wanton women—all negative portrayals. They were supposed to live in water, or in trees, attacking men in particular from these spots.[19] Berehinia during this season was often interchanged with the Rusalkii. In stories told to Professor Vasilenko in the 1930s, Berehinia lives in the water. "Don't swim in there, women told him pointing to the local swimming hole; Berehinia lives in there." But once the Rusalkii had passed from the water to the fields and had fertilized the grain, which began to sprout, it was safe to go swimming again.[20]

The festival of the ripened grain, usually in June, was Kupalo. Named for John the Baptist, whose religious feast comes at midsummer, the festivities encouraged human as well as crop fertility as celebrants jumped over bonfires, sent wreaths and a straw doll representing the goddess downstream, swam and slept in the woods all night. On the embroideries, the goddess of harvests, Mokosh, is shown with raised arms, holding up cups for offerings while sheaves of grain are depicted between them. In the lowered-arm position, she guards the crop. Beside her is a square-shaped fire symbol, with flames shooting out from it. These fires had been kindled from earlier times, not only in Russia but throughout Western Europe. Jumping over the fire was a way of purifying humans, just as the smoke purified the animals that were being taken to mountain pastures for the summer. On other embroideries, the "Ivan Kupala symbol," a stylized human figure with upraised arms and outspread legs, can be seen within the skirts of a large goddess figure or separately set up between trellises and flares. The motif is similar to the Berehynia motif on Ukrainian eggs.

This early harvest of first grain had been planted the fall before. It was followed by later harvests at which an image of Berehynia headed processions into the fields as the reaping began. She may have personified the grain goddesses. These large dolls, made from the final sheaves of wheat, were brought indoors and saved as seed for the following year. It was thought that the vital essence of the field became concentrated as the grain was cut, and that this last sheaf held the most potent seeds.

As winter neared, it was time for the Kolaida festival, usually held on Christmas Eve or between Christmas and New Year. People looked forward to the new agricultural year, foretold the future of family members, welcomed ancestors, and honored Rozhanitza, whose figure represented them. This motif, shown on cloth, has large deer horns, as is appropriate for a mother of the world. Rybakov recounts the Siberian myth of the mother deer and her daughter, the pole stars who created humans and deer to feed them in Paleolithic times.[21] Rozhanitza, with upraised arms and outspread legs, shows a tiny child emerging from her body or has two children in her outspread arms. As she is the embodiment of human fertility, it is appropriate that her feast be celebrated around Christmas, as is the birth of the Christian deity.

Contemporary Berehinia Views, Images and Rituals

Since Ukrainian independence in 1991, the goddess Berehynia has become closely identified with the national spirit, the guardian of the nation and the "hearth mother" of Ukrainians. With roots in the 1980s works of several Ukrainian writers, today Berehynia has a place in the national consciousness, feminism, and neopaganism. Indeed, in 2001 a large column with Berehynia at the top was proclaimed protector of Kiev and was installed on Independence Square (formerly the place of the Lenin monument) in the center of the city.

Berehynia's image has also been a source of inspiration to artists in the United States and in Ukraine. Contemporary painters, sculptors, and weavers find pleasure in repeating and recreating her figure in their work. In Kiev, S. G. Nechiporenko has woven more than 100 ritual cloths with this image, shown in his recent book, *My Berehynias*.[22] In the United States Ohio artist Aka Peremya makes sculpture depicting Berehynia, whom she sees as the fertile mother and protectress. Folk artists in Lviv, Ukraine, keep alive the practice of making decorated Easter eggs with Berehynia's image, as has been done for many hundreds of years. However, as all folk artists, they look for ways to create variants of the motif, showing solar crowns and wheat sheaves in their hands. An entire museum, the Pysanka Museum, is devoted to these productions in Kolomyia, Ukraine.

Museum exhibitions have featured both the Russian and Ukrainian Berehinia figures. In 1987 the Roberson Museum in Binghamton, New York, mounted the show *Goddesses and Their Offspring*, featuring primarily Russian ritual cloths. In 2007 the Ukrainian Museum in New York displayed Berehynia figures on eggs and textiles in *The Tree of Life, the Sun, and the Goddess*. In a catalog of the same name, Professor Natalie (Moyle) Kononenko draws attention to the many contemporary rituals where Ukrainian women play major roles. She says, "In addition to the numerous contemporary rituals in which women serve as facilitators of birth, protectors of human plant and animal fecundity, many folk art objects contain goddess images." On ritual eggs, cloths and breads, the goddess is portrayed by women to fulfill "their sacred, creative duties." Folk wisdom is embodied in the figure of the goddess, she says, and provides today an important symbol of "creation, not destruction, that has been honored thru the millennia."[23]

Notes

1. Lubow Wolynetz, "Rushnyky: Ukrainian Ritual Cloths," in *Goddesses and Their Offspring*, ed. Mary Kelly (Binghamton, NY: Roberson Center for the Arts and Sciences, 1986), 38.

2. Y. Pasternak, "The Neolithic Age," in *Ukraine: A Concise Encyclopedia*, ed. Volodymyrs Kubijovyc (Toronto: University of Toronto Press, 1963), 1:532, 534.

3. Natalie K. Moyle, "The Goddess: Prehistoric and Modern," in *Goddesses and Their Offspring*, ed. Mary Kelly (Binghamton, NY: Roberson Center for the Arts and Sciences, 1986), 17.

4. Roman Jacobson, "Contributions to Comparative Mythology," in *Selected Writings* (The Hague: Mouton, 1956), 7:5–22.

5. Esther Jacobson, *The Deer Goddess in Ancient Siberia* (Leiden: Brill, 1993), 27.

6. Victor M. Vasilenko, Folk Art Department, Moscow State University, personal interview, Moscow, March 9, 1982.

7. Victor M. Vasilenko, *Ruskii Prekladnoe Iskusstvo* [Russian Applied Art] (Moscow: Izdatelestvo Iskusstvo, 1977), 25.

8. Boris Rybakov, "Cosmogony and Mythology of the Agriculturalists of the Eneolithic," *Soviet Anthropology and Archeology* 4, no. 2 (1965): 25.

9. V. Sidamon-Eristoff and N. P. Shabelsky, *Antiquities Russe* (Moscow, 1910): 1–2.

10. Wolynetz, "Rushnyky," 37.

11. Raisa Zaharchuk-Chuhai, Ethnographic Museum in Lviv, Ukraine, personal interview, June 27, 1988.

12. V. Petrov, "The Elements of Pre-Christian Religion and the Peoples View of Life," in *Ukraine*, ed. Kubijovyc, 342.

13. Wolynetz, "Rushnyky," 12.

14. Sheila Paine, *Embroidered Textiles* (New York: Rizzoli, 1990), 68.

15. Lubow Wolynetz, *The Changeless Carpathians* (New York: The Ukrainian Museum, 1995), 8.

16. Boris Rybakov, *Iazychestvo Drevnikh Slavian* [Old Slavic Paganism] (Moscow: Izadatelestvo Nauka, 1981), 471–527.

17. Cleveland Museum of Art #31.123, #31.121; the Boston Museum of Art and the Brooklyn Museum also have holdings of this material.

18. Ludmila Kalymkova, curator at the State Art Museum at Zagorsk, Russia, personal interview, May 27, 1988.

19. Boris Rybakov, Archeological Institute, Moscow, personal interview, February 25, 1982.

20. Petrov, "Elements of Pre-Christian Religion," 358.

21. Rybakov, "Cosmogony and Mythology," 35.

22. S. G. Nechiporenko, *My Berehynias* (Kiev, 2007).

23. Natalie (Moyle) Kononenko, "Goddess Figures in Ukrainian Art," in *The Tree of Life, the Sun, and the Goddess* (New York: Ukrainian Museum, 2007), 66, 68, 70.

Bibliography

Jacobson, Esther. *The Deer Goddess in Ancient Siberia*. Leiden: Brill, 1993.

Jacobson, Roman. "Contributions to Comparative Mythology." In *Selected Writings*, vol. 7. The Hague: Mouton, 1956.

Kelly, Mary B. *Goddess Embroideries of Eastern Europe*. McLean, NY: Studiobooks, 1989.

Kelly, Mary B. *Goddess Embroideries of the Balkan Lands and Greek Islands*. McLean, NY: Studiobooks. 1999.

Kelly, Mary B. *Goddess Embroideries of the Northlands*. Hilton Head, SC: Studiobooks, 2007.

Kononenko, Natalie (Moyle). "Goddess Figures in Ukrainian Art." In *The Tree of Life, the Sun, and the Goddess*. New York: Ukrainian Museum, 2007.

Moyle, Natalie K. "The Goddess: Prehistoric and Modern." In *Goddesses and Their Offspring*, ed. Mary Kelly, 17–27. Binghamton, NY: Roberson Center for the Arts and Sciences, 1986.

Nechiporenko, S. G. *My Berehynias*. Kiev, 2007.

Paine, Sheila. *Embroidered Textiles*. New York: Rizzoli, 1990.

Pasternak, Y. "The Neolithic Age." In *Ukraine: A Concise Encyclopedia*, ed. Volodymyr Kubijovyc, 1:532–537. Toronto: University of Toronto Press, 1963.

Petrov, V. "The Elements of Pre-Christian Religion and the Peoples View of Life." In *Ukraine: A Concise Encyclopedia*, ed. Volodymyr Kubijovyc, 1:350–361. Toronto: University of Toronto Press, 1963.

Rybakov, Boris. "Cosmogony and Mythology of the Agriculturalists of the Eneolithic." *Soviet Anthropology and Archeology* 4, no. 2 (1965): 16–36.

Rybakov, Boris. *Iazychestvo Drevnikh Slavian* [Old Slavic Paganism]. Moscow: Izadatelestvo Nauka, 1981.

Sidamon-Eristoff, V., and N. P. Shabelsky. *Antiquities Russe*. Moscow, 1910.

Vasilenko, V. M. *Ruskii Prekladnoe Iskusstvo* [Russian Applied Art]. Moscow: Izdatelestvo Iskusstvo, 1977.

Wolynetz, Lubow K. *The Changeless Carpathians*. New York: The Ukrainian Museum, 1995.

Wolynetz, Lubow K. "Rushnyky: Ukrainian Ritual Cloths." In *Goddesses and Their Offspring*, ed. Mary Kelly, 36–43. Binghamton, NY: Roberson Center for the Arts and Sciences, 1986.

15

Sheela na Gig: Dark Goddess of Europe

Starr Goode

Sheela na gigs are mysterious. They engender an obsession not usually present in the study of architectural motifs carved on medieval churches. The debate about their meaning started in the 19th century when the Irish first began to catalog these figures adorning buildings throughout the islands of Ireland and Britain, and it continues to this day. Are the Sheelas incarnations of a devilish evil used to warn against the sins of the flesh, or are they part of the undying legacy of an ancient great goddess? Why should a bald, nude woman with genitals half the size of her body have been so popular in the Middle Ages, and why does she continue to fascinate today?

A Sheela na gig clearly offers up her sex. She tilts her hips forward in a sensual thrust—an open invitation. Yet she emanates menace from the upper half of her body. Often, she may be a fierce hag with withered breasts and a skull of death. Her image embraces a conundrum of opposites. Standing roughly in height from one to two feet, most Sheelas are carved from stone, be it red sandstone, limestone, or gray granite. She squats down, all the better to frame her most quintessential and notorious feature: her private parts, pulled open by her own hands. One almost winces—so fierce, so vigorous is this spreading open of the vulva. There is only one quality that makes a Sheela a Sheela: she must be exposing her genitals. All Sheela na gigs have this display to assert the powers of the female sex. Clearly, the Sheela na gig, who in her time

Figure 15.1 Replica of the Ballylarkin Sheela na gig by Starr Goode and Charles Sherman. (Photo by Starr Goode.)

has been called whore, devil, witch, and goddess, is no ordinary woman. One glance at her exaggerated genitals shows that, literally, she is a female, but figuratively, what concept does she embody?

Historical Overview

The first recorded reference to a Sheela occurs in the 19th century when interest in the ruins of the past spurred the age of the Antiquarians, those precursors to modern archeologists. John O'Donovan, hired to catalogue antiquities in the Irish countryside, writes in his *Ordnance Survey Letters* from 1840 of his encounter in Tipperary with a Sheela na gig on the Kiltinane Church. His Victorian sensibilities are quite undone as he describes a female sculpture "whose attitude and expression conspire to impress the grossest idea of immorality and licentiousness."[1] The man traveled around Ireland for thirteen years in his duties as a surveyor, yet he allotted more time to his comments on this Sheela than to any other single artifact.[2] Repelled though he may have claimed to be, he certainly was mesmerized. Like many others, he could not stop looking.

O'Donovan records the name of the figure as a Sulis Ni Ghee and a few pages later as Sheela ni Gig, words which seem to blend English and Gaelic (see Cheryl Straffon's chapter in this volume). The Irish behind the half-anglicized name is difficult to trace. The exact meaning of her name, like so many of her qualities, is elusive. Possible translations of *Sheela na gig* are "old hag of the breasts" or "old hag on her hunkers" *Sulis* means "hag" or "spiritual woman"; the term also relates to the words "fairy" or "sprite." *Gig* can be interpreted as Irish *Xoch* or *Gob*, "breasts" or "buttocks" or "vulva." The earliest form of the name dates to 1781 when, oddly enough, there was a British navy ship called *Sulis na Gig*, translated as "Irish Female Sprite." In one of the latest books on the Sheelas, scholar Barbara Freitag connects gig with jig (a lively dance) in her discovery of country folk dances known as Sheela na gigs. Certainly, some Sheelas stand on one foot, which can hint at a possible shaman's function, as if they dance between the worlds. The Kiltinan Sheela dances on one foot, echoing the stance of the hag in the Irish tale of the Destruction of Da Derga's Hostel as she delivers her prophecies. In a more contemporary usage, the name Sheila is still employed in Australia as a slightly derogatory slang for a woman.[3]

For centuries the Sheelas appeared on churches and castles as prominent figures, especially in Ireland, becoming increasingly powerful in whatever setting they appeared, until the 17th century when the image lost the power of its official sanction due to the rising tide of Puritanism and the Counter Reformation of the Catholic Church. Artists stopped creating her. At this time, the clergy, acting under "provincial statutes," destroyed Sheelas, often by burning the stones.[4] This destruction of the Sheelas continued into Victorian times. It is impossible to know how many Sheelas once adorned sacred architecture before these stone witch-hunts occurred. The invasion of Ireland by English troops under Elizabeth I and Oliver Cromwell in the late 16th and 17th centuries effectively marked the end of Gaelic Ireland and the era of Sheelas.

Today, the dedicated Sheela seeker can still find her on buildings in Ireland, a land possessing the greatest concentration of Sheelas with over 100 still existing. In Great Britain and Scotland, there are probably fewer than 40, and in France and Spain, where the earlier exhibitionist figures are much smaller and hidden among other church carvings, the numbers are even more difficult to ascertain. To aid a new generation of those interested in scouting for Sheelas, updated lists of locations and maps can be found in Jack Roberts's and Barbara Freitag's books. They expand the first comprehensive taxonomy complied by Edith Guest in

1935 which this author used in her adventures on the trail of the Sheelas beginning in the late 1980s.

Agreements and Disagreements

Several conflicting theories prevail as to the origins and functions of the Sheela na gig. Does she embody the power of the Celtic goddesses, first conjured on pagan soil and connected back to Stone Age female divinities of Old Europe? Or did she originate on the European continent as a decorative figure on medieval Romanesque churches, depicting the sin of lust? Jorgen Andersen, in the first comprehensive study of the subject, sees the Sheela's beginnings as an exhibitionist church motif that later blends with Irish traditions. Art historians Anthony Weir and James Jerman contend that Sheelas function strictly as images of lust and first appear in the 12th century as architectural motifs on Christian churches in northern Europe. Other more recent studies by Joanne McMahon and Jack Roberts, and by Maureen Concannon, hold that the image of the Sheela, rather than being a minatory one, was revered by country folk as a holdover from the earlier Celtic Christian era or an even earlier Celtic pagan period. The Church employed the Sheela figure as a means to convert the rural population; a carving of a familiar female divinity could entice the pagan countryfolk into the Christian churches. Barbara Freitag argues that sculptures were seen as magical birthing stones, representing folk deities and used to help women survive childbirth. Still other scholars like Marija Gimbutas link the Sheelas back to the earliest origins of art and religion, back to Paleolithic and Neolithic Europe.

No written records remain to unravel the mysteries of the Sheelas. No treatise from her time exists on the meaning behind the image, on what religious impulses or ideas inspired their creation. Furthermore, determining the date of many individual Sheela na gigs remains difficult to impossible. Records can reveal when some churches were built, but one cannot always tell if the Sheelas were part of the original construction. All interpretation is speculation, formed by the available evidence but also shaped by the bias of the observer. Many make claims that they cannot adequately back up. With the rise of feminist scholarship deconstructing the entrenched patriarchal concepts, a new analysis of the past shows the Sheelas in a different light. No one knows for sure. However, one can say with certainty that interest in Sheela na gigs continues to grow.

Medieval Theory: Pure Lust

The first dated female exhibitionist figures appear on early 12th-century Romanesque churches in France and Spain, among the fantastical stone carvings on the corbel tables, a ledge of decorative carvings that encircled the outside of the church. Corbels were not so important as to be under the careful scrutiny of the monks supervising the construction of a church, and the stone carvers could let their imaginations run unrestrained, creating a gallery of haunting figures.[5] The Sheelas fit in well with their misshapen neighbors: acrobats, entertainers, misers, clutching couples, tongue pullers, anus showers, and beasts of every kind as well as seductive mermaids whose dangerous sexuality echoes that of the Sheelas.

Earlier studies hold the view that the Sheela figure embodies the evils of the flesh. When Sheela na Gigs were carved out of stone by medieval masons, Christianity ruled Europe. The 12th century was a time of tremendous social upheaval. A complex cultural milieu of social and religious factors contributed to the expansion of the Romanesque school of architecture to the British Isles and Ireland such as the Norman invasions (first of England and a century later of Ireland). The Roman Church began to tighten its political grip with the goal of making Rome the center of religious power. One of its goals was to destroy the independence of the Celtic Christian church in Ireland. Unfortunately, it was also a time of intense misogyny.

The slaughter of witches would soon begin. In Rome it was debated whether women even had souls. There was no doubt, however, that women via Eve brought the downfall of "mankind." And what better way to demonstrate a woman's wickedness than a Sheela na gig? For what is the essence of the Sheela but her femaleness, her big rude vulva, the primal gateway to hell? Hence, some scholars' analysis of her origins believe that the Sheela na gig emerges as part of the religious architecture of the churches along the pilgrim routes and later migrated to the British Isles and Ireland. Born from lust, she embodies lust, the mortal sin of *luxuria*. She is there as a warning example to protect the good folk from eternal damnation. Thus, the Sheela supposedly functioned as a visual image to terrorize an illiterate populace.

Celtic Connection

The question arises: how could the Sheela na gig be purely a medieval figure born on the corbel tables of northern Europe when a body of evidence exists that links the Sheela na gig with pre-Christian Celtic traditions of stone sculptures, as well as goddesses and heroines found in mythic literature?[6] Contemporary scholars have connected the medieval Sheela with these earlier figures found in word and stone. According to this argument, the Irish adapted the Sheela na gig from earlier images, and she became the latest expression of traditions that never died in Ireland.

The Celtic precursors of the Sheela na gig have roots in pagan Ireland. Never occupied by the Romans, the Irish kept their tribal Celtic culture alive well into the Christian era, when pagan beliefs were Christianized rather than condemned. In Ireland, pre-Christian and early Christian carvings survive; these may have been harbingers of the medieval Sheela na gig. These prototypes color the character of the later Irish Sheelas, making them wilder, with a menacing strength. The Irish Sheelas show features such as lean ribs, tattooing, a certain grotesqueness, agonized looks, and headgear.

Some examples of these early Celtic and Celtic-Christian sculptures are found in the environs of Lough Erne in Northern Ireland. An early Christian stone carving called the Bishop's Stone has thick lips (as has the later Irish Sheela from Cavan), and one cheek is marked with a scar or tattoo (a mark echoed in the Kiltinan Sheela). Two similar stone carvings are located in a remote, atmospheric Victorian graveyard on Boa island in Lough Erne. They are pre-Christian figures thought to have been carved by Iron Age Celts.[7] Tattooing appears on the face of the bearded figure, a double-faced Janus; similar tattooing is found on the later Irish Sheelas such as the Fethard, Killinaboy, and Moate Sheelas, to name a few. The other sculpture, known as the Lustymore Idol, was transplanted from a nearby island. It is often described as a male figure; however, on close examination, one can see a faint inverted V that marks a vulva. Undeniable is the posture of her arms: in the characteristic Sheela gesture, they reach down toward the abdomen/genital area.

The Lustymore Idol, though carved in stone, is reminiscent of a much earlier female figure dating ca. 725 to 525 BCE, rendered in wood: the Ballachulish Statue. This figure gestures in a Sheela-like manner, placing both hands on her abdomen; she also has a pronounced, swollen pubic area. She was discovered in western Scotland, a Celtic region where three Sheelas were later found.[8] A similar wooden female figure is housed in the Colchester Castle Museum in eastern England, the Dagenham "Idol." According to the museum inscription by the figure, she is the second oldest human depiction in the country, found twenty feet down in an area of marsh at Dagenham on the north bank of the Thames.

The earliest Celtic prototype of the Irish Sheela na gig was discovered in an impressive Celtic grave dating to the fourth century BCE in Reinheim, Germany.[9] Carved on the terminal of a gold armlet, the female figure displays her genitalia in a fashion characteristic of the Sheela na gig, with her hands pulling open her labia. These images reveal a Celtic tradition of nude female figures, some of which predate the Romanesque carvings by millennia.

Medieval Mindset on Pagan Soil

It took the Roman Church centuries of concentrated warfare to conquer the traditions of pagan Europe. The artistic soil of Europe was pagan first. Taking the longest view, Christianity is a veneer, the last coat of varnish on the surface of a religious history that began in the Paleolithic period with the worship of a primal mother goddess. The mystery of the medieval Sheela na gig is not that she exists, but that she was created at the very time when the last vestiges of the Old Religion were being stamped out.[10] And not only did the Sheela burst forth in the midst of the misogyny of Catholic Europe but she did so in a startling, bold form. As far removed from the gentle, submissive ideal of the Virgin Mary as can be imagined, the Sheela is aggressive and sexual. She is not asking for permission to exist.

The Sheela na gig certainly excited the imaginations of those Irish artists who combined the medieval female exhibitionist motif with lingering pagan themes.[11] In her they saw the duality of their goddesses who had powers of both creation and destruction, which was conceptualized by the display of the gigantic vulva—an image of creativity and regeneration and the destructive forces mirrored in her hag-like appearance of old age and death. In Ireland the Sheela became a figure of great importance. The Irish Sheelas and later ones in Great Britain and Scotland are fiercer and wilder, more glorious in their display of themselves than their earlier continental sisters found in France and Spain. She was not one of a hundred figures on a corbel table but often the only figure on the building. With all of the rich images of Norman corbel motifs to choose from, the Irish had an affinity for the exhibitionist female. It is she they transformed into the Sheela na gig, selecting an image of aggressive female display to adorn the architecture throughout their country.

Although mainly set on the walls of churches and castles, the Irish Sheela na gig is also carved on towers, holy wells, menhirs (standing stones), and even the funerary monument of a bishop. She is often conspicuously placed by entrances—doors and windows—so that she may give protection and bring good luck through the apotropaic power of the naked vulva. Imagine the Killinaboy Sheela with her legs spread open and placed above the door of the south wall over 800 years ago. One enters the church as one enters through her legs, a threshold of transformation into sacred space.

The vulvas of many Sheelas, such as the Kilsarkin or Castlemanger who are within human reach, bear the evidence of centuries of being rubbed, of having received worshiping caresses because of a belief in the Sheelas' healing powers. Wherever she is placed on a building, be it the quoin (corner) or high on a wall to survey the land before her, she adds strength.[12]

But the Sheela na gig cannot fully be explained as medieval motif or solely from the pagan Celtic tradition or a blending of both; this chapter examines her roots, going back to the classical era and finally going back to the mists of prehistory, back to the first human cultures.

Classical Models

To trace her earliest historical forebears in terms of iconography, function, and spiritual essence, she is comparable to two strong figures found in the classical world of Greece and Rome: Baubo and the Gorgon Medusa.

Baubo plays a brief but transforming role in the story of Demeter and Persephone (see Dolores DeLuise's chapter in this volume). This mythic cycle of separation-then-reunion of mother and daughter was enacted in a secret ritual known as the Eleusisian Mysteries for close to 2000 years. The primeval myth tells of the grief of the grain goddess losing her daughter and the consequent barrenness of the world. It is Baubo, the old servant, who brings Demeter (and thus the neglected dying earth) back to life by making the goddess laugh. How does she accomplish what all the gods of Olympus have failed to do? By lifting her skirts, her *ana-suromai*, for a ceremonial gesture of naked display.[13]

Lest one think the pagan rites of classical Greece are a far cry from the activities of medieval masons carving Sheela na gigs on Christian churches, a connecting link can be found in the writing of the early church fathers. Clement of Alexandria was born ca. 150 CE and was "extremely knowledgeable" about Greek myths. He recorded the legend of Baubo, and there is a "strong likelihood" it survived down through the generations of ecclesiastical writers and monks so that "the tale of Baubo in Christian writings, and the figurines themselves, played a possible part in the creation of the female exhibitionist carvings."[14]

Over seventy years ago, Margaret Murray published an article on "Female Fertility Figures" in which she argued that the medieval Sheela was the descendent of the classical Baubo, a universal archetype that she names the "Personified Yoni." Murray analyzes the era of Egypt in the Roman period where figures of Baubo were found in the women's quarters as well as in women's graves, thus demonstrating the use of the regenerative vulva to the living as well as to the dead. She calls Baubo "an ancient goddess in a new form" and believes her meaning may be reflected in the meaning of the much later Sheela na gig. She then recounts a local tradition with the Sheela on St. Michael's Church in Oxford: "All brides were made to look at the figure on their way to church for the wedding." Murray connects this practice with "the fact that the ancient figures [of Baubo] were found almost exclusively in the rooms . . . of women[, which] seems to show that the use of such figures may have been to rouse and stimulate the sex desires of women.[15]

This woman scholar suggests an interpretation of the sexual qualities of the Sheela quite the opposite of many male scholars, that is, attraction to rather than repulsion from the erotic. Murray puts forth her ideas "as a basis for discussion, for so much of the published work on female psychology is founded on the masculine ideas of what a woman should feel or be."[16]

The second figure in the classical world similar to the Sheela is Medusa. As one of the three Gorgon sisters, Medusa is best known for her ability to turn men to stone. A figure with supernatural powers, she has an ancient lineage that connects her with the earliest roots of goddess culture. The later classical age depicts her as a menacing face with penetrating lethal eyes, open lips with protruding tusks, all framed by a head of writhing snakes. Her face becomes stylized as the Gorgon mask, and in the earliest Greek text, Homer's *Iliad*, she appears on the aegis of Athena: "and on it the Gorgon head of the terrible monster."[17]

Like the Sheela, images of the Gorgon Medusa are also placed on sacred buildings to serve as guardians of the gates. Because of her great apotropaic power, she watches over temple entrances so as to repel evil. In one of the most striking carvings of a full-bodied Medusa, she watches on high from the center of the pediment of an Artemis temple on the isle of Corfu. Yet another Gorgon rules from the pediment of the Temple of Athena on Sicily. Both figures are winged with snake motifs that connect them to Neolithic bird and snake goddesses, and both assume a posture of splayed legs with bent knees, reminiscent of the Sheelas. Patricia Monaghan contends that Medusa "may be one of the most ancient European symbols of women's spiritual abilities."[18] French scholar Jean Claire links Medusa and Baubo as "twin embodiments of female sexual power"; Medusa's face is a vulva while Baubo's vulva is made into a face.[19] To observe the different responses from each gender to this power makes one ponder cultural identities and natural instinct. The spirit of delight visits Demeter in the form of an outburst of pleasurable laughter when Baubo displays her naked femaleness. Yet this same exposed vulva terrorizes male warriors across the centuries from the Greek Bellerophon to the Irish Cúchulainn and causes them to back down in battle.[20] Murray insists on an enduring tradition of women's delight in Baubo and the much later Sheela because "it appears certain that the figures made and still make, an appeal to women's [sexual] nature. This then is the reason for their original use and long survival."[21] One final point: some modern scholars believe that Medusa petrified only males, and they know of no instance when her power is used against a female.[22]

Through the iconic visual metaphors of their female sex, Baubo stimulates pleasure and the return of life, and Medusa's fierceness can destroy threatening forces and thus protect those who need her. The magic power in the act of display began in prehistoric religions and never died; it is an elementary idea whose apotheosis in the classical world was animated in the figures of Baubo and Medusa and continued in time down through the boldness of the Sheela na gig. Baubo and the Gorgon Medusa can be seen as chronological mothers to the Sheela, for all their powers emanate from the transforming energy of female sexuality.

Back to the Beginning: The Dark Goddess of Old Europe

The iconography of the Sheela na gig links back to the earliest archetypes of European worship. Archeological breakthroughs in the last century have revolutionized the vision of the past. The deepest roots of European religion have been unearthed, revealing a great goddess of nature who, in myriad forms, ruled over all cycles of life. Indeed, the Sheela na gig cannot be understood without knowledge of the prehistoric goddess-centered civilization. With her hunched shoulders and hunkered-down posture, the Sheela physically resembles the ancient frog goddess, a hybrid frog-woman whose squatting frog body reveals a prominently marked human vulva. In her functions, the goddess is also a forebear of the powers of the Sheela as death wielder and restorer of life, that is to say, a goddess of death and regeneration.

From Paleolithic engravings of frog-women found in Les Trois Frères cave to 20th-century northern Italy where peasants carved frog votives to be blessed by the priest, the supernatural powers of the frog over life processes have held a place in human consciousness. Throughout Neolithic Europe, the frog goddess has been painted on temple walls, carved out of amber, alabaster, ivory, marble, or green or blue stone.[23] Toad sculptures created in materials from terracotta to bronze have been found in Bronze Age sanctuaries and graves in Greece and Rome.[24] At the temple of Çatal-hüyük in Turkey, archeologists have discovered a shrine dated from the seventh millennium BCE devoted to the frog goddess. Carved in relief on a wall, legs spread wide as if ready to give birth, her belly is marked in concentric red circles—symbols of the whirling life force.[25] Below the floor lay the dead. This goddess holds the promise, a yearning deep in the human heart, that life will come again. Through the magical portal of her vulva, she can take back the dead and birth new life.

In the continuum of life and death, the Sheela's monstrous appearance may tip her more to death imagery, and yet her squatting birth posture and exposed vulva give her a sexuality that points to regeneration. Likewise, according to Gimbutas, the frog and toad "were both funerary and life symbols at the same time."[26] Such enigmas can never fully be explained, but the continuity of the image over the millennia testifies to its mysterious power. The displayed vulva remains the quintessential image of the ever-renewing creative life force and at the same time an image of return as resting place for the dead. Dark goddesses wield the terrible necessity of their destructive forces to clear the space for something new.

With the rise of the Indo-European patriarchal culture, then later the Christian era, the powers of the dark goddess were demonized and forced underground, only to resurface in folktales, myth, and art as the evil witch, the ugly old hag, the Sheela na gig. She cannot be erased completely. She may be driven from the conscious to the storage bank of the unconscious mind where her image can erupt from the deep memory of a medieval mason when he carves a stone over the entrance to a church. The menacing Sheela guards over the threshold, a symbolic as well as literal entrance. Enter here those who dare to pass through her legs. Enter her to gain an altered state of consciousness through the primal forces of life, death, sex. Behind the mask of terror, lies a hope for transformation

The Sheela na gig's epoch lasted over four centuries, the manifestation in a particular form, in a particular time and space of an archetype. She reveals a universal motif of creation and destruction: the displayed vulva. Countless examples of this motif can be found all over the world throughout history. From gravestones in Ecuador to rock carvings in Siberia or Hawaii, or figures sculpted on a wooden door in Africa or over a door in Oceania or on a temple in Katmandu, all testify to the urge to express in image what humans experience in their lives. Looking at Ireland, where hundreds of Sheelas were created by artists with an unbroken connection to their past, one could say the ancient lineage of the Sheela na gig makes her a dark goddess of the West.

In the end, the concrete image remains. Possible interpretations come and go, rise and fall; new ones will surface as the recent books of female scholars testify to. Whatever contradictory meanings may be projected onto her, the image endures: powerful, mysterious, eternal.

Notes

Portions of this chapter are adapted from Starr Goode and Miriam Robbins Dexter, "Sexuality, the Sheela na gigs, and the Goddess in Ancient Ireland," *ReVision* 23, no. 1 (2000): 38–48. Copyright © 2000 Starr Goode and Miriam Robbins Dexter.

1. John O'Donovan, *Ordnance Survey Letters*, Tipperary Ms. (Dublin: Royal Irish Academy, 1840), 150.

2. James O'Connor, *Sheela na gig* (Fethard, County Tipperary: Fethard Historical Society, 1991), 5–7.

3. O'Donovan, *Ordnance Survey Letters*, 152–154; Jorgen Andersen, *The Witch on the Wall* (Copenhagen: Rosenkilde and Bagger, 1977), 22; Eamonn P. Kelly, *Sheela-na-gigs: Origins and Functions* (Dublin: County House, 1996), 5; Jack Roberts, *The Sheela-na-gigs of Britain and Ireland: An Illustrated Guide.* (Skibbereen, West Cork: Key Books Publishing, 1993), 8; O'Connor, *Sheela na gig*, 15; Barbara Freitag, *Sheela-nag-gigs: Unravelling an Enigma* (London: Routledge, 2004), 57; Goode and Dexter, "Sexuality, the Sheela na gigs, and the Goddess in Ancient Ireland," 44.

4. Anthony Weir and James Jerman, *Images of Lust: Sexual Carvings on Medieval Churches* (London: B. T. Batsford, 1986), 14.

5. Andersen, *Witch on the Wall*, 47–48.

6. Goode and Dexter, "Sexuality, the Sheela na gigs, and the Goddess in Ancient Ireland," 38–48.

7. Françoise Henry, *Irish Art in the Early Christian Period* (London: Methuen, 1965), 2.

8. Anne Ross, *Pagan Celtic Britain* (Chicago: Academy Chicago Publishers, 1967), 66.

9. Etienne Rynne, "A Pagan Background for Sheela-na-gigs," in *Figures from the Past: Studies in Figurative Art in Christian Ireland in Honor of Helen M. Roe*, ed. E. Rynne (Dublin: Glendale Press. 1987), 190.

10. Roberts, *Sheela-na-gigs of Britain and Ireland*, 5.

11. Andersen, *Witch on the Wall*, 77.

12. Ibid., 26, 107.

13. Winifred M. Lubell, *The Metamorphosis of Baubo: Myths of Women's Sexual Energy* (Nashville: Vanderbilt University Press, 1994), 17.

14. Weir and Jerman, *Images of Lust*, 111, 113.

15. Margaret. A. Murray, "Female Fertility Figures," *Journal of the Royal Anthropological Institute* 64 (1934): 93–100, and plates IX–XII, 95–99.

16. Ibid., 95.

17. Miriam Robbins Dexter, "The Ferocious and the Erotic: 'Beautiful' Medusa and the Neolithic Bird and Snake," *Journal of Feminist Studies in Religion* (Spring 2010): 2.

18. Lubell, *Metamorphosis of Baubo*, 244.

19. Ibid., 112.

20. Dexter, "The Ferocious and the Erotic," n. 7.

21. Murray, "Female Fertility Figures," 99.

22. Dexter, "The Ferocious and the Erotic," n. 22.

23. Marija Gimbutas, *The Language of the Goddess* (San Francisco: Harper and Row, 1989), 252.

24. Marija Gimbutas, *The Goddesses and Gods of Old Europe, 6500–3500 BC: Myths and Cult Images* (Berkeley: University of California Press, 1982), 177.

25. Ibid., 176.

26. Gimbutas, *Language of the Goddess*, 251.

Bibliography

Andersen, Jorgen. *The Witch on the Wall*. Copenhagen: Rosenkilde and Bagger, 1977.

Battaglia, Frank. "Goddess Religion in the Early British Isles." In *Varia on the Indo-European Past: Papers in Memory of Marija Gimbutas*, ed. M. R. Dexter and E. C. Polomé, 48–82. Journal of Indo-European Studies Monograph 19. Washington, DC: Institute for the Study of Man, 1997.

Brenneman, Walter, and Mary Brenneman. *Crossing the Circle at the Holy Wells of Ireland*. Charlottesville: University of Virginia Press, 1995.

Concannon, Maureen. *The Sacred Whore: Sheela Goddess of the Celts*. Cork, Ireland: The Collins Press, 2004.

Condren, Mary. *The Serpent and the Goddess*. San Francisco: Harper and Row, 1989.

Dexter, Miriam Robbins. "The Ferocious and the Erotic: 'Beautiful' Medusa and the Neolithic Bird and Snake." *Journal of Feminist Studies in Religion* (Spring 2010): 25–41.

Dexter, Miriam Robbins, and Starr Goode. "The Sheela na gigs, Sexuality, and the Goddess in Ancient Ireland." *Irish Journal of Feminist Studies* 4, no. 2 (2002): 50–75.

Erlande-Brandenburg, Alain. *Cathedrals and Castles: Building in the Middle Ages.* New York: Harry M. Abrams, 1993.

Ford, Patrick K. "Celtic Women: The Opposing Sex." *Viator* 19 (1988): 417–438.

Freitag, Barbara. "A New Light on the Sheela-na-gig." *Éire* (Fall/Winter 1998): 33–34.

Freitag, Barbara. *Sheela-nag-gigs: Unravelling an Enigma.* London: Routledge, 2004.

Gimbutas, Marija. *The Civilization of the Goddess: the World of Old Europe.* San Francisco: HarperSanFrancisco, 1991.

Gimbutas, Marija. *The Goddesses and Gods of Old Europe, 6500–3500 BC: Myths and Cult Images.* Berkeley: University of California Press, 1982.

Gimbutas, Marija. *The Language of the Goddess.* San Francisco: Harper and Row, 1989.

Goode, Starr, and Miriam Robbins Dexter. "Sexuality, the Sheela na gigs, and the Goddess in Ancient Ireland." *ReVision* 23, no. 1 (2000) 38–48.

Green, Miranda. *The Gods of the Celts.* Sutton: Gloucester, 1986.

Guest, Edith. "Ballyvourney and Its Sheela-na-gig." *Folklore* 48 (1937): 374–384.

Guest, Edith. "Irish Sheela-na-gigs in 1935." *Journal of the Royal Society of Antiquaries of Ireland* 66 (1936): 107–129.

Henry, Françoise. *Irish Art in the Early Christian Period.* London: Methuen, 1965.

Ilieva, Anna, and Anna Shturbanova. "Some Zoomorphic Images in Bulgarian Women's Ritual Dances in the Context of Old European Symbolism." In *From the Realm of the Ancestors: an Anthology in Honor of Marija Gimbutas,* ed. Joan Marler, 309–321. Manchester, CT: Knowledge, Ideas, and Trends, 1997.

Kelly, Eamonn P. "Sheela-na-gig: A Brief Description of Their Origin and Function." In *Beyond the Pale: Art and Artists at the Edge of Consensus.* Dublin: The Irish Museum of Modern Art, 1994.

Kelly, Eamonn P. *Sheela-na-gigs: Origins and Functions.* Dublin: County House, 1996.

Lamm, Robert C. *The Humanities in Western Culture.* 4th ed. Boston: McGraw-Hill, 2004.

Lippard, Lucy. *Overlay.* New York: Pantheon Books, 1983.

Lubell, Winifred M. *The Metamorphosis of Baubo: Myths of Women's Sexual Energy.* Nashville: Vanderbilt University Press, 1994.

Marler, Joan. "An Archaeological Investigation of the Gorgon." *ReVision* 25, no. 1 (2002): 15–23.

McMahon, Joanne, and Jack Roberts. *The Sheela-na-Gigs of Ireland and Britain: The Divine Hag of the Christian Celts—An Illustrated Guide.* Dublin: Mercier Press, 2000.

Monaghan, Patricia. *O Mother Sun!* Freedom, CA: Crossing Press, 1994.

Murray, Margaret. A. "Female Fertility Figures." *Journal of the Royal Anthropological Institute* 64 (1934): 93–100 and plates IX–XII.

O'Connor, James. *Sheela na gig.* Fethard, County Tipperary: Fethard Historical Society, 1991.

O'Donovan, John. *Ordnance Survey Letters,* Tipperary Ms. Dublin: Royal Irish Academy, 1840.

Roberts, Jack. *An Illustrated Map of the Sheela-na-gigs of Britain and Ireland.* Ireland: Bandia Publishing, 1997.

Roberts, Jack. *The Sheela-na-gigs of Britain and Ireland: An Illustrated Guide.* Skibbereen, West Cork: Key Books Publishing, 1993.

Roche, Richard. *The Norman Invasion of Ireland.* Dublin: Anvil Books, 1995.

Ross, Anne. "The Divine Hag of the Pagan Celts." In *The Witch Figure: Studies in Honor of Katharine Briggs,* ed. V. Newall, 139–164. Boston: Routledge and Kegan, 1973.

Ross, Anne. *Pagan Celtic Britain.* Chicago: Academy Chicago Publishers, 1967.

Rynne, Etienne. "A Pagan Background for Sheela-na-gigs." In *Figures from the Past: Studies in Figurative Art in Christian Ireland in Honor of Helen M. Roe,* ed. E. Rynne, 189–202. Dublin: Glendale Press, 1987.

Weir, Anthony, and James Jerman. *Images of Lust: Sexual Carvings on Medieval Churches.* London: B. T. Batsford, 1986.

16

The Goddess-Turned-Heroine of the Celts: Queen Medb and the Sovereignty of Ireland

Miriam Robbins Dexter

Queen Medb, pronounced and spelled in Anglicized form as Maeve, was a powerful and controversial female figure whose story is told in the medieval Irish epic the *Táin Bó Cúailnge*, the "Cattle Raid of Cooley." Early on in this epic, Queen Medb, the queen of Connacht and the epic version of the sovereignty of Ireland, the power that bestows the kingship, exclaims,[1]

> I demanded a wonderful bridal gift,
> which no woman ever before
> had asked of a man of the men of Ireland,
> that is, a husband without meanness, without jealousy, without fear.[2]

In order to eliminate any ambiguity about what she might mean by "jealousy," Medb elaborated:

> If the man with whom I should be
> were jealous,
> it would not be proper,
> for I was never before
> without a man
> waiting close by
> in the shadow of another.[3]

The Old Irish text dates to the medieval era, a time when, throughout Europe, women were practically the chattel of their husbands.[4] Therefore, it is rather interesting that Medb has a long line of lovers and husbands; in fact, one could not be king of Ireland without marrying her. A sexually autonomous European woman, demanding that her husband be without jealousy, was truly unusual in this era.

Queen Medb, the Honey-Drink, and the Sovereignty of Ireland

The sovereignty of Ireland was bestowed by female figures: in myth she was the goddess Flaith, and in epic she was Queen Medb.

Two Medbs appear in the texts. The one considered above was Medb of Connacht. Medb of Leinster or Medb Lethderg (Medb "Red-Side" or "Half-Red"), daughter of Conan of Cuala, was described in the *Book of Leinster*. It is clear that the two Medbs are regional variants of the same female figure.[5] Both Medb of Connacht and Medb of Leinster have a series of husbands: the Leinster Medb was wife first of Cu Corb, then of Feidlimid Rechtaid, father of Conn Cétchathach, then of his grandson Art, and finally Cormac mac Airt (son of Art).[6] Thus Medb was the wife of several generations of men, none of whom could become king unless he married her.

Queen Medb, in both her Connacht and Leinster forms, was the key to the sovereignty of Ireland. Medb's name comes from the Indo-European word for "honey," and it probably refers to a horse-ritual (confirming sovereignty) involving drunkenness due to an intoxicating honey-drink.[7] Another Indo-European female figure who has a relationship to a horse-ritual and has a honey name is the Indic Madhavī. These female figures were also connected with horses. Toward the end of the *Táin* when the Connacht warriors are losing badly, the hero Fergus—who has slept with Medb—comments, "We followed the rump of a misguiding woman . . . it is the usual thing for a herd led by a mare to be strayed and destroyed."[8] So Medb here is compared to a mare.[9]

Medb was related to Flaith, the goddess whose name, in its primary sense, means "lordship, sovereignty, rule."[10] A further connection of Flaith and Medb may be read into a text bearing upon sovereignty that describes the possession of several provinces, and who possessed them. Connacht, the text reads, was given to Medb before every other province; here Medb is used synonymously with Flaith.[11] In Old Irish sovereignty and intoxicating drinks are connected; the word *flaith* has the secondary meaning of "ale."[12] In fact, a ritual involving an intoxicating drink made of mead may have been connected with the bestowal of sovereignty among many Indo-European cultures; that is, Medb, being associated with both the honey-drink and the mare, is connected with the ritual that appears in India as the *Aśvamedha*, in Rome as the October Equus, and among the Celts as the ritual described by Geraldus Cambrensis.[13] In the original form of this ritual, the king mated with a mare (literally or metaphorically), who represented the goddess of sovereignty. In myth, Medb has intercourse with Fergus mac Roich, "Warrior Hero, son of Great Horse," a stallion-like warrior who has a penis "seven fist-lengths."

If Flaith was both sovereignty and ale, so was Medb. The Leinster Medb was "the daughter of Conan of Cuala,"[14] and it was said that

> [A man] will not be a king over Ireland
> if the ale of Cuala does not come to him.[15]

Thus, Medb is the "ale" of Cuala, without whom a man cannot be king. Eochaid Dala was the husband who preceded Ailill:

> At that time, Ailill, son of Máta,
> son of Sraibgind of the Erna,
> came to Cruachan (Connacht),
> and Ailill was at that time a young child.[16]

Máta was Ailill's mother; this then is a matronymic, indicating mother-descent. Medb's sister Ele was Ailill's grandmother, thus demonstrating the fact that Medb was considerably older than Ailill.[17] When he had attained the proper age for kingship, Ailill had to fight Eochaid Dala "for the kingdom and for his wife."[18] So, it was not her youthful charms that caused Ailill to be eager to take his place in line, although Medb was certainly famous for her sexuality; Ailill was much more interested in Medb's key to the kingship. Again in the *Táin*, Medb made several demands of her husbands—generosity, courage, and lack of jealousy—and her husbands took those demands seriously.

Queen Medb, Laws of Inheritance, and the *Táin*

Although Queen Medb on the mythic level was the goddess of sovereignty, she was viewed on many levels in the *Táin Bó Cúailnge*, a tale in which she and the hero Cú Chulainn were adversaries. The *Táin* is a literary work, and the character of Queen Medb has been artfully constructed, although it still has a mythic character: the *Táin* begins at Samain, the sacred pagan Irish holiday that marks the beginning of the Irish year. It is the time of year when the world of the living and the Otherworld were thought to be closest. In the *Táin*, in fact, not only the boundaries of the worlds but also the boundaries between goddess and mortal overlap; although Medb still represents sovereignty, it is her negative mortal qualities that are thrown into high relief. In this work, the *persona* of Queen Medb has been constructed as a caricature of goddess, queen, and even mother. This, at least in part, is a function of medieval Irish misogyny, found particularly in the *Book of Leinster* version of the *Táin*.[19]

The *Táin* is a saga that celebrates the battle of Queen Medb and her people of Connacht (the western province of Ireland), against King Conchobor and his people of Ulster (the northern province of Ireland), over the Brown Bull of Cooley, the *Donn Cúailnge*. Queen Medb, the fomenter of the cattle-raid, is an example of a woman who is autonomous, due to inherited wealth. In fact, Medb has enough money to wage war on her own, for the text says that

> Medb: she was capable, out of her house(hold),
> of plundering Cooley, a hundredfold."[20]

According to Irish law, if a woman had a greater fortune than her husband, he was called a *fer fognama* ("man of service" or "man without power over a wife"). If a woman had as much property as her husband, she was called a *bē cuitc[h]erns a* ("woman of equal rank"). According to Old Irish law, a daughter could inherit both goods and land ("movables and immoveable") from her father; if there was no male heir; she was then a *banchomarbae* ("female heir").[21] If she had no brothers, she could also inherit from her mother.[22] If two heirs married, their relationship was an equalitarian one. A female heir had veto power over most of her husband's contracts; even women with little or no property had veto powers.[23] In Irish marriage, unlike other Indo-European marriages such as that of *manus* in Rome, a woman was never completely separated from her kin group.[24]

An Intimate Conversation

So, power in a marital relationship could be related to material possessions, and at the beginning of the *Táin* (at least the *Book of Leinster* version), Queen Medb and her husband Ailill Mac Máta are lying in bed, having an intimate conversation. Ailill happens to mention that he thinks Medb is financially far better off now than she was before she married him. Medb bridles at this, communicating in no uncertain terms the extent of her lineage and wealth.

Since she was a propertied woman, Medb was autonomous as well, and she conveys her power in terms of the rules of behavior that she expects of a husband: he must never display jealousy, and he should know that he is just one of a series of husbands, one waiting in the shadow of another.

Although Medb is presented in the *Táin* as exceptionally sexual, her intimate discussion with Ailill—in bed!—is an economic one: they are cataloguing their separate property. After telling Ailill what she expects of a husband, Medb asserts that her fortune is greater than his. Ailill says that it is certain that he has the greater property and goods and precious things. So both bring out their separate property, their pots and pans, jewelry, multihued cloth, sheep and horses and pigs. Finally it is found that Ailill has one more bull than Medb; Ailill has the white-horned Finnbennach, and Medb has no bull its equal. What is she to do?'

A messenger tells Medb that there is indeed a bull the match of Finnbennach; it is to be found in the territory of Cooley, in the province of Ulster. Although at first Medb requests the bull as a loan, that does not work out. And so she decides to take the bull by force.

Medb has a great stake in this cattle-raid, because her whole marriage is at risk: if she is not the equal of Ailill in wealth, she will not be his equal in marriage. So throughout the *Táin*, she does whatever she can to gain the property that will make her at least her husband's equal, and, rather surprisingly, Ailill is committed to help her to obtain the bull and become his equal. Medb needs to induce her men to do single combat with the youthful warrior Cú Chulainn, who, due to a curse on the Ulstermen, is the only man related to the Ulstermen who is capable of fighting. To this end, she offers her own and her daughter's graceful thighs to whatever man of Connacht is willing to fight Cú Chulainn.

Thighs are quite pertinent: land could be inherited through "hand or thigh," that is, it could be inherited, given as a gift, or given in return for labor (service). The Laws of Inheritance state, "It is in the inheritable land of hand or thigh of her mother that she brings that act of taking possession, and there is no son out of it; or it is (on) the land of (his) father and grandfather, and there is not a male heir out of it."[25] Thus, Irish women had the potential of gaining property on which they had labored; they could thereby become economically viable.

The Authors of the *Táin*

To understand Queen Medb, one must ascertain the origin of the material in the *Táin*. Rather than being derived from early Irish oral tradition—that is, employing the pre-Christian tales of Medb and the others in the *Táin*—this epic in its various recensions is a product of late first millennium Irish *literati*: quite patriarchal, often misogynistic monks, well educated in Greco-Roman myth as well as the Judaeo-Christian Bible, and knowledgable about the forms of early Irish poetry and prose as well. These men sculpted tales that appeared to be archaic, but that in reality were filled with the politics of their own time.[26] Medb seems to have been created by these *literati* as an anti-heroine, to demonstrate the woes which would befall a people led by a woman. The vestiges of female power in the *Táin,* left over from the prepatriarchal era, are thus displayed in a degenerated form.

That does not at all subtract from the power of the earlier Irish female; indeed, that power is underlined by the vehemence with which Medb is derided. Nor does it detract from her role as sovereignty goddess, for it is only because of his marriage to Medb that Ailill is king of Connaught in the *Táin*. Further, it is precisely because of the power of the pre-Christian goddesses and the pre-Indo-European goddesses as well as mortal women that the later *literati* felt the need to ridicule them. One does not need to pay such attention to elements of society that are not threatening to the status quo. Thus the tales reflect not only the politics of Christianized medieval Ireland, but the social customs as well. In fact, this saga is most likely the attempt of a Christian composer to discredit not only female power but the power of the early Irish goddesses as well.

Indeed, as Sessle writes, Medb is still the sovereignty goddess; the negative interpretation of Medb "is a direct result of the failures of the men that she interacts with"—that is, Ailill and Fergus fail as kings.[27] When the sovereignty goddess met a true king of Ireland, she underwent a metamorphosis from hag to beautiful woman, as in the tale of "Niall of the Nine Hostages."[28] That is, "the goddess turns into a hag until she is united with her rightful mate."[29] When she is without her proper mate, the true king, the goddess may also undergo a mental or personality change for the worse. The kings of Ireland were required to be perfect, and both Ailill and Fergus were flawed. With flawed kings, the country could not prosper, and the sovereignty goddess reflected this lack of prosperity by becoming "a form of the anti-goddess," and in fact, as we have observed, Medb demonstrates many characteristics of the ancient sovereignty-goddess.

Early on in the *Táin*, Medb had been willing to give the owner of the Brown Bull of Cooley her graceful thighs in return for the loan of the bull. She stated this in front of her husband Ailill, who made no comment. Although the barter did not work out, it is clear that such behavior on the part of Medb was not considered devastating to the marriage or to the fabric of Connacht society. Indeed, throughout the *Táin*, Medb continually promises herself, and even her daughter Finnabair, to anyone willing to fight Cú Chulainn. She offers Finnabair to Nadcranntail, Ferbaeth, and several other warriors in turn—after Ailill gets them drunk. They all agree to fight Cú Chulainn in single combat, with Finnabair urging them on. However, all of them die, so Finnabair doesn't have to sleep with them.

Not only does Medb use her own and her daughter's sexuality as bait for those warriors unfortunate enough to agree to fight Cú Chulainn. During the course of the *Táin*, Ailill suspects that Medb and the hero Fergus are sleeping together. He asks his charioteer Cuillius to spy upon them. Cuillius finds the two, takes Fergus's sword and reports back to Ailill. Instead of exploding in self-righteous anger, Ailill says that it is all right, Medb is just sleeping with Fergus to make sure he helps on the cattle-raid. Then Ailill calls Fergus to play the board-game *fidchell* with him and he is rather sarcastic with him. Medb considers this unacceptable. Ailill should bear no grudge, says Medb.

Although Medb, throughout modern literary critiques of the *Táin*, is described in terms of her legendary "promiscuity," Medb's sexuality serves her desire to procure the Brown Bull of Cooley.[30] Further, the commentary about Medb's sex life, throughout the last millennium or so, is to be taken in the light of the sexual double standard of modern Western society. The Ulster King Conchobor, for example, had the right to sleep with all of the brides-to-be in his land, but some male scholars have seemed to think that Queen Medb as a woman was not supposed to be sexual.

Notwithstanding labels affixed to her behavior, Medb is sexually autonomous. And in this fact she, along with other Irish female figures, is an anomaly in Indo-European myth and saga. The women of other Indo-European cultures—those of the Greek, Roman, and Germanic cultures, for example—were required to be chaste.[31] Why was this chastity necessary to the other Indo-European cultures? The explanation may be found in the economic needs deriving from patrilinear inheritance. Since goods in these cultures were inherited through the paternal line, it was important for a man to be able to ascertain fatherhood. Only by being certain that he was indeed the father could a man feel comfortable about passing his material goods on to his children. In Ireland, where inheritance could take place through the paternal *and* maternal lines, the identity of the father perhaps became less significant.

Thus it was not only Medb's function as sovereignty that rendered her so autonomous, but also her financial power. Other Indo-European female figures also personified sovereignty but none of them were sexually autonomous.[32] In contrast, the Irish personification of sovereignty, Medb, was in complete control of her sexuality. What was the societal difference between the Greek and Indic female figures and the Irish? The answer, again, is financial; it is to be found in the pre-Indo-European background of the Irish, particularly in the matri/patrilinear patterns of Irish inheritance.

The subject of Irish inheritance cannot be clearly understood without taking into account the composition of the various peoples who settled in Ireland. The population of Connacht, the home of Ailill and Medb, included a subject group called in Old Irish the *Cruithin*. These were called the *Picts* (Latin for "the painted ones") by the Romans, and the *Prytani* by the Greeks and, from the time of Julius Caesar on, the *Brytanni* or *Bryttani*. Eoin MacNeill cites both archaeological and lexical evidence for this group, remnants of whom settled particularly in Connacht, and also in Ulster and Leinster.[33] The evidence of Pictish king lists shows that the Picts selected their kings from the *female* royal line.[34]

When the descendants of the Cruithin (the Picts), who may have practiced matrilineal or matri/patrilineal descent, met the patrilinear Indo-Europeans, the result was a complex interweaving of matriliny and patriliny among the Irish. The assimilation need not have been friendly; there is evidence of many battles and skirmishes between the Cruithin and other Irish tribes, and of a final victory over the Cruithin.[35] In Ireland, by the time the *Táin* was written, the patriarchality of the Indo-Europeans was underscored by the patriarchality of the Christian Church; the religion and equalitarian character of the Pictish culture were buried under many layers of male-centeredness.

Thus in the *Táin,* Queen Medb is a paradox. She is a powerful woman who is both wealthy and a warrior. She has inherited wealth, in keeping with matrilinear inheritance patterns. But such female power was not a force to be understood or accepted by the new order. Therefore, Medb becomes a caricature of a powerful woman who but dimly reflects the grandeur of her role as both wealthy queen and goddess of sovereignty. She is larger than life, because she probably has more powers than any mortal queen ever had. And she is smaller than life because she makes deadly mistakes during the battles of the *Táin* and she is characterized by greed and foolishness, as when she offers her daughter Finnabair up to all who would meet Cú Chulainn in single combat.

Medb is the example of what a sovereign, and a mother, ought not to be; to the creators of the *Táin* what a sovereign ought not to be is a woman. Medb, in reflecting the powers of early Irish goddesses before the advent of Indo-European patriarchy and particularly before the advent of Christianity, reflects in an exaggerated manner a prehistoric female autonomy. The *Táin* turns the goddess of sovereignty into a figure to be derided, much as patriarchal societies turned former great goddesses such as the Greek Circe or Medea or the Furies into witches and monsters; the once-potent goddess is diminished not only in power but, more important, in reverence.[36] But again, despite this derision, there is no question that Medb is wealthy, powerful, and autonomous.

Perhaps because of this intermixture of matrilineal and patrilineal traditions, even after the advent of Christianity, Irish women had some legal ability to inherit and thus gain wealth, or at least the ability to sustain themselves economically. Economic viability seems always to lead to power within a community. And Medb, even as a caricature of a heroine in a saga written by a patriarchal writer, demonstrates the power born of economic viability.

The power of the Irish female thus must predate the earliest Irish legal texts. The female economic power indicated in these texts must be a dim reflection of their prepatriarchal, prepatrilineal financial strength. In fact, these texts demonstrate the fact that Indo-European patriliny largely superseded the matri/patriliny of tribes such as the Picts. In what are perhaps the earliest Irish laws, women may have had little more power than those in the sister cultures of India and Greece. In the *Dire* Text,

> Her father looks after her (when she is) a young woman;
> her husband (*cétmuinter*) looks after her (when she is) the wife of a
>   *cétmuinter*;
> her sons look after her (when she is) a woman with children;
> her tribe looks after her (when she is) a woman of the tribe;
> the Church looks after her (when she is) a woman of the Church.[37]

This text postdates the rise of Indo-European patriliny and patriarchy, and even Christianity. Such medieval Irish texts, late and Christianized though they may be, demonstrate that patriliny and patriarchy never completely supplanted the prepatriarchal, matrilinear elements that made up the complexity of Irish society. In these texts, women do have some autonomy and some financial power. Both the Indo-European tradition of female dependency and the pre-Indo-European tradition of female strength, particularly economic strength, come together in the Old Irish legal texts.

Thus, in the legal text called the *Cáin Lánamna*, women have considerable veto power in the selling of household goods. According to Dillon the earliest legal texts discuss the *banchomarbae* ("women of property"). Moreover, both men and women had separate property, which each could dispose of as they chose. Furthermore, even the early Irish laws provide ample evidence of the woman's right to divorce her husband: if he failed to support her, if he tricked her into marriage, if he was impotent, if he broadcast the secrets of their intimate life. In fact, if *either* partner was infertile, the other could leave the marriage temporarily, the man in order to beget a child, the woman in order to become pregnant.[38] This freedom for the female is in sharp contrast to the lack of availability of divorce for other Indo-European women, such as the upper-class woman in classical Greek society.[39]

Thus the laws, and the society which they reflected, were complex. On one level, some laws related to the cognate Indo-European belief systems in which women were the property of their male relatives. On another level, women could inherit, and they could control their separate property; there was some latitude for a woman to have economic viability and other forms of autonomy, including sexual autonomy. This seems to provide the greatest difference between the women of ancient Ireland and most of the related Indo-European cultures. Again, perhaps the different strata of Irish society, that is, the matrilineal (or matri/patrilineal), matrilocal, perhaps equalitarian pre-Indo-Europeans, and the patriarchal, patrilineal, patrilocal Indo-Europeans, gained ascendancy at different times, and in different parts of Ireland. This phenomenon can also be observed in more modern Western societies, where for the past 100 years there has been an ebb and flow in the feminist movement.

Thus, Irish female figures such as Medb were quite powerful; it was only through the goddess Flaith and her humanized avatars, such as Queen Medb, that a man might attain sovereignty. The systems of education and inheritance in Irish myth and saga reflect an underlying matrilineality. There is a final indicator of matriliny: Irish is replete with female eponyms; just as Ailill son of Máta carries his mother's name, so the Túatha Dé Danann carry the name of their eponymous mother Danu, and so the Goddess Ériu gives her name to the land of Éire.

Notes

1. Translations from the Old Irish are by the author, except for the Bowen translation noted below. This passage and the following one are taken from the 12th-century *Book of Leinster* version of the *Táin*. For the texts in the Old Irish

language, see Miriam Dexter, "The Brown Bull of Cooley and Matriliny in Celtic Ireland," in *From the Realm of the Ancestors: Essays in Honor of Marija Gimbutas,* ed. Joan Marler (Manchester, CT: Knowledge, Ideas, and Trends, 1997), 218–236; and Miriam Dexter, "Queen Medb, Female Autonomy in Ancient Ireland, and Matrilineal Traditions," in *Proceedings of the Ninth Annual UCLA Indo-European Conference, 1997,* ed. Karlene Jones-Bley, Angela della Volpe, Miriam Robbins Dexter, and Martin Huld, Journal of Indo-European Studies Monograph 28 (Washington, DC: Institute for the Study of Man, 1998), 95–122. The author thanks the UCLA Center for the Study of Women for supporting her work as a Research Scholar.

2. Cecile O'Rahilly, ed., *Táin Bó Cúailnge,* Recension II, 27–28.

3. Ibid., 36–37.

4. The exact date is controversial. See J. P. Mallory, "The World of Cú Chulainn: The Archaeology of *Táin Bó Cúailnge,*" in *Aspects of the Táin,* ed. J. P. Mallory (Belfast: December Publications, 1992), 103–159; and J. P. Mallory and G. Stockman, eds., *Ulidia* (Belfast: December Publications, 1994).

5. Miriam Robbins Dexter, *Whence the Goddesses: A Source Book,* Athene Series (New York: Teachers College, 1990), 149–150.

6. Tomás Ó Máille, ed., "Medb Chruachna," *Zeitschrift für Celtische Philologie* 17 (1927): 138, 143.

7. E. G., Quin, ed., *Dictionary of the Irish Language* (Dublin: Royal Irish Academy, 1976), 3:78. Ó Máille ("Medb Chruachna," 144) calls her "the intoxicating one"; Jaan Puhvel, "Aspects of Equine Functionality," in *Myth and Law Among the Indo-Europeans,* ed. Puhvel (Los Angeles: University of California Press, 1970), 167; Edgar C. Polomé, "Some Reflections on the Vedic Religious Vocabulary," in *Studies in Honor of Jaan Puhvel,* Part 2: *Mythology and Religion,* ed. John Greppin and Edgar C. Polomé, Journal of Indo-European Studies Monograph 21 (Washington, DC: Institute for the Study of Man, 1997), 225.

8. R. I. Best and Osborn Bergin, eds., *Book of Leinster* (Dublin: Thom and Co., 1954), 4846–4851; Charles Bowen, "Great-Bladdered Medb, Mythology and Invention in the *Táin Bó Cúailnge,*" *Éire* 10, no. 4 (1975): 32.

9. For a discussion of female figures who act as horses, see Miriam Robbins Dexter, "The Hippomorphic Goddess and Her Offspring," *Journal of Indo-European Studies* 18, nos. 3–4 (1990): 137–144.

10. Quin, ed., *Dictionary of the Irish Language,* 2:160.

11. *Lebor na hUidre: Book of the Dun Cow,* ed. R. I. Best and Osborn Bergin (Dublin: Royal Irish Academy, 1929), 51a15; cf. Ó Máille, ed., "Medb Chruachna," 144–145.

12. Quin, ed., *Dictionary of the Irish Language,* 2:161. Cf. P. S. Dineen, *An Irish-English Dictionary* (Dublin: Educational Co. of Ireland, 1927), 462.

13. *Giraldus Cambrensis in Topographia Hiberni:* "De Novo et Enormi Regni et Dominii Confirmacionis Modo," ed. John O'Meara, Royal Irish Academy Proceedings 52 C4 (Dublin: Hodges, Figgis & Co., 1949), 168.

14. Best and Bergin, eds., *Book of Leinster*, 6416.

15. Daniel A. Binchy, ed., *Scéla Cano Meic Gartnáin* (Dublin: Institute for Advanced Studies, 1963), 452–453.

16. "Cath Boinde Andso" 351b–353a; *The Yellow Book of Lecan*, ed. R. Atkinson (Dublin: Royal Academy House, 1986).

17. Cf. Ó Máille, ed., "Medb Chruachna," 134.

18. *Book of Lecan*, "Cath Boinde Andso" 351b–353a.

19. Cf. E. M. Greenwood, "Some Aspects of the Evolution of *Táin Bó Cúailnge* from TBC I to LL TBC," in *Ulidia*, ed. J. P. Mallory and G. Stockman (Belfast: December Publications, 1994), 47–54.

20. *Metrical Dindshendchas IV*, ed. Gwynn, Edward. "Ath Luain," Royal Irish Academy, Todd Lecture Series, vol. 11 (Dublin: Hodges, Figgis & Co., 1924), 41–42.

21. *Cáin Lánamna*, articles 4–5, H.3.18,221a3; Miles Dillon, "The Relationship of Mother and Son, of Father and Daughter, and the Law of Inheritance with Regard to Women," in *Studies in Early Irish Law*, ed. R. Thurneysen et al. (Dublin: Hodges, Figgis and Co, 1936), 129–179.

22. Dillon, "Relationship of Mother and Son," 136ff., 168–169.

23. Fergus Kelly, *A Guide to Early Irish Law* (Dublin: Dublin Institute for Advanced Studies, 1988), 76–77.

24. Daniel A. Binchy, "Family Membership of Women," in *Studies in Early Irish Law*, ed. R. Thurneysen et al., 182.

25. Dillon, "Relationship of Mother and Son."

26. Cf. Joan N. Radner, "'Fury Destroys the World': Historical Strategy in Ireland's Ulster Epic," *Mankind Quarterly* 23, no. 1 (1982): 44; Katherine Simms, "Propaganda Use of the *Táin* in the Later Middle Ages," *Celtica* 15 (1983): 142–149; Ruairi Ó hUiginn, "The Background and Development of the *Táin Bó Cúailnge*," and Patricia Kelly, "The *Táin* as Literature," both in *Aspects of the Táin*, ed. Mallory, 29–67 and 69–102, respectively; Pádraig Ó Riain, "The *Táin*: A Clue to Its Origins," in *Ulidia*, ed. Mallory and Stockman, 31–37.

27. Erica Sessle, "Misogyny and Medb: Approaching Medb with Feminist Criticism," in *Ulidia*, ed. Mallory and Stockman, 135–138.

28. Dexter, *Whence the Goddesses*, 148–149.

29. Sessle, "Misogyny and Medb," 135–138.

30. Bowen, "Great-Bladdered Medb," 29.

31. Cf. Dexter for a discussion of virgin goddesses and heroines. Miriam Robbins Dexter, "Indo-European Reflections of Virginity and Autonomy," *Mankind Quarterly* 26, nos. 1–2 (1985): 57–74.

32. Dexter, *Whence the Goddesses*, 146–152.

33. Eoin MacNeill, "The Pretanic Background in Britain and Ireland," in *A Celtic Reader: Selections from Celtic Legend, Scholarship and Story*, ed. John Matthews (Wellingborough: Aquarian Press, 1991), 127–147.

34. W. A. Cummins, *The Age of the Picts* (Far Thrupp, Gloucestershire: Alan Sutton, 1995), 32–34.

35. MacNeill, "Pretanic Background in Britain and Ireland," 129 et passim.

36. Miriam Robbins Dexter, "The Frightful Goddess: Birds, Snakes, and Witches," in *Varia on the Indo-European Past: Papers in Memory of Marija Gimbutas,* ed. Miriam Robbins Dexter and Edgar C. Polomé, Journal of Indo-European Studies Monograph 19 (Washington, DC: Institute for the Study of Man, 1997), 124–154.

37. Daniel A. Binchy, "The Legal Capacity of Women in Regard to Contracts," in *Studies in Early Irish Law,* ed. R. Thurneysen et al., 213. The Old Irish text is on p. 37. Binchy considers this one of the earlier Irish legal texts.

38. Thus, in the legal text, the Cáin Lánamna, women have considerable veto power in the selling of household goods (cf. *Cáin Lánamna*, article 6). According to Dillon, "Relationship of Mother and Son," 134, the earliest legal texts discuss the banchomarbae, women of property. Moreover, both men and women had separate property, which each could dispose of as they chose (cf. Binchy, "Legal Capacity of Women," 228). Furthermore, even the early Irish laws provide ample evidence of the woman's right to divorce her husband: if he failed to support her, if he tricked her into marriage, if he was impotent, if he broadcast the secrets of their intimate life (Kelly, *Guide to Early Irish Law,* 74). In fact, if either partner was infertile, the other could leave the marriage temporarily, the man in order to beget a child, the woman in order to become pregnant (Kelly, *Guide to Early Irish Law,* 75). This freedom for the female is in sharp contrast to the lack of availability of divorce for other Indo-European women, such as the upper-class woman in Classical Greek society (see, for example, Plutarch's Life of Alcibiades VIII:3–5).

39. See, for example, Plutarch's *Life of Alcibiades* (VIII.3–5). Plutarch (Ed. Stereotypa). *Bioi Paralleloi (Vitae Parallelae. Ad optimorum librorum fidem accurate editae)* (Leipzig: Tauchnitz, 1829).

Bibliography

Best, R. I., and Osborn Bergin, eds. *The Book of Leinster (LL)* I-II-III. Dublin: Thom and Co., 1954.

Best, R. I., and Osborn Bergin, eds. *Lebor na hUidre: Book of the Dun Cow.* Dublin: Royal Irish Academy, 1929.

Binchy, Daniel A. "Family Membership of Women." In *Studies in Early Irish Law,* ed. R. Thurneysen et al., 180–186. Dublin: Hodges, Figgis and Co, 1936.

Binchy, Daniel A. "The Legal Capacity of Women in Regard to Contracts." In *Studies in Early Irish Law,* ed. R. Thurneysen et al., 207–234. Dublin: Hodges, Figgis and Co, 1936.

Binchy, Daniel A., ed. *Scéla Cano Meic Gartnáin*. Dublin: Institute for Advanced Studies, 1963.

Bowen, Charles. "Great-Bladdered Medb, Mythology and Invention in the *Táin Bó Cúailnge*." *Éire* 10, no. 4 (1975): 14–34.

Cummins, W. A. *The Age of the Picts*. Far Thrupp, Gloucestershire: Alan Sutton, 1995.

Dexter, Miriam Robbins. "The Brown Bull of Cooley and Matriliny in Celtic Ireland." In *From the Realm of the Ancestors: Essays in Honor of Marija Gimbutas*, ed. Joan Marler, 218–236. Manchester, CT: Knowledge, Ideas, and Trends, 1997.

Dexter, Miriam Robbins. "The Frightful Goddess: Birds, Snakes, and Witches." In *Varia on the Indo-European Past: Papers in Memory of Marija Gimbutas*, ed. Miriam Robbins Dexter and Edgar C. Polomé, 124–154. Journal of Indo-European Studies Monograph 19. Washington, DC: Institute for the Study of Man, 1997.

Dexter, Miriam Robbins. "The Hippomorphic Goddess and Her Offspring." *Journal of Indo-European Studies* 18, nos. 3–4 (1990): 137–144.

Dexter, Miriam Robbins. "Indo-European Reflections of Virginity and Autonomy." *Mankind Quarterly* 26, nos. 1–2 (1985): 57–74.

Dexter, Miriam Robbins. "Queen Medb, Female Autonomy in Ancient Ireland, and Matrilineal Traditions." In *Proceedings of the Ninth Annual UCLA Indo-European Conference, 1997*, ed. Karlene Jones-Bley, Angela della Volpe, Miriam Robbins Dexter, and Martin Huld, 95–122. Journal of Indo-European Studies Monograph 28. Washington, DC: Institute for the Study of Man, 1998.

Dexter, Miriam Robbins. *Whence the Goddesses: A Source Book*. Athene Series. New York: Teachers College, 1990.

Dexter, Miriam Robbins, and Edgar C. Polomé, eds. *Varia on the Indo-European Past: Papers in Memory of Marija Gimbutas*. Journal of Indo-European Studies Monograph 19. Washington, DC: Institute for the Study of Man, 1997.

Dillon, Miles. "The Relationship of Mother and Son, of Father and Daughter, and the Law of Inheritance with Regard to Women." In *Studies in Early Irish Law*, ed. R. Thurneysen et al., 129–179. Dublin: Hodges, Figgis and Co., 1936.

Dineen, P. S. *An Irish-English Dictionary*. Dublin: Educational Co. of Ireland, 1927.

Greenwood, E. M. "Some Aspects of the Evolution of *Táin Bó Cúailnge* from TBC I to LL TBC." In *Ulidia*, ed. J. P. Mallory and G. Stockman. 47–54. Belfast: December Publications, 1994.

Kelly, Fergus. *A Guide to Early Irish Law*. Dublin: Dublin Institute for Advanced Studies, 1988.

Kelly, Patricia. "The *Táin* as Literature." In *Aspects of the Táin*, ed. J. P. Mallory, 69–102. Belfast: December Publications, 1992.

MacNeill, Eoin. "The Pretanic Background in Britain and Ireland." In *A Celtic Reader: Selections from Celtic Legend, Scholarship, and Story,* ed. John Matthews, 127–147. Wellingborough: Aquarian Press, 1991.

Mallory, J. P. "The World of Cú Chulainn: The Archaeology of *Táin Bó Cúailnge.*" In *Aspects of the Táin,* ed. J. P. Mallory, 103–159. Belfast: December Publications, 1992.

Mallory, J. P., and G. Stockman, eds. *Ulidia.* Belfast: December Publications, 1994.

Ó hUiginn, Ruairi. "The Background and Development of the *Táin Bó Cúailnge.*" In *Aspects of the Táin,* ed. J. P. Mallory, 29–67. Belfast: December Publications, 1992.

Ó Máille, Tomás, ed. "Medb Chruachna." *Zeitschrift für Celtische Philologie* 17 (1927): 129–146.

O'Neill, Joseph, ed. "Cath Boinde Andso." *Eriu* 2 (1905): 174–185.

O'Rahilly, Cecile, ed. *Táin Bó Cúailnge, from the Book of Leinster.* Reprint, Dublin: Dublin Institute for Advanced Studies, 1984.

Ó Riain, Pádraig. "The *Táin*: A Clue to Its Origins." In *Ulidia,* ed. J. P. Mallory and G. Stockman, 31–37. Belfast: December Publications, 1994.

Plutarch (Ed. Stereotypa). *Bioi Paralleloi (Vitae Parallelae. Ad optimorum librorum fidem accurate editae).* Leipzig: Tauchnitz, 1829.

Polomé, Edgar C. "Some Reflections on the Vedic Religious Vocabulary." In *Studies in Honor of Jaan Puhvel.* Part 2: *Mythology and Religion,* ed. John Greppin and Edgar C. Polomé, 225–234. Journal of Indo-European Studies Monograph 21. Washington, DC: Institute for the Study of Man, 1997.

Puhvel, Jaan. "Aspects of Equine Functionality." In *Myth and Law Among the Indo-Europeans,* ed. Jaan Puhvel, 159–172. Los Angeles: University of California Press, 1970.

Quin, E. G., ed. *Dictionary of the Irish Language (RIA).* Dublin: Royal Irish Academy, 1976.

Radner, Joan N. "'Fury Destroys the World': Historical Strategy in Ireland's Ulster Epic." *Mankind Quarterly* 23, no. 1 (1982): 41–60.

Sessle, Erica. "Misogyny and Medb: Approaching Medb with Feminist Criticism." In *Ulidia,* ed. J. P. Mallory and G. Stockman, 135–138. Belfast: December Publications, 1994.

Simms, Katherine. "Propaganda Use of the *Táin* in the Later Middle Ages." *Celtica* 15 (1983): 142–149.

Thurneysen, R., Nancy Power, Myles Dillon, Kathleen Mulchrone, D. A. Binchy, August Knoch, and John Ryan. *Studies in Early Irish Law.* Dublin: Hodges, Figgis and Co., 1936.

17

Sulis (Minerva) and Other "Celtic" Goddesses: The Native Tradition in Pre-Roman Britain

Cheryl Straffon

Before the Roman invasion of what is now called Britain (England, Wales, and Scotland) in the first century CE, the country comprised a number of so-called Celtic tribes, each with its own territorial boundaries. From the Cornovii of northeastern Scotland to the Dumnonii of southwest England (now Devon and Cornwall), these tribes included the Brigantes of northern England, the Iceni of eastern England, and the Silures of south Wales. Each of these tribal groups probably had its individual territorial goddesses: some of these are known from inscriptions, some from stories and legends recorded hundreds of years later, and some from excavated remains. Some are comparatively well known, such as Sulis from present-day Bath, others hardly known at all outside Britain, and others have doubtless been lost forever. Occasionally, one not known before turns up, as did Senuna a few years ago. This chapter will identify the ones that are known, recorded, or inferred from the available evidence, and reconstructs a picture of goddess worship and celebration before the Romans arrived and before Christianity came.

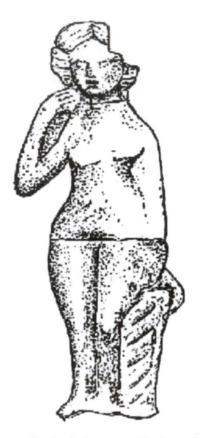

Figure 17.1 In southwestern England, the town of Bath was built around a shrine to a Celtic goddess named Sulis, called Minerva by invading Romans after their healing goddess. Such goddesses of healing waters are known throughout Celtic Britain. (Art by Cheryl Straffon. Used by permission.)

Goddesses and Water Cults

For the native British people (commonly called the Celts), springs, wells, and rivers were of primary importance, and many of these were given names that suggest that they were seen as physical embodiments of goddesses. This may have been partly because they were thought of as liminal places, marking tribal boundaries or delineating sacred areas, and partly because water was seen as the source of life and nourishment and therefore its presence was thought of as a gift of the goddess. Examples from textual evidence of river goddesses include the goddess Deva, who gave her name to the River Dee at Chester; Clotna, who gave her name to the River Clyde in Scotland; Sabraan or Sabrina of the

River Severn in Bristol and Gloucestershire; Verbeia, after whom the River Wharfe in Yorkshire was probably named; and Brigantia, the goddess of the Brigantes tribe, whose name may be found in the River Braint in Anglesey and River Brent (formerly called Briganti) in Middlesex. This process also took place in Gaul and Ireland. Little is known about these goddesses apart from their names, except for one or two cases where a little flesh can be put on the bones of the name.

For example, an altar carving of the goddess Verbeia was found at Ilkley in Yorkshire and still resides today inside Ilkley Church. She is depicted carrying two long undulating serpents, one in each hand. There may have been a connection between snakes and water cults for the Celtic peoples, and Martin Henig has suggested that the name "Verbeia" may mean "winding river."[1] If this is the case, the undulating snakes in her hands may be personifications of the nearby river Wharfe itself. In central and southern Britain, the River Severn, one of Britain's longest rivers, flows in a huge loop through Shropshire, Herefordshire, Worcestershire, and Gloucestershire to discharge into the Bristol Channel at Avonmouth. At a small place on the riverbank called Aust-on-Severn, a bronze statuette five inches tall was found depicting a goddess with eyes inset with glass beads. She wears a crescent-shaped headdress, her hands are at her sides, her buttocks are well developed, and her breasts are firm and pronounced. The style is Cycladic (Mediterranean) and, given the location, she may have been a prized imported or traded artifact. There is evidence of Romano-British occupation there, so she may have been a representation of, or offering to, the British goddess Sabraan, later Romanized into Sabrina and later still into the name of the river Severn. The deity of the river found at its mouth was perhaps ritually placed there as a thanksgiving and/or a protective talisman. Further up the river, the Romans built temples at Lydney and Little Dean, which may have been founded on the sites of pre-existing Celtic British shrines.

Goddess Shrines in Britain

In London, the Walbrook stream was probably sacred in pre-Roman times, and many skulls found from the river attest to a sacrificial spot, dedicated by the Iceni tribe under Queen Boudicca, who made her stand here against the Romans. After her defeat the site continued in sacred use by the Romans, as the discovery of many pipe-clay figurines of Venus-style goddesses shows. These goddess figurines may have been mass-produced, probably in Gaul, and made available to the ordinary people to give as votive offerings. Continuity of religious practice was important to the Romans, and many Roman religious shrines and temples in Britain were undoubtedly built on sites that had been dedicated to Celtic goddesses.

One such place was at Buxton in Derbyshire, whose Roman name was Aquae Arnemetiae ("the waters of the Goddess Arnemetia"). The name is Latin combined with a Celtic term, deriving from *ar (e) nemeton* ("in front of a sacred grove"). Recently, archaeological excavation at Poole's Cavern, a natural cave in the nearby Peak District, has revealed evidence for a shrine that may have been dedicated to this little-known goddess. The finds included a large number of brooches found deposited under a stalagmite in a kind of antechamber to the main chamber that was Roman in date (second and third centuries CE). The excavators comment: "The ritual area forms a most attractive watery grotto: conceivably it was regarded as a genius loci, possibly the abode of a nymph or river god to be worshipped with ceremony and votive offerings."[2] Given the proximity of the cavern to Buxton nearby, it seems a reasonable assumption that the shrine would have been dedicated to Arnemetiae herself.

The same root word as Arnemetiae also gave rise to the Roman goddess Nemetona, a relief of whom was found at Bath. But behind Arnemetia and Nemetona undoubtedly lies a pre-Roman Celtic goddess whose name is now lost. We know that sacred groves were important in Britain to the Celtic peoples, and their priesthood the Druids, because the Roman historians Lucan and Tacitus both say so. Therefore it seems probable that native British goddesses were worshiped in sacred groves, often beside rivers and streams. Queen Boudicca offered up sacrifices to the goddess Andraste in a sacred grove. Dio Cassius, another Roman historian, says that Boudicca released a hare before setting out on a campaign, while invoking Andraste.

Other Romanized names of goddesses associated with waters include two from Hadrian's Wall in Northumberland. An inscription to the goddess Latis, whose name means "Goddess of the Pool [or Beer?]" was found at Birdoswald and Fallsteads. A major shrine to a Romanized Celtic goddess Coventina was found at Carrawbrough. Here, a spring that fed a small pool or well was enclosed by a high sanctuary wall that dates to about 130 CE. It remained an open-air shrine, perhaps indicating that it was a Celtic structure which was never fully Romanized. Coventina's name is also recorded at Narbonne in Gaul and in northwest Spain, but she appears to have been predominantly a British goddess. It is likely that there was already an important shrine to her when the

Romans arrived. Recognising her significance, they dedicated altars to her, with names such as Augusta ("most venerable") and Sancta ("sacred"), the only native British goddess to be designated with such terms. She was undoubtedly a goddess of healing, as revealed by the vast number of offerings found here, which included more than 16,000 coins, votive beads, a bronze dog and horse, brooches and glass pottery, shrine bells, and a fragment of a female skull. There were also many pins found, indicating that Coventina may also have been a goddess of childbirth, as pregnant women would throw pins, hoping for a successful delivery. The original meaning of this became lost, but up until the early 20th century women continued to throw pins into holy wells such as Madron in Cornwall for good luck and as a presage of the future. Whether the pins rose or fell would indicate good or bad fortune.

There were no statues found of the goddess at Coventina's Well, but there were dedications to her, reliefs that may depict her, and a bronze mask that may be attributed to her. On one relief, the goddess is depicted semi-naked, reclining on lapping waves, holding a water-lily leaf in one hand and resting one elbow on an overturned pitcher. On another she is represented as a triple nymph, pouring water from a beaker. Of these sculptures Miranda Aldhouse-Green says: "While her imagery owes its form to Graeco-Roman iconography, the style of the Goddess' representations is Celtic, with little attention being paid to realism in anatomical proportions and rudimentary facial features."[3] Today, the site is nothing but a sad and neglected swamp, but in its time it was one of the most important goddess shrines in Britain, with a continuity that undoubtedly stretched from Celtic into Roman times.

Sulis Minerva and Her Shrine at Bath

All of this now leads to Bath and the shrine of the goddess Sulis Minerva, another Romanisation of a pre-existent native British site. In this case the Celtic name of the goddess is known: Sulis, to which the Romans added the dedication of their tutelary goddess of war and territory, Minerva. Bath was clearly already an important shrine for the local Celtic tribe there, who may well have been the Silures, who occupied much of Somerset and South Wales; it is possible that Sulis gave her name to the Silures themselves.

The fame of Bath attracted pilgrims from all over Celtic Britain. The hot mineral waters rise from a deep natural spring at a rate of a quarter of a million gallons a day, at a temperature of 49°C (120°F). The site was probably venerated from Neolithic times onwards, and may have been dedicated to a sun goddess, the memory of which is contained in the name Sul or Sulis. By the Celtic period it was called Aquae Sulis— the waters of the goddess Sul(is), whose name may come from a root word *sil* or *sul* ("eye"). By the time the Romans came, it was such an important sacred place that they grafted their own goddess Minerva on to the native goddess and built a shrine to the now-renamed Sulis Minerva.

From the first century CE the site became a huge temple complex, consisting of a Roman temple, sophisticated bath buildings, a great altar, and a reservoir for the sacred spring water. This steaming water was viewed as the living body of the goddess and became the focal point of the complex. The temple, now buried under Stall Street, was dedicated to Sulis Minerva; a gilded bronze head of the goddess, found under the street in 1723 CE, would have been part of a cult figure of the temple. Other finds from the site have included model bronze and ivory breasts, indicating either that Sulis was a nurturing goddess or that the supplicant was a nursing mother. Also found were many inscribed stone, lead, and pewter tablets that had been cast into the waters, which ask the goddess for her help in finding lost items or in cursing those who had stolen personal possessions. On epigraphic dedications to the goddess, where both Celtic and Roman names are mentioned, that of the indigenous goddess Sulis is always put first, emphasizing that she was the original matron of the site. Some 16,000 Celtic and Roman coins were also discovered, similar to the number found at Coventina's Well in Northumberland. The habit of throwing coins into wells and fountains for good luck, which continues today, goes back into Celtic times. At Bath, certain coin types seem to have been specifically chosen, and some were deliberately damaged. Miranda Aldhouse-Green suggests that this may have been a ritual act to remove the offerings from the mundane world and make them suitable for acceptance into a supernatural realm.[4]

As the site was such a large and complex one, its uses were multifarious. The temple shrine was doubtless also a healing sanctuary, and supplicants would have come to bathe in the waters and perhaps undergo sleeping and dreaming therapy in the hope of a curative vision. This may offer an explanation of the root *sil* as meaning "eye" and, by extension "vision"—a goddess of visionary trances. There would also have been appropriate rituals and festivals at this important place. The original spring was later enclosed, making access available only through a dim passageway—perhaps an attempt to replicate initiation ceremonies into the caves and tombs of the prehistoric ancestors. There was also an ornamental pool, now situated beneath the main bath, that was surrounded by several smaller baths with water at different temperatures, the whole forming a great water and healing complex.

The remains from the site show an interesting mix of Celtic and Roman motifs. One carving discovered was of a Medusa-style head with staring hypnotic eyes and snake hair, clearly influenced by classical stories of the Gorgon. But its style is unmistakeably Celtic, with hair and beard harking back to Celtic heads found elsewhere, depicting solar gods and ancestral heads; some were thought to have apotropaic powers, the power to avert an evil influence or bad luck. Celtic heads were frequently horned and were often associated with thermal waters. A fragment of a female skull was found at Coventina's Well, as well as several small heads in bronze. Another pediment found at Bath, now beneath the Pump Room, depicts a moon goddess, with her head surrounded by a double-crescent moon, appearing as a kind of horned crown. She may be connected to moon rituals performed at the site, the moon governing the ebb and flow of the waters of the earth. Her iconography could as easily have been influenced by Celtic motifs as classical Roman ones. Also found at the site were dedications to the goddess Nemetona with her consort Leucetius, which, although probably brought by Roman visitors, could originally have come from Gaul, where Nemetona was a native Celtic goddess. Anne Ross points out that Celtic and Roman aquatic cults had much in common, and in places like Bath, the two traditions could be easily be united to satisfy all tastes.[5]

Senuna and Her Shrine

There may well have been many such shrines all over Britain in Celtic times, many now lost and destroyed. In 2002 one was discovered by chance by a metal-detectorist in a field near Ashwell in Hertfordshire. He found twenty-six pieces of gold and silver, including silver plaques with gold highlights, a set of jewellery pieces that included a brooch and cloak clasps, and a silver figurine. When experts from the British Museum cleaned up these badly corroded pieces, they found to their amazement that the base of the statuette had an inscription on it to a hitherto-unknown local goddess, Senuna. These were clearly objects from a temple, one that was built around a shrine, probably a ritual pool, at the place where the finds were made. Ralph Jackson, Roman curator at the British Museum, commented: "To find a hoard of a temple treasure, such as this one, is incredibly rare, not just in Britain but anywhere. To give Britain a new goddess is extraordinary."[6]

Senuna, formerly identified as Senua, was undoubtedly a native British goddess, worshiped at a spring on the site, who was subsequently adopted and Romanized, and then twinned with the Roman goddess Minerva, just as at Bath. A silver figurine of the goddess was found, with its base nearby inscribed with the words "D[ea] Senun[a]e Flavia Cunoris v[otum] s[olvit] l[ibens] m[erito]", which translates as "To the goddess Senuna, Flavia Cunoris has paid her vow, willingly, deservedly."[7]

At least twelve votive plaques were also found, showing classical images of Minerva, with spear, shield, and owl, but many of these carry an inscription dedicated to Senuna rather than Minerva. These dedications all state the name of the person who "makes [or willingly fulfills] her/his vow to the goddess Senuna," and they vividly bring to life the names of those who made the offerings. These are Claudius Celsius, Carita Ressa, Bellicus Memorianus, Lucilia Sena, Herbonianus, Servandus, and Firmanus. The names are a mixture of Latin and Celtic forms, showing that the native Celtic peoples had by this time adopted Roman names and customs.

The name Senuna is perhaps linked to that of that of the river Senua, at an unknown location in southern Britain, mentioned in the Ravenna Cosmography, an early eighth-century CE text listing place names and rivers in Britain. If the goddess's name is etymologically identical with that of a nearby river, then it is likely that the river took its name from the goddess, who was perceived as a manifestation of the river itself. Subsequent to the discovery of the hoard, the name Senuna was identified in the inscription on a silver finger-ring found in Kent, so the worship of this hitherto-unknown goddess may have been widely spread throughout southeastern Britain.

The site at Ashwell was subsequently excavated and revealed an open-air shrine, possibly at a former springhead, making a direct parallel to both Bath and Coventina's Well on Hadrian's Wall. The shrine enclosure had been formalized in the Roman period by a chalk pebble surface encircling an area about fourteen meters across. Beyond this shrine enclosure lay a graveled surface, probably a courtyard, where the hoard deposit was found. Within the shrine enclosure other ritual deposits were found scattered throughout the soil filling, but mostly near the perimeter. These included Romano-British pottery, coins, brooches, dress-pins, glass shards, fragments of pipe-clay figurines, animal bones and oyster shells. One deposit, dating from the first to second century CE, included eight axe-heads, thirteen spearheads, two chisels, two awls, a gouge, a dagger, and sword blade fragments. The implication is that they were all collected from local burial mounds and settlements in the pre-Roman Iron Age, displayed, and then cast into the enclosure at some special event, probably as an offering to the goddess Senuna. Within the enclosure was found the remains of a small building, which the excavators suggest may have been a shrine that housed a statue of the goddess herself. It was an extraordinary find and a site that sheds much light on the native British worship of goddesses in pre-Roman and Roman Britain.

*Sillina and the Isles of Scilly

From goddesses whose names are attested by dedications, inscriptions, and statuary, analysis now moves on to one whose existence can only be inferred from linguistic reconstruction. Some twenty-eight miles off the tip of the southwest coast of Cornwall lie the Isles of Scilly, an archipelago of some 200 individual rocks and islands, with five main inhabited ones. One of the now-uninhabited eastern isles is Nornour, but it was not always so deserted. In fact, in a period lasting from the Bronze Age (second millennium BCE) to the Romano-Celtic period (fourth century CE), Nornour housed a comparatively large and busy settlement. Excavated in 1962, eleven circular stone huts were found, extending over a strip of ground fifty meters wide. The main characteristics of the buildings consisted of roughly circular main rooms, about five meters in diameter, usually having a smaller annex alongside. The original settlement probably consisted of one extended family, with different generations occupying the three main houses. Later, during the Romano-Celtic period (approx. 500 BCE–500 CE) the site became a shrine centered on two buildings, while the rest of the site was unoccupied. Here were found a large number of votive offerings: 300 brooches, 35 bronze rings, 11 bronze bracelets, 84 Roman coins, 24 glass beads, and fragments of several clay figurines, including a mother-goddess and a so-called Venus figurine. This was clearly a significant goddess cult center, and one that must have existed long before the Romans occupied Britain. From linguistic clues, Professor Charles Thomas suggested that her name was *Sillina (the asterisk indicating a hypothesized name) and that she was an Iron Age deity worshiped there who ultimately gave her name to the islands.[8]

This little-known goddess has an interesting link to Sulis, for the root of both of their names is *sil* or *sul*. Charles Thomas suggests that the name *Sillina may mean "She-who-looks-out" or simply "the Watcher," an appropriate name for a goddess who looked out over the sea passage from Ireland, Wales, Cornwall, and Brittany.[9] She may have been a local marine goddess who guarded the Iron Age sea routes, to whom the mariners came to give thanks for a safe passage or to ask for one as they traveled onwards. This would explain the comparatively numerous offerings found at the shrine on Nornour, many more than could be expected simply from the number of people occupying the two huts. There may have been a shrine to the goddess, tended by a select number of priest/esses, at which sailors and travelers called to give votive offerings and thanks.

There may have been a link between Sulis at Bath and *Sillina at Nornour. Both goddesses were connected with water, the hot springs and baths at Bath, and the ocean at Nornour. Other goddess centers, such as Sabraan at the mouth of the Severn and Coventina and Senuna with their shrines beside sacred springs, were also intimately connected with water and healing. Jocelyn Toynbee suggested that the Gorgon's Head discovered at Bath actually depicts a water deity and that Sulis Minerva was the daughter of a water-god.[10] In Greek mythology the three Gorgons were daughters of an archaic sea-god, Phorcys, and the Romans, recognizing the essential attributes of these native British goddesses, added their own iconography.

Other Goddess Names and Places

These above goddesses—Brigantia, Verbeia, Sabraan, Arnemetia, Sulis, Senuna, *Sillina, and other minor ones—are the principal divinities linked to specific places, shrines, and temples that probably existed in pre-Roman Britain. About others, whose names are known from perhaps a single inscription, next to nothing else is known. One is Setlocenia, whose name may mean "she of the long life." A relief of a goddess was found in Maryport, Cumbria, and a dedication to Setlocenia was found at the same site. A dedication to a goddess Saitada was found in the Tyne Valley. Anne Ross raises the possibility that her name may be connected with the Welsh word *hoed*, meaning "grief."[11] Also, a few fragments of statues and one complete figurine have been found, representing the Celtic horse goddess Epona, whose name is derived from Gaulish *epos* ("horse"). The complete figurine is a bronze statuette that depicts her in a sitting position, with what has been variously interpreted as a cornucopia, a serpent, or a yoke on her left arm. The two ponies flanking her emphasize her divine status. Her provenance is unknown, but may have come from Wiltshire. Many representations of Epona show her feeding her horses or depict young ponies suckling the mare or sleeping beneath her. Figures also show her with a dog and a key, suggesting otherworld associations as a goddess who presides over the journey of the soul through life and the next world. She may have been a Celtic goddess of horses and the other world, whose original name and attributes persisted into Roman times.

Horses were important to the Celts, and Epona has her equine equivalents in Ireland, where Macha appears in the early tales, and in Wales, where Rhiannon features in the early text *The Mabinogi*. The material, which was not written down until the 14th century CE, tells of a Celtic world of around the fifth and sixth centuries CE. The stories are about kings and queens and mythological beings, but most scholars agree that behind these beings lie original gods and goddesses. These stories provide a reverse telescope for seeing some of the original goddesses of the inhabitants of pre-Roman Britain, who were increasingly driven to the "Celtic" fringes of Britain—Wales, Scotland, and Cornwall—by successive waves of invaders.

One goddess figure, found in the Welsh text *The Tale of Culhwch and Olwen*, is Modron, whose name seems to mean simply "Mother." She may have been the mother goddess of the British peoples, remembered in the Welsh saint Madrun (Maddern, Madron). This goddess-saint was brought to Cornwall by Welsh incomers in the fifth–sixth centuries CE and the name given to a holy well dedicated to Saint Maddern, now known as Madron well. The well was associated with healing, so the link with a native British mother goddess may be very likely. Another possible goddess name from Scotland is Scáthach (Skiach or Sgathach), whom legend says fought a battle with Cúchulainn, hero of Ulster, and settled on the Isle of Skye, which still bears her name. The figure of the Cailleach or hag is also known from Irish and Scottish myth. Very often she is represented as an ancestral goddess who strides across the land, dropping rocks from her apron, which form the hills and tors and cairns on the land. These stories may be the nearest thing remaining of a pre-Christian creation myth in Britain.

From the sites known and named to the distant Celtic twilight of legend and myth, the goddesses of pre-Roman Celtic Britain are elusive but nevertheless also real and tangible. They may not have many stories, and the ones who have stories may not have many identifiable sites, but nevertheless they are a rich cultural heritage, and a reminder that before the Romans came, Britain had a vibrant goddess-celebrating tribal society.

Notes

1. Martin Henig, *Religion in Roman Britain* (London: Batsford, 1984), 17.
2. D. Bramwell et al., "Excavations at Poole's Cavern, Buxton," *Derbyshire Archaeological Journal* 103 (1983): 70–72.
3. Miranda J. Green, *Dictionary of Celtic Myth and Legend* (London: Thames and Hudson, 1992), 68.
4. Ibid., 201.
5. Anne Ross, *Pagan Celtic Britain* (London: Constable, 1992), 56.
6. Maev Kennedy, "Senua, Britain's Unknown Goddess Unearthed," *The Guardian*, September 1, 2003.
7. Ralph Jackson and Gilbert Burleigh, "The Senuna Treasure and Shrine at Ashwell Herts," *Journal of Roman Archaeology* 17 (2007): 39.
8. Charles Thomas, *Exploration of a Drowned Landscape* (London: B. T. Batsford, 1985), 154, 158; the asterisk in front of the name indicates that it is hypothetical.
9. Ibid., 154.
10. Jocelyn Toynbee, *Art in Roman Britain* (London: Phaidon, 1962), 163.
11. Ross, *Pagan Celtic Britain*, 291.

Bibliography

Allason-Jones, Lindsay, and Bruce McKay. *Coventina's Well*. Chesters: Chesters Museum, 1985.
Bramwell, D., K. Dalton, J. F. Drinkwater, K. L. Lorimer and D. F. Mackreth. "Excavations at Poole's Cavern, Buxton." *Derbyshire Archaeological Journal* 103 (1983): 70–72.
Branston, Brian. *The Lost Gods of England*. London: Thames and Hudson, 1974.
Green, Miranda. *Celtic Goddesses*. London: British Museum Press, 1995.
Green, Miranda. *Dictionary of Celtic Myth and Legend*. London: Thames and Hudson, 1992.
Henig, Martin. *Religion in Roman Britain*. London: Batsford, 1984.
Jackson, Ralph, and Gilbert Burleigh. "The Senuna Treasure and Shrine at Ashwell." *Journal of Roman Archaeology* 17 (2007).
Matthews, Caitlin. *Mabon and the Mysteries of Britain*. London: Arkana, 1987.
Matthews, Caitlin. *The Mabinogian*. Translated by Gwyn Jones and Thomas Jones. London: Dent, 1972.
Ross, Anne. *Pagan Celtic Britain*. London: Constable, 1992.
Straffon, Cheryl. *The Earth Goddess*. London: Blandford, 1997.
Thomas, Charles. *Celtic Britain*. Londong: Thames and Hudson, 1997.
Thomas, Charles. *Exploration of a Drowned Landscape*. London: Batsford, 1985.
Toynbee, Jocelyn. *Art in Roman Britain*. London: Phaidon, 1962.

18

The Rhineland Deae Matronae: Collective Female Deity in Germanic Europe

Dawn E. Work-MaKinne

In the rolling uplands of the German region known as *die Eifel*, on a green and golden hill amidst the surrounding farmland, the remains of a Roman-era temple complex are spread out under the sun. Less than five kilometers away, atop another green hill, an even larger temple complex lies in a shady forest glade. Yet another few kilometers away, tucked inside a tiny village, a small shrine is overgrown with wildflowers. Each temple has one or more carved votive altar stones bearing an inscription and the image of three goddesses, the Deae Matronae. These are the shrines of Nettersheim, Pesch, and Zingsheim, and the Deae Matronae are the Matron Goddesses of the Roman-era Rhineland. The Deae Matronae are a collective deity, defined as: (1) a group of sacred or super-natural beings, (2) collected under one group name (3) but not generally conflated into one being, (4) worshiped collectively, (5) who act and wield their powers collectively and by extension consensually. The collective sacred female is a recurring theme in Germanic religious history.[1]

The Deae Matronae of the German Rhineland are a potent ethnic mix of Celtic, Germanic, and Roman. At base the Matronae are a Celtic phe-nomenon, and examples of the Matronae or Matres are found in Gaul, Italy, Spain, and even Africa. But the Matronae were also a Germanic expression of religion, with extensive Roman practice. In an area of lower

Figure 18.1 The Deae Matronae or "mother goddesses" were honored along the German border during the Roman Empire. They represent a melding of Germanic, Celtic, and Roman religion and, in altered form, survive today. (Photograph © Dawn E. Work-MaKinne. Used by permission.)

Germany, in and around the cities of Bonn and Köln and in the nearby uplands of the Eifel, Matronae worship by the Germanic Ubii people flourished. The Romans had entered the region with the arrival of Julius Caesar in 58 BCE, and the Ubii people moved into the region from their former home on the east bank of the Rhine around 51 BCE. It is unclear from the historical record whether the Germanic Ubii people adopted the religion of the Matronae upon their relocation to the west bank of the Rhine, or whether they had worshiped the Matronae previously, and brought their religion with them. In any case, the Germanic Ubii and the frontier Romans enthusiastically practiced the worship of the Rhineland Matronae.

There is no written record of the mythology of the Deae Matronae. Their story is largely told in stone. Stone votive altars provide artwork depicting the three goddesses, their attributes, their veneration, and their worshipers. Stones in the landscape indicate the remains of temples, cult worship, and gathering places. The stone votive altars also present inscriptions to the goddesses, inscriptions that give descriptive epithets to the name "Matronae" as well as solemn vows to the goddesses and names of worshipers. These stones are guides to the world of the Deae Matronae.

Votive Altar Artwork

The first stone stories are told by the artwork on the votive altar stones. At important life junctures, Ubii and frontier Roman worshipers of the Matronae made prayers and vows to the Deae Matronae. As these prayers were answered or vows fulfilled, worshipers commissioned Roman stonecutters to fashion votive altar stones. Most of these votive altar stones simply refer to the Matronae without artwork, adding a descriptive epithet naming and describing the goddesses, as in Matronae Aufaniae ("matrons of the remote fen"). Over 1000 votive altar stones have been discovered in the Rhineland area, most with just the title "Matronae" in some form, together with an epithet. Matronae votive altar stones have been found in temple sites, cemeteries, and pits, as well as in excavations of assumed temple sites such as under the Cathedral in Bonn. Matronae votive altars were sculpted from native limestone or sandstone, and are of widely varying sizes. The largest stones, with long inscriptions and representational artwork, can be over a yard high, several feet wide, and a foot thick. The dated altars are clustered in the years 164–251 CE.

The most striking of the surviving altars, with the finest carving, was commissioned by Q. Vettius Severus to the Matronae Aufaniae. The earliest of the datable stones, at 164 CE, it was discovered under the Bonn Cathedral. This "Vettius" Stone depicts the Matronae as three seated goddesses, the flanking outer goddesses wearing the large bonnet head-dress of the Ubii married woman, and the center goddess with the long flowing hair of the unmarried younger woman. The feet of this central goddess rest on a small footrest. All the goddesses hold offering baskets filled with fruit in their laps. They are seated on a long curved bench covered with cloth, with decorated pillars at each end, flanked by what appear to be diminutive attendants. Above the goddesses are three small figures, presumably the family of Q. Vettius Severus. Atop the picture is a ceiling, which in other stones is replaced by a shell, gable, or *aedicu-lum* (small Roman shrine). The dress of the goddesses is peculiar to Ubii women. They wear an ankle-length underskirt, a belted dress, and an over-cape with open-ended bell-like sleeves, with a rectangular fibula-type or brooch closure. The goddess on the right wears a necklace with a crescent.

Although most of the surviving Matronae votive altars do not have the fineness of carving of the "Vettius" Stone, and details are often obscured, the basic outline of the Matronae artwork is held in common. There are always three goddesses, and they are always seated. There are two goddesses with large bonnet headdresses flanking a central goddess with loose flowing or decorated hair. The collectivity of the Deae Matronae is emphasized by two facets in the artwork: their consistent representation as a group of three, and their representation as three separate goddesses, not conflated into a single being or a single being replicated three times.[2] The dress of the goddesses is that of the Ubii woman, including the various dresses and robes, the rectangular fibula-clasp, and the necklace or torque. The goddesses may hold any of a wide variety of gifts. Generally, the offerings are baskets of fruits, which may be apples, pears, quinces, or walnuts. More seldom seen are bundles of sheaves, bunches of grapes, blossoms or twigs, cornucopias, or steering rudders and globes, reminiscent of the Roman Fortuna and of the Frisian Nehalennia.

Some of the stone votive altars speak of rituals, through such scenes carved into the artwork. Donors gave the votive altars in the context of the Roman-style ceremony of the *votum*, the ritual of the vow. In this long-term ritual, a supplicant would make a contract with a deity, often for the term of one year. The ritual would open with the naming of the deities, the favors requested, and the offerings proposed if the requests were granted. The ritual would end, in the Roman world, with an animal sacrifice at an altar to the deity.

The Matronae votive altar stones show several parts of this ritual: the image of the deities, the inscription of the fulfillment of the vow, an image of the ritual concluding the vow and an image of the temple in which the deities are housed. One altar depicts the three Matronae goddesses seated on a forward-thrusting bench above a simple ritual scene involving several participants: a ritual specialist along with a family consisting of father, mother, and daughter. The specialist performing the ritual stands behind a small model of the altar. To the left, in Roman dress, stands the father. To the right, in Ubii dress and the large bonnet of the married woman, is the mother. Immediately above the woman and to the right of the Matronae goddesses is a young woman, also dressed in Ubii costume, who is presumably the daughter, with hair unbound and uncovered. This simple ritual scene reveals something of the society in which men and women dwelt along the Roman frontier. Germanic men

often adopted Roman dress, attitudes, and even names more readily than
women; also Roman men along the frontier took Germanic women in
marriage. Germanic women were more likely to retain native (in this case,
Germanic Ubii) names, customs, and dress.[3]

An altar to the Matronae Aufaniae given by C. Candidinius Verus dating from 220–230 CE is unique for its portrayal of ritual scenes. The
Matronae at the top of the altar are flanked by two figures stepping
lightly on their globes, the figure on the left holding a palm in her hand.
The ruins of the walls of the aediculum surrounding the Matronae show
that the walls were decorated with fruits and vines. The lower portion of
the front of the same altar depicts a complex ritual scene. To the right
of a small model of the altar is the donor, presumably C. Candidinius
Verus. Three figures, ritual specialists, stand to the left. The furthest left
is holding a jug for libations in his right hand and a *patera* in his left
hand; a patera is a specialized Roman bowl or ladle for pouring libations.
The ritual specialist in the center is playing a flute during the animal sacrifice to cover any sounds of the animal's death. The ritual specialist at
the altar is probably burning incense prior to burning portions of the
animal for sacrifice. One side-panel of the altar shows a pig being
brought for sacrifice, while the other shows the cooking pot being prepared for cooking the animal. These ritual scenes demonstrate that ceremonies to the Matronae followed ritual practice common throughout
the Roman world, with libations, music, incense, and animal sacrifice.[4]
These examples indicate that the collective was venerated as a collective
and not as one of the goddesses or one being. The ritual is offered to
the collective of three.

In the ritual scenes depicted thus far, the ritual specialists have been
male. This by no means exhausts the possibilities for participation and
leadership in rituals to the Matronae. Side-panels of other altars depict
both male and female attendants. One altar shows a female offering
attendant or ritual specialist holding a basket with fruit and a small flask
of liquid for libations, while the other side-panel depicts her counterpart,
a male offering attendant or ritual specialist, holding a basket of fruit.
The famous "Vettius" Stone has only women on the side panels and
depicts no other ritual specialists. Women were major participants in rituals to the Matronae, in addition to their participation in family rituals.
A unique stone votive altar includes women ritual participants only. The
Matronae goddesses are seated upon a raised plinth, their hands and
laps empty and awaiting offerings. To the right of the goddesses is a
procession of six or seven Ubii-dressed women carrying offering gifts.

There do not appear to be any men in this procession, although it is possible that a man stands to the left of the Matronae. Perhaps this was a peculiarly Ubii celebration of the Matronae, held in addition to the Roman rituals seen on previous votive altars.

Sides of altars often depict naturalistic scenes such as trees, plants, or vines. One side-panel shows a tree with a snake winding around the trunk and up toward the leaves. This is not the only depiction of tree and snake iconography to be depicted on Matronae altars; several of the altars found under the cathedral at Bonn show the tree with the snake creeping out of a hole in the trunk.[5] A spectacular scene is found on a votive altar to the Matronae Aufaniae given by Statilius Proculus and his wife Sutoria Pia. A large tree dominates a rocky landscape, and a snake emerges from a hole in the trunk. Most of the branches are bare until ending in large leaves. Among the leaves at the very top of the tree is a nest with four birds. At the foot of the tree is something arresting: a three-bodied goat with a single head. Each goat has obvious udders. Bird and snake imagery is ancient imagery of rebirth and regeneration.[6] Since no written mythology belongs to the cult of the Matronae, it is unknown whether this tree-and-snake imagery, perhaps including birds and the occasional goat, is Germanic in origin, whether it hearkens back to Rome and the Mediterranean, or whether it may precede either. There is no known Roman myth that includes all elements of this particular pictorial story.

Temple Sites

The votive stones above were primarily unearthed at known temple sites in the basin and upland areas west of Köln and Bonn, and in the cities themselves. Archaeologists found a cache of stones under the Bonn Cathedral, where no temple has been located. Votive stones were reused to create later buildings, pits, or funeral stones. Three temple precincts from the Eifel uplands provide examples of Matronae veneration during the early centuries of the Common Era. Votive altars were found in these temple precincts—Nettersheim, Zingsheim, and Bad Münstereifel-Nöthen (Pesch)—some in temples, some in cult settings, some used as foundation stones for later buildings. Zingsheim is the smallest and least complex of the sites, Pesch by far the largest and most complex. The three sites are within five kilometers of each other.

The tiny village of Zingsheim is located on a flat plain near the river Urft. Its site was discovered in 1960, and excavated in 1963 and 1975; the period of the temple was the second to fourth centuries CE, with the height of temple activity in the third to fourth centuries CE. Since the dates of the stone votive altars examined above can be ascertained only to 164 to 251 CE, activity at the Zingsheim site extends probable Matronae veneration in the area by another century, although it is possible that the site was put to other uses later in its history. Excavated at Zingsheim were the flat outlines of a Gallo-Roman temple: a rectangular inner sanctum or *cella* with high clerestory roof and windows, surrounded by an "ambulatory," a covered walkway in which one could walk around the central cella. Surrounding the ambulatory was a low wall holding up the walkway roof. The long sides of the temple were aligned northeast-southwest. The outer walls of the ambulatory were 8.4 meters across by 8.7 meters long. The stone used in the building was quarried limestone, with some greywacke, a form of masonry with small rounded rocks or pebbles packed tightly in sand.[7] There are some traces of other structures on the site, but they have not been excavated. It is possible that stone votive altars rested on the low walls of the ambulatory, or were deposited within the central cella. Perhaps some form of ritual circumambulation took place at the temple. Again, ritual was apparently performed to the goddesses collectively.

The Matronae worshiped at the Zingsheim temple were the Matronae Fachinehae ("matrons at the river near the fish-catching device," or alternately, "Gladsome Ones"). One of the votive altar stones at the Zingsheim temple reads: *Matronis Fachineis Lucius Celeris pro se et suis Libens Merito.* Translated, the inscription says, "To the Matronae Fachineis has Lucius Celeris for himself and for his family fully and freely fulfilled his vow." The date for this votive altar stone is the end of the second century or beginning of the third century CE, which places the altar within the time-frame of the dated stone votive altars examined above. Matronae votive altar stones were often reused as grave covers, and at least one of the Matronae Fachinehae stones had been recarved as a funerary stone.

A few kilometers away from Zingsheim, at Nettersheim, a temple complex to the Matronae sits atop a hill called the Görresburg. Excavated in 1909 and again in 1976–1977, this complex contains a Gallo-Roman temple with ambulatory and two small side buildings, all enclosed in a *temenos*: a piece of land marked off, in this case by a wall, for ritual use. The purpose of the two small side buildings is unknown, but they may be shrines or storage buildings for cult materials or cult offerings. There was also a pit in front of the Gallo-Roman temple for offerings. Most of the votive altars were discovered in front of the main Gallo-Roman temple, on or near the outer wall of the ambulatory.[8] The altars found there were dedicated to the Matronae Aufaniae, who were venerated by the *beneficiarii*, as they were by their superiors at Bonn. The majority of the Matronae altars at Nettersheim date from 150–250 CE, which puts them firmly into the second–third century veneration seen in other votive altar stones.

During Roman times the Nettersheim site was a *statio*, or outpost for legionaries at the rank of *beneficiarii consulares*, especially common along the Roman road system. The most common tasks for the beneficiarii were to patrol the roads and collect tolls. The temple precinct is on a hilltop again near the river Urft and was next to a Roman *vicus* (village) on the Junkerath to Bonn Roman road, or perhaps the Trier to Köln road.[9] A very unusual votive altar stone from Nettersheim to the Matronae Aufaniae dates from 205 CE and says, "to the Holy Aufanis, T. Flavius Severus, beneficiarius consularis and Successinia Tita, for him and his family, willingly and rightly fulfilled his vow, in the time of the second consulship of Antonius and of Geta."[10] There are several points of interest about this inscription. First, the Matronae are referred to as Aufanis Sanctis instead of Matronis; this occurs on only a few other inscriptions. This is the only stone at Nettersheim to be given by a husband-and-wife couple. The husband's name is fully Romanized, but the wife's name, Successinia Tita, is apparently Germanic (the *-inia* ending is telling, similar to the Germanic *-inja*). Women were more likely to preserve native Germanic names than their male spouses or relatives. Geta was murdered by his older brother, and his name was erased from inscriptions, including this one.[11]

The largest temple complex of these examples was at Bad Münstereifel–Nöthen (Pesch), on a hill called the Addig. The goddesses venerated at Pesch were the Matronae Vacallinehae (either those "of the tribe Vacalli," "where the coltsfoot grows" or "of the river Waal"). The site was excavated in 1913, 1918, and 1962. The temple precinct, much larger than the previous two discussed, was built in more phases and used over a longer period of time. The first building period (mostly in wood) dates from the middle or second half of the second century CE. There were simple rectangular wooden buildings with a temenos wall and a simple cella. The second period at Pesch dated from 150 to 200 CE, and the third period begins with the second quarter of the fourth century CE. These later phases featured the stone buildings that are now visible at the site. The cella for the later temple is positioned over the cella of the first structure.[12]

The building of the second layer of the temple precinct seems likely to have coincided with the known dates of Matronae veneration in the area. The buildings from the latest period that have been excavated and are currently visible in their foundations or partial reconstructions were built around 330 CE and destroyed around 450 CE. Nearly 300 Matronae votive altars were found on the site, many recovered from the foundations of the later buildings where they had been used as fill. These altars were presumably on view during the second phase of the site's use. Matronae veneration may have disappeared from the site circa 325 CE, which still places the veneration almost a century later than the known dated votives of 164–251 CE.

This is the only one of the three temple precincts to have a well on site, probably from the earliest phase of use. All of the doors to the buildings are oriented to the east. There were three main buildings or cult areas in the latest phase of building. The furthest north was a typical Gallo-Roman temple with columned and pillared ambulatory. Here were found at least seven altars to the Matronae Vacallinehae. Window glass was also found on the site. In the center of the site was an enclosed cult courtyard ("Kulthof"). This was a large courtyard, a simple, low-walled area, with two small buildings at the two front corners. It is possible, like the small buildings at the Nettersheim complex, that these were small shrines, or that they were used to store cult ceremony objects or particularly valuable religious offerings. Also excavated in this courtyard was a small six-sided, open pillared temple, dated to sometime after the third century CE, built for the Roman god Jupiter. Many of the votive altar stones were found in this Kulthof. Interestingly, only one stone of the hundreds at Pesch can be affirmed as donated by a member of the military. Unlike other sites, at Pesch there is basically no evidence of a military presence. Furthest south of the excavated buildings is a building called the "Basilika" or "Versammlungshaus" (assembly-house). It is an early example in the north of what became the three-naved churches during the early Christian era and was known architecturally as a basilica throughout the Greco-Roman world. The building was possibly used for religious or civic gatherings.

The three example temple precincts offer some commonalities. All three feature a Gallo-Roman temple with ambulatory, common across Gaul and Britain. Both Nettersheim and Pesch are hilltop shrines, with buildings oriented to the east. At no site is there evidence for residence of ritual specialists, priests, or offering attendants, although such are pictured on Matronae votive altars, and presumably the worship at the temples included such rituals as portrayed on votive altar scenes. There is a village next to the Nettersheim site, probably for the lodging of the beneficiarii. The evidence of these three temples supports the importance of the worship of the Matronae by a wide variety of people in all walks of life (military, ranking military, villager). The Nettersheim temple was mainly staffed by military members of the beneficiarii class, fairly high ranking, who copied their superiors in Bonn by worshiping the Matronae Aufaniae. The temple at Pesch appears to have been created by local villagers, keeping Germanic names, and not members of the military. This did not deter them from building a large and complex temple site.

Inscriptions and Epithets

The story in stone of the Deae Matronae would not be complete without a discussion of the actual words carved in stone describing the Matronae. These fall into two categories. First, there are the inscriptions themselves. Second, as a subset of the inscriptions, there are the Matronae "epithets," the descriptive names given to each collective.

Of the first case, the inscriptions themselves, the "Vettius" Stone provides an idealized inscription, as it also provided an idealized artistic image. The inscription can be translated as "Q Vettius Severus, quaestor of Köln, has willingly and rightfully fulfilled his vow to the Aufanian Mothers in the year of the consulships of Macrinius and Celsus."[13] This idealized inscription provides the name of the Matronae and their epithet, the name of the donor of the altar, a formula concerning the fulfillment of a vow, and an indication of the date. The inscriptions show that part of the worship of the Matronae included making a vow to the goddesses, then devoting an altar and celebrating a ritual when the vow has been achieved or the prayer answered. The inscriptions do not indicate the nature of the vow, so it is unknown if the prayer was for advancement, protection, healing, or some other specific help requested of the goddesses. The inscriptions indicate that the Deae Matronae are a collective: the inscription is written to the goddesses in the plural, not conflated into one being, and they were venerated collectively for their collective action on behalf of their worshipers.

Most Matronae goddess names are paired with a descriptive epithet: they carry epithets that describe their activities, their work, their place in the landscape, their relationship with a group of people, a clan or tribe. In the inscriptions, the goddesses are named by the Latin Matronae (nominative plural) or Matronis (dative plural, indicating "for the goddesses Matronae"), and a second word, an epithet describing the goddesses in some way. The Germanic Matronae epithets are among the earliest attested writing in any Germanic language, roughly comparable with the oldest Runic inscriptions from further north. This gives these epithets a linguistic importance in addition to their religious-historical importance.

The veneration of the Rhineland Matronae was the worship by a Germanic Ubii tribe and its Roman military neighbors, at the frontier of the Roman empire, in an area that had possibly been held by Celts. The same ethnic mix can be seen in the Matronae epithets. Having been created in a syncretized Roman religious culture and carved by Roman stonecutters, the names and inscriptions are in Latin. At root, some of the epithets are Germanic, some are Celtic, and some are Germanicized Celtic, as befits a Germanic religion on soil that had possibly been held by a Celtic tribe. The words underlying the Matronae epithets from this area are either Germanic or Celtic, depending on the indigenous collective deities being honored by that particular altar or inscription.

For linguistic analysis of the Matronae epithets, the most important recent work is that of Günter Neumann.[14] Examples chosen here are goddesses of the three temple sites, the Matronae Aufaniae, the Matronae Fachinehae, and the Matronae Vacallinehae. The epithet Aufaniae is one of the most-attested, with over seventy examples on votive altars. According to Neumann, the prefix *au-* can be seen in the adjective *auþja-* ("far, remote"). The primary word, Germanic **fanja-* ("bog, fen"), is widely attested in place-names. **Au-fanja-* would be the "remote fen," and the Matronae Aufaniae would be the "matrons of the remote fen." Their primary source of worship appears to have been in Bonn, the home of the highest-ranking Roman military and their families. The site of excavation in Bonn, under the Bonn Cathedral, is near the Rhine River, so perhaps the "remote fen" refers to swampy riverland.

The Matronae Fachinehae were worshiped at the temple at Zingsheim. The presence of the Latin spelling *-ch-* or *-h-* points to an underlying Germanic- χ-. The root is **faχ-*, Indo-European *pa-* ("mooring"). In Germanic, the meaning can be seen most clearly in the Gothic noun *gafah* ("the catch, especially of fish"). To the Indo-European root *pa-* there is the Old Saxon variant, *fac* ("perimeter, enclosure") and OHG *fah* ("wall"). The Old High German noun *fah* also designates in West Germanic a weir or device for catching eels in the river. Neumann suggests that **Fachina-* is the course of a river with such a catching device in place; he also notes older analysis that suggests this epithet might come from Gothic *faheps* ("joy") and the related verbs *-fahjan* ("to satisfy, to please, to content") and *faginon* ("to be glad").[15] This offers the translation "Gladsome Ones."

The Matronae Vacallinehae may bear a Germanicized Celtic name.[16] In the Rhine region, the Germanic settlers took many of the native Celtic deity names and used them in Germanic word building, making hybrid word formations. The Gallic *callio marci "testiculus equi"* translates to German "*Huflattich*," or the botanical coltsfoot. This could be a site name, "place where the coltsfoot grows." However, there are other options for Matronae Vacallinehae. Perhaps it is a watercourse name, the river Waal, Gallic *Vacalus*, Germanic *Vahalis*. Although the river Waal in modern times runs considerably northward of the Matronae temple at Pesch, the name Vacalus once applied to the entire lower-Rhine region.[17] Finally, it is also possible that the name Vacallinehae is derived from the name of a local tribe, the Vacalli.

The Deae Matronae of the Romano-Germanic Rhineland are probably the earliest, but by no means the only, example of the collective sacred female in Germanic religious history. There are the powerful Old Norse collectives, including the Norns, the Dísir, and the Valkyries. Later, during the Christian era, there are collectives of saints, as well as folkloric women like witches, godmothers, and wood-wives. The collective sacred female is not limited to Germania; it is found throughout Europe and is especially widespread in Greece. The Deae Matronae are the earliest historical articulation in Germanic religious history. All votive altar artwork, epithets, inscriptions, and temple worship point to goddesses venerated by all the people, whether military or native, high-ranking nobility or village inhabitant. The Deae Matronae in their collective work of provision gave help and fulfilled promises to all.

Notes

1. Cf. Dawn E. Work-MaKinne, "Deity in Sisterhood: The Collective Sacred Female in Germanic Europe," PhD diss., Union Institute and University, 2009, and Karen Bek-Pedersen on the Norns (next chapter in this volume).

2. Note that the collective is a group of adult women, perhaps a sisterhood. There is no indication of a Maiden-Mother-Crone triplicity in the Matronae goddesses.

3. Vincent T. Burns, "Romanization and Acculturation: The Rhineland Matronae," PhD diss., University of Wisconsin, 1994, 302.

4. Sarah Iles Johnston, *Religions of the Ancient World: A Guide* (Cambridge: Belknap Press of Harvard University Press, 2004), 346.

5. Christoph B. Rüger, "A Husband for the Mother Goddess: Some Observations on the Matronae Aufaniae," in *Rome and Her Northern Provinces*, ed. Brian Hartley and J. S. Wacher (Gloucester Gloucestershire: A. Sutton, 1983), 214.

6. Cf. Miriam Robbins Dexter, "The Frightful Goddess: Birds, Snakes and Witches," in *Varia on the Indo-European Past: Papers in Memory of Marija Gimbutas*, ed. Miriam Robbins Dexter and Edgar C. Polomé (Washington, DC: Institute for the Study of Man, 1997), 124–154.

7. Peter D. Horne and Anthony C. King, "Romano-Celtic Temples in Continental Europe: A Gazetteer of Those with Known Plans," in *Temples, Churches, and Religion*, ed. Warwick Rodwell (Oxford: BAR, 1980), 492.

8. Burns, "Romanization and Acculturation," 101.

9. Alex Gustav Garman, *The Cult of the Matronae in the Roman Rhineland: An Historical Evaluation of the Archaeological Evidence* (Lewiston, NY: Edwin Mellen Press, 2008), 70.

10. Burns, "Romanization and Acculturation," 172.

11. Ibid., 173.

12. Horne and King, "Romano-Celtic Temples," 447.

13. Burns, "Romanization and Acculturation," 152.

14. Günter Neumann, "Die Germanischen Matronen-Beinamen," in *Matronen und Verwandte Gottheiten*, ed. Gerhard Bauchhenss and Günter Neumann (Köln: Rheinland-Verlag, 1987), 103–132.

15. Ibid., 119.

16. Karl Horst Schmidt, "Die Keltischen Matronennamen," in *Matronen und Verwandte Gottheiten*, ed. Bauchhenss and Neumann, 145.

17. Siegfried Gutenbrunner. *Die Germanischen Götternamen der Antiken Inschriften* (Halle: M. Niemeyer, 1936), 180.

Bibliography

Burns, Vincent T. "Romanization and Acculturation: The Rhineland Matronae." PhD diss., University of Wisconsin, 1994.

Dexter, Miriam Robbins. "The Frightful Goddess: Birds, Snakes, and Witches." In *Varia on the Indo-European Past: Papers in Memory of Marija Gimbutas*, ed. Miriam Robbins Dexter and Edgar C. Polomé, 124–154. Washington, DC: Institute for the Study of Man, 1997.

Garman, Alex Gustav. *The Cult of the Matronae in the Roman Rhineland: An Historical Evaluation of the Archaeological Evidence*. Lewiston, NY: Edwin Mellen Press, 2008.

Gimbutas, Marija, and Miriam Robbins Dexter. *The Living Goddesses*. Berkeley: University of California Press, 1999.

Green, Miranda J. *Celtic Goddesses: Warriors, Virgins, and Mothers*. 1st ed. New York: G. Braziller, 1996.

Gutenbrunner, Siegfried. *Die Germanischen Götternamen Der Antiken Inschriften*. Halle: M. Niemeyer, 1936.

Horne, Peter D., and Anthony C. King. "Romano-Celtic Temples in Continental Europe: A Gazetteer of Those with Known Plans." In *Temples, Churches, and*

Religion: Recent Research in Roman Britain: With a Gazetteer of Romano-Celtic Temples in Continental Europe, ed. Warwick Rodwell, 369–585. Oxford: BAR, 1980.

Johnston, Sarah Iles. *Religions of the Ancient World: A Guide.* Harvard University Press Reference Library. Cambridge: Belknap Press of Harvard University Press, 2004.

Neumann, Günter. "Die Germanischen Matronen-Beinamen." In *Matronen und Verwandte Gottheiten: Ergebnisse Eines Kolloquiums Veranstaltet von der Göttinger Akademiekommission für die Altertumskunde Mittel-und Nordeuropas*, ed. Gerhard Bauchhenss and Günter Neumann, 103–132. Köln: Rheinland-Verlag, 1987.

Rüger, Christoph B. "A Husband for the Mother Goddess: Some Observations on the *Matronae Aufaniae.*" In *Rome and Her Northern Provinces: Papers Presented to Sheppard Frere in Honour of His Retirement from the Chair of the Archaeology of the Roman Empire, University of Oxford, 1983*, ed. Brian Hartley and J. S. Wacher, 210–221. Gloucester: A. Sutton, 1983.

Schmidt, Karl Horst. "Die Keltischen Matronennamen." In *Matronen und Verwandte Gottheiten: Ergebnisse Eines Kolloquiums Veranstaltet von der Göttinger Akademiekommission für die Altertumskunde Mittel-und Nordeuropas*, ed. Gerhard Bauchhenss and Günter Neumann, 133–154. Köln: Rheinland-Verlag, 1987.

Work-MaKinne, Dawn E. "Deity in Sisterhood: The Collective Sacred Female in Germanic Europe." PhD diss., Union Institute and University, 2009.

19

The Norns: Representatives of Fate in Old Norse Tradition

Karen Bek-Pedersen

The Norns (*nornir*) are probably one of the best-known groups of female supernatural beings in Old Norse tradition.[1] Turning up only a handful of times, yet strangely pervasive, these shadowy figures are closely connected to ideas about fate and destiny. Most of their appearances consist of brief references to their secretive dealings behind the backs of human beings, yet they loom in the background, intangible and mostly out of focus—intriguingly difficult to grasp.

Although they are not particularly prominent in the sources, they come across as powerful beings and are often referred to in scholarship as "goddesses of fate."[2] However, they are not "goddesses" in the sense of belonging to the Old Norse pantheon proper, nor is there much evidence of any formal worship or cult activities relating specifically to the Norns in the heathen belief system as now understood. The Norns share certain aspects with a number of Old Norse goddesses (*ásynjur*), such as Frigg, Freyia, Iðunn, and Sága, as well as several other female supernatural beings from the same tradition, but they seem to have been considered a separate group of beings.

On a few occasions, the Norns appear to be somehow connected to the god Óðinn, but never as his subordinates;[3] indeed, attempting to establish any hierarchy between Óðinn and the Norns may be a mistaken interpretation of the link between them. The overlapping of the Norns and the above-mentioned goddesses, as well as other groups of female beings, particularly Valkyries (*valkyrjur*) and Dísir, means that it can be difficult in some instances to establish absolute clarity with regard to what type of being is presented in a given context, also because of the Old Norse convention of frequently using synonyms (*heiti*) and kennings, especially in poetic language. It is nevertheless possible to draw some lines among Norns, Valkyries, Dísir, and goddesses (ásynjur), yet such lines will never be absolutely clear; there will always be grey areas between these different groups of beings.

The Norns are mentioned predominantly in skaldic and eddic poetry and in a few prose texts. The most important source is the Edda, an anonymous collection of mythological and heroic poems from Iceland, of which the earliest version is from circa 1270.[4] Snorra-Edda, a prose collection of mythological material, is thought to have been written around 1220 by the Icelander Snorri Sturlusson, though the earliest surviving manuscript dates from ca. 1300–1325.[5] The skaldic poems, composed by poets of the Viking and early medieval period, ca. 800–1300, may well constitute the chronologically oldest material, but they survive predominantly in sagas that were written down several centuries after the poems were allegedly composed. As far as dating this material is concerned, it must be kept in mind that while the manuscripts, the language, and the external poetic forms can be dated, this is not the case for the meanings and narratives. In other words, the wrappings are dateable, but not the contents.

In Old Norse poetry, the Norns are often associated with violent death, with transition of various kinds, and with battle. Different aspects of their nature are portrayed in different contexts. For instance, the saga hero Kveldúlfr laments the loss of his son Þórólfr, who has died in battle. Kveldúlfr says that Óðinn has chosen Þórólfr much too soon and that the Norn "is grim to me."[6] There are strong emotions involved in the scene, a sense of personal tragedy on the part of the father who has lost his son, but also the notion that Þórólfr has been chosen, presumably as a worthy warrior. The emotional cost brought about by the involvement of the norn is high, but it is noteworthy that Kveldúlfr says that she "is grim to me," whilst nothing is said about her being grim to Þórólfr.

Another poem shows a somewhat different aspect of the Norns although this, too, concerns a battle wherein men have been killed. Torf-Einarr rejoices in the fact that he has won the battle, stating that "the Norns settled this right" (or "with justice"). He appears to say that now that he has carried out his share of the revenge of his father, he is also due his share of the inheritance after the father. The looming dispute over the inheritance between Torf-Einarr and his half-brothers is of a legal nature and it is interesting that he mentions the Norns in this context—as if they have an involvement in such matters—while stating that they "settled it right."[7]

In poem *Ynglingatal*, which essentially lists the deaths of several more or less mythical Swedish kings, the Norns are mentioned when Hálfdanr "enjoyed the judgment of the Norns," referring to his death.[8] This use of the noun *dómr* ("judgment") brings in a quasi-legal aspect of the dealings of the Norns, not unlike the reference in Torf-Einarr, whilst the verb *njóta* ("enjoy") may indicate that the death was timely or somehow appropriate. The connotations of this verb may, however, also recall the notion of death as a sexual encounter with a supernatural female being—although one would rather expect the term *valkyrie* to be employed in such alluring circumstances.[9]

An unusual reference shows the Norns in a different light, when Hallfreðr describes his conversion to Christianity, clearly a transitional point in his life. From his newly (and, it seems, reluctantly adopted) Christian perspective he looks back on his heathen beliefs, stating:

So is the custom at the Sygna king's place
that sacrifice is forbidden;
most of us must avoid
the ancient norn decisions;
all men leave behind
Óðinn's sacrifice;
I, too, am forced from Njörðr's kin
to worship Christ instead.[10]

It is interesting that Hallfreðr refers to the heathen belief system as "the ancient Norn decisions." The fact that he mentions the Norns alongside the gods (*æsir*, such as Óðinn, and *vanir* including Njörðr or Freyr depending on which manuscript is quoted), gives the impression that the Norns are as important and central to the heathen religious beliefs as the gods. Considering that Hallfreðr does not mention the goddesses here may justify the question of what he really means by the term *nornir*. Is he perhaps using it as a *heiti* for goddesses (ásynjur)?

The connection of Norns and water is often emphasized. One stanza says that: 'Urðr comes out of the well / spring."[11] Urðr, a noun meaning "fate," is used in some texts as a proper name for a Norn. The well or spring, important in relation to the Norns and to ideas about fate, is found in a number of texts that refer to Urðarbrunnr ("the well of fate") and this stanza serves to reinforce this link. It is noteworthy that the connection between the Norns and a source of water is repeated on the part of several other supernatural female figures in many poems, eddic and skaldic. Frigg is said to dwell in Fensalir ("Hall in the Fens"), Sága in Søkkvabekkr ("Sunken Benches"), Iðunn in Brunnakr ("Field of Wells/Springs"), and in one instance the name Sökkdalr ("Sunken Glen") is used to name the dwelling place of Gunnlöð. She is not usually considered a goddess, but Gunnlöð does share important facets with the above-mentioned ásynjur, particularly regarding her links to Óðinn whom she grants a special drink during his stay in her dwelling place. All of these female figures overlap with the Norns. This does not mean that distinctions are not relevant or that they cannot be made, but this overlap may well say something about the female principle in general in Old Norse tradition.

In the story of Óðinn's visit to Gunnlöð, an important reference describes the well of fate as a source of secret knowledge.[12] By extension, this would seem to connect Urðr, and probably the Norns as a collective whole, to notions of otherworldly knowledge. The scene is not unlike that of an initiation or an inauguration.[13]

A passage of particular interest in relation to the Norns appears in the eddic poem Völuspá 19–20:

I know an ash that stands
called Yggdrasill,
a tall tree, watered
with white silt;
from there come the dews
that fall in the valleys;
it stands eternally, green
over the well of Urðr.

From there come maidens,
very knowledgeable,
three, from that lake
which stands under the tree;
one they called Urðr,
another Verðandi,
-they carved on slips of wood-
Skuld the third one.
They laid down laws,
they chose life
for the children of men,
the fate of men.[14]

This is a remarkable passage, partly in being so detailed in its description of these "maidens" and partly in being so different from other references to the Norns. It is generally accepted that this passage does refer to Norns although the term is not actually employed. Such is also Snorri's interpretation; when he quotes this passage, he adds: "We call them Norns."[15]

These two sources are the only ones that refer specifically to three individually named Norns: Urðr, Verðandi, and Skuld. The name Urðr does appear to be strongly linked to the Norns and to the concept of fate in Old Norse tradition. The name Verðandi is suspicious because it is exactly the present extended form of the verb *verða* ("to become") and is nowhere else attested as a name of a Norn or of any other kind of being. The name Skuld is given later in Völuspá as the name of a Valkyrie;[16] the name also occurs in other texts attached to female figures possessing magical skills or of supernatural descent. The noun *skuld* means "debt" or "something owed."

Often, these three names are understood to refer to time, with Urðr representing the past, Verðandi the present, and Skuld the future. This interpretation is not impossible, as the etymologies of the names could be seen to have certain links to aspects of chronology, most convincingly on the part of Verðandi. But the interpretation raises serious questions inasmuch as neither the words nor the names of Urðr and Skuld are ever used to denote the chronological periods of past and future. Although etymological considerations allow for the possibility of making the connections, the names do not in themselves carry these meanings. It seems more sensible to read the three names in their literal senses, as meaning Fate, Becoming, and Debt, while noting that they potentially have an additional layer of meaning relating to chronology, especially given the presence of Verðandi in between Urðr and Skuld.[17]

The actions carried out by Urðr, Verðandi, and Skuld seem to center on creating and maintaining some sort of order.[18] Notions of making choices, making decisions, and laying down the ground rules are strongly present and may recall the quasi-legal vocabulary surrounding the Norns elsewhere. It is remarkable that violent death, or even death at all, is not mentioned here while it is a feature often evident in other texts that mention the Norns; the description seems to focus much more on life-enhancing aspects.

The idea that there are three Norns and three Norns only is present only in these two sources. Elsewhere, reference is made simply to *nornir* in the plural, as a collective whole, occasionally to *norn* in the singular, as though there were only one. Traditions about their enumeration may well have varied over time and from one geographical location to the next; three may have been the number most often associated with the Norns—as triple figures are common in many European traditions—but the evidence from Old Norse tradition does not really allow any firm conclusions regarding this point.

It is, for example, noteworthy that one eddic poem mentions, not three Norns, but three groups of Norns:

> Of different origins
> are the Norns, I say,
> they are not related;
> some are of the æsir,
> some are of the álfar,
> some are the daughters of Dvalin.[19]

It seems odd to describe the Norns in terms of belonging to *æsir, álfar,* and *dvergar* (Dvalin being the name of a dvergar), as if Norn describes an occupation or status, rather than a separate class of being.[20] Phrases very similar to this one are found in some other poems, and the division into three may be formulaic or traditional. Snorri, while naming three individual ones, divides the Norns into two groups, one of which one is good and allots good fates, the other being evil and allotting evil fates.[21] This very rational division of their protective and destructive aspects into two separate groups of Norns is hardly heathen in origin. The attitude behind a runic inscription dated to circa 1180 CE seems somewhat more authentic in that it attaches both good and evil to the same one group of Norns: "the Norns decide over both good and evil, for me they have decided much suffering."[22]

Another reference to Norns is somewhat enigmatic: "who are those Norns who go to those in need and separate mothers from sons?"[23] It has often been taken to refer to the Norns' involvement in childbirth, but given the fact that the word *nauðgönglar* ("those that go to those in need") is a hapax legomenon—which means that it occurs nowhere else—it is difficult to reach any firm conclusion regarding the context of it here. The meaning of "those in need" and the separation of mothers and sons could just as well refer to mothers losing their sons in battle, thus pointing toward the transition from life to death rather than the transition into life at birth. To read the stanza as a reference to childbirth is at best conjectural, though it is natural to assume that the Norns would be linked to the beginning of life and not just to its end.

One eddic poem does show the Norns in connection with birth, but they attend the birth in order to decide on the child's fate, not to help out.[24] A few references from 19th-century folk tradition in Setesdal, Norway, and in the Faroe Islands speak of a certain food called "norn porridge" that was prepared after childbirth, but this does not necessarily constitute evidence for any ancient custom.[25]

The context of battle and violent death is prevalent also in a number of eddic poems. The hero Helgi brings his Valkyrie lover Sigrún the news that he has killed her brother and father, stating, "though I say the Norns decided some of it." With these words, he seems to indicate that he had no desire to kill them but was obliged to do so, almost as if it were not in his power to do otherwise. The conflict is deeply emotional on the part of both Helgi and Sigrún; the complex divided loyalties to their kin on the one side and to their love for each other on the other side leads them into a situation where all possible ways out will bring them tragedy.[26]

In another poem, warfare is again the issue:

It were better, brother,
if you had come in armour,
like eagle-carved helmets,
to see Atli's home,
had you sat in the saddle
through sun-heated days,
made the Norns weep
at corpses deathly pale,
taught Hunnish shield-maidens
how to work the fields,
and Atli himself
you could have put in a snake pit,
now that snake pit
is reserved for you.[27]

The poem appears to suggest that the Norns would have wept over the great number of men Gunnarr would have killed had he only come to Atli's place armed and prepared for war. While this reveals that the Norns feel pity for human lives, it does make them seem somewhat gloomy if it takes something of such a scale to make them show their pity. The descriptions of shield-maidens working the fields may enhance the notion that these events are unlikely to take place. No other instances of weeping Norns are found.

In another battle, we hear the heroes Hamðir and Sörli speaking:

We have fought well,
we stand on Goth corpses
weary of sword-edge
like eagles on a branch.
We have won great renown
whether we die now or yesterday,
no man lives out the evening
after the Norns give their verdict.[28]

While the phrase "verdict of the Norns" undoubtedly refers to death
(and here specifically to the death of the two heroes), it is not all gloom.
The feeling conveyed seems to be satisfaction for a job well done. The
stanza describes a great victory on the part of Hamðir and Sörli, hinting
at the heroic reputation they have gained from it, and it is not unlikely
that such a reputation is worth paying for with life. Although death is
not infrequently the context in which the Norns are mentioned, that in
itself needs not be considered negative. Their nature is more nuanced.

Another reference occurred in the immediately preceding stanza: "We
are not the ones to follow the example of wolves . . . like the Norns'
dogs."[29] The wolves referred to may be literally the beasts of the battlefield
from whose ferocious behavior the speaker, Sörli, distances himself. But
the stanza may also be interpreted as he felt that he was not in charge of
his own actions but acted in accordance with the commands of the Norns,
much as a dog obeys the commands of its master. Norns, however, are
not normally portrayed as giving commands directly to people; instead,
they make decisions without people knowing about it until the effects
become clear. No other sources link the Norns to wolves, but it is noteworthy that troll-women are sometimes portrayed with close connections
to wolves.[30]

In another eddic poem, the Norns are mentioned in connection with
runes.[31] Clearly, the talk is of rune-magic rather than mere literacy, but
there is no apparent basis for connecting Norns closely with the runes;
they are simply mentioned as part of a long list of how to use runes and
which runes have what effect. Runes should be cut "on the nail of the
Norn" for protection against deception, with the addition: "and mark
your nail with nauð," presumably the N-rune, though as a noun nauð
means "need, necessity, distress."[32]

One poem about the Norns is unusual in describing what the Norns do and how they go about allotting fate:

Night fell on the place,
the Norns came,
those who were to shape
fate for the prince;
they said the king
should be most famous
and that he would be thought
the best of leaders.

They twisted very strongly
the strands of fate,
as the fortification broke
in Brálundr;
they arranged
golden threads
and fastened them in the middle
of the moon's hall.

East and west
they put the ends,
the prince should have
the land between;
the kinswoman of Neri
to the north
threw one fastening;
bade it hold forever.[33]

This is the only source that unequivocally connects the Norns to textile work, an activity commonly accepted as being typical of Norns. But when the source material is consulted and scrutinized, it would seem to be, in fact, quite uncommon; textile work such as weaving and spinning is by no means what dominates references to the Norns.[34] It is hardly hinted at elsewhere, though the poem connects fate and warfare to the act of weaving, mentioning Valkyries instead of Norns. There are indications that textile work was considered related to the concept of fate in Old Norse tradition, at least during the early medieval period, but the evidence does not seem to allow for direct links to the Norns without making assumptions based on extratraditional material, for example from Roman and Greek mythology.[35] The dominant metaphors for fate appear to draw on images relating to some quasi-legal sphere, probably also to issues pertaining to speech and communication of secret knowledge.

Outside the Eddas and skaldic poems, the Norns make few appearances, but some other sources merit a mention. Regarding the idea that fate may be linked to the spoken word this verse appears: "the words of Urðr no man can hinder, though it was flawed in its creation."[36] The poem is closely related to the eddic poems in terms of style, form, and content, but it only survives in a 17th-century manuscript and is therefore often regarded as too late to be trustworthy. In the cited stanza, fate is described as something spoken. This may link up with the notion of fate as a quasi-legal matter given that law was spoken, not written, in the oral, preliterate society of Scandinavia prior to the adoption of Christianity. It also appears to relate closely to ideas about prophecy, which similarly is a matter of words spoken out loud and considered to be particularly powerful.[37]

Finally, a short tale makes reference to the Norns.[38] It tells the story of Gestr, who is known as Norna-Gestr because three mysterious women came to his cradle to predict his future when he was born. The tale has many of the qualities of a folktale rather than of mythology,[39] and it employs the term *Norn* only about one of the three women, the one who gives an evil prediction while the other two have given good ones. The other two are called seeresses (*völur*) and speywives (*spákonur*). In this way, it may be that the tale slips into what became the common usage of the term *Norn* in later times, namely as meaning "witch" or "hag" rather than "goddess of fate."

Information about the Norns that can be obtained from available sources is fragmentary and incomplete, and it seems advisable to avoid making too many assumptions. Such a narrow base of evidence does undeniably lend itself more easily to conjecture than to firm conclusions; it is hard to tell what the Norns stood for in the heathen worldview, and it must be kept in mind that, whatever it was, it was both provisional and revisable. Ideas about the Norns may well have changed through time as well as between different geographical regions—the Icelandic perception of Norns around the year 1000 CE need not be exactly the same as the one current in southern Sweden 300 years earlier. From the material discussed in this chapter, it appears that there are several unusual references to the Norns, describing features not mentioned elsewhere. It is difficult, indeed risky, to generalize on the basis of such singular occurrences; are they representative of a greater picture now lost, or of the chance survival of oddities? It is very hard to tell.

Notes

1. The term "Old Norse" refers to the languages, cultures, and traditions of the Scandinavian cultural area during the period ca. 800–1100 CE. The Scandinavian cultural area at this time includes the "homelands" of Denmark, southern and middle Norway, and southern and middle Sweden, but also the new settlement areas of the Faroe Islands, Iceland, and Norse Greenland, as well as the Scottish archipelagos of Orkney and Shetland.

2. The Old Norse sources that deal with the Norns consists almost entirely in literary material produced in early medieval Iceland; especially relevant are the *Poetic Edda* (ca. 1270 CE), *Snorra-Edda* (ca. 1325 CE; supposedly written ca. 1220 CE) and skaldic poetry (ca. 1250–1400 CE). For a discussion of these, see Terry Gunnell, "Eddic Poetry," in *A Companion to Old Norse-Icelandic Literature and Culture*, ed. Rory McTurk (Oxford: Blackwell, 2005).

3. Óðinn seems to have been a very important deity in Old Norse culture. He has been mistakenly regarded as father of all the other gods, an error based on a reinterpretation of his character going back to the early Middle Ages (see Mathias Strandberg, "On the Etymology of Compounded Old Icelandic Óðinn Names with the Second Component—Föðr," *Scripta Islandica* 59 (2008): 93–120). Óðinn was a figure closely connected to issues of wisdom, poetry, magic, violent death, gold, warfare, and numinous knowledge. One expression of his grim aspect was that he was thought to ensure the death of great heroes deliberately because he wanted them to join his chthonic army in his otherworldly abode Valhöll ("Hall of the Slain"). He seems to have been a god especially favored by war-bands, kings and leaders.

4. Gunnell, "Eddic Poetry," 82.

5. Ibid., 83.

6. Occasional stanza (*lausavísa*) 5 in Egils saga Skallagrímssonar 24. *Lausavísur* are single strophes (rather than longer poems) composed by saga heroes about special situations in the sagas of Icelanders and in the sagas of the kings. This source clearly refers to one Norn (*norn*), with a grammatically singular form, though most other sources refer to norns (*nornir*) in the plural form.

7. "Lausavísa" by Torf-Einarr, in *Haralds saga ins hárfagra* 30.

8. Stanza 24 in *Ynglingasaga* 47.

9. Gro Steinsland, *Eros og død i norrøne myter* (Oslo: Universitetsforlaget, 1997), 97–123; Judy Quinn, "The Gendering of Death in Eddic Cosmology," in *Old Norse Religion in Long-Term Perspectives: Origins, Changes, and Interactions,* ed. A. Andrén, K. Jennbert, and C. Raudvere (Lund: Nordic Academic Press, 2006), 54.

10. All translations from the Old Norse are my own unless otherwise stated.

11. Third section of Snorra-Edda, Skáldskaparmál, stanza by Kormákr.

12. Stanza 111 of the eddic poem Hávamál.

13. Svava Jakobsdóttir, "Gunnlöð and the Precious Mead (Hávamál)," in *The Poetic Edda—Essays on Old Norse Mythology,* ed. Paul Acker and Carolyne

Larrington (New York: Routledge, 2002), 31–34. It should be said that Snorri also relates Óðinn's visit to Gunnlöð in Skáldskaparmál G57–G58, but his version, although more detailed, is quite different in a number of points, and it is advisable not to assume that the two versions necessarily employ the same perspective or attach the same significance to the story as a whole or to the individual details of it.

14. Völuspá 19–20. All translations of eddic poetry are by Bek-Pedersen and are based on Neckel and Kuhn's edition of the original manuscript.

15. Gylfaginning 15.

16. A double-identity also portrayed in Gylfaginning 36, which groups Skuld both with the Norns and with the Valkyries.

17. Another problem with the temporal interpretation is that time and fate are not really the same concept at all; cf. Anthony Winterbourne, *When the Norns Have Spoken. Fate and Time in Germanic Paganism* (Madison: Fairleigh Dickinson University Press, 2004), 18.

18. Völuspá 19–20.

19. Fáfnismál 13.

20. The terms *æsir, álfar,* and *dvergar* refer to three separate groups of supernatural beings in Old Norse cosmology. The æsir constitute a group of beings clearly regarded as deities and worshiped in various ways; alongside the somewhat similar beings called *vanir* they make up the Old Norse gods. The álfar form a group of beings only vaguely portrayed in the mythology as now known, but they seem to have very close affiliations to both æsir and vanir and may have been a third group of gods (or the term *álfar* may have operated as an alternative term for *vanir*). The dvergar seem to have been an exclusively male race of supernatural beings, wherefore it is surprising that they should have daughters. They appear to have been subterranean or to have lived inside of rocks and large stones; they are portrayed as excellent blacksmiths and smiths of precious metals. The noun *dvergur* is cognate with the English "dwarf," but whether they were thought of particularly as being small is uncertain.

21. Gylfaginning 15.

22. Number IV from Borgund, Norway; see Magnus Olsen, ed., *Norges Innskrifter med de Yngre Runer* 4. XI: Hordaland Fylke XII: Sogn og Fjordane Fylke XIII: Møre og Romsdal Fylke (Oslo: Bokcentralen, 1957), 149.

23. Fáfnismál 12.

24. Helgakviða Hundingbana I 2–4.

25. Johannes Skar, "Bygdeliv," *Gamalt or Sætesdal* IV (Kristiania: Olaf Norlis Forlag, 1909), 120; Mads Andreas Jacobsen and Christian Matras. *Føroysk—Donsk Orðabók* (Færøsk–Dansk Ordbog, Tórshavn: Føroya Fróðskaparfelag, 1961), 299.

26. Helgakviða Hundingsbana II 26.

27. Atlakviða 16.

28. Hamðismál 30.

29. Hamðismál 29.

30. Hyndluljóð 5; Gylfaginning 12 and 49; perhaps also the Hunnestad picture stone in Skåne, Sweden; see Catharina Raudvere, "Kunskap och Insikt I Norrön Tradition," in *Mytologi, rituler och trolldomsanklagelser, Vägar till Midgård*, vol. 3 (Lund: Nordic Academic Press, 2003), 34–35.

31. Sigrdrífumál 17. Runes are the characteristically angular letters of the alphabet indigenous to ancient Scandinavia. It appears that the individual signs were considered to have not just practical but also magical properties; especially the description of how Óðinn acquired knowledge of the runes in the eddic poem *Hávamál* 138–139 contributes to an impression of runes as magical. They continued to be in use in Scandinavia long into the Middle Ages, side by side with the Roman alphabet, which was brought into the region with Christianity.

32. Sigrdrífumál 17.

33. Helgakviða Hundingsbana I 2–4.

34. Karen Bek-Pedersen, "Are the Spinning Nornir Just a Yarn?" *Viking and Medieval Scandinavia* 3 (2007): 1–3. Helgakviða Hundingsbana I describes neither spinning nor weaving, but it clearly involves some related activity, probably twining or braiding.

35. Bek-Pedersen, "Are the Spinning Nornir Just a Yarn?" 4–7; Gerd Wolfgang Weber, "Wyrd: Studien zum Schicksalbegriff der altenglischen und altnordischen Literatur," *Frankfurter Beiträge zur Germanistik* 8 (Berlin: Gehlen, 1969), 124.

36. Fjölsvinnsmál 47.

37. Raudvere op Cit: 42.

38. Norna-Gest þáttr, one of the þættir or shorter tales included in Óláfs saga Tryggvasonar hin mesta,

39. It conforms to the pattern of tale-type ATU 410 in the international folktale index. For a discussion of the index, see Hans-Jörg Uther, "The Types of International Folktales: A Classification and Bibliography Based on the System of Antti Aarne and Stith Thompson," *FF Communications* nos. 284, 285, 286 (Helsinki: Suomalainen Tiedeakatemia, 2004).

Bibliography

Bek-Pedersen, Karen. "Are the Spinning Nornir Just a Yarn?" *Viking and Medieval Scandinavia* 3 (2007): 1–10.

Bek-Pedersen, Karen. "Weaving Swords and Rolling Heads: A Peculiar Space in Old Norse Tradition." In *Space and Time in Europe: East and West, Past and Present*, ed. Mirjam Mencej, 167–180. Ljubljana: Univerza v Ljubljani, Filozofska fakulteta, 2008.

Gunnell, Terry. "Eddic Poetry." In *A Companion to Old Norse-Icelandic Literature and Culture*. ed. Rory McTurk, 82–100. Oxford: Blackwell, 2005.

Jacobsen, Mads Andreas, and Christian Matras. *Føroysk—Donsk Orðabók*. Færøsk—Dansk Ordbog, Tórshavn: Føroya Fróðskaparfelag, 1961.

Neckel, Gustav, ed. *Edda. Die Lieder des Codex Regius nebst verwandten Denkmälern.* Revised by Hans Kuhn. 1: Text, Heidelberg: Carl Winter Universitätsverlag, 1962.

Olsen, Magnus, ed. *Norges Innskrifter med de Yngre Runer* 4. XI: Hordaland Fylke XII: Sogn og Fjordane Fylke XIII: Møre og Romsdal Fylke. Oslo: Bokcentralen, 1957.

Page, R. I. *Runes.* London: The British Museum Press, 1987.

Quinn, Judy. "The Gendering of Death in Eddic Cosmology." In *Old Norse Religion in Long-Term Perspectives: Origins, Changes, and Interactions,* ed. A. Andrén, K. Jennbert, and C. Raudvere, 54–57. Lund: Nordic Academic Press, 2006.

Raudvere, Catharina. "Kunskap och Insikt I Norrön Tradition." *Mytologi, rituler och trolldomsanklagelser, Vägar till Midgård,* vol. 3. Lund: Nordic Academic Press, 2003.

Skar, Johannes. "Bygdeliv." *Gamalt or Sætesdal* IV. Kristiania: Olaf Norlis Forlag, 1909.

Sturluson, Snorri. *Edda: Prologue and Gylfaginning.* Viking Society for Northern Research. London: University College London, 2005.

Sturluson, Snorri. *Edda: Skáldskaparmál,* ed. Anthony Faulkes. Viking Society for Northern Research. London: University College London, 1998.

Steinsland, Gro. *Eros og død i norrøne myter.* Oslo: Universitetsforlaget, 1997.

Strandberg, Mathias. "On the Etymology of Compounded Old Icelandic Óðinn Names with the Second Component—Föðr." *Scripta Islandica* 59 (2008): 93–120.

Svava Jakobsdóttir. "Gunnlöð and the Precious Mead (Hávamál)." In *The Poetic Edda—Essays on Old Norse Mythology,* ed. Paul Acker and Carolyne Larrington, 27–57. New York: Routledge, 2002.

Uther, Hans-Jörg. "The Types of International Folktales: A Classification and Bibliography Based on the System of Antti Aarne and Stith Thompson." *FF Communications,* nos. 284, 285, 286. Helsinki: Suomalainen Tiedeakatemia, 2004.

Weber, Gerd Wolfgang. "Wyrd: Studien zum Schicksalbegriff der altenglischen und altnordischen Literatur." *Frankfurter Beiträge zur Germanistik* 8. Berlin: Gehlen, 1969.

Winterbourne, Anthony. *When the Norns Have Spoken. Fate and Time in Germanic Paganism.* Madison, NJ: Fairleigh Dickinson University Press, 2004.

20

Danu, Raetia, Marisa: Mountain Goddess of the Alps

Claire French

The names of the Alpine mountain goddess are well known from local myth and legend. To this day she is still revered under the guise of the Christian Virgin Mary and a number of female saints throughout the Alps. Her sanctuaries include wayside shrines and chapels, usually built on pre-Christian sites of worship. On fieldtrips through the Alps researcher Hans Haid collected a long list of goddess names: Raetia, Samblana, Nossa Dunna delle Glisch (Our Lady of the Glaciers), Matreia, Madrisa, Dea Noreia, Tanna, Donna Dindia, Dea Matreia, Verena, Veldidena, Virginal, White Lady, Donna Kenina, and the goddess manifesting as the Three Holy Virgins variously known as Margaret, Catherine, and Barbara, or Ambet, Cubet, and Borbet.[1]

The question of the identity of the original Alpine settlers is a subject of scholarly dispute. Some contend that the area was settled by immigrants from the Altai mountains of central Asia, while the southern slopes of the Alps and the left shore of the Po were inhabited partly by Etruscans, Veneto-Illyrians, and the enigmatic Raetians. On the northern and western slopes the Celtic element was prevalent in the Cottian Alps in eastern Gaul. In the Upper Rhine and Danube valleys lived the Celtic Helvetians in present-day Switzerland, and the Norici and Vindelici in what is now Austria and Bavaria respectively.

But by etymological comparisons, Swiss linguists Linus Brunner and Alfred Toth have theorized that the very earliest Alpine pastoralists came from the eastern Mediterranean and spoke Akkadian, an ancient Semitic language. The name Alp (pl. *Alpen*) is said to be derived from Akkadian *alpu* ("bull"), and in the same language the word *reitia* has the meaning of "shepherdess."[2] According to Brunner and Toth, settlement of the Alps occurred over several millennia, beginning in the fifth millennium BCE, after the last Ice Age. As Semitic loan words in Alpine pastoral and dairy industries show, these immigrants seem to have come from Mesopotamia, probably from the area of Ur. They brought with them the cultivation of cereals, such as the wheat varieties einkorn and emmer as well as barley; they introduced dairy farming, sheep breeding, and beekeeping.

Their goddess Reitia, the lady shepherdess, retained her earlier role as lady of the beasts. Narratives show her as protector of the Alpine fauna, particularly of chamois and ibex. She watches the hunter, often in her triple manifestation as the Saligen Fräulein ("the Blessed Ladies"), and any hunting crime is severely punished. She also protects the dangerous work of transhumance, the droving of cattle and sheep from winter quarters to summer pastures, a practice that has allowed the survival of human and beast in the Alps for thousands of years.

The Alpine Arc, extending over 80,000 square miles across the center of Europe from Slovenia in the east to France in the west, cuts the continent into halves and represents a considerable hindrance for trade and traffic. The glacier region of the Inner Alps appears like an unexplored continent, a literal and figurative "white spot" on the map of Europe. Poor in economic assets, the region is nevertheless rich in natural beauty, history, and cultural values. After many armed conflicts in the past, the mountains are now peacefully shared by Latins (French, Italians, Romanches, and Ladinians), Teutons (Bavarians and Suebians), and Slavs (Slovenians), and the mountain dwellers consider themselves a people apart. Although they speak different languages and follow different religions, there is an overall sense of unity and a feeling of common interests.

Apart from localized mining activities Alpine dwellers have contented themselves for millennia with subsistence farming and pastoral activities. They maintain their herds of sheep, goats, and dairy cattle through extensive transhumance to summer pastures called *Alm* (pl. *Almen*), which in most cases can only be reached after many days of droving. There is a marked difference in population on the valley floors, on the foothills and on higher altitudes, where the earliest strata of population had withdrawn before the Teutonic immigration in the Middle Ages.

Religious Life in the Area

To judge from the numerous shrines dotted over the mountains, the Alpine population must count among the most pious in Europe. Yet theirs is a kind of nature religion, based on water, rocks, trees, and animals. Their shrines, often built on the most inaccessible sites, are usually dedicated to Mary or other female saints. Archaeological finds of pre-Christian cultures are relatively rare. An extensive study by Ludwig Pauli, however, mentions some prehistoric finds pointing to early religious activities: a few female figurines of "Venus" type from the Upper Paleolithic found in the cave Barma Grande near Ventimiglia in Liguria and a recently discovered bone tablet representing a woman with accentuated pudenda found in a rock shelter of Riparo Gaban at Martignano, Trento Province, a shelter inhabited from 4500 to 3500 BCE. But pride of place among archaeological finds must be accorded to the cult wagon of Strettweg in Styria. This is a small effigy of the goddess who seems to bless a young couple surrounded by warriors and stags, dated to between the eighth and the fifth centuries BCE.

The Alps have been continuously inhabited for 10,000 years, yet the earliest human finds go back 50,000 years when hunters stalked cave bears and left sacrificial offerings of bear skulls in the Drachenloch in the Swiss Canton of St. Gall and in other caves. In later centuries votive deposits became more frequent in the vicinity of important passes from Italy to Switzerland such as at St. Gotthard and St. Bernhard, at the Stilfser Joch, and at Mitterberg near the Grossglockner Massive in the Salzburg region. Other preferred places for sacrificial deposits were wells with medicinal qualities, lakes such as Lake Neuchatel, and the confluence of rivers.

It is now generally recognized that most Alpine tribes had a matrilineal and matrifocal social organization. They worshiped a goddess under different names and different manifestations.[3] This was originally the earth goddess, in her manifestation as nubile virgin in spring, mature woman and mother in summer, and death goddess in fall and winter. Her consort was an earth spirit, the wild man or green man, a disguised youth who still appears in some places during Alpine spring celebrations. Over the millennia the persona of the goddess has changed considerably, yet even Christianity was unable to completely obliterate her image and absorbed it in the form of Mary, St. Anne (mother of Mary), and the trinity of the Three Holy Virgins (Catherine, Margaret, and Barbara).

The Goddess Raetia, Protector of Alpine Pastures

After the Roman conquest of the Alps, a better knowledge of Alpine culture and religion can be traced. Writers of antiquity called the people of the Alps "Raetians," after their tribal goddess Raetia, Reita, or Reeta. She had her central shrine at Este in the valley of the Po River. In addition to Raetia, the name Esti (Estu) occurs, possibly another name or title for Raetia related to the Akkadian Ishtar. In Celtic Noricum, the protective divinity was Dea Noreia, after whom their city was named.

After the victory of the Roman generals Drusus and Tiberius over the Alpine tribes, the area from the Po Estuary to Lake Constance was established as Provincia Raetia. At that time the Alpine region was still largely unknown to Roman administration and relatively sparsely populated. To be posted there was regarded as a punishment because of the wildness of the region and its harsh climatic conditions. Rome only kept small military units there for securing the roads to the northern and western provinces of the empire and for the most important Alpine passes.

Through phonetic changes particularly in the Swiss regions of Tessin, Grison, and Wallis the name of the tribal goddess Raetia or Reisa changed to Risa, Madrisa/Matreia, or Mother Risa. Many place names throughout the Alps include the name Reita, Risa, or similar formations.

Remnants of Goddess Worship in Raetian Switzerland

The authority for the Swiss Grison region is Mgr. Christianus Caminada (1876–1962), Bishop of Chur, the son of a mountain farmer. His book *Die verzauberten Täler* is a good introduction to Swiss nature religion.[4] Caminada describes Saint Margaret (Margarita), a name that may have evolved from Raetia, Reita, or Risa. In the Romanche language, an amalgamation of Latin with the pre-Latin local idiom, her name was Sontga Margriata, with phonetic affinity to the word Raetia. Like the goddess Raetia in antiquity, Sontga Margriata was the unseen protector of the Alm, the summer pasture where cows, goats, and sheep are milked and cheese produced according to age-old rituals. The head shepherd and cheesemaker is called the Senn and, like the captain of a ship, he has absolute authority over human and beast.

According to an ancient rule the Alm was strictly off limits for women. Yet the ancient Swiss folk song "Canzun de la Sontga Margriata," recorded by Caminada, tells of a beautiful woman called Margriata who is discovered by the youngest shepherd boy.[5] She pleads with him not to reveal her presence to the Senn. With every stanza she promises him ever-greater treasures if he will not betray her. But he does not listen and runs to tell the Senn of the beautiful girl he has discovered. Therefore to her great regret Sontga Margriata must leave the Alm forever, taking her blessings with her. The mysterious woman is the goddess Raetia in her late manifestation as protectress of the mountain pastures.

Caminada was so moved by the melody of the song, which he acquired by taping an old woman's performance, that he had it analyzed by Swiss musicologist Fr. Ephrem Omlin of the Monastery of Engelberg. Without actually declaring the song of pagan origin, Omlin certified that it had affinities with pagan liturgical music and must be older than medieval hymns. After this verdict Caminada suggested that it be sung at special occasions as the national hymn of the Raetian cantons "standing upright and with hat in hand."

Eduard Renner describes an ancient Alpine evensong that must be performed each night by the Senn for the protection of the Alm, its shepherds, and the cattle. Using a large milk funnel as a megaphone he sings a long prayer over the pasture, ending each stanza with the refrain:

> Around this pasture there is a golden ring
> And there sits Maria with her dearest little child.

The prayer has many verses and is accompanied by a symbolic gesture signifying a "ring pass not" spell over the Alm. This ritual blessing has been discussed by Alpine anthropologist Hans Haid, who observed that without the change of "Marisa" to "Maria," the ritual would have long ago been prohibited by church authorities.[6]

The Many Manifestations of the Alpine Goddess

Many other names can be found for the goddess of the Alps. The ancient European goddess *Dana (the asterisk indicates a hypothesized form) can be found in the hamlet of Danay, at an altitude of 1500 meters above sea level in the glacier region of the Alpine watershed. Other names known from the legends of South Tyrol are Tanna, Samblana, Bona Gaia, Donna Kenina, and the White Lady. On the northern slopes of the Alps, Frau Berchta is commemorated in the name Berchtesgaden.

The goddess also appears in her triple form as *die drei Saligen Fräulein* ("the three Blessed Ladies") Ambet, Cubet, and Borbet, also found as the triad of saints Catherine, St. Margaret, and St. Barbara, and even personified as the Christian virtues of Hope, Faith and Charity. The effigies of the three Holy Virgins adorn most Alpine churches, particularly in

Catholic Austria and Bavaria. School children learn to distinguish them by their attributes:

Sankt Margareth mit dem Wurm	St Margaret with the worm (the dragon)
Sankt Barbara mit dem Turm	St Barbara with the tower
Sankt Kathrin mit dem Radl	St Catherine with the wheel (the sun wheel)
Das sind die drei heiligen Madl.	These are the three holy lasses.

On the eve of the sixth of January, Epiphany and Feast Day of the Three Wise Men, the farmers smoke the house with burning herbs and write over each door the initials of the three Magi Caspar, Melchior, and Balthasar, thus: C + M + B. But it is well known that these letters also refer to Catherine, Margaret and Barbara.

Dana, Tanna, Samblana, St. Anna

The hamlet of Danay consists of a few chalets and stables at the northern end of the Matsch Valley, a point that marks the watershed between southern and northern Europe, at an altitude of 1500 meters. In close proximity to the hamlet there exist several shrines of pilgrimage, Catholic mountain sanctuaries dedicated not to the Holy Virgin but to St. Anna, a name close to that of the goddess Anu (*Dana). Most researchers agree that these shrines are of pagan origin and were established by a people who worshiped a woman as supreme deity.[7]

Locally, the name *Dana was pronounced "Tanna." She was a goddess of glaciers with a heart of ice whose throne can be found on the highest peaks. She wore a mantle of snow and a crown of blue ice. Her servants were the fearsome Croderes, elementals without a human heart, who carried out her orders. These nature spirits had power to destroy the valley floors with avalanches, mudslides, rock falls, and raging torrents.

Legend tells that Tanna was once in love with a prince from Aquileja by whom she had a son. To the fury of the Croderes she renounced her crown of ice and, taking pity on humans, forbade the destructive work of the elementals. The walls of ice grew higher and higher, the avalanches enormous, and the waters of the glacier lakes threatened to overflow. When she discovered that the prince had betrayed her, Tanna returned to the mountain peaks and ordered the Croderes to resume their work, wreaking worse havoc in the valleys of men than ever before.

It is said that Tanna possesses a mirror of blue ice with which to observe the work of humans. She gathers the souls of babies who die before baptism and keeps them under her mantle of ice and snow. The Alpine population sees a great unfairness in the Christian teaching that unbaptized children cannot go to heaven. There are several places of pilgrimage where parents take stillborn babies and deposit them on the altar in the hope that the infant may give a sign of life and hence can be baptized. It is said that the winter goddess Tanna takes pity on them and favors little girls to carry her long train of ice and snow.

Two little girls that the Ladinians call *les yemeles* ("the twin girls") are in Tanna's service. Lonely wanderers may meet them on dangerous mountain paths. They warn humans of threatening blizzards, avalanches, rock falls, and other mountain dangers. Many legends show that Samblana and Tanna are different aspects of the same goddess. She is the divine queen of the glacier regions, the realm of eternal ice, but she still has a motherly heart for children.

The Curse of the Alpine Goddess

In the vicinity of the Danay hamlet, legend tells of the accursed city of Tannaneh. Its rich burghers had hearts of stone and never gave alms to the poor. Once an old beggar, who had been chased from their doors, cursed the city with the words:

Tannaneh, Tannaneh,	Tannaneh, Tannaneh,
Es schneibt an Schnee	It will snow a snow
Der apert nimmermeh!	Which will never melt again!

And so it happened. Tannaneh vanished under a thick cover of snow and was never found again. Other legends tell about accursed farms or townships whose inhabitants were punished for their sins. Upon investigation these places usually turn out to have been pagan cult shrines condemned by the church. Perhaps Tannaneh, as the name suggests, had originally been a sanctuary dedicated to Tanna.

The Goddess and the Man in the Ice

The goddess of the Alps is connected with the discovery, two decades ago, of *homo tyrolensis*, the Man in the Ice, nicknamed Ötzi because he was found near a glacier in the Ötztal, on the Austro-Italian border. Discovered by tourists on July 19, 1991, the Man in the Ice became a cause célèbre. Although situated in the geographic center of Europe, the locality of the find is so remote and the border between Italy and Austria so ill-defined that the discovery almost provoked a diplomatic conflict.

It was initially assumed that the man had been the victim of misadventure, leading to the transport of the body to the Innsbruck coroner. Only when it was understood that the body had been in the ice for over 5000 years was he transferred to the archaeological team of Innsbruck University. When X-rays revealed a stone arrowhead under his shoulder blade it became clear that the man had met with a violent death.

None of the official publications referring to the glacier mummy noted that the man lived in a society where human sacrifices in honor of the goddess were most probably practiced. This connection was first pointed out by German ethnologist Heide Göttner-Abendroth.[8] She suggests that the man's final resting place beneath the sacred mountain throne Similaun would almost certainly point to a human sacrifice. Human sacrifices to the goddess were offered yearly until relatively recent times. In the case of the Ice Man his death may have been a staged hunting accident.

Since the discovery of the Man in the Ice the strikingly regular glacier pyramid that dominates his resting place has been the object of folkloric and etymological studies. The name Samblana is associated with the Similaun glacier. According to Kurt Derungs, the mountain's original name was Sam-Alu-Ana, which translates as *sam* ("white") *alu* ("deity") and Ana (the name "Anna"). The same name occurs in the Himalayas, where a peak close to Mount Everest is called Ana-Purna. The name Similaun therefore signifies White Goddess Anna, a name befitting this beautiful glacier.[9]

Hans Haid, who lives in the glacier region of the Ötztal, concludes that Ötzi may have been a shepherd priest or a shaman. This can be inferred from his elaborate netted mantle, his feather-lined shoes, and the magical tools and hallucinogenic mushrooms in his pouch. Either voluntarily or by the verdict of his tribe he must have suffered a sacrificial death. His burial place beneath the Similaun, literally at the feet of the goddess Samblana, suggests that he was to be especially honored in death.

The Goddess of the Weather

The role of the goddess to control the weather, preserved in many local legends, can be seen in is the story of Cian Bolpin, "Little Fox Dog," beloved by Ladinian storytellers. The young man Cian Bolpin discovers the dwelling of the weather goddess Donna Kenina high in the mountain wilderness of the Dolomites, where he takes the low-hanging clouds for her bed linen hung out to dry. With great difficulty he finds the access to her castle in the clouds, and she invites him to stay with her. After they have lived happily together for some time, Cian Bolpin wishes to visit his friends in the valley. She graciously permits it but forbids him to tell anybody about her. She also gives him a magic ring to help him return to her. Unfortunately the young man cannot refrain from bragging about her beauty. Donna Kenina appears amid a thunderclap, demanding the return of her ring. Cian Bolpin has proved his point to his friends but has lost his beloved. Without the magic ring, he can no longer find her castle in the clouds. After many adventures he becomes the storm wind's servant and with his help is able to rediscover Donna Kenina. In the meantime she has become the mother of his child and gladly forgives him. The reunited couple shares a cake called Strauben, a baked replica of the labyrinth, the ancient symbol of human fate.[10]

The Kingdom of Fanes

If the Canzun de la Sontga Margriata hides the connection with the goddess for the people of Grison in Switzerland, the story of the Kingdom of Fanes serves the same purpose for the Ladinians of the Dolomites in Italy. This saga was discovered and saved from oblivion by Karl Felix Wolff of Bolzano, a dedicated collector of folk customs and sagas of the Dolomite valleys.[11] At the beginning of the 20th century, Wolff postulated a matriarchal society for the valleys of the Dolomites and their Ladinian (Raetian) population. Having been denied a college education he was accused for decades of inventing his material, and the authentic sagas he published were long regarded as fabrications. Only toward the end of his life did he find recognition. Wolff reconstructed the story of Fanes from the fragments he and his friend Hugo von Rossi had collected in the Dolomite valleys of Ampezzo and Fassa.

In the tale, a strange woman called Molta gives birth to a little girl on a mountain peak and dies. The infant is adopted by an *aguana*, a wise woman, who calls the child after her mother, Moltina. The child grows up among marmots, learning their ways, their language, and their salute to the morning sun. She finds she has the power to change into a marmot. She marries a prince from a foreign country and, having given asylum to a tribe of refugees, Moltina and Prince Landro found the Fanes Realm. Moltina is revered as queen, and the marmots are the realm's secret totem. The people of Fanes live happily and in peace for many generations.

There comes a day when a queen of Fanes marries a king who disturbs the old order of the queendom. He first woos the queen's sister Tsikuta, a priestess, and fathers a son with her, before turning his attention to the queen. The king abolishes the marmot totem and introduces the totem of the eagle. The queen does not protest. To his disappointment she gives birth to twin girls, Luyanta and Dolasilla. Luyanta is presented as a totem exchange to the marmot people. Dolasilla grows up to become a famous archer and warrior woman who wins many lands and treasures for her father.

Eventually Dolasilla falls in love with her shield bearer Ey-de-Net (Night Eye) and wants to marry him. Ey-de-Net does not know he is Tsikuta's son and Dolasilla's half-brother. In their matrilinear society, which insists on exogamy, their marriage would amount to the greatest crime. In vain Tsikuta tries to warn her son. The king has other reasons to fear the marriage. According to the mother-line, Dolasilla is the rightful heiress of the realm, as her daughters would be after her. In order to secure the crown for his younger son with the queen, the king sends Ey-de-Net into exile. In his greed, the king plans to win the goldmine Aurona in the Padon mountain and for this purpose is prepared to betray his own people. Compelled to fight without her shield bearer, Dolasilla is killed in battle. The wicked king is changed into a rock and the realm falls into ruin. Luyanta, who has been living with the marmots, reappears to lead the remaining people into the caverns of the Fanes Mountains, where they turn into marmots.

Ulrike Kindl has analyzed this story as a tragedy of ancient Mother Right.[12] Apart from the marmot totem, she found many other ancient features in this story. One of them is the queen's friendship with a vulture who breathes a blue flame and keeps alive the memory of fallen heroes. Kindl points out that the story must be understood in the light of the demise of matrifocality and exogamy, in favor of the patriarchal attitudes and male lineage represented by the king.[13] Under patriarchy the old marriage law of exogamy (girls marrying men from outside the tribe) changed into endogamy (marrying within the tribe). As long as there was no land property to share it was better for the tribe to bring in genetic biodiversity via exogamy and property was irrelevant. When land became more valuable girls were forced to marry within the tribe in order to keep the tribal land property whole and undivided.

The heroine Dolasilla with her silver bow and arrows represents the goddess in her virginal state. Her thirteen magical arrows, one of which kills her, represent the thirteen months of the lunar year. When she changes into a nubile woman and wants to marry her chosen hero Ey-de-Net, whose name connects him with the moon, he is found unsuitable, because he is of the same totem and hence her brother. Their marriage would represent incest.[14] Ey-de-Net's mother Tsikuta, who always wears red and carries red poppies, represents the goddess in her summer aspect. When the king's betrayal hastens Dolasilla's death and the ruin of the realm, her sister Luyanta appears as death goddess to lead the vanquished people into the mountain caves. In this story it is first the figure of Moltina, then Tsikuta, later Dolasilla and finally Luyanta, her alter ego, who display characteristics of the Alpine goddess.[15]

A Continuing Tradition

To say that the people of the Alps still worship a goddess would be an exaggeration. However, most of their churches and sanctuaries are dedicated to Our Lady in her various guises. Whole countries and regions, like Austria, Bavaria, and the Tyrol placed themselves under her protection, and soldiers' prayers before battle are addressed to her.[16] After World War II it was not unusual for mothers to dedicate statues of the Mater Dolorosa in thanksgiving if their sons had safely returned home. Famous shrines like Altötting in Bavaria and Maria Einsiedeln in Switzerland are proud of their Black Madonnas, effigies with pagan connotations. All this seems to betray a preference for feminine values that can be traced back to pre-Christian times.[17]

From the proto-European *Dana to Saint Anna of today, there was never a time without the goddess in the Alps, nor a mountain peak that was not sacred to her. No matter how much Christianity has tried to chase her away, the goddess still resides on the Alpine mountain peaks, and the ancient cult places deserve to be approached with the same respect that is accorded other places of worship.

Notes

1. Hans Haid, *Mythen der Alpen—Von Saligen, Weißen Frauen und Heiligen Bergen* (Vienna: Böhlau Verlag, 2006).

2. Linus Brunner and Alfred Toth, *Die rätische Sprache enträtselt* (Chur: Amt für Kulturpflege des Kantons St. Gall, 1987), 99. Alpu is also known as Aubet, Cubet, Guere/Quere. Karl Gruber, *Aubet, Cubet, Quere: Die Wallfahrt zu den Heiligen drei Jungfrauen von Meransen* (Bolzano: Arunda, 1978), 6/78. According to linguist Linus Brunner the name Reitia as found in ancient inscriptions is the correct name of the tribal goddess of ancient Raetia. Her alternative name Esti may refer to her sanctuary at Este, near the ancient estuary of the Po River. Other variations may be due to phonetic differences of the language in different valleys. Due to the paucity of the research material inscriptions differ and there are no strict rules for the spelling.

3. Gruber, *Aubet, Cubet, Quere*, 124.

4. Pauli Ludwig, *The Alps, Archaeology and Early History* (London: Thames and Hudson, 1984).

5. Hans Haid, *Mythos und Kult in den Alpen*, Myth and Cult in the Alps (Bad Sauerbrunn: Edition Tau, 1992), 148.

6. Christian Caminada, *Die verzauberten Täler: Die urgeschichtlichen Kulte und Bräuche im alten Rätien* (Chur: Desertina, 2006); originally published by Walter Olten, Freiburg/Breisgau, 1961.

7. Ibid., 265.

8. Eduard Renner, *Goldener Ring über Uri* (Zürich: Ammann Verlag, 1991) .

9. Haid, *Mythos und Kult.*

10. Ibid., 152–153.

11. Heide Göttner-Abendroth, "Auf den Spuren der Göttin [In the Wake of the Goddess]," *Planet Alpen* 8, no. 1 (2002): 3–40.

12. Hans Haid, *Aufbruch in die Einsamkeit: 5000 Jahre Überleben in den Alpen* (Start into Solitude) (Rosenheim: Rosenheimer Verlagshaus, 1992).

13. Ulrike Kindl, *Märchen aus den Dolomiten* (Munich: Diederichs Verlag, 1992), 18.

14. Karl Felix Wolff, *Dolomitensagen* (Innsbruck: Tyrolia Verlag, 1974); also published in Italian and English.

15. *Kritische Lektüre der Dolomitensagen von Karl Felix Wolff*, vol. 2 (San Martin de Tor: Istitut Ladin Micurà de Rü, 1997).

16. Marija Gimbutas, *The Language of the Goddess* (New York: HarperCollins, 1991).

17. In her two volumes *Kritische Lektüre der Dolomitensagen von Karl Felix Wolff*, 2 vols. (San Martin de Tor: Istitut Ladin Micurà de Rü, 1983 and 1997).

Bibliography

Brunner, Linus, and Alfred Toth. *Die rätische Sprache enträtselt.* Chur: Amt für Kulturpflege des Kantons St Gall, 1987.

Caminada, Christian. *Die verzauberten Täler: Die urgeschichtlichen Kulte und Bräuche im alten Rätien.* Chur: Desertina, 2006.

French, Claire. *The Celtic Goddess: Great Queen or Demon Witch?* Edinburgh: Floris Books, 2001.

French, Claire. *Das Reich der Fanes—eine Tragödie des Mutterrechts* (The Realm of Fanes—A Tragedy of Mother Right). Der Schlern: Bolzano, 1975, 49:4–12.

French, Claire. *Mutmaßungen über den Namen Danay* (Musings about the Name "Danay"). Der Schlern: Bolzano, 1999, 73/3:183–187.

French, Claire. *Mythische Wurzeln in Volksmärchen und höfischer Epik* (Mythic Roots in Popular Tales and Court Epic). Der Schlern: Bolzano, 1999, 73/12:759–764.

Gimbutas, Marija. *The Language of the Goddess.* New York: HarperCollins, 1991.

Göttner-Abendroth, Heide. "Auf den Spuren der Göttin (In the Wake of the Goddess)." *Planet Alpen* 8, no. 1 (2002): 3–40.

Göttner-Abendroth, Heide. *Frau Holle—Das Feenvolk der Dolomiten.* Königstein/ Taunus: Verlag Ulrike Helmer, 2005.

Göttner-Abendroth, Heide. *The Goddess and Her Hero.* Stow, MA: Anthony Publishing, 1995.

Gruber, Karl. *Aubet, Cubet, Quere: Die Wallfahrt zu den Heiligen drei Jungfrauen von Meransen.* Bolzano: Arunda, 1978, 6/78.

Haid, Hans. *Aufbruch in die Einsamkeit (Start into Solitude).* Rosenheim: Rosenheimer Verlagshaus, 1992.

Haid, Hans. *Mythen der Alpen—Von Saligen, Weißen Frauen und Heiligen Bergen* (Myths of the Alps). Vienna: Böhlau Verlag, 2006).

Haid, Hans. *Mythos und Kult in den Alpen.* Bad Sauerbrunn, Germany: Edition Tau, 1992.

Kindl, Ulrike. *Kritische Lektüre der Dolomitensagen von Karl Felix Wolff.* Vol. 1, *Einzelsagen.* San Martin de Tor: Istitut Ladin Micurà de Rü, 1983.

Kindl, Ulrike. *Kritische Lektüre der Dolomitensagen von Karl Felix Wolff.* Volume 2: *Sagenzyklen—Die Erzählungen vom Reich der Fanes.* San Martin de Tor: Istitut Ladin Micurà de Rü, 1997.

Kindl, Ulrike. *Märchen aus den Dolomiten.* Munich: Eugen Diederichs Verlag, 1992.

Pauli, Ludwig. *Die Alpen in Frühzeit und Mittelalter.* Munich: Beck Verlag, 1980.

Pauli, Ludwig. *The Alps, Archaeology and Early History.* London: Thames and Hudson, 1984.

Renner, Eduard. *Goldener Ring über Uri.* Zürich: Ammann Verlag, 1991.

Wolff, Karl Felix. *Dolomitensagen.* Innsbruck: Tyrolia Verlag, 1974.

Wolff, Karl Felix. *The Dolomites and Their Legends.* Bolzano, Italy: Verlagsanstalt Athesia, 1958.

About the Editor and Contributors

PATRICIA MONAGHAN is professor of interdisciplinary studies at DePaul University in Chicago and Senior Fellow at the Black Earth Institute in Wisconsin. She is the author of more than a dozen books, including *The Encyclopedia of Goddesses and Heroines* (Greenwood) and *The Red-Haired Girl from the Bog* (New World Library). She is an officer of the Association for the Study of Women and Mythology. Monaghan has published four books of poetry and has won numerous prizes for her literary work, including a Pushcart Prize.

KAREN BEK-PEDERSEN works as a lecturer in Scandinavian studies at the University of Aberdeen in Scotland. Her research interests are centered on Old Norse mythology but also include Celtic mythology, Old Norse sagas, and folklore. She holds an MA in ethnology and wrote her PhD thesis on the Norns of Old Norse mythology.

CRISTINA BIAGGI, PhD, scholar, writer, editor, and lecturer on pre-historic cultures, the goddess, and the history of patriarchy, discusses the ancient female deity figurines from Malta between 3500 and 2500 BCE. Biaggi is author of *Habitations of the Great Goddess* and editor of *In the Footsteps of the Goddess* and *The Rule of Mars: Readings on the Origins, History and Impact of Patriarchy.*

DANIEL COHEN is an independent theologian who has been part of the goddess movement since the late 1970s. He is a storyteller, particularly interested in using the insights of feminism and goddess theology to rewrite myths of heroes. For over twenty years, he co-edited *Wood and Water*, a British goddess-centered magazine.

DOLORES DELUISE holds a PhD and a certificate in women's studies from the Graduate Center of CUNY. She is an associate professor, teaching writing and literature at BMCC/CUNY, specializing in developmental writing and creative nonfiction. Her areas of research and publication are pedagogy, women's literature, and women's spirituality.

MIRIAM ROBBINS DEXTER holds a BA in classics and a PhD in ancient Indo-European languages and linguistics, both from UCLA. Her doctoral dissertation, "Indo-European Female Figures," along with comparative mythology courses she has taught and is still teaching at UCLA, evolved into her book, *Whence the Goddesses: A Source Book*. She is the author of over twenty scholarly articles and nine encyclopedia articles on ancient female figures, and she has edited and co-edited sixteen scholarly volumes; she edited and supplemented Marija Gimbutas's *The Living Goddesses*.

CLAIRE FRENCH was born in 1924 into a family of South Tyrolean sculptors and studied modern languages and literature at Innsbruck and Melbourne universities. Her doctoral thesis was a study of the mythological background of the Welsh Mabinogion. She migrated to Australia in 1951, where she married and has three children. Since 1965 she has been a lecturer with the Melbourne Council of Adult Education. She has published extensively about goddess mythology both in English and in German.

STARR GOODE, a poet and writer, teaches literature at National University. Her work on the Sheelas has been published in *Irish Journal of Feminist Studies* and *ReVision*. Winner of the David L. Kubal Memorial Essay Prize, she is also a recipient of the Henri Coulette Memorial Poetry Award from the Academy of American Poets. Her poetry has appeared in numerous publications, most recently in *Expanding Circles: Women, Art & Community* and *Sage Woman*. She has been profiled for her work as a cultural commentator in the *LA Weekly*, the *Los Angeles Times*, and the *Wall Street Journal*.

KATHRYN HENDERSON is an associate professor of sociology at Texas A&M University and ordained clergy in the Reformed Congregation of the Goddess, International. Her research has included, among others, the visual culture of engineers, the straw-bale building movement, and the visual memories of Katrina survivors. Her current research is concerned with the coping strategies of those suffering from environmental illness in the face of medical failure. In the clergical domain her research has included interviews with practitioners of living spiritual traditions in order to engage them with respect.

M. KELLEY HUNTER, PhD, CAP, is a depth astrologer and mythologist who enjoys creative expression in the dramatic and visual arts. She has served on the faculties of Vermont College, Goddard College, and Burlington College. She favors research methodologies that engage the intuition and imagination. Feature writer for *The International Astrologer*, Kelley is author of *Living Lilith: Four Dimensions of the Cosmic Feminine* and *Black Moon Lilith*.

ZÜHRE INDIRKAS is a graduate of Ankara University where she studied classical archaeology and art history. She began working on her doctorate in the Department of Archaeology and Art History of İstanbul University in 1985. She did research for a time in London on a grant received from the British Council in Turkey and was awarded her doctoral degree in 1990. She is now a professor of art history at İstanbul University. The author of *Ana Tanrıça Kybele ve Çağdaş Türk Resmindeki İzdüşümleri, Türklerde Hükümdar Tacı Geleneği, Die Alttürkischen Mythen in Mittelasien und Ihr Weiterleben inb Anatolien*, and *Türk Mitosları ve Anadolu Efsanelerinin İzsürümü*, she has also published numerous articles on the subjects of pre-Islamic Anatolia, Turkish culture, and mythology.

MARY B. KELLY, professor emerita of art, author, artist, and weaver, has written a trilogy on embroideries that explores goddess motifs in Eastern, Central and Northern Europe. Her books include *Goddess Embroideries of Eastern Europe, Goddess Embroideries of the Balkan Lands and Greek Islands*, and *Goddess Embroideries of the Northlands*. She also writes articles for textile magazines and lectures at conferences, symposia, and on textile tours.

SUSAN LITTLE of Seattle has been a student of Mary Magdalene for fifteen years and a student of the Bible for more than forty. As an undergraduate at Harvard, she learned how to use scholarship to enhance the power and beauty of sacred texts. An assignment with the U.S. Foreign Service took her to the Holy Land in 1967, and subsequently she went back there to walk in the footsteps of Mary Magdalene beside the Sea of Galilee. In addition to writing Susan embodies the life of Mary Magdalene through a sacred dance ministry.

GLENYS LIVINGSTONE holds a PhD in social ecology; she has been academically and culturally involved in the resurgence of female imagery for the sacred for over three decades. She is the author of *PaGaian Cosmology: Re-inventing Earth-based Goddess Religion*. She was born in Australia, where she continues to live.

BETTY DE SHONG MEADOR, a Jungian analyist, is a member and past president of the C. G. Jung Institute of San Francisco. Her translations of all the known works of the Sumerian high priestess Enheduanna, the first author of record, appear in her books *Princess, Priestess, Poet—The Sumerian Temple Hymns of Enheduanna* (2009) and *Inanna—Lady of Largest Heart* (2000). In *Uncursing the Dark* (1992), she includes translations of Sumerian love songs and myths among the collection of essays.

BRENDA PETERSON is a nature writer and novelist, author of fifteen books, including *Duck and Cover*, a New York Times Notable Book of the Year. Her ten nonfiction books, including *Living by Water* and the National Geographic book *Sightings: The Gray Whale's Mysterious Journey* established her as a prominent creative nonfiction writer, extensively profiled in America's Nature Writers. Peterson's most recent novel was *Animal Heart*; her most recent nonfiction book, *I Want to be Left Behind*.

JUDITH ROCHE is the author of three poetry collections, most recently *Wisdom of the Body*, an American Book Award winner. She has published widely in various journals and magazines, and has poems installed on several Seattle area public art projects. As Literary Arts Director for One Reel she produced the Bumbershoot Bookfair and Literary Program for over twenty years. She was Distinguished Northwest Writer-in-Residence at Seattle University in 2007 and currently teaches at Hugo House Literary Center and at Cornish College of the Arts. She is a Fellow at the Black Earth Institute.

BORIA SAX is the author of many books including *The Serpent and the Swan, Animals in the Third Reich, The Mythical Zoo*, and *Crow*, as well as a memoir of growing up in the shadow of atomic espionage entitled *Stealing Fire*. He is completing a history of the ravens in the Tower of London. He teaches courses online for the State University of Illinois at Springfield and Mercy College, and in person at Sing Sing Prison.

CHERYL STRAFFON graduated with a degree in English and comparative religion at King's College London University. She did a postgraduate education diploma at Cambridge University, then taught for some years before taking up librarianship. For the last thirty years she has been researching the beliefs of ancient peoples in Cornwall and elsewhere. She is the author of several books, including *Pagan Cornwall—Land of the Goddess, The Earth Goddess—The Pagan and Celtic Legacy of the Land* and *Daughters of the Earth*, and editor of the magazine *Goddess Alive!* She grew up in Cornwall and returned there to live in 1986, where she is chair and project manager of the Cornish Ancient Sites Protection Network, co-organizer of the annual Goddess in Cornwall event, and Trainer on the Priestess of Kernow training course.

JOHANNA STUCKEY received degrees from the University of Toronto and her PhD from Yale University. Currently University Professor Emerita at York University in Toronto, Canada, she is a retired member of York's interdisciplinary Division of Humanities and Programs in Women's Studies and Religious Studies and still active in the Program in Women's Studies in the Faculty of Graduate Studies. She has also taught continuing education courses on goddesses and goddess worship at the University of Toronto. She is the author of numerous learned articles, papers, book reviews, and a text book on feminist spirituality and is at present working on another book, tentatively titled *Goddesses and "Dying Gods."*

DAWN E. WORK-MAKINNE holds an MS from Indiana University, an advanced diploma from the Women's Theological Institute and a PhD in women's studies in religion from the Union Institute and University. Dr. Work-MaKinne is a founding member of the Association for the Study of Women and Mythology and is on the faculty of the Women's Theological Institute.

Index